Pavan Pod
Kevin Hoff

WPF Control
Development

UNLEASHED

Building Advanced User Experiences

SAMS | 800 East 96th Street, Indianapolis, Indiana 46240 USA

WPF Control Development Unleashed

Copyright © 2010 by Pearson Education, Inc.

ISBN-13: 978-0-672-33033-9
ISBN-10: 0-672-33033-4

Library of Congress Cataloging-in-Publication Data:

Podila, Pavan.
 WPF control development unleashed : building advanced user experiences / Pavan Podila, Kevin Hoffman.
    p. cm.
 ISBN 978-0-672-33033-9
 1. Windows presentation foundation. 2. Application software—Development. 3. User interfaces (Computer systems) 4. Microsoft .NET Framework. I. Hoffman, Kevin. II. Title.
 QA76.76.A65P64 2009
 006.7'882—dc22
              2009032558

First Printing September 2009

Trademarks

Warning and Disclaimer

Bulk Sales

Sams Publishing offers excellent discounts on this book when ordered in quantity for bulk purchases or special sales. For more information, please contact

   U.S. Corporate and Government Sales
   1-800-382-3419
   corpsales@pearsontechgroup.com

For sales outside of the U.S., please contact

   International Sales
   international@pearson.com

Editor-in-Chief
Karen Gettman

Executive Editor
Neil Rowe

Development Editor
Mark Renfrow

Managing Editor
Kristy Hart

Project Editor
Andy Beaster

Copy Editor
Geneil Breeze

Indexer
Brad Herriman

Proofreader
Water Crest Publishing

Publishing Coordinator
Cindy Teeters

Book Designer
Gary Adair

Compositor
Jake McFarland

Contents at a Glance

Table of Contents

About the Authors

Pavan Podila, Architect at NYC's Liquidnet Holdings, has worked extensively with many leading UI technologies, including WPF/Silverlight, Flash/Flex/AIR, and DHTML. In the past, he has worked with Java Swing, Eclipse SWT, and TrollTech/Nokia Qt. His primary interests include 2D/3D graphics, data visualization, UI architecture, and computational art. He created FluidKit (http://fluidkit.codeplex.com), an open-source WPF library of controls such as ElementFlow, TransitionPresenter, etc. He is a Microsoft MVP for Client App Dev and blogs actively at http://blog.pixelingene.com.

Kevin Hoffman got his first computer, a Commodore VIC-20, when he was 10 years old and has been hopelessly addicted to programming ever since. He has written desktop applications, web applications, distributed enterprise applications, VoIP software, and pretty much everything else in between. He is currently a .NET Architect in New England building large-scale, next-generation web applications.

Dedications

Pavan:

I dedicate this book to my parents, my grandparents, my brother, and my loving wife Sirisha, who seeded the idea of writing a book.

Kevin:

I would like to dedicate this book to the women in my life, from age 8 to 98, who have inspired me and kept me going when I would've given up otherwise. My daughter Jerrah is continually amazed that someone like me could contribute to a book that appears in her favorite place (the book store!), and my wife Connie is constant proof that there is no upper bound to the limits of human patience. And my grandmother Lillian who, at the age of 98, sends e-mails and surfs the web like a pro. She is proof that geek is universal :)

Acknowledgments

Pavan:

I want to acknowledge all my teachers who have helped me grow as an individual and shaped my thinking throughout my academic years. I want to make a special mention of Mr. Bapat, who transformed me from a math-hating kid to someone who enjoyed solving challenging math puzzles and eventually appreciating the beauty of Calculus. I could not have made it into Computer Science without his math classes. I want to thank Mr. D.B. Kulkarni, who taught me the essentials of Organic Chemistry and in the process made me realize that there is value in everything you learn. I am very fortunate to have a professor, graduate-advisor, and a friend like Dr. Venkat Subramanium, who helped me fill some serious gaps in my OO programming knowledge. It is amazing what I have learned about software development in one semester than the four years I spent in CS undergrad. He is truly an exceptional teacher and I would never pass up the opportunity of attending any of his classes.

When I was still climbing the ropes of WPF, I got the chance to do a project with Andrew Whiddett, a veteran at the art of building jaw-dropping user interfaces. Since then he has been my mentor and a good friend, always willing to share a few tricks up his sleeve. Thanks Andrew, I have learned a lot from you.

I want to thank all the reviewers of the book who were very kind to take time out from their busy schedules: Bart De Smet (of Microsoft), who reviewed the first nine chapters of the book and was very prompt with his feedback, and Jaime Rodriguez (of Microsoft), who challenged me with tough questions on some of the content, which greatly improved the quality of the chapters. Jaime also helped in getting Rath Shetty of the UI Automation team to review the chapter on automation. I want to thank John Gossman (Microsoft Architect for WPF and SilverLight), Jonathan Russ, Marlon Grech, Cory Plotts, Kent Boogart, and Lester Lobo (of Microsoft), who all shared their real-world experiences with WPF and reviewed several chapters.

I want to acknowledge Kevin Hoffman, my co-author, who once told me that he will never write his 15th book but graciously made an exception. He is a real craftsman at making dull sentences spring to life with full vigor and energy. Some tough concepts in this book were made surprisingly easy to follow because of his tactful writing skills. I want to thank my manager at Sams, Neil Rowe, for giving me the opportunity to write this book, and the Sams editorial team, Andrew Beaster, Geneil Breeze, and Mark Renfrow, who have painstakingly edited every chapter and helped me maintain a consistent quality.

I want to thank my manager Brett Kotch at Liquidnet Holdings for giving me the freedom to explore WPF and go crazy with ideas.

I would like to extend my thanks to all the bloggers, book authors, article writers, community contributors, and speakers who have shared their knowledge on WPF and software development, enriching this field with great ideas and practices. They have made programming all the more fun. Finally, huge props go to everyone on the Microsoft WPF team for building an awesome UI technology. It's a real thing of beauty and a joy for every UI developer.

Kevin:

I want to acknowledge Pavan Podila. Hopefully readers will figure this out by reading this book, but there are probably 2 or 3 people on the planet with the kind of raw WPF talent that he has, and I consider it an honor that I was able to help bring his talent to the world by working with him on this book. He is a true User Interface genius, and there are great things in store for him and those lucky enough to work with him.

We Want to Hear from You!

As the reader of this book, *you* are our most important critic and commentator. We value your opinion and want to know what we're doing right, what we could do better, what areas you'd like to see us publish in, and any other words of wisdom you're willing to pass our way.

You can email or write me directly to let me know what you did or didn't like about this book—as well as what we can do to make our books stronger.

Please note that I cannot help you with technical problems related to the topic of this book, and that due to the high volume of mail I receive, I might not be able to reply to every message.

When you write, please be sure to include this book's title and authors, as well as your name and phone or email address. I will carefully review your comments and share them with the authors and editors who worked on the book.

Email: feedback@samspublishing.com

Mail: Neil Rowe
Executive Editor
Sams Publishing
800 East 96th Street
Indianapolis, IN 46240 USA

Reader Services

Visit our website and register this book at informit.com/register for convenient access to any updates, downloads, or errata that might be available for this book.

CHAPTER 1

The WPF Design Philosophy

Imagine that you are an architect who has been asked to build a house on an empty lot in a fairly well-established neighborhood. You take a look at the nearby buildings to make sure that the colors you use on the outside of your house don't conflict with the aesthetics of the neighborhood. When you are done with your masterpiece of a new house, you stand back and marvel at what you've accomplished. It is a brilliant-looking four-story structure with huge open glass walls to afford the owners a great view of the surroundings. The rest of the house has many beautiful features such as an open porch, bay windows, balconies, skylights, and virtually everything else a new homeowner could want.

Six months go by and you receive a call saying that your fabulous house has basically been reduced to rubble. It turns out that in your original assessment of the neighborhood, you didn't think much of the fact that the existing houses were built from brick with extremely thick (hurricane-proof, to be exact) windows, no skylights, and no balconies. Also, the houses were predominantly ranch homes with basements made from strong foundations. What you didn't take into account was the *design philosophy* of the neighborhood. In ignoring that, you didn't realize that during the rainy season in that neighborhood, the area is frequently hit with torrential downpours, hurricanes, and multiple tornados. Without knowing *why* the other houses were built the way they were, you built a house that looked great the day after you built it, but would never survive the rainy season.

A similar mistake is often made when building software. Think of the neighborhood in this analogy as the framework upon which your application is built. While it is certainly possible to build applications upon that framework with little to no knowledge of the inner workings of it or its design philosophy, doing so runs the risk of creating unusable, unstable, or ineffective applications.

Before we even show you a single line of Windows Presentation Foundation (WPF) code or markup, we want to make sure that you know *why* WPF applications work the way they do and that you know how the myriad moving parts in a WPF application interact with each other to produce what the end user experiences and manipulates. Knowing the WPF design philosophy will make your future WPF applications more reliable, more robust, and have far better user experiences because you will be less likely to build a glass house in a hurricane-prone neighborhood.

The topics that are covered briefly and in summary in this chapter will be covered at length throughout the rest of this book and will become second nature to you by the time you reach the last chapter.

Data and Behavior

User interfaces are all about visually representing data and taking action on it. This section looks at the different kinds of data that you will typically see and also the notion of interacting with the data (aka actions).

When users look at an application, they see information that they feel is pertinent to getting a particular task done. Whether that task is annihilating the nearest spaceship as indicated by their radar screen or entering another line item in an accounts payable sheet, your users see information, meaning, and cues for potential interaction. What *you*, the developer, often see are rows, columns, gradients, cells, buttons, list boxes, scrollbars, and much more. What neither you nor the user usually take the time to think about is that there is much more to it than that—there are layers upon layers between the developer view of the world and the user view of the world. We can actually break down these layers into two main categories: data and behavior.

When we build user interfaces, what we're usually doing is putting a skin on top of data. The data can be everything from a high-level model object like a customer or a simple Boolean value. Data is the single largest influencer on our user interfaces and can take many shapes. The following is a list of the main types of data that are presented by modern applications:

- ▶ **Primitive data**—Atomic data at the lowest level, which includes primitives such as strings, booleans, integers, and decimal values.

- ▶ **List data**—Data that appears in collections. This data can be of the same or varying data type and includes arrays, lists, and so on.

- ▶ **Hierarchical data**—Complex graphs of data that can be represented by a tiered hierarchy such as a tree or lists of lists, graphs, and so on.

- ▶ **Composite data**—Data made up of more than one of the preceding types of data.

As the power of user interface (UI) and data-access technology increases, it becomes easier and easier to go from raw data to rendered output. Windows Forms allowed us to often drag and drop individual controls and quickly point that control at the underlying data to render it. However, building custom controls in Windows Forms was a complex task and required the skills of a Graphics Device Interface (GDI) Zen master. WPF strikes at the sweet spot and by giving developers flexibility while still making it easy to go from data to rendered output.

When building a user interface, we often make the mistake of thinking that it is the button or the grid or the ListView that is the most important. However, it isn't the button that is king, but rather *what the button allows the user to do* that is king. This means taking action in response to data that is presented. These are application and control *behaviors*.

Interaction with UI controls isn't limited to just clicking with the mouse. In addition to being able to react to keyboard hotkeys, modern user interfaces can respond to complex gestures made with the mouse as well as alternative input devices like pens (such as a pen from a Wacom tablet), styli, and even touches directly from the user.

The truly great user experiences come when the developers reach a harmony between *data* and *behaviors*. The following sections of the chapter provide an introduction to the terminology WPF uses to deal with data and behaviors and the architecture and design philosophy of each within the context of WPF.

Working with Data

Here we will delve further into how WPF helps in transforming raw-data into a shiny visual representation.

Data can take virtually any form—everything from a single number to a model object like a customer or an entire complex graph containing customers, orders, and order items. This means that any UI control that displays data really needs to be able to handle *any* kind of data.

This is the crux of why so many UI frameworks have historically been so difficult to use and why WPF is so powerful. Many WPF controls assume that the default data type of its content is System.Object. If a control's content can be of *any* data type, how do controls know how to render their own content? How does WPF take raw data of any type and flow that through a control hierarchy and eventually convert that into something visible, tangible, and responsive to user interactions?

The first answer is through the use of *templates*.

Templates

Think of templates as cookie cutters. Whenever WPF needs a new cookie, it asks a template for one. The template then stamps a nice fresh shape out of the dough and gives it to WPF. WPF then bakes up the cookie and hands it to the user in the form of a steamy fresh user interface.

WPF provides two different kinds of templates that operate on two different kinds of cookie dough—control templates and data templates.

A control template is used when WPF wants a visual representation of a control. This template is completely related to the user interface and generally does not involve any *data*. The default control template for a button looks like a rectangle with rounded edges.

A data template is used when WPF has a piece of raw data and needs to know how to represent that data. In this case, you can think of the data as the cookie dough and the data template as the cookie cutter. The end result, after stamping the cutter (template) into the dough (data) is the visual representation of the data that the developer has provided.

For example, let's say that you have a Person object as your raw data. As a WPF developer, you might provide a data template that indicates that a person's name should appear in a text box, a picture of the person's face should appear as a small image in the left-hand corner of a panel, and other personal information should appear in a scrolling region of the panel on the right side. WPF takes the raw data and maps that to a visual representation.

Presenters

So far we have just a little piece of the picture. We know that a control template is used to form the base visualization of a control and that a data template defines how a particular piece of data needs to be displayed. However, how do we go from a data template to a visual representation? The answer is with a content presenter. The content presenter creates screen real estate inside which the UI dictated by the data template is presented.

While presenters allow developers to create complex visualizations with ease, WPF also allows you to use lower-level graphics primitives to build your UI. Here, you can create your own lines, polygons, ellipses, arcs, custom text, and so on. Each of these techniques becomes useful in certain scenarios and having all these tools at your fingertips makes WPF incredibly powerful.

Binding and Converters

We have seen the different types of data that can be represented and also the mechanism of data templates for visually describing this data. However, we need some essential glue for connecting them together. This glue is called *data binding*. Data binding in WPF is more powerful than in many other UI frameworks because it can be unidirectional or bidirectional. The UI can automatically update itself as bound objects change, and the data objects can change immediately in response to user actions. Data templates in WPF provide all the flexibility you need to visually represent any shape of data that you have in your application.

Sometimes the data that your templates need to present isn't in a format that is as user friendly as it could be. For example, you might be storing a phone number in a string that has no parentheses or dashes in your database, but you want the version of that string that is presented to the user to be formatted with parentheses and dashes. You aren't limited to just converting data of a given type to something else of that type. In fact, you can convert any piece of data into any representation. Common uses of this are converting Boolean values into images like a colored light bulb, converting numbers into an appropriate currency form, or even converting a series of numbers into points on a poly line to create line graphs.

Converters can be invoked both when going from data to presentation and when going from presentation to data through the channel provided by data binding.

Layout

Finally, once the templates have been stamped out, data has been plugged in, converters have been invoked, and presentation containers have been created, there is one last step before the user sees anything. That step is *layout*.

Layout provides the sizing and positioning for all of the UI controls created in the previous steps. It is also used for organization and keeping relevant elements together.

The layout step in WPF is more important than it might seem because, if you play your cards right, you can create a WPF UI that is entirely resolution independent. This makes the layout step *supremely important* because the layout step becomes the step where the relative coordinates and relative sizing information defined by your templates and presenters become actual physical pixel coordinates on the user's screen.

In WPF, the *panel* and classes that descend from it are responsible for providing layout functionality. They are responsible for grouping relevant elements with each other (by storing relevant controls as children of the panel) and by dictating the final size and position of elements contained within.

> **NOTE**
>
> **Layout Is a UIElement Feature**
>
> Although panels make it easier to lay out your user interface, note that every UIElement in the visual tree participates in layout. Without layout, there would be no screen space for that UIElement.

Finally, once the panels have determined where everything is going to be and how big everything needs to be, all of that content has to go somewhere. That content ends up in a *window*. A window is a top-level container that acts as the root of the visual tree. Visual trees are explained in lengthy detail throughout this book. Data that needs to be displayed on the screen will finally reside within a window after having passed through data templates, being placed into a presentation container, and finally passing through a layout container.

Styles

Throughout the entire chain of events where data flows from raw data objects through logical organization elements up to visually rendered elements, we have the ability to dictate the *style* of a control. Styles in WPF serve the same purpose as Cascading Style Sheets (CSS) for web applications. Styles can be applied at any level from template to content presenter to layout panel so that you can provide a cohesive look and feel for related elements. They provide an abstraction that gathers up all of the properties of an element so that those same properties can be applied to multiple elements throughout your application without having to specify them individually for every control. Styles are loaded from a resource dictionary, which could be anywhere in the element hierarchy, application level or at the theme level. The default styles that dictate the default look and feel for WPF applications are defined in a separate assembly.

Figure 1.1 summarizes the flow from raw data up through data templates, converters, data binding, presenters, and layout panels finally becoming a tangible user interface.

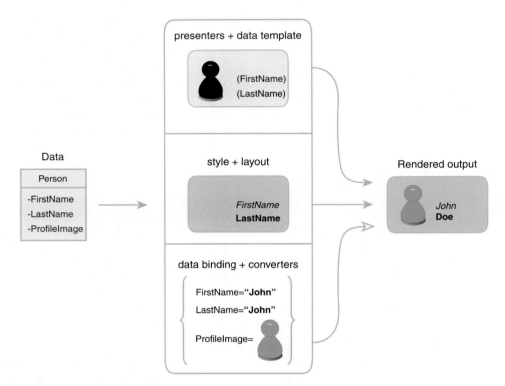

FIGURE 1.1   Illustrating the flow of data toward the user through WPF's layers.

Working with Behaviors

So now that you have a better idea of how data becomes a tangible user interface, we need to cover the various ways in which user input can be translated into actions that your application performs. Getting data to the user as a compelling UI is only *half* of the work. The other half revolves around giving the user compelling, easy, intuitive ways to interact with your application.

Behaviors give us a way to manipulate the data that created the UI being presented to us. Data manipulation and user behaviors are becoming more powerful and more innovative

1

and new interaction paradigms are being created all the time. The most common of these are the mouse, keyboard, and stylus. Touch computing is also gaining both in popularity as well as cost effectiveness. Not only can we now interact with our computers using just our hands, but others near us can interact with the same computer using their hands at the same time, such as with devices such as Microsoft's Surface.

The input device is no longer going to be limited to just something we rest our hands upon on our desks; it could be our hands themselves. Dealing with these numerous simultaneous inputs is something that many modern UI frameworks are simply not equipped to deal with. Thankfully WPF's behavior model works well for keyboard, mouse, and other input types such as touch.

The user's interaction with your application begins with some user input through any of the devices mentioned already. This input takes the form of an event. Windows responds to the low-level input signal and sends a message to your application, which WPF then turns into a high-level *event*. These events can be of different types such as mouse move events, key press events, stylus tap, and so on. The event is then wrapped up with some basic information that describes the context in which the event occurred. For example, two quick mouse-click events become a double-click event, when WPF generates the high-level event.

Identifying events is the first step toward allowing your application to respond to user behavior. The next step after identification is to map the input events to an action, which is some code that will be executed. An action can be triggered by a single input event or a combination of events. For example, the user pressing F5 to refresh a web page is an event, and a user holding down the Ctrl key while dragging a UI element across the screen is an example of a combination of events. In general, WPF treats these user events as RoutedEvents, which are specialized events propagated through the visual elements in a WPF application. Keep in mind that the user may not necessarily be the sole source of events. Network servers can send your application messages that can be turned into events; internal events within your application can notify other parts of your application of critical events. In all of these cases, your application can respond to these events with actions.

The action that your application takes in response to an event generally occurs in an event handler. However, you can also specify actions using a *command*. Commands are powerful tools that allow you to decouple the actions an application takes from the event that triggered it, allowing the application to easily respond the same way to multiple different user stimuli. For example, you could wrap a block of code that copies a piece of text to the Clipboard in a command. This command could then be invoked both by the Ctrl+C key combination and by a right-click contextual menu. This way, the logic for the text-copy action can be encapsulated at one single place, making it easier for code maintenance.

Events and actions are the core of how the user interacts with your application, but there are more complex means of interaction that involve multiple command and event primitives. These include drag and drop, the Tab key changing focus between input elements, Ctrl-clicking to select multiple items within a container control, and so on. All of these interaction paradigms are available to WPF programmers and are generally far easier to implement than their Windows Forms predecessors.

Figure 1.2 illustrates how user input events as well as other events get into your application to invoke the appropriate code.

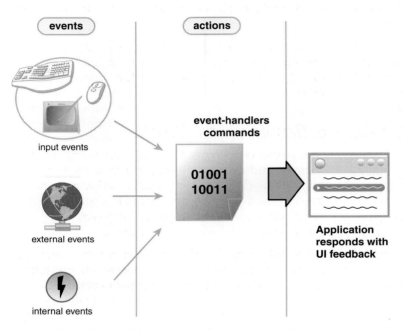

FIGURE 1.2   How information from user input flows through WPF.

The User Experience

So far the discussion in this chapter has touched on the concepts involved in taking raw data and presenting it to the user, as well as responding to user events with code that performs some action. Taken separately, they seem like pretty manageable components of a good application.

The problem is that you *cannot* take them separately. All too often people think they're done if they have conquered the problem of displaying data or if they have conquered the problem of responding to user input.

The overall experience is more than just input and output. It is how the user feels when using your application. The greatness of a user experience can be measured by how intuitive it is to perform an action and see the results. If your application forms a barrier or provides resistance to the user's natural tendencies, the user's experience will be a bad one. On the other hand, if the application seems to step aside and simply let the user do what she wants to do, the experience will be a great one. With a little thought, effort, and knowledge of some of WPF's finer points such as the ones presented in this book, you can create amazing, compelling, and memorable user experiences.

We need additional building blocks above and beyond what we've been doing with Windows Forms and other UI technologies to provide the user with a rich and engaging user interface. Fortunately, WPF has such building blocks in place in the form of storyboards and animations. We can also easily mix media such as video, audio, and high-end scalable graphics using WPF.

Controls are fairly dynamic in nature and can go through a variety of state changes throughout their lifetime. One way of making a user interface more engaging is to use subtle animations to depict those state changes visually rather than just shocking the user with a state change without a transition.

The User Experience Benevolent Circle

When we build an application that presents data to the user in a way that is elegant, intuitive, and well-designed, that user is encouraged to interact with the data. If the way in which that user interacts with the data is handled responsively and smoothly by our application, the user will be encouraged to continue using the application, and the data that changes as a result will have even more meaning than it did just moments ago because the user is now having a positive experience with the application.

The combination of features provided by WPF, plus the ability to smoothly and elegantly respond to user behavior, and the ability to dynamically provide beautiful renderings of raw data make WPF a fantastic toolkit for building the best applications available on Windows today.

A Note on Sample Source Code

All of the source code for this book can be downloaded at the following website: informit.com/title/9780672330339.

To browse through the various examples in this book, we have included a custom WPF application called BookExplorer, shown in Figure 1.3. It presents a master-detail view with the navigation section on the left, showing the examples grouped by chapters and the actual content on the right.

Many of the examples discussed in this book will not have the entire source code in printed text. It would be advisable to first run the example, have a quick glance at the code and then read up the example in the book. After that you can go back to source code to look at some of the intricate details. We as authors believe that it is best to only discuss the most important parts of the example instead of going through every single line of code.

For some chapters we have also included bonus examples that build on the ideas discussed in that chapter. They are not discussed in the book but the source code should give all the details. These examples have been marked as "BONUS" in the navigation section of the app.

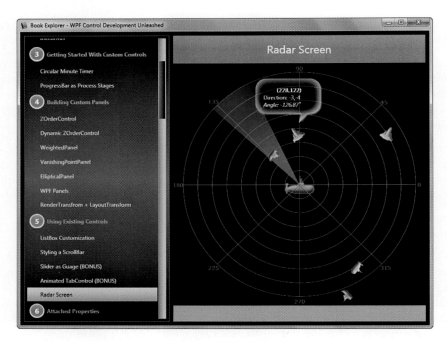

FIGURE 1.3   The BookExplorer application for browsing example source code.

Summary

This chapter provided an essential overview of the design philosophy and architecture of the Windows Presentation Foundation. As mentioned at the beginning of the chapter, without the essential knowledge of how and why foundations are built, developers are likely to build on top of structures that will not stand the test of time (or the test of cranky users!). Knowing the structure of what's underneath and why it has that structure is crucial to being able to distinguish your application from all the other applications available as a truly remarkable, world-class application that provides a beautiful user experience.

Throughout this book, you are presented with a tremendous amount of detail on how to do all manner of amazing things using WPF. However, as you progress through the book, keep in mind that you should always strive to provide the least resistance to user behavior and to provide the best skin possible on top of the raw data. WPF provides these tools, but it is up to you, the developer, to use them wisely.

CHAPTER 2

The Diverse Visual Class Structure

In the first chapter, we talked about how the construction of a framework like WPF is much like the construction of a house. If you don't know why certain things are built the way they are, you are likely to use them improperly and break something.

This chapter is all about the tools you use when building your house. Every craftsman (including programmers!) knows that picking the right tool for the job is essential to the success of the project. If you use a tool that has too much power, you're likely to break something or punch a hole through a wall. Go with something that doesn't have enough power and you won't be able to get the job done either.

WPF provides a rich and diverse set of classes that allow you to create everything from simple visuals to complex layered visuals and components. This is possible because of the precision with which the class structure of WPF was built. There are dozens of tools, but it is up to you to pick the right one for the job. Each class has a specific purpose and unique strengths that separate it from other classes. This allows us to mix and match classes to fit our particular needs.

Figure 2.1 shows the visual hierarchy of classes that we examine in detail in this chapter.

Introducing the Visual Classes

WPF has a rich, diverse set of building blocks and tools that you can use to create amazing interfaces. Knowing which tool to use and when to use it is absolutely invaluable to

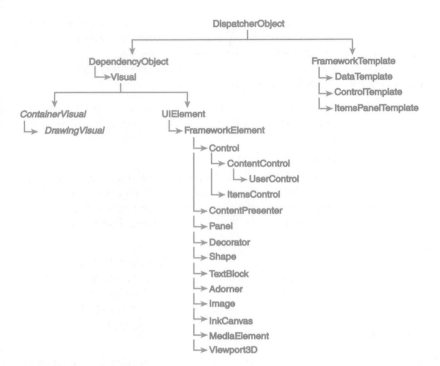

FIGURE 2.1   The visual classes.

creating next-generation applications. What follows is a brief overview of the most important classes in WPF. These are the classes that you will use most often as you progress
through this book and as you create your own applications.

The DispatcherObject Class

The DispatcherObject class can be found in the System.Windows.Threading namespace.
It provides the basic messaging and threading capabilities for all WPF objects. The main
property you will be concerned with on the DispatcherObject class is the Dispatcher
property, which gives you access to the dispatcher the object is associated with. Just like
its name implies, the dispatching system is responsible for listening to various kinds of
messages and making sure that any object that needs to be notified of that message is
notified on the UI thread. This class does not have any graphic representation but serves
as a foundation for rest of the framework.

The DependencyObject Class

The DependencyObject class provides support for WPF's dependency property system. The
main purpose behind the dependency property system is to compute property values.
Additionally, it also provides notifications about changes in property values. The thing
that separates the WPF dependency property system from standard properties is the

ability for dependency properties to be data bound to other properties and automatically recompute themselves when dependent properties change. This is done by maintaining a variety of metadata information and logic with the DependencyProperty. DependencyObject also supports attached properties, which are covered in Chapter 6, "The Power of Attached Properties," and property inheritance.

The DependencyObject class is part of the System.Windows namespace and has no graphic representation. It is a subclass of DispatcherObject.

The Visual and DrawingVisual Classes

The System.Windows.Media.Visual abstract class is the hub of all drawing-related activity in WPF. All WPF classes that have a visual aspect to their nature are descendants in some way from the Visual class. It provides basic screen services such as rendering, caching of the drawing instructions, transformations, clipping, and of course bounding box and hit-testing operations.

While the Visual class contains a tremendous amount of useful functionality, it isn't until we get down to the DrawingVisual class in the hierarchy that we start seeing concrete implementations that we can work with. DrawingVisual inherits from ContainerVisual, a class that is designed to contain a collection of visual objects. This collection of child visuals is exposed through the Drawing property (of type DrawingGroup).

DrawingVisual is a lightweight class specifically designed to do raw rendering and doesn't contain other high-level concepts such as layout, events, data binding, and so on. Keep in mind the golden rule of this chapter: *Pick the right tool for the job.* If you need to simply draw graphics and the extent of user interaction with that object is simple hit testing, you can save a lot on overhead by using DrawingVisual.

A great example of where DrawingVisuals would be an excellent choice is in a charting application. You can build a variety of charts by using the drawing primitives such as lines, beziers, arcs, and text and fill them with colors using a solid brush or even more advanced fills such as linear and radial gradients.

You might be wondering what to do for your charting application if you need the charts to be data bound. You see more about how to do this later, but remember that the output of processing a data template can be simple drawing visuals, allowing you to create data-bound charts that produce only the functionality you need.

Listing 2.1 shows an example of drawing a sector in a chart. In charting terms, a sector is a closed region that looks like a pizza slice. It has two straight lines that form the two sides of a triangle, but the last piece of the shape is closed by an arc rather than another straight line.

LISTING 2.1   A "Pizza Slice" Sector Visual Class

```
public class SectorVisual : DrawingVisual
{
    public SectorVisual
```

```
    {
        StreamGeometry geometry = new StreamGeometry;
        using (StreamGeometryContext c = geometry.Open)
        {
            c.BeginFigure(new Point(200, 200),
                    true /* isFilled */, true /* isClosed */);

            // First line
            c.LineTo(new Point(175, 50), true /* isFilled */, true /* isClosed
➥*/);

            // Bottom arc
            c.ArcTo(new Point(50, 150), new Size(1, 1), 0, true,
                SweepDirection.Counterclockwise, true /* isFilled */, true /*
➥isClosed */);

            // Second line
            c.LineTo(new Point(200, 200),
                true /* isFilled */, true /* isClosed */);
        }

        // Draw the geometry
        using (DrawingContext context = RenderOpen)
        {
            Pen pen = new Pen(Brushes.Black, 1);
            context.DrawGeometry(Brushes.CornflowerBlue, pen, geometry);
        }
    }
}
```

When rendered, the preceding class creates a visual that looks like the one shown in Figure 2.2.

If you have done any graphics programming for other platforms before, the concept behind the DrawingContext class should be pretty familiar to you. It is essentially an entry point into the conduit between your code and the actual rendered pixels on the user's monitor. As WPF is a retained graphics system, it caches all the drawing instructions and renders them whenever a refresh is required. The DrawingContext is used as the cache from which these instructions are picked up. In the preceding code, we start by building the geometry of the sector using the StreamGeometryContext. We then use the DrawingVisual's RenderOpen method to obtain a reference to the current DrawingContext instance and draw the geometry. The DrawingContext class contains methods for drawing lines, rectangles, geometry, text, video, and much more. Using these methods, you can build up a shape like the sector in Listing 2.1.

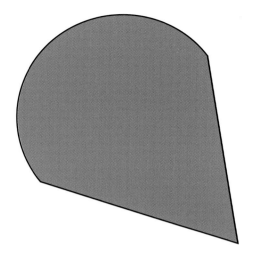

> **NOTE**
>
> **Retained Mode Graphics**
>
> Remember that WPF is a retained-mode graphics system, which means all of the drawing instructions are cached and you do not need to call any kind of update graphics API to force a visual refresh, as in an immediate mode graphics system. Although the API around `DrawingVisual` and `DrawingContext` resembles something you find in an immediate mode graphics system, beware of using it like one. You should never have to call any kind of update-my-graphics API to force a visual to redraw.

FIGURE 2.2   A sector visual class.

While the `DrawingVisual` class is ideally suited to scenarios in which you just need to do basic drawing and hit testing, it still needs a container that is responsible for placing those graphics on the screen. One such container is the `FrameworkElement` class.

The `FrameworkElement` Class

`System.Windows.FrameworkElement` derives from `UIElement`, which actually provides the core services such as layout, eventing, and user input that are used by rest of the framework. Although `UIElement` is a public class you would typically not derive from it. Instead, the `FrameworkElement` makes a better choice since it exposes the previous services (that is, layout, styles, triggers, data binding) in a user-customizable way.

`FrameworkElement` is also a lightweight container host for a set of visuals. Because it is a descendant of `UIElement` it is free to participate in the logical tree and can provide container support for more primitive visual elements (such as the `DrawingVisual` from the preceding example). The `FrameworkElement` class can be used in the following ways:

1. Provide simple visual representations of data by overriding the `OnRender` method.

2. Compose custom visual trees, making the `FrameworkElement` an excellent container class.

3. Provide custom layout logic (sizing and positioning) for the contained visuals.

4. A combination of the above.

For the pie slice control to be displayed onscreen, we need to build a container in which the `SectorVisual` class (refer to Listing 2.1) is the lone visual child, as shown in Listing 2.2.

LISTING 2.2   Creating a Container for the **SectorVisual** Class

```
public class VisualContainer : FrameworkElement
{
    private SectorVisual _visual = new SectorVisual();

    protected override Visual GetVisualChild(int index)
    {
        return _visual;
    }

    protected override int VisualChildrenCount
    {
        Get
        {
            return 1;
        }
    }
}
```

It is worth pointing out that the preceding VisualContainer class could also have been a subclass of UIElement instead of FrameworkElement, since it is not doing any custom layout. A FrameworkElement is best suited when you also want to provide custom sizing and positioning of elements, data binding, and styles.

> **NOTE**
>
> **The Spine**
>
> Inside the WPF team, a specific term is used for the set of classes comprised of DispatcherObject, DependencyObject, Visual, UIElement, and FrameworkElement. They call it the *Spine* and rightfully so. It is the backbone of WPF and provides the solid foundation to build more advanced functionality.

The Shape Class

The Shape class provides yet another mechanism to enable primitive drawing in WPF applications. If we already have the DrawingVisual, which we have seen can be used to draw lines, arcs, and "pie slice" wedges, what do we need the Shape class for?

The Shape class actually provides a level of abstraction slightly above that of the DrawingVisual. Rather than using the primitives of the DrawingContext as we have already seen, instead we can use the concept of *geometry* to determine what is going to be drawn.

As a developer creating a custom shape, you use the DefiningGeometry property on your custom shape class. This geometry defines the raw shape of the class, and other properties such as the stroke, stroke thickness, and fill determine the rest of the information needed to render the shape. If you have ever used shapes, strokes, and fills in Adobe Photoshop or Illustrator, these concepts should already be familiar to you. Whatever you create using DefiningGeometry can also be done using the more primitive DrawingVisual class, but using the geometry allows your custom shape class to be inserted more easily into a logical tree, making it more flexible and more amenable to reuse and packaging.

Shape is a subclass of FrameworkElement, a base class used by most container-type classes such as Panel to render child elements. This lets Shape instances participate in the layout pass and allows for easier event handling. Shape also defines the Stretch property, which allows you to control how a shape's geometry is transformed when the dimensions of the Shape object change.

Figure 2.3 illustrates a sector shape and how it can be transformed automatically using the Stretch property.

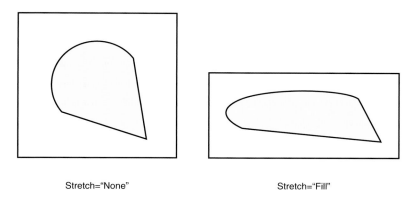

Stretch="None"   Stretch="Fill"

FIGURE 2.3   Stretching a shape's **DefiningGeometry**.

Taking the previous example of the sector and upgrading it this time to inherit from the Shape class, we end up with the code in Listing 2.3.

LISTING 2.3   Making the SectorVisual into a Shape

```
public class SectorShape : Shape
{
    protected override Geometry DefiningGeometry
    {
        get { return GetSectorGeometry(); }
    }

    private Geometry GetSectorGeometry()
    {
        StreamGeometry geometry = new StreamGeometry();
        using (StreamGeometryContext c = geometry.Open())
        {
            c.BeginFigure(new Point(200, 200), true, true);
            c.LineTo(new Point(175, 50), true, true);
```

```
        c.ArcTo(new Point(50, 150), new Size(1, 1), 0, true,
         SweepDirection.Counterclockwise, true, true);
        c.LineTo(new Point(200, 200), true, true);
    }
    return geometry;
  }
}
```

As you can see from the preceding code, the construction of the shape is exactly the same as constructing a visual-based sector. The difference here is that for a Shape we stop after creating the geometry and setting that to the DefiningGeometry property. With the SectorVisual, we must both construct the geometry and render it. The core difference is basically a difference in responsibilities. The Shape knows how to render itself in its container using the geometry defined in DefiningGeometry.

When creating a shape's defining geometry, the most commonly used geometry classes are PathGeometry, StreamGeometry, GeometryGroup, or CombinedGeometry. You learn more about these types of geometry in more detailed examples later in the book.

The Text Classes

Developers often overlook fonts when they are digging in their toolbox for something to get the job done. WPF actually has robust support for drawing text, laying out text, and working with documents. Text can be displayed onscreen in multiple ways and ranges from simple text to text with complex layout and formatting support.

At the most primitive level, we have GlyphRuns and FormattedText. These can't be used declaratively; rather, you need to use the DrawingContext to display them onscreen. This can be done using the DrawingContext.DrawGlyphRun and DrawingContext.DrawText APIs.

In today's modern age of globalized applications, you need more than just the ability to blindly throw text onto the user interface. You need to be able to do things like display text that runs from right to left, display Unicode characters, and much more. For example, when you draw text into a drawing context, not only do you supply font information, but you also supply the text, text culture, flow direction, and the origin of the text:

```
drawingContext.DrawText(
        new FormattedText("Hello WPF!",
        CultureInfo.GetCultureInfo("en-us"),
        FlowDirection.LeftToRight,
        new Typeface("Segoe UI"),
        36, Brushes.Black),
        new Point(10, 10));
```

Text can also be displayed declaratively and easily using the TextBlock and Label classes. TextBlocks (and Labels) are generally useful for a single line of text with fairly rich formatting and simple alignment support. For more complex text display, you can use the FlowDocument and FixedDocument classes that have more elaborate features to handle dynamic layouts, paragraphs, and mixing of rich media.

FlowDocument handles automatic layout and sizing of text and graphics as you resize the document. They are most useful for viewing newspaper-style text that can flow into columns and multiple pages. FixedDocuments are useful for programmatically generating a document with precise control over sizes of the textual elements, hence the name. These documents use two kinds of elements: blocks and inlines. Blocks are container elements that contain the more granular inline elements. Typical block-related classes include Paragraph, Section, List, and Table. Some of the common inline classes are Run, Span, Hyperlink, Bold, Italic, and Figure.

Although TextBlock, Label, FixedDocument, and FlowDocument are useful for displaying static text, WPF also provides interactive controls for editing text. These include the classic TextBox, which has limited formatting capabilities, and the RichTextBox, which as the name suggests has richer editing capabilities.

Most of these text-related classes expose properties to control alignment, fonts, font styles, and weights. Additionally, there is a class called Typography under the System.Windows.Documents namespace that has a rich set of properties to specifically control the various stylistic characteristics of OpenType fonts. They are available as attached properties, which can be set on text-related classes that use OpenType fonts. A sampling of the properties include Capitals, CapitalSpacing, Fraction, Kerning, and NumeralAlignment.

The Control Class

The Control class is pretty close to the top of the food chain of visual classes. It provides a powerful Template property (of type ControlTemplate) that can be used to change the entire look and feel of a control. Knowing that control templates can be changed during design time and at runtime can make for some amazingly powerful applications and compelling UIs. Designing with a Control allows developers and designers to quickly and easily define visual elements.

A rich set of classes that derive from the Control class provide specialized functionality and increasing complexity and level of abstraction. Choosing the right subclass of Control goes back to the analogy of *choosing the right tool for the job*. You need to make sure that you don't take something overly complex as well as not picking something that is too simplistic and doesn't offer the functionality you need. Choosing the wrong subclass can dramatically increase the amount of work you need to do.

For example, if you are building a control that needs to display a list of child items, you should start with ItemsControl or ListBox instead of starting with the comparatively low-level functionality of the Control class.

Unlike the earlier UI frameworks, the `Control`-related classes in WPF can be used directly without subclassing. Because of the powerful features such as `Styles` and `Templates`, you can customize the look and feel of a control declaratively. The subclasses of `Control` deal with the shape of the data rather than the appearance. A `Button` deals with singular data. `ScrollBars`, `Sliders`, and so on work with range data. `ListBox` and `ListView` work with collections. `TreeView` works with hierarchical data. It is up to the development team to decide how best to visually represent the data using these controls. In most cases, you do not have to subclass a control, rather you only have to change its `Style` and `Template`.

The `ContentControl` Class

The `ContentControl` class is ideal for displaying singular content, specified via the `Content` property. The content's look and feel can be customized using its `ContentTemplate` property, which is of type `DataTemplate`. Remember back in Chapter 1, "The WPF Design Philosophy," how plain data gets transformed into a visual representation through data templates.

The container that hosts the content can also be customized using the `Template` property of type `ControlTemplate`. This way you actually have two levels of customization available to you: You can customize the outer containing frame (via the `Template` property), and you can customize how the content within the frame is rendered (via the `ContentTemplate` property).

Controls derived from `ContentControl` are used to represent individual items that are displayed within list-based controls such as a `ListBox`, `ItemsControl`, `ListView`, and so on. The `Template` property is used for user interaction features such as showing selections, rollovers, highlights, and more. The `ContentTemplate` property is used for visually representing the data item associated with the individual element.

For example, if you have a list of business model objects of type `Customer` that you are displaying inside a `ListBox`, you can use its `ItemTemplate` property (of type `DataTemplate`) to define a visual tree that contains the customer's picture, home address, telephone number, and other information. Optionally you can also customize the item container holding each `Customer` object. As mentioned, a `ContentControl` derived class is used for wrapping each item of a `ListBox`. We can customize this `ContentControl` derived container using its `Template` property, which is of type `ControlTemplate`.

Some of the most powerful tricks in WPF revolve around control templates, content controls, and content presenters, so it is well worth the effort of learning them in detail.

The `ContentPresenter` Class

The `ContentPresenter` class is the catalyst that brings a data template to life. It is the container that holds the visual tree of the data template. `ContentPresenters` are used inside the `ControlTemplates` of `Control`, `ContentControl`, or any other custom control that exposes a property of type `DataTemplate`. It may help to think of the role of the `ContentPresenter` as the class that is responsible for *presenting* the visual tree of a data template within its container.

Within the `ControlTemplate`, you associate the `DataTemplate` property of the template control with the `ContentTemplate` property of the `ContentPresenter`. You might do this in XAML (eXtensible Application Markup Language) this way:

```
<ContentPresenter ContentTemplate={TemplateBinding ContentTemplate} />
```

In the preceding snippet, we are template binding the `ContentTemplate` property of the `ContentPresenter` to the `ContentControl`'s `ContentTemplate` property.

In general, you can think of a presenter element as a shell or container for the actual content. It instantiates the template tree and applies the content to it. As you may recall from Chapter 1, you can think of the content as being a piece of cookie dough, the template is the cookie cutter, and the presenter pushes down on the dough and presents the end result of a nicely shaped cookie.

The `ItemsControl` Class

As this class's name suggests, the `ItemsControl` class is ideally suited to displaying a list of items. More specifically, those items are interactive controls.

Not so long ago, when the main framework for building Windows applications was Windows Forms using .NET, controls were almost always too specialized. A `ComboBox` would display a drop-down list of items, but those items were *always* text, unless you rolled up your sleeves and did some serious work. This same problem occurred in virtually every place where Windows Forms displayed a list of items—the type and display of each item in a list was fixed unless you practically rewrote the control.

With WPF, the `ItemsControl` allows you to present a list of items that can have any visual representation you choose and can be bound to any list-based data you want. Finally we have both the flexibility we have always wanted and the power we have always needed.

Frequently used derivations of the `ItemsControl` class include the `ListBox`, `ListView`, and `TreeView`. The `ItemsControl` class exposes a wide variety of properties for customizing the look of the control and also of its contained items. Because these properties are exposed as `DependencyProperties`, they can be data-bound to other properties. These properties include the following:

- **`ItemsPanel`**—The `ItemsControl` needs a panel to lay out its children. We specify the panel using an `ItemsPanelTemplate`. The `ItemsPanelTemplate` is then applied to an `ItemsPresenter`.

- **`ItemTemplate`**—The `ItemTemplate` is the `DataTemplate` for the items being displayed. This template may be applied to a `ContentPresenter` or a `ContentControl`.

- **`ItemContainerStyle`**—This property indicates the style for the UI container for each individual item. Note that an `ItemControl` wraps each data item within a UI container such as a `ContentPresenter` or a `ContentControl`-derived class.

- **`Template`**—This defines the `ControlTemplate` for the `ItemsControl` itself.

If this seems like a lot to take in, don't worry. The concepts behind content controls, presenters, and data templates can seem daunting at first, but we use them so extensively throughout this book that their use will quickly become second nature to you. We cover the `ItemsControl` in greater detail in Chapter 5, "Using Existing Controls," and Chapter 8, "Virtualization."

The `UserControl` Class

The `UserControl` class is a container class that acts as a "black box" container for a collection of related controls. If you need a set of three controls to always appear together and be allowed to easily talk to each other, then a likely candidate for making that happen is the `UserControl` class.

Creating your own `UserControl` is an easy first start at creating your own custom controls. It provides the familiar XAML + Code-Behind paradigm that you can use to define your control's appearance and associated logic. The `UserControl` class derives from `ContentControl` and makes a few additions to `ContentControl`'s stock dependency properties.

The first thing you may notice about a user control is that the control itself cannot receive keyboard focus nor can it act as a Tab stop. This is because in the static constructor for `UserControl`, the `UIElement.Focusable DependencyProperty` and the `KeyboardNavigation.IsTabStop` property have been set to false.

This makes complete sense when you think about the idea that the primary function of a `UserControl` is to wrap a set of related controls and not act as an interactive control on its own.

To make things more clear, let's take a look at an example. Suppose that you have to create a search bar for your application that looks something like the one in Figure 2.4.

FIGURE 2.4   A sample interactive search bar for a WPF application.

The search bar in Figure 2.4 is comprised of a `TextBox` and a `Button`. When a user types a keyword or set of keywords and then presses the Enter key, the search functionality is invoked. The same functionality is invoked if the user types in a keyword and clicks the Search button.

While you can place these two controls individually in your window, their purpose and functionality are so interconnected that you would never really use them separately. This makes them ideal candidates for being placed inside a `UserControl`.

To further enhance the encapsulation, you could write your `UserControl` such that it doesn't tell the hosting container when the user presses Enter or when the user clicks the Search button; it simply exposes a single event called `SearchInvoked`. Your window could listen for that event and, in an ideal Model-View-Controller world, pass the search request on to a search controller for processing.

Within the UserControl, you have the ability to improve the look and feel of that single element without affecting the UI definition of the window and enabling your control for reuse in multiple locations throughout your application. Additionally, wrapping a set of related controls and giving them a purpose-driven name such as SearchBar makes your XAML and your code easier to read, maintain, and debug.

Similar to the way refactoring allows you to incrementally improve your C# code to make it more understandable, maintainable, and testable, refactoring the UI provides the same benefits and is much easier to do within the bounds of a UserControl. This is often called *view refactoring*.

> **NOTE**
>
> **Customizing UserControls**
>
> A UserControl doesn't allow customization of its look and feel because it does not expose properties for templates, styles, or triggers. You will have the best luck with UserControls if you think of them as faceless containers for logically and functionally related controls.

The Panel Class

The Panel class is an element that exists solely to provide the core layout functionality in WPF. Powerful, dynamic layout capability has always been something that was missing in Windows Forms, and now that WPF has dynamic layout features, the world is a much happier place.

Think of the Panel as a "layout brain" rather than something that actually produces its own UI. Its job is to size the child elements and arrange them in the allocated space, but it has no UI of its own. WPF ships with a powerful set of panels that handle many of the common layout scenarios that developers run into on a daily basis. These include the Grid, StackPanel, DockPanel, and the WrapPanel. The following is a brief description of each layout pattern (don't worry, you see plenty more of these classes in the code samples throughout the book):

- ▶ **Grid**—Provides a row/column paradigm for laying out child controls.

- ▶ **StackPanel**—Child controls are laid out in horizontal or vertical stacks.

- ▶ **DockPanel**—Child controls are docked within the container according to the preferences specified by each child control.

- ▶ **WrapPanel**—Child controls in this panel wrap according to the specified wrapping preferences.

Another panel called the Canvas provides static, absolute coordinate-based layout. Panels can be nested within each other to create more complex layouts. Layout in WPF is handled using the two-phased approach of measure and arrange.

During the measure phase, the parent requests that each of its children supply their minimum-*required* dimensions. The parent then applies additional requirements such as margins, alignment, and padding.

Once each child has been measured, the parent panel then performs the arrange phase. During this phase, the parent panel places each child control in its actual position in the final dimensions. The final position and size of the child element may not be what the child element requested. In these scenarios, the parent panel is the final authority on where the child controls are and how much space they take up.

`Panels` also have some extra functionality that you might not want to supersede, such as built-in ability to work with `ItemsControls` and the ability to dynamically change the z-order of a child element with the `Panel.SetZIndex` method.

The Decorator Class

A `Decorator` class is responsible for wrapping a UI element to support additional behavior. It has a single `Child` property of type `UIElement`, which contains the content to be wrapped. A `Decorator` can be used to add simple visual decoration, such as a `Border`, or more complex behavior such as a `ViewBox`, `AdornerDecorator`, or the `InkPresenter`.

When you subclass a `Decorator`, you can expose some useful `DependencyProperties` to customize it. For example, the `Border` class exposes properties like `BorderBrush`, `BorderThickness`, and `CornerRadius` that all affect how the border is drawn around its child content.

The Adorner Class

If we already have an additive decoration class in the form of the `Decorator`, why do we need an `Adorner` class? As mentioned earlier, every single class in the class hierarchy that makes up WPF has a specific purpose. While a `Decorator` is responsible for drawing decoration *around* the *outside* of a piece of child content, the `Adorner` class allows you to overlay visuals *on top of* existing visual elements. An easy way to think of adorners is that they are secondary interactive visuals that provide additional means to interact with the primary visual. That might seem complex, but think about widgets such as resizing grips that appear on elements in a typical diagramming program. Those are a secondary visual that sit *on top of* the elements that they are adorning and provide additional functionality and interaction. By clicking and dragging the resizing-handles, the user can resize the underlying control.

Adorner classes work in conjunction with the `AdornerDecorator`, which is an invisible surface on which the adorners rest. To be part of the visual tree, adorners have to have a container. The `AdornerDecorator` acts as this container.

`AdornerDecorators` are generally defined at the top of the visual tree (such as the `ControlTemplate` for the `Window` control). This makes all adorners sit on top of all of the `Window` content. We explore the use of adorners throughout the book, but you see them specifically in Chapter 6, "The Power of Attached Properties," and Chapter 9, "Creating Advanced Controls and Visual Effects."

The `Image` Class

You might be a little surprised to see the `Image` class mentioned here among all of the other highly interactive visual controls. In most frameworks, images contain just enough functionality to display rasterized (nonvector) images and maybe support reading and writing streams of image data, but that's about it.

`Image` classes can actually provide control-like capabilities for some specific scenarios. `Image` derives from `FrameworkElement`, so it can be composed in logical trees and has rich support for event handling and layout. It encapsulates the functionality to render an instance of an `ImageSource`, specified via the `Source` property. The `ImageSource` class can represent a vector image like `DrawingImage` or a raster/bitmap image like the `BitmapSource`.

Images can be useful when you want to visualize a large amount of data for which you have limited interaction. Some situations where this might come in handy are when you are visualizing high-volume graphs or network monitoring tools that are visualizing thousands of network nodes. In cases like this, even `DrawingVisuals` become extremely expensive because each data item is a separate visual and consumes CPU and memory resources. Using an image, and knowing that each data point doesn't need to be interactive, you can visualize what you need without bringing the host computer to its knees.

Since the `Image` class also has event handling support, we can attach handlers for mouse events that can query the pixel at the mouse's current coordinates and report information about that data item. With a little bit of creativity and forethought, the `Image` class can be a powerful tool in any developer's toolbox.

The Brushes

The `Brush`-related classes in WPF represent a powerful way of drawing simple to complex graphics with extreme ease of use. A brush represents static noninteractive graphics that serve mostly as backgrounds on visual elements. You can use a basic brush like `SolidColorBrush`, which only draws solid colors like Red, Blue, LightGray, and so on, and also gradient brushes like a `LinearGradientBrush` and `RadialGradientBrush`. The gradient brushes have additional properties to control the style of drawing the gradient. Figure 2.5 shows you various kinds of gradient brushes.

Although solid and gradient brushes are available in previous UI technologies, the real power comes with the `TileBrush` classes such as `ImageBrush`, `DrawingBrush`, and `VisualBrush`. An `ImageBrush` as the name suggests allows you to create a `Brush` out of an image. This is useful since it allows you to use an image without using the `Image` class. Since it is a brush, you can use it wherever a `Brush` type property is expected.

`DrawingBrush` gives you the power of defining complex graphics as a simple brush. Using `DrawingGroups` and `GeometryDrawings`, you can define nested graphics that can provide elegant backgrounds to your visuals. In Figure 2.6, you can see a nested set of graphic elements to create the final `DrawingBrush`. With clever use of `DrawingBrushes`, you can simplify the way you define some `ControlTemplates`.

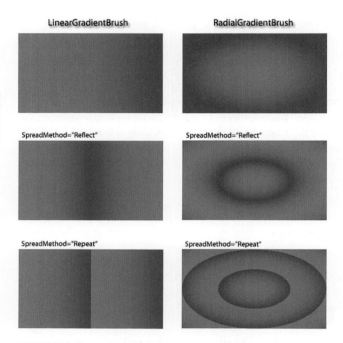

FIGURE 2.5   Linear and radial gradient brushes.

FIGURE 2.6   The swoop seen in Word 2007, created using a DrawingBrush.

A `VisualBrush` gives you a live snapshot of a rendered element from the visual tree. We see many uses of `VisualBrush`es in later chapters, such as using `VisualBrush` as a texture on a 3D model or creating reflections.

The TileBrush can also be stretched and tiled to fill the bounds of the visual. You can also cut out a rectangular section of the brush using the Viewport and ViewBox properties. Just like regular visuals, you can also apply transforms. Brushes have two kinds of transform properties: RelativeTransform and Transform. The RelativeTransform property scales the brush using the relative coordinates of the visual ([0,0] to [1,1]). It is useful if you want to transform the brush without knowing the absolute bounds of the visual on which it is applied. The Transform property works after brush output has been mapped to the bounds of the visual—in other words, after the RelativeTransform is applied.

The DataTemplate, ControlTemplate, and ItemsPanelTemplate Classes

WPF has a set of template classes that are used to represent visual trees. Templates are never actually rendered directly; rather, they are applied to other container classes like a ContentPresenter, ItemsPresenter, or a Control.

Each template class derives from the FrameworkTemplate class. These include the DataTemplate, ControlTemplate, and ItemsPanelTemplate classes. There is also a HierarchicalDataTemplate that is used for representing hierarchical data. It takes a little getting used to, but once you are, it is an invaluable tool for representing multilevel or tiered data. HierarchicalDataTemplates are used for controls such as the TreeView.

Each of these three templates contains a visual tree that can be greater than one level. The exception here is that the ItemsPanelTemplate can only contain a Panel-derived class as the root (there is a hint to this exception in the name of the template class itself).

The Viewport3D Class

So far every class that we have discussed so far has been a flat, two-dimensional control. WPF also gives developers unprecedented power and accessibility into the world of 3D programming. The Viewport3D class (see Figure 2.7) gives developers the ability to work in three dimensions without having to deal with complex game-oriented frameworks such as Direct3D or OpenGL.

The Viewport3D class is a container for a 3D world that is comprised of 3D models, textures, cameras, and lights. Viewport3D derives from the FrameworkElement class instead of Control. This makes a good deal of sense because FrameworkElement works great as a visual container, and the Viewport3D class is a visual container for an interactive 3D scene.

The Viewport3D class also has no background. As a result, you can place a 3D viewport on top of 2D elements and create stunning effects by mixing and matching 2D and 3D visual elements. Just keep in mind that the 3D world must reside in a completely different container. For example, you can use a VisualBrush to take a 2D visual and apply it to the surface of a 3D model as a material. The .NET Framework 3.5 introduced additional classes that allow you to have live, interactive 2D visuals on a 3D surface. For example, you can place a Button visual as a material for a Sphere and interact with it like a regular button, even if the Sphere is spinning and being dynamically lit by a light source.

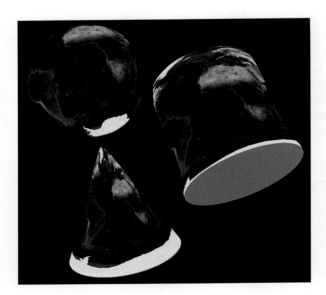

FIGURE 2.7   A sample of the **ViewPort3D** class.

The MediaElement Class

Many of today's modern applications are more than just static controls and grids and buttons. Many of them contain multimedia such as sounds, music, and video. WPF not only lets you play audio and video, but gives you programmatic control of the playback.

WPF gives you this multimedia programming experience with the MediaElement class. You indicate the source of the media using the Source property. You can control the media playback using the Play, Pause, and Stop methods. You can even control the volume and skip to a specific time in the playback using the Position property.

Figure 2.8 shows a simple WPF application that contains a media element and some controls for manipulating the video.

FIGURE 2.8   A simple **MediaElement** application.

The InkCanvas

The Tablet PC introduced a more widespread use of the stylus as a means to interact with the applications. The strokes created using the stylus were treated as ink, which could also be mapped to application-specific gestures. Although the stylus is treated as the default device, a mouse makes a good substitute.

WPF has the `InkCanvas` class that provides most of the features available on the Tablet PC. In fact the `InkCanvas` becomes the slate on which we can scribble either with the mouse or with the stylus. `InkCanvas` can be created declaratively and exposes a variety of events related to strokes. It also has built-in gesture recognition for some standard gestures. By overlaying an `InkCanvas` on some UI elements, you can add some interesting features to an application. For example, for a photo-viewing application, you can overlay an `InkCanvas` on a photo to annotate parts of the picture, as shown in Figure 2.9.

2

FIGURE 2.9   A simple **InkCanvas** application.

Summary

With the diverse range of classes available to use within WPF, we can see that WPF is a great toolset for creating interesting, compelling, and visually stunning interfaces and controls.

Understanding and respecting this diversity and knowing which is the best tool for any given situation will make your development experience more rewarding and enjoyable and will ultimately improve the quality of your applications.

Table 2.1 presents a summary of the classes discussed in this chapter.

In the next chapter, we discuss creating controls and some best practices for approaching control creation. We build on the foundations from this chapter and the previous chapter as we venture into the world of creating exciting, modern interfaces with WPF.

TABLE 2.1   Summary of WPF Classes

Class	Description
DispatcherObject	Provides threading and messaging control
DependencyObject	Provides hosting for dependency properties, a core building block for many of WPF's advanced features, such as data binding
Visual, DrawingVisual	Provide functionality for drawing simple graphics
Shape	Provides functionality for drawing geometry-based graphics
Decorator	Draws decorations around a contained UIElement
Adorner	Provides a decorative overlay on top of other controls
FrameworkElement	A container for other visual elements
GlyphRuns, TextBlock, FlowDocument	Provide text support with increasingly complex set of features for formatting and layout
Panel	The "layout brain" container for other elements
Control	A UI component that supports templating
ContentPresenter	Container for holding a DataTemplate
ItemsPresenter	Container for holding an ItemTemplate
ContentControl	A control that contains a single child
ItemsControl	A control that displays a list of items
UserControl	A "black box" container for multiple logically and visually related controls
DataTemplate, ControlTemplate, ItemsPanelTemplate	Reusable visual tree templates
Image	A high-performance graphics control for high-volume data visualization or display of raster and vector images
Brush	Provides static graphics for backgrounds, ranging from the simple SolidColorBrush to the complex TileBrushes
Viewport3D	A container for an interactive 3D world
MediaElement	Plays audio and/or video within a container
InkCanvas	For creating Tablet PC-like strokes and gestures

CHAPTER 3

Getting Started Writing Custom Controls

WPF represents a fundamental change in how user interfaces are built for the Windows platform. It provides so much more flexibility than its predecessors that one of the worst mistakes a WPF developer can make is assuming that something you had to do in WinForms is also something you have to do with the Windows Presentation Foundation.

One of the biggest pitfalls any of us can make is to create a custom control when we don't need to create one. Surprisingly, there is a multitude of scenarios where our first instinct is to create a custom control, yet the flexibility of WPF's templates attached properties make that instinct wrong more often than not.

This chapter provides clear guidelines and the tips and tricks available that actually negate the need for a custom control. When you finish this chapter, you will have a set of questions that you can ask of your requirements that will help you determine whether you really do need a custom control. The rest of the book teaches you some of the most important WPF techniques through custom control creation.

Overcoming the "Start from Scratch" Instinct

Creating a control in WPF is both interesting and challenging. The challenge comes not from the difficult implementation, but rather from the difficult time many developers have in deciding on the best option from the hundreds of available options. WPF controls can be designed in many different ways, but more importantly, you can customize and extend existing controls without ever writing your own control.

WPF is a rich and powerful platform that gives you many controls straight out of the box. In the majority of cases, these out-of-the-box controls should fit your requirements well. If the changes that you need to make to an existing control are cosmetic, usually you can make those changes using the control's own properties. For example, a Button exposes properties such as Background, BorderThickness, and BorderBrush. These properties can be used to quickly and easily change the appearance of a button. For more advanced changes to a control that involve modifying the visual tree, you can use a ControlTemplate or a DataTemplate (or both) to satisfy your UI requirements.

Using a ControlTemplate can radically alter the appearance of an existing control. The ControlTemplate allows you to include most of the classes in the WPF hierarchy in your modified visual tree, resulting in a rich look and feel. You can enhance the look of the control using a mix of opacities, shader effects, and animations.

Most of the controls in WPF follow a pattern called *lookless controls*. This means that a control's appearance is separated from its behavior, and the control makes no assumptions about its own appearance. The control is defined only in terms of logical properties, events, and behavior. A control's appearance can be specified using a combination of a ControlTemplate and/or a DataTemplate or just using the control's properties. The separation of appearance and behavior in controls allows developers to enhance the appearance and even modify the behavior of a control without resorting to subclassing.

This section of the chapter takes you through an overview of the many different techniques at your disposal for creating the functionality and appearance that you need without creating a new control class. When selecting the tools you need, think about which behaviors you want and what base appearance you need and work outward from there.

Using Data Transformations

Sometimes a ControlTemplate gets you most of the way to your goal, but there still may be a small cosmetic gap between the end result and your requirements. This usually happens when you are trying to bind to a data value that doesn't lend itself to direct rendering. Instead you want an interim step to convert the value to which your GUI is bound into something more pleasing to the user. Transformations are not limited to just domain-specific data but can also be used in the UI layer. In WPF, you use ValueConverters and TypeConverters to solve this problem.

Using Value Converters

Value converters are great for transforming data from one domain to another. One thing that developers often realize is that the more optimized a back-end data source is, the less human-readable the contents. A value converter can be used to do anything from convert simple Boolean values into Yes/No text to turn a bitmask-packed integer into a series of graphically rendered on/off switches. You can also use value converters to take user input or user gestures and convert that into something usable by the bound data source.

Value converters work exclusively with the WPF data binding facilities. This means that they work within the {Binding ... } syntax in XAML but can also be created programmatically using the Binding class. The Binding class exposes a property called Converter, which is of type IValueConverter. Using the converter, it is possible to apply a transformation on the bound value.

Formatting is a classic example of using converters with bound values. If you have data values that need to be displayed in a human-readable fashion then a ValueConverter is the right tool for the job. Value converters work on more than just plain data and can be used in many other places where bindings are applied. Using a TemplateBinding inside a ControlTemplate is a good (and often overlooked) place to use value converters.

Using TypeConverters

TypeConverters are useful when setting values of complex properties inside XAML. By associating a TypeConverter with a particular type, it is possible to take the string values entered by developers in the XAML and convert them into more concrete types used by the underlying object tree.

For example, if a control that you created exposes a property that is an enum, you still want to be able to set the value on that control, but in XAML you want to be able to set it as a simple string and have the control understand your intent. TypeConverters make this possible.

Consider the example of the BrushConverter. Most of us use this converter on a daily basis when building WPF applications, but we take its existence and utility for granted. The BrushConverter makes it possible for us to type freeform strings like "Red", "Green", or "Blue" when setting a property of type Brush:

```
<Grid Background="Blue" ... />
```

The Background property of the Grid class is of type Brush. The BrushConverter takes the string "Blue" and turns it into an instance of the SolidColorBrush class and initializes that color to System.Windows.Media.Colors.Blue.

TypeConverters and ValueConverters add a level of indirection or abstraction that simplifies setting properties in XAML and dramatically increases our ability to show users what they expect to see and not force them to look at data that only a database could love.

You can also add conditional logic inside these converters to create some powerful interfaces. Consider an example where you want to change the ItemsPanel of a ListBox based on some criteria. In other words, based on something that happens in your UI, you want to dynamically change the panel container holding the list box items.

You can do this using a Style trigger that looks at a particular property on the ListBox and changes the ItemsPanel. In this example, the plain property value is not enough to make the decision, and we need more information to decide on an appropriate panel. We can add this additional information using a ValueConverter and supply it to the style trigger:

```
<Style.Triggers>
    <Trigger Property="SwitchToBigPanel"
                 Value="True">
        <Setter Property="ItemsPanel"
            Value="{Binding RelativeSource={RelativeSource Self},
                        Converter={StaticResource Conv}}" />
    </Trigger>
</Style.Triggers>
```

The `{StaticResource Conv}` inside the binding refers to an instance of an `IValueConverter` that performs some logic, examines additional criteria, and returns an instance of the `ItemsPanelTemplate` class (the property `ItemsPanel` is of type `ItemsPanelTemplate`). As you can see, using value converters like this can be *extremely* empowering to the WPF developer.

One practical use for a converter and trigger like this might be to dynamically change the containing panel when the number of items in the `ListBox` exceeds some threshold. For example, you could use the default container panel when there are fewer than 50 child items, but you might dynamically change to a different container to hold medium, large, and enormous data sets to provide the user with the best possible item navigation experience. The `ValueConverter` might also have additional logic to check available system resources or user preferences for the number of items they want to deal with at any given time. The possibilities are endless!

Find the Behavior You Want, Then Extend

When deciding where to start customizing existing controls, you need to find a control that has the behavior you're looking for first. Generally, visual elements are far easier to customize and extend than behavior. For example, you can change the panel that contains items in an item-rendering control, but you don't want to try and turn a list-type control into a singular-type control.

The controls in the WPF hierarchy are defined based on the shape of the data they represent. The following is a brief recap of the data shapes supported by controls within WPF:

- ▶ **Singular controls**—Button, RadioButton, CheckBox
- ▶ **Range-based controls**—Slider, ProgressBar
- ▶ **List-based controls**—ItemsControl, ListBox, ListView, ComboBox
- ▶ **Hierarchy-based controls**—TreeView
- ▶ **Composite data-based controls**—UserControl

When you start to represent data in your application, these controls are the ones that you start with. If the shape of the data that you are trying to represent doesn't map directly to the controls, it is still possible to use the stock controls with judicious use of data templates, control templates, and converters. Throughout the rest of this chapter, you see various techniques for presenting a custom UI using the stock controls.

The Power of Attached Properties

So you're building an amazing new application and you need a behavior for a typical type of control that isn't available out of the box. You're absolutely convinced that there's no way to extend the existing control functionality without subclassing and creating a pile of work for yourself. Time to subclass, right?

Maybe not. There is still a chance that you can add the behavior you need without creating a new control. WPF provides an innovative feature called *attached properties*, which can be used to add behavior to existing controls. These new properties are not defined on the control being extended, but rather they are defined on a separate object (generally a `DependencyObject`). Thus, we end up with a *source* object that defines the attached properties and a *target* object on which you attach these properties. The target is the object being extended with new functionality contained in the source. When the attached property is set on the target object, a property change event is fired on the source. The event handler is passed information about the target and the new and old values of the property.

By hooking up property changed handlers, we can add additional behavior by calling methods on the target, changing properties, and listening to events. We look at more detailed examples of using attached properties in Chapter 6, "The Power of Attached Properties." Keep in mind that attached properties are only a means to extend functionality; the original target control still needs to be considered a "black box," and its internals cannot be modified.

Let's consider a simple example that illustrates the use of attached properties. Let's say you want to represent the progress of a particular workflow process. Although the progress is internally represented as a percentage, the user interface guidelines call for displaying the progress in stages, of which there are five, each stage representing 1/20 of the 100% completion.

Looking at the previous list of data shapes, we know that we're probably interested in the `ProgressBar` control for this, but the default UI for this control renders a solid bar, as shown in Figure 3.1, and doesn't know about stages.

FIGURE 3.1 Default display form of a **ProgressBar**.

Rather than the default display, we want our "staged" progress bar to look like the one displayed in Figure 3.2.

FIGURE 3.2 Custom display of a "staged" progress bar.

This can be achieved by using a combination of a `ControlTemplate` for the progress bar and an interesting use of attached properties. The `ControlTemplate` defines the visuals for the `ProgressBar`. `Triggers` are used to highlight the current stage. Since triggers work only on a single value comparison (for example, trigger when PropertyX equals ValueY) rather than a range comparison, we cannot directly use the `ProgressBar`'s `Value` property to highlight the current stage.

What would be great is to actually augment the `ProgressBar` so that it has a `Stage` property. This would make the rest of the control extension much easier. To do this, we need a helper class called `ProcessStageHelper` that maps the range of progress values to a custom `ProcessStage` enum. We pick the correct `ProcessStage` based on the current progress value. This can be seen in Listing 3.1.

The `ProcessStageHelper` class exposes two attached properties: one for receiving the progress value and one for giving out a read-only `ProcessStage` enum value.

The code in Listing 3.1 shows the definition of the `ProcessStageHelper` class.

LISTING 3.1   The **ProcessStageHelper** Class

```
public class ProcessStageHelper : DependencyObject
{
    public static readonly DependencyProperty
        ProcessCompletionProperty = DependencyProperty.RegisterAttached(
          "ProcessCompletion", typeof(double),
          typeof(ProcessStageHelper), new PropertyMetadata(0.0,
            OnProcessCompletionChanged));

    private static readonly DependencyPropertyKey
      ProcessStagePropertyKey =
          DependencyProperty.RegisterAttachedReadOnly(
            "ProcessStage", typeof(ProcessStage),
            typeof(ProcessStageHelper),
              new PropertyMetadata(ProcessStage.Stage1));

    public static readonly DependencyProperty ProcessStageProperty =
        ProcessStagePropertyKey.DependencyProperty;

    private static void OnProcessCompletionChanged(DependencyObject d,
        DependencyPropertyChangedEventArgs e)
    {
      double progress = (double)e.NewValue;
      ProgressBar bar = (d as FrameworkElement).TemplatedParent
          as ProgressBar;
      if (progress >= 0 && progress < 20)
        bar.SetValue(ProcessStagePropertyKey, ProcessStage.Stage1);
      if (progress >= 20 && progress < 40)
```

```
                bar.SetValue(ProcessStagePropertyKey, ProcessStage.Stage2);
        if (progress >= 40 && progress < 60)
                bar.SetValue(ProcessStagePropertyKey, ProcessStage.Stage3);
        if (progress >= 60 && progress < 80)
                bar.SetValue(ProcessStagePropertyKey, ProcessStage.Stage4);
         if (progress >= 80 && progress <= 100)
                bar.SetValue(ProcessStagePropertyKey, ProcessStage.Stage5);
}
```

The preceding code is a little more complex than it needs to be just to help illustrate the additional functionality that you can add to existing classes. The `OnProcessCompletionChanged` handler sets the `ProcessStage` read-only attached property. Since this read-only property is attached to the `ProgressBar` class, it can now be used in the `ControlTemplate.Triggers` section to provide a custom UI based on the current workflow process stage, as shown in Listing 3.2.

LISTING 3.2   ControlTemplate for the Process Workflow ProgressBar

```xml
<ControlTemplate x:Key="ProcessStageTemplate"
            TargetType="ProgressBar">
            ...
            ...
    <ControlTemplate.Triggers>
    <Trigger
            Property="Chapter_CustCtrl:ProcessStageHelper.ProcessStage"
        Value="Stage1">
    <Setter Property="Fill"
        Value="{StaticResource SelectedStageBrush}"
        TargetName="Stage1" />
    <Setter Property="Stroke"
        Value="#bb2d00"
        TargetName="Stage1" />
    </Trigger>
    <Trigger Property="Chapter_CustCtrl:ProcessStageHelper.ProcessStage"
        Value="Stage2">
    <Setter Property="Fill"
        Value="{StaticResource SelectedStageBrush}"
        TargetName="Stage2" />
    <Setter Property="Stroke"
        Value="#bb2d00"
        TargetName="Stage2" />
    </Trigger>
    <Trigger Property="Chapter_CustCtrl:ProcessStageHelper.ProcessStage"
        Value="Stage3">
    <Setter Property="Fill"
```

```
        Value="{StaticResource SelectedStageBrush}"
        TargetName="Stage3" />
    <Setter Property="Stroke"
        Value="#bb2d00"
        TargetName="Stage3" />
</Trigger>

...

...

</ControlTemplate.Triggers>

</ControlTemplate>
```

In Listing 3.2, we created multiple triggers. Each one is triggered when the process stage is set to a specific value. This then allows the code to set the `Fill` and `Stroke` property of the appropriate "stage" box.

Remember that this is just one small example of the ways that you can extend the behavior and visuals of a control without creating your own.

Custom Control Creation Checklist

Now that you have seen many of the alternatives to creating custom controls, we can summarize the process of elimination used to determine whether you should create a new custom control.

The following is a summary of the decision process:

▶ Use the framework as much as possible. WPF provides a variety of extensible controls, so make sure that the functionality you want doesn't already exist in a WPF control.

▶ In many cases, the data structure you're working with requires different visual representation. Using `ControlTemplates` and `DataTemplates` can often get you the functionality you need.

▶ Look at `ValueConverters` to see whether they can help bridge the gap between the stock functionality and what you need.

▶ Finally, see whether you can't extend existing behavior with attached properties.

A universal fact about all frameworks such as .NET, WPF, WinForms, or any other is that there is only so much you can do out of the box. The stock controls supplied by WPF may be sufficient to handle 90% of what you want your application to do. There are always those cases that require some feature in the last 10%. If after going through the preceding checklist you determine that none of the techniques will solve your problem, you are ready to build your own control. The rest of this book focuses on a variety of techniques and scenarios for building your own controls that also help improve your overall WPF skills.

Thinking in Layers—The Art of Decomposition

When we build a house, we don't simply walk up to an empty plot of land and build a house. First, the land is prepared to support the foundation. Then the foundation is poured. Once the foundation has set and is ready, then we set up the framing or the skeleton of the house. From there, you can worry about rooms, walls, plaster, electricity, plumbing, and everything else. The point is that you don't walk up to the empty plot of land and start laying down wires for the full-featured home officeΔhome theater you're planning on building (no matter how attractive that idea might be).

We need to think in layers and think compositionally. The software that we build needs to be looked at in terms of multiple layers to decompose the problem into a set of smaller problems. This task of breaking down a large project into smaller individual projects is commonplace for most developers. If done properly, this can give us better clarity of vision, purpose, and even reduce the overall project risk.

The concept of a layered structure is useful when building user interfaces or custom controls. The UI, is nothing more than a visual layering of graphical components. When we interact with the UI, we are dealing with a flattened interface that hides the layers and presents us with the digital equivalent of a flat piece of colored paper. Even though we may not be able to see them, the layers are still there contributing to the overall user experience. In WPF, we treat these visual layers in terms of a tree of components: the visual tree and the logical tree.

Thinking in layers is perhaps one of the most important steps in building your controls. If you can decompose the final visual representation into a collection of layered graphics, you will have a much clearer idea of how to build that control. In the real world, interface development often happens by looking at a wireframe or mockup image. As developers we are supposed to look at that picture and transform it into an interactive component. A developer accustomed to thinking in layers would immediately begin carving up the image and determining the layer hierarchy required to produce the design image.

It is beneficial to train our minds to think compositionally and in terms of layers. Not only does it help in creating custom components but it also helps in understanding the visual structure of other controls.

The remainder of this chapter is dedicated to an example designed to train your mind to think in terms of visual layers of interactive components. This compositional thinking process helps you to *think in WPF*.

Sample: Building a Circular Minute Timer

Imagine that you have been asked to build a circular timer like the one shown in Figure 3.3. It starts at 0 seconds and counts up to 60. This control could have a wide variety of applications, so it sounds like an interesting project.

At first glance, looking at the image given to you by a designer (such as the image in Figure 3.3), you think this is a

FIGURE 3.3   A circular minute timer.

job for a custom control since WPF doesn't have any controls that count time in a circular fashion. You could definitely build this as a custom control, but let's take a step back and go through some of the thought process from the checklist in the previous section of this chapter. Perhaps we don't need a new control at all and might be able to create this by enhancing an existing control.

Dissecting the requirements a little, we can abstract the requirements down to the fact that we need a control that can display a value somewhere within a given range (in our case, a value between 0 and 60). WPF actually *does* have many controls that fit the requirement of a range-based control, including ScrollBar, Slider, and ProgressBar.

The ScrollBar is probably not a good candidate since we want to display the value; we don't necessarily want an interactive way to control the current progress/stage. This actually eliminates the Slider as well, which is also an interactive value-changing control that modifies a value within a given range.

That leaves us with the ProgressBar. We want to represent the concept of a timer, which can be thought of as *progress on a time axis*. Thinking of it this way, the ProgressBar is beginning to look more promising. We could, as an alternative, create a new control that derived from RangeBase, but that would require reimplementing a lot of the functionality in ProgressBar.

> **NOTE**
>
> **Don't Reinvent the Wheel**
>
> If you ever get to the point in your code where you feel you are spending more time reinventing the wheel than you are extending and enhancing existing functionality, there's a good chance you chose to extend at too low a level. Check the WPF control hierarchy to see whether there is a better match for what you're trying to accomplish.

Enhancing and Extending the ProgressBar

It seems pretty clear at this point that we can probably create the radial minute timer by extending and enhancing the ProgressBar control. By default, the ProgressBar is displayed as a vertical or horizontal bar with a differently styled bar contained within to show the current progress. What we need to display looks like a ring. First we need to decide whether the ring is part of the control or the data contained within it. In this case, the ring is the control container so looking at the ControlTemplate to create the ring seems like a promising start.

How do we create a control template that creates a "progress ring"? Let's explore a couple of options and see which one best fits our needs:

▶ The circular ring that represents the progress is technically an arc that spans from 0 degrees to 360 degrees. This arc can be represented as either a thick stroke, as in Figure 3.4, or as a combination of a pie shape and an overlay circle, as in Figure 3.5. The latter is a case for CombinedGeometry with a custom pie shape and a circular Ellipse.

FIGURE 3.4   An arc shape.

▶ We need to create the geometry somewhere. This could either be in a class that derives from FrameworkElement or a Shape.

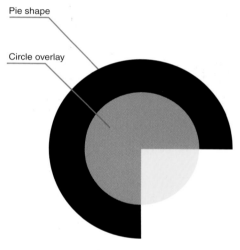

▶ Deriving from Shape automatically gives us some dependency properties such as Stroke, Fill, and StrokeThickness, and all we have to do is override the protected property: DefiningGeometry. We also get some bonus features such as Stretch, which can stretch the shape to fit in its parent container's bounds.

FIGURE 3.5   A pie shape with a circular overlay.

▶ Deriving from FrameworkElement can make it more lightweight. All the geometry construction would happen in its OnRender method. Note that we have to set up our own dependency properties for Fill, Stroke, StrokeThickness, and so on. We would also need to use the MeasureOverride and ArrangeOverride methods to set the bounds properly.

From what we can see for this particular sample, it looks like using the Shape derived class to deal with the arc is a good idea. This allows us to concentrate more on the geometry instead of worrying about setting up dependency properties or creating overrides for Measure and Arrange and so on.

Creating the Arc Shape

To simplify the creation of our ProgressBar's ControlTemplate, we are going to create a building block, the arc shape, which can then be used to assemble our ControlTemplate.

The Arc class will have two dependency properties: StartAngle and EndAngle. These two act as the start and stop points for the arc. By specifying the start and end as degree angles, we get a really good abstraction with which to work. The angle needs to be specified in degrees with the regular Cartesian convention of describing angles. In other words, these angles are increasing in the counterclockwise direction with the positive X axis representing 0 degrees, as shown in Figure 3.6.

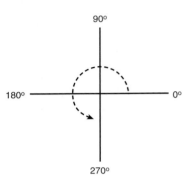

FIGURE 3.6   Illustration of WPF angle of rotation.

With the two angle properties, we can specify the arc in Figure 3.4 as a StartAngle of 0 and an EndAngle of 270. Now that we know what it will take to draw the arc, let's put it into code. We are going to take the approach of using StrokeThickness instead of CombinedGeometry because of its simplicity and ease of implementation. As a result, our arc implementation only needs to provide the geometry for the arc outline.

The bulk of the work for the Arc class happens in the two methods shown in Listing 3.3.

LISTING 3.3   Creating the Arc geometry

```
private Geometry GetArcGeometry()
{
    Point startPoint = PointAtAngle(Math.Min(StartAngle, EndAngle));
    Point endPoint = PointAtAngle(Math.Max(StartAngle, EndAngle));

    Size arcSize = new Size(Math.Max(0, (RenderSize.Width -
                                StrokeThickness)/2),
        Math.Max(0, (RenderSize.Height - StrokeThickness)/2));
    bool isLargeArc = Math.Abs(EndAngle - StartAngle)    180;

    StreamGeometry geom = new StreamGeometry();
    using (StreamGeometryContext context = geom.Open())
    {
        context.BeginFigure(startPoint, false, false);
        context.ArcTo(endPoint, arcSize, 0, isLargeArc,
                    SweepDirection.Counterclockwise, true, false);
    }
```

```
        geom.Transform = new TranslateTransform(StrokeThickness/2,
                                                 StrokeThickness/2);
        return geom;
}


private Point PointAtAngle(double angle)
{
        double radAngle = angle*(Math.PI/180);
        double xRadius = (RenderSize.Width - StrokeThickness)/2;
        double yRadius = (RenderSize.Height - StrokeThickness)/2;

        double x = xRadius + xRadius*Math.Cos(radAngle);
        double y = yRadius - yRadius*Math.Sin(radAngle);

return new Point(x, y);
}
```

The private `PointAtAngle` method calculates the X and Y location of a point given the degree angle. This is called twice from the `GetArcGeometry` method: once for the start angle and once for the end angle. Note the way we adjust the arc size. We are reducing the bounds by half of the `RenderSize` and the `StrokeThickness`. In WPF, strokes on the shapes are drawn such that the stroke falls midway on the outline. This means that half the stroke width is inside the shape and half of it is outside the shape, as shown in Figure 3.7.

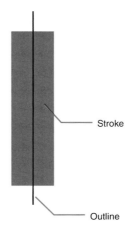

FIGURE 3.7   WPF stroke and outline locations.

We are adjusting the bounds such that the stroke completely falls inside. So far, with the code shown in Listing 3.3, we've taken care of drawing the `Arc` shape. By specifying the `StartAngle` and `EndAngle` we can make the arc look like any of the shapes in Figure 3.8.

Working with the `ControlTemplate`

Now that we've created the `Arc` class, the rest of the work of bending the functionality of a `ProgressBar` into a circular minute timer should be fairly straightforward. The next step is to replace the `ProgressBar`'s default `ControlTemplate` with one of our own that utilizes the newly created `Arc`.

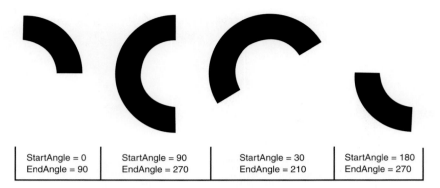

| StartAngle = 0 | StartAngle = 90 | StartAngle = 30 | StartAngle = 180 |
| EndAngle = 90 | EndAngle = 270 | EndAngle = 210 | EndAngle = 270 |

FIGURE 3.8   Creating different arc shapes by varying start and end angles.

Remember that earlier in this section of the chapter we mentioned that the art of decomposition and thinking in terms of layers allows you to create some jaw-dropping user interfaces with much less effort than you might otherwise think. Figure 3.9 shows the circular minute timer ProgressBar decomposed into the different parts required for rendering.

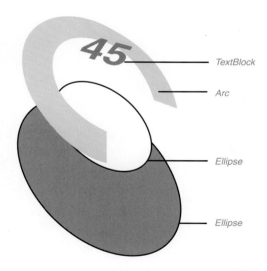

TextBlock

Arc

Ellipse

Ellipse

FIGURE 3.9   Layering for a custom **ProgressBar ControlTemplate**.

Listing 3.4 illustrates the XAML for the new ControlTemplate.

LISTING 3.4   ControlTemplate for the Circular Minute Timer

```
<Runner:ProgressToAngleConverter x:Key="ProgressConverter" />
<Style TargetType="ProgressBar">
    <Setter Property="Template">
        <Setter.Value>
```

```xml
<ControlTemplate TargetType="ProgressBar">
<Grid>
<Ellipse Stroke="Black"
    Fill="{TemplateBinding Background}"/>
<Ellipse Stroke="Black"
    Margin="40"
    Fill="White"/>
<Controls:Arc StrokeThickness="30"
    Stroke="{TemplateBinding BorderBrush}"
    Margin="5">
<Controls:Arc.StartAngle>
    <MultiBinding Converter="{StaticResource ProgressConverter}">
    <Binding Path="Minimum"
    RelativeSource="{RelativeSource TemplatedParent}" />
    <Binding Path="."
    RelativeSource="{RelativeSource TemplatedParent}" />
    </MultiBinding>
</Controls:Arc.StartAngle>
<Controls:Arc.EndAngle>
    <MultiBinding Converter="{StaticResource ProgressConverter}">
        <Binding Path="Value"
        RelativeSource="{RelativeSource TemplatedParent}" />
        <Binding Path="."
        RelativeSource="{RelativeSource TemplatedParent}" />
    </MultiBinding>
</Controls:Arc.EndAngle>
</Controls:Arc>
<TextBlock Text="{Binding Value,
    RelativeSource={RelativeSource TemplatedParent}, StringFormat=\{0:0\}}"
Foreground="{TemplateBinding Background}"
VerticalAlignment="Center"
HorizontalAlignment="Center"
FontSize="72"
FontWeight="Bold"/>
</Grid>
</ControlTemplate>
</Setter.Value>
</Setter>
</Style>
```

A couple of really important things are going on in Listing 3.4. First there is a ProgressToAngleConverter class that, as the name suggests, converts from a progress value to an angle between 0 and 360. The angle chart from Figure 3.6 should show you the math required to do this conversion. The ControlTemplate contains an instance of the Arc class, whose StartAngle and EndAngle are bound to the Minimum and Value properties, respectively.

We used a MultiBinding because we also need a reference to the ProgressBar, obtained via the {RelativeSource TemplatedParent} block of XAML. The following code from the converter should make the need for this reference clear:

```
public class ProgressToAngleConverter : IMultiValueConverter
{
    public object Convert(object[] values, Type targetType,
        object parameter, CultureInfo culture)
    {
        double progress = (double)values[0];
        ProgressBar progressBar = values[1] as ProgressBar;

        return 359.9999 * (progress / (progressBar.Maximum - progressBar.Minimum));
    }

    public object[] ConvertBack(object value, Type[] targetTypes,
        object parameter, CultureInfo culture)
    {
        throw new NotImplementedException;
    }
}
```

One thing that might look odd is the use of 359.9999 as the destination angle instead of 360. This is a quirk of modulo arithmetic. When code, including WPF (but not limited to WPF, I've seen this in several animation frameworks), considers drawing from 0 to 360, since 360 is actually at the same location as 0, "optimizations" often decide to do no drawing at all. So to force the drawing to take place, we use "almost 360."

With the combination of the Arc class (a class that we created quickly and easily), the ProgressToAngleConverter class, and a custom ControlTemplate, we were able to turn a standard straight-line progress bar into a circular minute timer. We strongly urge you to play with the fully functional sample code that comes with the book. Experiment with changing values and tweaking the visual tree to see how fancy you can make the minute timer.

Note how we broke down the problem of the circular minute timer into primitives such as the Arc and the ProgressToAngleConverter. Building on those, we created the ControlTemplate. In addition, a TextBlock shows the countdown value.

> **NOTE**
>
> **Challenge**
>
> Use the techniques you learned from the beginning of the chapter to create a segmented workflow-style progress bar and combine them with the tools you used to create the circular minute timer to create an hour and minute timer. Use a "staged" approach to segment the minute arc into ten 6-minute stages.

Summary

This chapter provided an introduction to the task of building custom controls. Before you can get started building your own custom controls, you actually need to know when *not* to build those controls. The first part of this chapter covered a set of interrogations you can do on your requirements that will help you determine whether you need to create a custom control.

Figure 3.10 shows a recap of the decision process for determining whether you should build a custom control that was mentioned earlier in the chapter.

If you don't need to create a custom control, this chapter showed you a variety of techniques to create amazing UI and behavior using the built-in extensibility mechanisms of WPF. These include attached properties, `ControlTemplates`, `DataTemplates`, and Value Converters.

In the following chapters, we show you increasingly detailed and powerful techniques for custom control building and other advanced development scenarios.

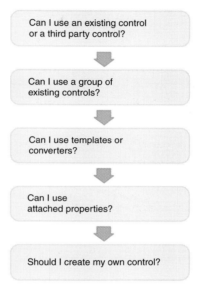

FIGURE 3.10   Determining whether to build a custom control.

CHAPTER 4

Building Custom Panels

In the chapters leading up to this, we have explored how all of the visual elements within WPF work together, how they are structured, and how they can be enhanced with concepts such as templates. The next thing that we need to explore is the concept of layout.

This chapter provides a thorough walkthrough of exactly what layout is and what it means to developers building WPF applications. In addition, this chapter contains a detailed walkthrough of how layout works and how you can harness all of that power for your own applications and controls by creating your own custom panels.

Even if your end goal is not to build a custom panel, this chapter is still valuable. By the time you finish this chapter, you will have in-depth knowledge of layout in WPF and how to customize that layout functionality. In addition to being able to create custom panels, you will also be well prepared to deal with any layout problems that come your way in the future.

Layout Defined

Before we get down into the dirty details of creating custom panels, we need to know exactly what it is we're talking about when we refer to *layout*. The short answer is that layout is simply the act of arranging a set of rectangles on the screen. For the most part, this is exactly what layout does, but it is a bit of an oversimplification.

An overarching principle needs to be remembered whenever working with layout: Every visual element that requires layout is considered in terms of the size and position of its rectangular bounds. Even if the element has an irregular shape, its layout is still calculated based on a bounding rectangle.

While at first this might seem limiting, the standardization upon a uniform geometric model for layout is actually a good thing. Learn to embrace your inner rectangle and you will be a master of WPF layout.

The most primitive element in WPF that can participate in the layout process is the UIElement class. The UIElement class defines the core of the layout process that is used by all derived classes. It is assumed in the layout process that all the visuals being arranged are instances of the UIElement class or any of its derivatives. Therefore, the Panel class (the class responsible for handling the layout of its children) stores its children in a UIElementCollection, a collection class containing only instances of UIElement.

The output of the panel layout process is a set of rectangles representing the layout of the panel's children. Different panels lay out their children according to different rules. For example, a UniformGrid calculates the layout rectangles of its children such that each child has the same size. A StackPanel that lays out its children vertically will assign the rectangles such that each of them will be as wide as the containing panel and as tall as the child's desired height. More stock layout options are available to you, and as this chapter explains, you can create your own layout rules. Figure 4.1 illustrates the difference in layout rules between the StackPanel and the single-columned UniformGrid.

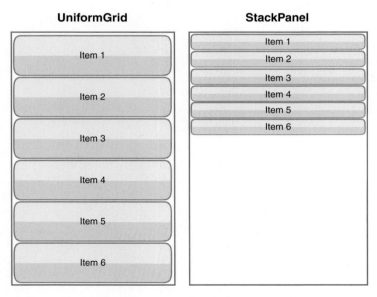

FIGURE 4.1   StackPanel and UniformGrid layout styles.

How Layout Works

The layout system in WPF is a conversation between the layout container and its children. This conversation takes place in two stages that are often referred to as *passes*. This two-pass approach starts at the root of the visual tree and recursively traverses the tree until all containers have been given the chance to perform the layout process with their children.

In the first pass of the conversation, the parent asks its children how much space they need to display themselves. The parent informs each child about the available size based on constraints such as margin, alignment, and so on. This is the *layout space* allocated to the child. Based on this layout space, the child responds to the container, indicating the total space (remember, these are rectangles) it needs to display itself.

Programmers often cringe when they see or hear the word "recursion," so we'll keep this paragraph short. This process is recursive. Before the child responds to its parent indicating how much space it needs, it asks all of its children how much space *they* need. Once all of the children respond, that information is aggregated according to the rules that are part of that control and then passed up to the parent. This occurs when you have nested layout controls, say a WrapPanel that contains multiple StackPanels.

At the end of the first phase, the parent determines the total size that can be allocated to the child for its layout. This is the final size that will be assigned to the child. In the second phase, the parent informs the child of its final size.

Figure 4.2 illustrates the conversation flow between parent and child during a layout pass.

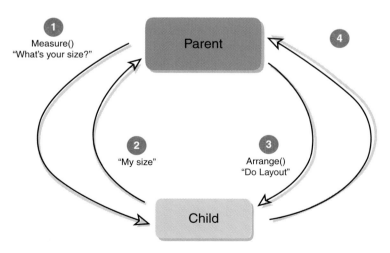

FIGURE 4.2   Conversation between parent and child during layout pass.

The first pass is characterized by the Measure call issued by the parent. Internally, the Measure call then invokes the MeasureOverride method in descendants. Similarly, the second pass is characterized by the call to `Arrange`, which then invokes `ArrangeOverride` on the children. Here are the signatures for the two methods:

```
protected override Size MeasureOverride(Size availableSize);
protected override Size ArrangeOverride(Size finalSize);
```

The actual layout (remember, it's all about the rectangles) of the control happens in the `ArrangeOverride` method implementation. The really crucial thing to be aware of is that the size sent in the arrange pass might not be the same as the size passed in `MeasureOverride`.

For example, if the size of the parent is 400x400 and its only child has a margin of (20,20,20,20) set on it, the size passed to its `MeasureOverride` method will be 360x360. The child may report a size other than 360x360 depending on its layout logic or the layout logic of its children. This could happen if the child control decides that it doesn't need all the space it has been given and can lay itself out in a smaller space. Therefore, `ArrangeOverride` may see a different final layout size. The significance of this fact is subtle, but if you're aware of it, you can save yourself some trouble. If you are precalculating rectangles within `MeasureOverride`, you might have to recalculate them again within `ArrangeOverride`. It is always a safer bet to never blur the responsibilities of the methods. Make sure the measurement pass only determines required sizes and the arrangement pass performs the actual layout. In other words, do not share any state between `MeasureOverride` and `ArrangeOverride`.

Once the `Measure` method has executed on a child, the child's `DesiredSize` property is set. A `Panel` can determine its required size by aggregating the `DesiredSize` properties of its children according to its own layout rules.

Another thing to keep in mind is that if the child has *explicitly* set its own height or width, the layout pass of the containing panel respects the explicit size.

Working with Visual Children

Before getting into the details of creating a custom panel, we need to stop briefly to talk about visual children and how they relate to the rendering of child elements within a layout panel.

In addition to `Measure` and `Arrange`, one more method and one more property need to be discussed:

```
protected override Visual GetVisualChild(int index)
protected override int VisualChildrenCount
```

These aren't features that you will be overriding all that often in your own controls, but knowing what they are and how they affect the rendering of the visual tree can be helpful.

Before we can really understand what these methods do, we need to understand why they exist. You have probably noticed already that throughout WPF, controls expose their children in wildly varying ways. A `Panel` class uses the `Children` property to expose its child items. A `Decorator` does the same with the `Child` property, and a `ContentControl` achieves the same through the use of the `Content` property. You get the idea. The problem is how does a framework universally deal with layout for all of these different controls when they don't expose their children with the same types of properties?

This is where these two class members come in. `VisualChildrenCount` gives a count of the number of visuals contained within the control. The `GetVisualChild` method acts as an indexed method to access these visual children. Since they are defined almost at the top of the hierarchy by `FrameworkElement`, they are available to virtually all classes inside the framework. These two members combine to provide a common way for WPF (and curious developers) to traverse the visual tree.

An interesting side-effect of the use of `GetVisualChild` is that it controls the Z-order ("distance" from the user relative to other controls on the screen) of the children. This is the technique that the `Panel` class uses to dynamically change the visual ordering (aka stacking order) of its children. If we look at the signature of `GetVisualChild`, we can see that there is an index parameter.

The default implementation of this method would return the child at the same index requested by the method call. However, if you get a little creative with which control you return, you can manipulate which control appears on "top" and which control appears on the "bottom"—the Z-order.

We're going to build a custom control called `ZOrderControl` that does just that. In our custom `GetVisualChild` implementation, when the 0th element is requested, we return the (n-1)th element. For the 1st child, we return the child at index (n-2) and so on. This implementation looks like this:

```
protected override Visual GetVisualChild(int index)
{
  if (index < 0 || index >= Children.Count)
  {
    throw new ArgumentOutOfRangeException("Bad Index");
  }

    // Reverse the Z order
  if (IsOrderReversed)
  {
    return Children[Children.Count - 1 - index];
  }

  // Normal Z order
  return Children[index];
}
```

The `IsOrderReversed` property is one that we defined on our custom control. This provides a declarative means of setting the behavior of this panel directly in the XAML.

```
public bool IsOrderReversed {get; set; }
```

By default, the Z-order reversal feature is disabled. If the property is set to true, then the next time the control loads, it will reverse the Z-ordering of its children. Figure 4.3 shows the ZOrderControl with the default and reversed order.

Default Order

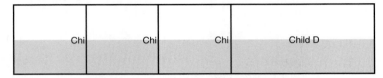

Reversed Order

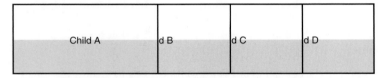

FIGURE 4.3   ZOrderControl with default and reversed order.

This is a neat little trick, but what happens if you want to change the Z-order direction of a control's children dynamically at runtime? To do this, we need to do a little more work, but the exercise is worth it. To start, we need to convert the IsOrderReversed property into a DependencyProperty. This allows us to do dynamic data binding on that property and also gives us the ability to listen to changes made to that property.

```
public static readonly DependencyProperty IsOrderReversedProperty =
  ➡DependencyProperty.
    Register("IsOrderReversed", typeof (bool), typeof (ZOrderControl2),
    new FrameworkPropertyMetadata(false, OnIsOrderReversedChanged));
```

Take note that the default value has been specified as false and the property changed handler (OnIsOrderReversedChanged) has been connected. The On<PropertyName>Changed naming convention is not only good practice but is used consistently throughout the .NET Framework and WPF.

The custom implementation of GetVisualChild stays the same as the one in the previous listing. The interesting part is in the property changed event handler:

```
private static void OnIsOrderReversedChanged(DependencyObject d,
                                DependencyPropertyChangedEventArgs e)
```

```
{
    ZOrderControl2 control = d as ZOrderControl2;
    Reparent(control);
}

private static void Reparent(ZOrderControl2 control)
{
    for (int i = 0; i < control.Children.Count; i++)
    {
        control.RemoveVisualChild(control.Children[i]);
    }

    for (int i = 0; i < control.Children.Count; i++)
    {
        control.AddVisualChild(control.Children[i]);
    }
}
```

The detaching and subsequent reattaching of the child controls causes the invalidation of the child ordering in the visual tree. This is how the Z-order can be reversed at runtime. Of course, this is mostly an exercise designed to illustrate how the visual tree is queried and the impact of the order in which children are assigned.

If you need more fine-grained (and practical) control over the Z-order, your best bet is to use the Panel class. By associating the Panel.ZIndex attached property with the children, you can cause dynamic changes to the visual ordering.

Here is the definition of the ZIndex property:

```
public static readonly DependencyProperty ZIndexProperty =
DependencyProperty.RegisterAttached("ZIndex",
    typeof(int), typeof(Panel),
    new FrameworkPropertyMetadata(0, new
PropertyChangedCallback(Panel.OnZIndexPropertyChanged)));
```

You can set the value of this property with the following code:

```
Panel.SetZIndex(child, 3);
```

Or with XAML as shown here:

```
<StackPanel>
            <Button Panel.ZIndex="3">WPF</Button>
            <Button>Beyond</Button>
            <Button>the</Button>
            <Button>Basics</Button>
</StackPanel>
```

Creating a Custom Panel: The VanishingPointPanel

You have seen how Measure and Arrange methods control the layout of children and how the VisualChildrenCount property and the GetVisualChild method provide a unified means by which code can traverse the visual tree. With that knowledge, we're ready to start exploring the power of building custom panels.

As a sample, we're going to build a panel that sizes the child elements such that it creates a sense of depth or perspective distortion. Basic drawing class 101 tells us that objects that are closer to the viewer (in most cases, our eyes) appear to be larger than objects that are farther away. For this panel, we are going to simulate this effect by gradually reducing the size of distant children while making the closest children larger.

The VanishingPointPanel takes its name from the concept of vanishing points used in drawing and painting. A vanishing point is an imaginary point that represents the point at which objects in the distance appear to fade away or *vanish*. Objects that far in the distance are so small that they can only be represented by a point. Take a look at the picture in Figure 4.4. As the road fades away in the distance, it eventually becomes nothing more than a single point.

FIGURE 4.4   A picture that illustrates the concept of a vanishing point.

To create this sense of depth, we've created a DependencyProperty called ZFactor on the VanishingPointPanel. Remember that the primary task of a panel is to come up with a rectangle for each of its children. A rectangle in WPF is represented by an instance of the Rect structure, which is defined by its location (the Left and Top properties) and its size (Width and Height properties). We use the ZFactor property to calculate the location and size of the child control's rectangle. We don't need to set the Left property because the child control is going to be centered horizontally within the containing panel.

ZFactor is defined as a percentage. In typical WPF fashion, we represent this percentage as a number between 0 and 1. In other words, this is a scaling factor for the child elements. If the value is 1, the element is allowed to render at its full size. If the value is 0, the element will be invisible.

The scaling of the children is compounded from the nearest to the farthest from the perspective of the viewer. Thus, if we set the ZFactor to 0.5, the sizes for a set of three children would be 1.0, 0.5, and 0.25 times the maximum size. A similar compounding effect is applied to the Rect.Top property. We use the panel's Width as the maximum width for each child. The maximum height of a child is defined by a separate DependencyProperty called ItemHeight. Thus, the compounded scaling effect happens on the maximum size of (panelSize.Width,ItemHeight). The nearest child gets the full size (panelSize.Width,ItemHeight), and it continues decreasing as the view progresses toward the farthest item, each time reducing it by the ZFactor.

Figure 4.5 illustrates how all this comes together visually.

FIGURE 4.5   The **VanishingPointPanel** in action.

The core of the work that needs to be done for this custom panel is to calculate the rectangles for each of the children based on the ZFactor. The following code snippet contains the implementation of the CalculateRect method:

```
private Rect CalculateRect(Size panelSize, int index)
{
    double zFactor = Math.Pow(ZFactor, index);
    Size itemSize = new Size(panelSize.Width*zFactor, ItemHeight*zFactor);

    double left = (panelSize.Width - itemSize.Width)*0.5;
    double top = panelSize.Height;
        for (int i = 0; i <= index; i++)
    {
        top -= Math.Pow(ZFactor, i)*ItemHeight;
    }

    Rect rect = new Rect(itemSize);
    rect.Location = new Point(left, top);
    return rect;
}
```

In this custom panel, MeasureOverrride uses the maximum size for each child when called. ArrangeOverride uses the value returned by CalculateRect to lay out the child control. This method also does the job of arranging from the last item to the first item. Looking at the definition of `CalculateRect` in the preceding code, you can make out that the last item is actually the nearest and the first item is the farthest away. This makes sense because you want newer (recently added) items to appear closer and push the older items farther away, closer to the vanishing point.

The following are the definitions of `MeasureOverride` and `ArrangeOverride` for the `VanishingPointPanel` control. Notice how the `ArrangeOverride` calls `CalculateRect` starting from the last item and going to the first:

```
protected override Size MeasureOverride(Size availableSize)
{
    foreach (UIElement child in InternalChildren)
    {
        Size childSize = new Size(availableSize.Width, ItemHeight);
        child.Measure(childSize);
    }

    return new Size(availableSize.Width, ItemHeight *
InternalChildren.Count);
}

protected override Size ArrangeOverride(Size finalSize)
{
    int currentIndex = 0;

    for (int index = InternalChildren.Count - 1; index >= 0; index--)
    {
        Rect rect = CalculateRect(finalSize, currentIndex);
        InternalChildren[index].Arrange(rect);

        currentIndex++;
    }
    return finalSize;
}
```

This custom panel gives you an idea of what you can do simply by overriding the default implementations of `MeasureOverride` and `ArrangeOverride`. In the next section of the chapter, you see how to take this one step further.

Building a Panel with Attached Properties: `WeightedPanel`

The `VanishingPointPanel` is an example of a panel that does not impose any panel-specific constraints on its children. The size of a child depends on its index within the `UIElementCollection`. The last child has the largest size, and the first child has the smallest size (because it is the farthest from the viewer and the closest to the imaginary vanishing point).

What if you wanted to set additional panel-specific constraints on the children that could change the way the panel sizes those children? This behavior can be established using attached properties.

WPF already provides panels that use attached properties to set constraints on children. DockPanel and Grid are two examples of panels that use attached properties to control the layout behavior of their children. DockPanel uses the DockPanel.Dock property to position a child to the left, right, bottom, or top of the container. The Grid control uses the Grid.Row and Grid.Column attached properties to determine the appropriate location of a child element within the grid.

The code in the following listing illustrates the use of attached properties with a Grid and a DockPanel:

```
<DockPanel Grid.Column="0" Margin="0,0,20,0">
    <Button DockPanel.Dock="Top">Top</Button>
    <Button DockPanel.Dock="Bottom">Bottom</Button>
    <Button DockPanel.Dock="Right">Right</Button>
    <Button DockPanel.Dock="Left">Left</Button>
    <Button>Center</Button>
</DockPanel>

<Grid Grid.Column="1">
    <Grid.RowDefinitions>
        <RowDefinition Height="0.4*" />
        <RowDefinition Height="0.6*" />
    </Grid.RowDefinitions>

    <Grid.ColumnDefinitions>
        <ColumnDefinition />
        <ColumnDefinition />
    </Grid.ColumnDefinitions>

    <Button Grid.Row="0"
        Grid.Column="0">[0, 0]</Button>
    <Button Grid.Row="0"
        Grid.Column="1">[0, 1]</Button>
    <Button Grid.Row="1"
        Grid.Column="0">[1, 0]</Button>
    <Button Grid.Row="1"
        Grid.Column="1">[1, 1]</Button>
</Grid>
```

Figure 4.6 shows this XAML in action.

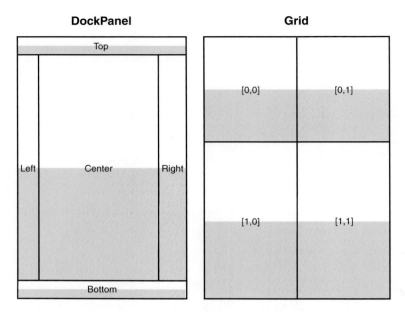

FIGURE 4.6   The **DockPanel** and **Grid** controls using attached properties.

As an example, we are going to create a panel called WeightedPanel that uses attached properties to constrain the sizes of its children.

WeightedPanel is a panel class that uses the relative weights of its children to size them appropriately. This is done by exposing an attached property called Weight that determines the size of the child in relation to the rest of the children. If you have two children in the panel with equal weight, both of them will be the same size. However, if you have one child with a weight of 6 and another with a weight of 4, the sizes would be 60% and 40%, respectively, of the panel size, as shown in Figure 4.7. Note that when you specify weights, they do not need to be percentage-based. Internally the WeightedPanel normalizes the weights of the child controls so that they are stored as fractions with values between 0 and 1. Thus for the previous example, the internal weights would be 0.6 and 0.4.

This is how the Weight attached property is defined:

```
public static readonly DependencyProperty WeightProperty =
DependencyProperty.RegisterAttached(
          "Weight", typeof (double), typeof (WeightedPanel),
                new FrameworkPropertyMetadata(1.0,
FrameworkPropertyMetadataOptions.AffectsParentMeasure |
   FrameworkPropertyMetadataOptions.AffectsParentArrange));
```

Note that the Weight property has additional metadata associated with it that might look strange to you if you haven't used more advanced dependency properties in the past.

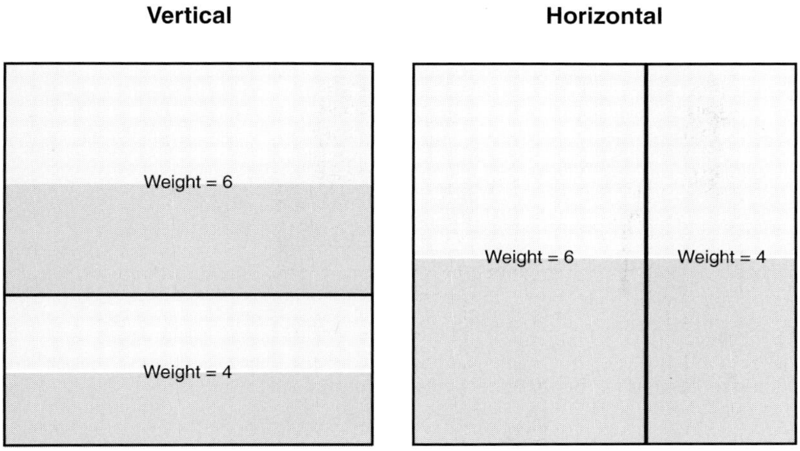

Vertical   **Horizontal**

FIGURE 4.7   The **WeightedPanel** custom panel.

The `AffectsParentMeasure` flag tells WPF that every time this property is changed, the `Measure` method on the parent should be invoked. Likewise, the `AffectsParentArrange` flag tells WPF that every time the property is changed, the `Arrange` method on the parent should be invoked.

In addition to the `Weight` attached property, an attached property called `Orientation` defines the direction that the weighted children flow within the panel. It can be either Horizontal or Vertical. Note that the metadata on this attached property is actually setting the flags for `AffectsMeasure` and `AffectsArrange`. These are different than `AffectsParentMeasure` and `AffectsParentArrange` as they affect the panel itself, not the parent of the panel:

```
public static readonly DependencyProperty OrientationProperty =
DependencyProperty.Register(
        "Orientation", typeof (Orientation), typeof (WeightedPanel), new
FrameworkPropertyMetadata(Orientation.Horizontal,
FrameworkPropertyMetadataOptions.AffectsMeasure |
FrameworkPropertyMetadataOptions.AffectsArrange));
```

Each time a layout pass happens (remember, a layout pass is the combination of a `Measure` and an `Arrange` call done recursively on all children), the normalized weights of the children are calculated. This is then used in determining the final `Rect` for each child. If the `Orientation` property is set to horizontal, the normalized weights are used to determine the width of each child. In the case of a vertical orientation, the normalized weights are used to define the height of each child. The following `CalculateItemRects` code shows how this process works:

```
private Rect[] CalculateItemRects(Size panelSize)
{
    NormalizeWeights();
```

```
        Rect[] rects = new Rect[InternalChildren.Count];
        double offset = 0;
        for (int i = 0; i < InternalChildren.Count; i++)
        {
            if (Orientation == Orientation.Horizontal)
            {
                double width = panelSize.Width*_normalWeights[i];
                rects[i] = new Rect(offset, 0, width, panelSize.Height);
                offset += width;
            }
            else if (Orientation == Orientation.Vertical)
            {
                double height = panelSize.Height*_normalWeights[i];
                rects[i] = new Rect(0, offset, panelSize.Width, height);
                offset += height;
            }
        }

        return rects;
    }


    private void NormalizeWeights()
    {
        // Calculate total weight
        double weightSum = 0;
        foreach (UIElement child in InternalChildren)
        {
            weightSum += (double) child.GetValue(WeightProperty);
        }

        // Normalize each weight
        _normalWeights = new double[InternalChildren.Count];
        for (int i = 0; i < InternalChildren.Count; i++)
        {
            _normalWeights[i] = (double)
InternalChildren[i].GetValue(WeightProperty)/weightSum;
        }
    }
```

Both the MeasureOverride and the ArrangeOverride use CalculateItemRects prior to call-ing the child's Measure and Arrange, as shown in the following code:

```
protected override Size MeasureOverride(Size availableSize)
{
```

```
    Rect[] rects = CalculateItemRects(availableSize);
    for (int i = 0; i < InternalChildren.Count; i++)
    {
        InternalChildren[i].Measure(rects[i].Size);
    }
    return availableSize;
}

protected override Size ArrangeOverride(Size finalSize)
{
    Rect[] rects = CalculateItemRects(finalSize);
    for (int i = 0; i < InternalChildren.Count; i++)
    {
        InternalChildren[i].Arrange(rects[i]);
    }
    return finalSize;
}
```

The WeightedPanel control is an example of how you can use a combination of overriding MeasureOverride and ArrangeOverride with your own custom attached properties to create compelling, reusable layout controls for your applications.

Using Transformations with Layout

Now that you've seen how Arrange, Measure, and visual tree manipulation and traversal work together to allow you to create new layouts, the next step is to take a look at modifying existing layouts through transformation.

When you are calculating rectangles for child elements during a layout pass, you normally wouldn't apply any render transformations to the children. However, for some special layouts and special circumstances, the simple layouts that we have experimented with so far in this chapter are insufficient.

For example, what do you do if you need a panel that positions and orients its children along the circumference of an ellipse? Such a layout cannot be achieved using simple rectangles. You might also want to apply a rotational transformation to each child to orient them along the curvature of the ellipse.

This really boils down to two different kinds of circular layouts: the "Ferris Wheel" and the traditional circle. In a traditional circle, all of the elements are simply placed along the edge of an ellipse and are rotated accordingly about their own center axis. In this kind of layout, any text or graphics would likewise be rotated and potentially look awkward.

In the Ferris Wheel rotation, elements are still placed along the circumference of an ellipse, but their rotation about their own central axis remains fixed, allowing text and graphics within those elements to remain clear and useful. I call this the "Ferris Wheel" rotation because humans in Ferris Wheel cars (think of each car as a child of the panel) remain upright relative to the earth while their position relative to the center of the Ferris Wheel is rotated along the outer ellipse. If you were to simply rotate the panel children with respect to the center of the ellipse and also allow the children to rotate independently, the poor humans contained within would fall out.

In Figure 4.8, we see several examples of traditional (non-Ferris Wheel) and Ferris Wheel transformed layouts along an ellipse.

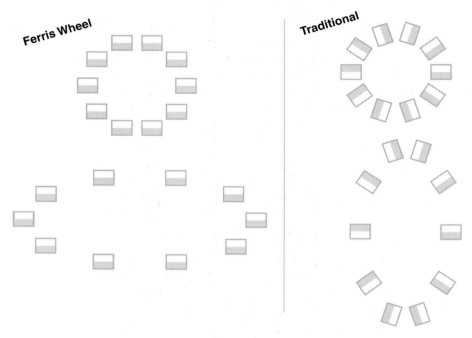

FIGURE 4.8   Transformation applied to layout.

For panels that need to lay out children with affine transforms, a recommended approach is to use the UIElement.RenderTransform property inside the ArrangeOverride. For the EllipticalPanel shown in Figure 4.7, the ArrangeOverride looks as follows:

```
protected override Size ArrangeOverride(Size finalSize)
{
    // Calculate radius
    double radiusX = (finalSize.Width - ItemWidth) * 0.5;
    double radiusY = (finalSize.Height - ItemHeight) * 0.5;

    double count = InternalChildren.Count;

    // Sector angle between items
    double deltaAngle = 2 * Math.PI / count;
```

```
// Center of the ellipse
Point center = new Point(finalSize.Width / 2, finalSize.Height / 2);


for (int i = 0; i < count; i++)
{
    UIElement child = InternalChildren[i];

    // Calculate position
    double angle = i * deltaAngle;
    double x = center.X + radiusX * Math.Cos(angle) - ItemWidth / 2;
    double y = center.Y + radiusY * Math.Sin(angle) - ItemHeight / 2;

    if (UseFerrisWheelLayout)
    {
        child.RenderTransform = null;
    }
    else
    {
        child.RenderTransformOrigin = new Point(0.5, 0.5);
        child.RenderTransform = new RotateTransform(angle * 180 /
➥Math.PI);
    }

    child.Arrange(new Rect(x, y, ItemWidth, ItemHeight));
}
return finalSize;
}
```

To switch between the two different layouts, we use a Boolean DependencyProperty called UseFerrisWheelLayout. This property has the AffectsArrange flag set in its metadata.

An interesting thing to note here is that the RenderTransform is applied only after the layout pass is completed. So the layout engine only sees a simple rectangle and not a rotated rectangle. It is only when the visual tree gets rendered that the transformations will be applied and take effect.

NOTE

Do Not Factor in RenderTransforms During Layout

For a panel author, it is absolutely crucial that you remember that the children should be positioned and sized according to what it would look like before the transformation. If you start writing code based on foreknowledge of transformations about to happen, you could get into serious trouble and create odd displays.

In our case, the RotateTransform is being applied with a RenderTransformOrigin of (0.5, 0.5). This means that the axis of rotation is the center of the layout rectangle. This means that we should be positioning the child element so that its center falls along the circumference of the circle. If we didn't put the center of the child item along the circumference, when the rotation is applied, the child elements would no longer look like they were on the smooth edge of a circle.

Affine Transformations for Mere Mortals

If you've always wanted to know exactly what an affine transformation was but didn't want to ask, here's the cheat sheet: An *affine transformation* is any transformation that preserves collinearity and distance ratios. Collinearity refers to the fact that all points that were in a line before the transformation remain on a line afterward. As such, common examples of affine transformations are scales, translations, and rotations.

Enter the LayoutTransform

In addition to the RenderTransform, WPF also provides a LayoutTransform that takes into account the effect of applying a transform on the child during the layout pass. This changes the rectangular size of the child by adjusting to the size of the convex hull of the transformed rectangle. A *convex hull* is a bounding rectangle that completely contains the transformed rectangle. Figure 4.9 should make the difference between the two types of transforms clear.

The main difference between the RenderTransform and the LayoutTransform is that the former considers the rectangular size after the layout pass while the latter actually changes the size of the rectangle. This makes LayoutTransform useful for scenarios where you don't want to re-layout a child using its Width and Height properties. A change in the child's LayoutTransform can get you the desired result.

For most scenarios, a RenderTransform is the better choice when compared to the LayoutTransform. LayoutTransforms have a specific use, and you should be aware of the performance implications of using LayoutTransform as it causes an additional layout pass after the regular layout has completed.

Additionally, RenderTransform is available for UIElements, and LayoutTransform is available only to FrameworkElements.

Layout Events

Before wrapping up the chapter, there are a few events related to layout of which you should be aware.

A layout pass is generally triggered when the size of a container changes, a property change occurs, or when an item comes into view. When the dimensions of a FrameworkElement change, the SizeChanged event gets fired. The SizeChangedEventArgs passed as a parameter to the event handler contain the new size and previous size associated with the control.

```
public delegate void SizeChangedEventHandler(object sender, SizeChangedEventArgs e)
```

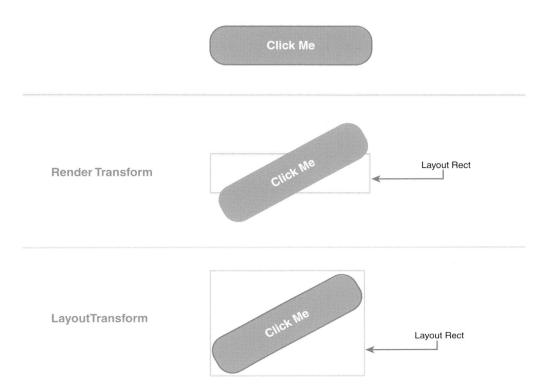

FIGURE 4.9   The difference between a **RenderTransform** and a **LayoutTransform**.

A global LayoutUpdated event is fired each time a layout pass runs on any of the
UIElements on the current Dispatcher. Since it is a global event, it does not contain any
information about the visuals that were involved, but is used instead to allow code to be
notified in general when the layout has changed.

The LayoutUpdated event is useful for carrying out layout animations. Instead of positioning and sizing the elements immediately in the ArrangeOverride method, you can cache
the new positions of controls and then play the layout changes in the form of animations
when the LayoutUpdated event is fired. To keep your event handler optimized, you can do
some housekeeping to ensure that it was really the control you are interested in that
caused the layout change in the first place (remember, it's a global event and gets called
every time *any* layout is changed).

A more granular event, CompositionTarget.Rendering, gets fired for each frame of
rendering that takes place. This happens after all the changes (including animation,
layout, and so on) are applied to the visual tree and are about to be sent over to the
render thread. This is a frame-by-frame event, so you can expect it to be called with very
high frequency. Generally you wouldn't use this event except in special circumstances
where you need extremely smooth animations with fine-grained control over individual

frames. Note that such custom animations are not compatible with storyboards. We will be covering custom animations in more detail in Chapter 12, "Custom Animations."

Figure 4.10 illustrates the difference in invocation frequency of the different layout events.

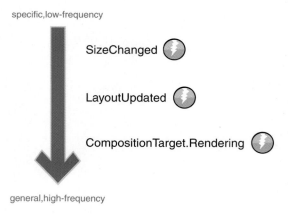

FIGURE 4.10   Layout event frequencies.

Summary

This chapter provided a glimpse of some of the powerful functionality that you can create by manipulating and customizing panels within WPF. Using transformations, attached properties, and a deep knowledge of the layout pass functionality in WPF, you can create incredible custom panels.

CHAPTER 5

Using Existing Controls

This chapter is all about *not* reinventing the wheel. Something has always seemed a little wrong with that phrase. First, in the grand scheme of things, wheels are a known commodity. It isn't as though someone could retreat to his cave, think a while, come out, and say, "I have invented the wheel!" without being accused of all manner of mental illnesses. What we are truly talking about here is making a better wheel out of the one we've been given.

Think about it this way: You've been given a boring, humdrum wheel from the factory. In this case, by "wheel," we mean the hub, the rim, and the tire. Now you decide to take off the rims and replace them with free-spinning chrome rims. Then you take the regular tire off and replace it with run-flat racing slicks. And, just to make things interesting, you take off the lug nuts and replace them with auto-extending razor blades, just in case you find yourself driving the minivan in the general vicinity of a James Bond villain.

What you've done is taken a boring wheel and injected it with pure awesome. This is what you want to do to the WPF controls given to you by the factory (Microsoft). You didn't have to go to a machine shop and refabricate the core of the wheel itself because it would be too time consuming, too costly, and produce little to no visible benefit to you. If you *really* need a new wheel, countless vendors specialize in building niche wheel types. When you get *their* boring humdrum specialist wheel, you can then add all the bling you like.

With WPF, if control vendors are adhering to guidelines and patterns, the process of adding your custom spinners and racing slicks should work the same with a factory (Microsoft) tire as it would with a specialist (third-party) tire.

This chapter shows you how to take boring humdrum controls and create amazing new features and functionality by reusing them instead of refabricating their core (note how we didn't say *reinvent*).

Customizing Existing Controls

WPF provides a rich set of controls that can be readily used for most scenarios faced by developers on a day-to-day basis. One of the features of WPF from the beginning has always been its flexibility and extensibility. Using its extensible nature, you can present the user with amazing, visually stunning features without having to build new controls from scratch.

Countless customization options are available that can be used to tailor the appearance and behavior of your controls. The rest of this chapter is devoted to showing you how to take existing WPF controls, swap out default behavior and appearance, and replace it with your own enhanced customizations.

Customizing Controls Using Properties

In the chapters preceding this one, you saw the diversity of classes available in WPF, including what you can accomplish just by modifying some key properties. There are primitive controls like `DrawingVisual` and complex controls like `ItemsControl` and everything in between.

The basic controls all have a set of properties that you can use for customization that don't support templating. Such controls include the `TextBlock`, `Shapes`, `Panels`, and much more. Table 5.1 shows the classes that support simple property-based customization and the relevant properties.

Customization Using Control Templates

You've seen a little bit of this already, but this chapter goes into much more detail. You can completely customize the appearance of some controls by modifying the `ControlTemplate`. Controls that support this kind of customization are lumped into a category called *lookless controls*. This means that the control behavior continues to function regardless of the skin you're draping on top of it. These kinds of controls are an absolute dream to customize because you get to change all of the stuff the user sees without having to redo any of the internal plumbing.

The behavior of a lookless control is defined by a set of semantic properties. These properties can be set using `TemplateBinding` inside the `ControlTemplates`. You got a taste of how this works with the `ProgressBar` customization back in Chapter 3, "Getting Started Writing Custom Controls."

The real power of WPF comes from the abstraction that separates the behavior of the control from its appearance. We take full advantage of this separation of concerns throughout this chapter.

TABLE 5.1   Customization of Basic Controls Via Properties

Control	Common Properties
Border	BorderThickness, BorderBrush, Background, CornerRadius
TextBlock	FontSize, FontWeight, FontFamily
Shape (Rectangle, Ellipse, Path, Polygon)	Fill, Stroke, StrokeThickness
StackPanel	Orientation
DockPanel	Dock
UniformGrid	Rows, Columns
WrapPanel	ItemWidth, ItemHeight, Orientation
Grid	Row, Column, ColumnSpan, RowSpan

Customization with Data Templates

Using a ControlTemplate, we can define the appearance of a control. With a DataTemplate, we can define the visual appearance of data contained within a control. DataTemplates on their own aren't so useful—they need a catalyst to bring them to life. That catalyst is the ContentPresenter. A content presenter exposes the Content and ContentTemplate properties that point to the data and the data template, respectively. In general, WPF uses the suffix "Presenter" to indicate a visual container for data templates. ContentPresenter is a container for singular data, whereas ItemsPresenter is a container for list-based data that is used with ItemsControl. Later in this chapter, you see detailed examples of data template-based customization.

Using a ControlTemplate and a DataTemplate

If you really want to tweak every aspect of a control (again, remember that you don't have to rewrite it from scratch!), you can use both a ControlTemplate and a DataTemplate and customize not only the shell container within which the data is rendered, but the way in which the data is rendered as well. Controls that can be customized this way are generally ones responsible for rendering singular data as well as being interactive. These include Button or a ContentControl.

Each of these controls has a Template property that is used for setting the ControlTemplate and a ContentTemplate property that is used for specifying a DataTemplate. The ControlTemplate generally contains an instance of a ContentPresenter within it, the properties of which are template-bound to the ones exposed on the control.

The following code is a simple `ControlTemplate` for a `Button`. The `ContentPresenter` binds to the `Button`'s `Content` and `ContentTemplate` properties to fetch its values:

```
<ControlTemplate x:Key="TestTemplate"
        TargetType="Button">
<ContentPresenter Content="{TemplateBinding Content}"
                ContentTemplate="{TemplateBinding ContentTemplate}" />
</ControlTemplate>
```

Customizing the `ItemsControl`

Customization of the `ItemsControl` deserves its own special section in this chapter because it combines the three different types of control customization into a single package that (as you see later) provides developers with amazing potential. It allows you to perform customization using all of the methods previously discussed.

Even though `ItemsControl` and its derived controls represent the most complex controls available in WPF, that doesn't mean they are difficult to customize. They have a number of properties that are used for customizing various aspects of the appearance and behavior.

Each `ItemsControl` is used for representing a list-based data set. The external container that holds all the items can be customized via the `Template` and `Style` properties. The container for each individual item can be customized using the `ItemContainerStyle`, and the actual data that is put in this container can be customized with the `ItemTemplate` property. Finally, the layout used for displaying the items can be customized using the `ItemsPanel` property. Since the `ItemsControl` control is also a data-bound control, there is an `ItemsSource` property that points to the bound list data. Some commonly used `ItemsControl`-derived classes are `ListBox`, `ComboBox`, `ListView`, and `TreeView`. Once you learn how to customize one of these controls, you should have a good idea of how to customize all of the other `ItemsControl`-based controls.

Additionally, `TreeView` uses a specialized form of `DataTemplate` called `HierarchicalDataTemplate` for defining the appearance of its child items. A `HierarchicalDataTemplate` defines the visual tree for each tree node and also contains an `ItemsPresenter` that points to the subtree used for displaying that node's child items. This template is evaluated recursively to generate a complete visual tree.

The following snippet of XAML shows a sample implementation of a `HierarchicalDataTemplate`:

```
<HierarchicalDataTemplate x:Key="BookTemplate"
            ItemTemplate="{StaticResource ChapterTemplate}"
            ItemsSource="{Binding XPath=Chapter}">
    <StackPanel>
```

```
        <DockPanel>
            <Image Source="Resources/book.png"
                    DockPanel.Dock="Left"
                        Width="22" />
            <TextBlock Text="{Binding XPath=@Title}"
                            VerticalAlignment="Center"
                            FontWeight="Bold" />
        </DockPanel>
        <ItemsPresenter />
    </StackPanel>
</HierarchicalDataTemplate>
```

A common theme that emerges from `ItemsControl`-based controls is that the control itself is built by assembling many smaller controls. Each of these smaller parts can be customized individually by using a `ControlTemplate`, a `DataTemplate`, or both. The diagram in Figure 5.1 shows how an `ItemsControl` is constructed.

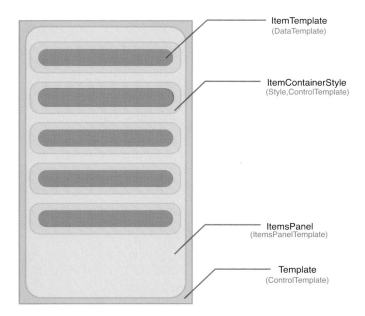

ItemTemplate
(DataTemplate)

ItemContainerStyle
(Style,ControlTemplate)

ItemsPanel
(ItemsPanelTemplate)

Template
(ControlTemplate)

FIGURE 5.1   The visual composition of an **ItemsControl**.

In addition to the layers of visuals, you can also add animations to make a rich and beautiful control. Animations can be triggered both in code and within XAML. However, doing it in XAML is definitely the preferred approach because of its flexibility and friendliness to designer tools. `Styles`, `ControlTemplates`, and `DataTemplates` support a property called `Triggers` that is a collection of `System.Windows.TriggerBase` elements that allow you to make visual state changes. These visual changes can be done via property setters or using `TriggerActions`. Setters are used for making property changes on the visuals, whereas `TriggerActions` are used for controlling storyboard animations.

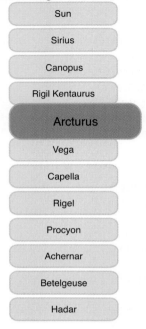

Customizing a ListBox

Let's take a look at one of the most common `ItemsControl`-derived classes, the `ListBox`. The visual composition of a `ListBox` is similar to the one seen in Figure 5.1. A `ListBox` uses the `ListBoxItem`, a `ContentControl`-derived type, as a container for each of its items. This means that the `temContainerStyle` property of the `ListBox` actually pertains to this container. Figure 5.2 shows the kind of customization that we want to do on a list box.

FIGURE 5.2   A customized list box.

The following is a list of the parts of the `ListBox` that we will customize to achieve the effect in Figure 5.2:

- ▶ The `ListBoxItem` using the `ItemContainerStyle` property
- ▶ The `ItemTemplate`
- ▶ The `ItemsPanel` using the `ItemsPanelTemplate` property

Customizing the `ItemContainerStyle`

In customizing the item's container style, we are going to set the style for the `ListBoxItem` and customize its visual tree using the `ControlTemplate`. The `ControlTemplate` needs to contain a `ContentPresenter` that finally contains the visual tree for the data item (specified using the `ItemTemplate` property).

There are three different states that we want to model for our custom list box, items. The first is the normal state, which is the default state for an item. The second state is a custom look for when the mouse is currently hovering over an item. Finally, the third state is when the item is selected.

Figure 5.3 shows the different states that we want to create for the custom list box item.

To create the selected state for an item in the custom list box, we need to use a scaling animation that scales the item to 1.25 times its width and 1.5 times its height. The appearance and state changes are all encapsulated inside a Style resource. The `ControlTemplate` defines the appearance, and the `ControlTemplate.Triggers` section handles the state changes. Note the use of `TriggerActions` for handling the selected state where we start and stop the storyboard responsible for the animated scaling:

FIGURE 5.3   Custom states for a list box item.

```
<Style x:Key="ListBoxItemStyle"
   TargetType="ListBoxItem">
<Setter Property="FocusVisualStyle"
    Value="{x:Null}" />
<Setter Property="Margin"
    Value="5,5,5,0" />
<Setter Property="RenderTransformOrigin"
    Value="0,0.5" />
<Setter Property="RenderTransform">
    <Setter.Value>
    <ScaleTransform ScaleX="1"
    ScaleY="1" />
    </Setter.Value>
</Setter>
<Setter Property="Template">
    <Setter.Value>
    <ControlTemplate TargetType="ListBoxItem">
            <Border x:Name="Root"
            BorderBrush="#bdc1a3"
            BorderThickness="1"
            CornerRadius="5"
            Background="{StaticResource NormalBrush}">
            <ContentPresenter
            Content="{TemplateBinding Content}"
            ContentTemplate="{TemplateBinding ContentTemplate}"
            HorizontalAlignment="Center"
            VerticalAlignment="Center" />
            </Border>
    <ControlTemplate.Triggers>
            <Trigger Property="IsMouseOver"
                Value="True">
                <Setter Property="BorderBrush"
```

```
                              Value="#2a849d"
                              TargetName="Root" />
                    </Trigger>
                    <Trigger Property="IsSelected"
                        Value="True">
                        <Setter Property="Panel.ZIndex"
                        Value="1" />
                        <Setter Property="BorderBrush"
                                Value="#2a849d"
                                TargetName="Root" />
                        <Setter Property="Background"
                                Value="{StaticResource SelectedBrush}"
                                TargetName="Root" />
                    <Trigger.EnterActions>
                        <BeginStoryboard>
                                <Storyboard>
                                    <DoubleAnimation
                                        To="1.25"
                                        Duration="0:0:0.25"
                                        Storyboard.TargetProperty=
                                "RenderTransform.(ScaleTransform.ScaleX)" />
                                        <DoubleAnimation To="1.5"
                                        Duration="0:0:0.25"
                                        Storyboard.TargetProperty=
                                "RenderTransform.(ScaleTransform.ScaleY)" />
                                </Storyboard>
                        </BeginStoryboard>
                    </Trigger.EnterActions>
                    <Trigger.ExitActions>
                        <BeginStoryboard>
                        <Storyboard>
                                    <DoubleAnimation To="1"
                                    Duration="0:0:0.25"
                                    Storyboard.TargetProperty=
                                    "RenderTransform.(ScaleTransform.ScaleX)" />
                                    <DoubleAnimation To="1"
                                    Duration="0:0:0.25"
                                    Storyboard.TargetProperty=
                                "RenderTransform.(ScaleTransform.ScaleY)" />
                        </Storyboard>
                        </BeginStoryboard>
                    </Trigger.ExitActions>
            </Trigger>
        </ControlTemplate.Triggers>
</ControlTemplate>
```

```
    </Setter.Value>
  </Setter>
</Style>
```

For the selected state, in addition to the animated scale transformation, we are also setting the attached property `Panel.ZIndex` to 1. You have already encountered Z indexing earlier in this book, so it should be no surprise that this ensures that inside the `ItemsPanel`, the selected `ListBoxItem` will be displayed on top of all other items nearby. This is essential because after scaling it to a larger size, if it had a low Z-order, the larger item would appear below its nearby peer items, obscuring the scaled edges.

Customizing the `ItemTemplate` and the `ItemsPanelTemplate`

For this particular customization, the `ItemTemplate` is going to be a simple `DataTemplate` that contains a `TextBlock`. For the `ItemsPanel`, we use a vertically oriented `WrapPanel`.

The following XAML shows how this is done:

```
<DataTemplate x:Key="ItemTemplate">
    <TextBlock Text="{Binding}"
            FontSize="18" />
</DataTemplate>

<ItemsPanelTemplate x:Key="PanelTemplate">
    <WrapPanel ItemWidth="200"
            ItemHeight="50"
            Orientation="Vertical"
            IsItemsHost="True"
            Margin="0,10,0,0" />
</ItemsPanelTemplate>
```

Now that we've got all of these customizations, we need to attach them to a `ListBox`, as shown in the following XAML:

```
<ListBox ItemsSource="{StaticResource DataSource}"
        ItemContainerStyle="{StaticResource ListBoxItemStyle}"
        ItemTemplate="{StaticResource ItemTemplate}"
        ItemsPanel="{StaticResource PanelTemplate}"
        HorizontalAlignment="Center"
        Width="250"
        BorderThickness="0"/>
```

Because the `ListBox` is data bound (in this case, to a resource we called `DataSource`) the UI container for each item (`ListBoxItem`) is automatically generated by a helper class that implements the interface `IItemContainerGenerator`. If you want to access a particular container, you need to go through the `ListBox`'s `ItemContainerGenerator` property.

For example, if you needed programmatic access to the 0th `ListBoxItem` in the list of items contained in a given control, you could access it like this:

```
ListBoxItem item =
    _listBox.ItemContainerGenerator.ContainerFromIndex(0)
        as ListBoxItem;
```

The `ItemContainerGenerator` is used not only for generating containers but it also aids in the virtualization features of `ItemsControl`, which allow for better memory management while still binding to large data sets. Chapter 8, "Virtualization," provides better coverage of virtualization techniques.

Creating a Custom `ScrollBar`

If you have ever owned a home, then you might be able to sympathize with this situation: You've remodeled, cleaned, and repainted the living room. It looks fantastic and you are proud of your work. Everybody who sees the living room is impressed, but there's a problem. Now the rest of your house looks like it is in bad shape simply because it is now being compared to the shiny new living room. Everyone who sees your living room immediately comments on how the rest of your house "needs work" and no one really notices all the hard work you put into the living room.

This is true with customizing user interfaces in WPF as well. Imagine that you have learned all of the amazing techniques covered in this book and you are customizing your application's GUI. You have created custom templates for your controls, made really nice backgrounds, and efficiently used transparencies and layered visual trees... and everyone ignores all your hard work and comments on how plain and ugly your scrollbars look.

This is actually a really common UI design problem. If you don't make your customizations complete and consistent throughout your application, they will look out of place and irritate your users rather than please them. A common source of frustration is an unstyled scrollbar that is scrolling highly customized content.

The `ScrollBar` is actually comprised of multiple smaller parts; some of which might not be so obvious at first glance. The diagram in Figure 5.4 shows the visual composition of a vertical `ScrollBar`. Horizontal `ScrollBars` are similarly structured.

NOTE

Reader Challenge

After you have finished building the custom vertical `ScrollBar` in this sample, take that knowledge and apply it to a horizontal `ScrollBar`. See whether there are other customization techniques from previous chapters that you can apply to this exercise.

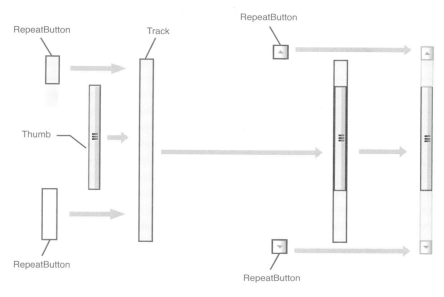

FIGURE 5.4   Visual composition of a vertical **ScrollBar**.

The smaller RepeatButtons are used to scroll up or down by small increments while the RepeatButtons inside the track are used for scrolling by pages or larger increments. The reason they are called RepeatButtons is because they raise a *repeated* Click event as long as the mouse is pressed on that button. In our custom ScrollBar sample, we deal with vertical orientation.

The style that we want to achieve for our custom control is shown in Figure 5.5.

FIGURE 5.5   A custom vertical **ScrollBar**.

The first thing that you will notice about this custom style is that certain parts are not present in the template. That is, the line up/down buttons responsible for small scrolling increments aren't included. The paging RepeatButtons are indeed there; they are just transparent to allow the track to show beneath them. You can see that even though we have missed a few parts, the ScrollBar still works. This is a great example of how lookless controls can downgrade themselves when certain parts are missing. It also gives the designer a lot of flexibility when it comes to designing the template.

A `ControlTemplate` that achieves the desired effect from Figure 5.5 is shown in the following XAML:

```xml
<ControlTemplate x:Key="VerticalScrollBarTemplate"
        TargetType="ScrollBar">
<Grid>
    <Border CornerRadius="30,5,5,30"
        Background="{StaticResource TrackBrush}"
        BorderBrush="#999999"
        BorderThickness="1"
        Padding="1">
        <Track x:Name="PART_Track"
        IsDirectionReversed="True">
        <Track.DecreaseRepeatButton>
                <RepeatButton Command="ScrollBar.PageUpCommand"
                  Template="{StaticResource RBTemplate}" />
        </Track.DecreaseRepeatButton>
        <Track.Thumb>
                    <Thumb Template="{StaticResource ThumbTemplate}"
                        Background="{TemplateBinding Background}"
                    BorderThickness="1"
                    BorderBrush="{TemplateBinding BorderBrush}" />
        </Track.Thumb>
        <Track.IncreaseRepeatButton>
                <RepeatButton Command="ScrollBar.PageDownCommand"
                  Template="{StaticResource RBTemplate}" />
        </Track.IncreaseRepeatButton>
        </Track>
    </Border>
</Grid>
</ControlTemplate>
```

The `Border` element is used to get the tube inside which the thumb is maneuvered. A large `CornerRadius` is applied to get the artistic curved look on the top and bottom. Inside this tube-like `Border` is a `Track` element, which contains the two-page `RepeatButtons` and the scrollbar `Thumb`. Because we want transparent visuals for the page `RepeatButtons`, we use a custom `ControlTemplate` named `RBTemplate`. This template is made up of a simple transparent rectangle. By attaching the `ScrollBar.PageUpCommand` and `ScrollBar.PageDownCommand`, we get the page movement functionality on the `RepeatButtons`.

The following snippet shows the `RBTemplate` in XAML:

```xml
<ControlTemplate x:Key="RBTemplate"
        TargetType="RepeatButton">
    <Rectangle Fill="Transparent" />
</ControlTemplate>
```

The rounded blue thumb is also a result of applying a custom `ControlTemplate`, this one is called `ThumbTemplate`. Notice how we apply a large `CornerRadius` to get the same curved look that we got for the `Track`. It also makes the thumb fit nicely inside the tube-like `Track`:

```
<ControlTemplate x:Key="ThumbTemplate"
        TargetType="Thumb">
    <Border Background="{TemplateBinding BorderBrush}"
        CornerRadius="30,5,5,30"
        BorderThickness="0"
        Padding="1">
    <Border Background="{TemplateBinding Background}"
        CornerRadius="30,5,5,30"
        BorderThickness="0" />
    </Border>
</ControlTemplate>
```

Two nested `Border` elements are used to get a more antialiased looking border on the outside of the `Thumb`. We could have achieved a similar effect using a `BorderBrush` on a single `Border` element, but that's really a matter of personal preference and has little visual impact on the final result.

> ## Use `TemplateBinding` for Property Values Inside a `ControlTemplate`
>
> Try to use `TemplateBinding` in most of the property values inside a `ControlTemplate` instead of setting hard values. This allows you to tweak the visuals outside the template. If you wanted to change the `Thumb` background, you could do that by specifying the property at a much higher level instead of having to go deep into the visual tree to make the change.

Finally, we tie the `ControlTemplate` to the `ScrollBar` by specifying a style, as shown in the following XAML:

```
<Style x:Key="{x:Type ScrollBar}"
    TargetType="ScrollBar">
    <Setter Property="MinWidth"
        Value="22" />
    <Setter Property="Background"
        Value="{StaticResource ThumbBrush}" />
    <Setter Property="BorderBrush"
        Value="#999999" />
    <Setter Property="Template"
        Value="{StaticResource VerticalScrollBarTemplate}" />
</Style>
```

> **Bonus Material**
>
> The code included for this chapter in the code downloads for this book has bonus samples that show even more creative uses for `ControlTemplate` to achieve amazing-looking controls without having to write your own from scratch. These bonus samples include a `TabControl` that is styled with animations and extra visuals and a `Slider` that looks like a gauge.

Note that we are specifying all of the brushes in the `Style` instead of doing so inside the `ControlTemplate`. This is possible because we built our templates to use `TemplateBinding` wherever possible. Now if we wanted a red colored `Thumb`, changing that style would be trivial.

Using Brushes to Create Advanced Visuals

Most of the controls and visuals have `Brush`-based properties that can be used to create pleasing effects. For example, `Shapes` support `Brush`-based properties like `Fill` and `Stroke` that can be used to create interesting shapes. The `Control` class has the `Background`, `Foreground`, and `BorderBrush` properties. Traditionally when you see these properties

FIGURE 5.6   A needle-shaped **DrawingBrush**.

used in simple samples, you see solid color brushes, or maybe you see the occasional gradient brush. WPF allows for so much more power and flexibility than that.

The `Brush` class is a base class for many useful brush types such as `LinearGradientBrush`, `RadialGradientBrush`, `ImageBrush`, `VisualBrush`, or `DrawingBrush`. By applying brushes that have transparent regions, you can achieve some cool effects without having to write any code at all. These brushes can be applied to rectangular bounded visuals to give them irregular shapes. For example, you can take a `DrawingBrush` that looks like the one in Figure 5.6 and apply it as a `Fill` on the rectangle.

Since the `Rectangle` class supports interaction via the mouse or keyboard, you can have a visual that looks like a needle without writing a custom `Shape` or `Decorator`. The `DrawingBrushes` can be designed in Expression Blend or Expression Design, and the corresponding XAML can be used as a resource in your application. Or, if you started your WPF career writing XAML in Notepad, then you can, in theory, create the brushes entirely in XAML by hand.

Using the `VisualTreeHelper` and `LogicalTreeHelper`

XAML definitely simplifies the creation of complex and nested visual hierarchies and also maintains good readability. With designer tools like Expression Blend or Expression Design, you could make even more elaborate visuals without looking at the XAML, but many developers prefer the tight control they have by hand-editing the XAML. It really is a matter of preference.

There may be times when you need to programmatically probe into the visual or logical tree at runtime to do some introspection or even manipulation. You might have attached a MouseLeftButtonDown event handler for the ListBoxItem, but you want to climb all the way up to the ItemsPanel to make some visual changes. This kind of "tree walking" can be done with the helper classes VisualTreeHelper and LogicalTreeHelper. Appropriately enough, these classes ease the traversal of the visual and logical trees, respectively. Some of the tree traversal methods that you might be interested in are the following:

- ▶ **VisualTreeHelper**—GetParent(), GetChild(), GetChildrenCount()

- ▶ **LogicalTreeHelper**—GetParent(), GetChildren()

Additionally, the VisualTreeHelper class has methods that query visual properties and can perform hit testing. A useful subset of these methods is as follows:

- ▶ GetEffect()

- ▶ GetContentBounds()

- ▶ HitTest()

- ▶ GetTransform()

- ▶ GetOpacity()

Using the tree helpers, in addition to all of the customization options you have seen so far, you can do some amazing things with WPF that you might have previously thought to be impossible or too difficult.

Customization Sample—The Radar Screen

So far the customizations of existing controls have been partial customizations. As we mentioned earlier, if you go to the trouble of redecorating your main living room, you had better be prepared to do that to your whole house because people are going to notice the "old" rooms.

So that's just what we're going to do: Redecorate the *entire* control. When you normally think of a ListBox, you probably think of this fairly plain and ordinary box that contains some other boxes that represent the items in the list. We've already seen how you can spice that up a little bit by making the selected item in the ListBox scale, but this time we're going to go all the way.

Instead of a boring box, we're going to make a circular display with concentric circles radiating out of the center, and the items in the list are going to be displayed at X and Y coordinates. In short, we're going to convert a simple ListBox into a fully functioning radar display. When you select an object on the radar display, a talk bubble appears showing you information about the object. This could potentially be used in a game for issuing commands to units or for IFF (Identify Friend or Foe) signals. Figure 5.7 shows all of the customizations in action.

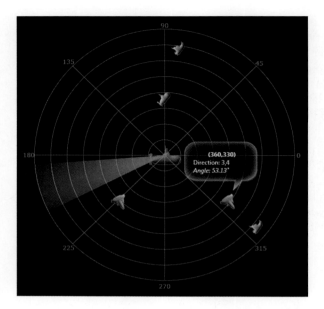

FIGURE 5.7   A completely customized **ListBox** converted into a radar screen.

At first glance, you might be thinking, "How could that possibly be a ListBox?!" On second glance, you might be thinking, "How can I possibly create something that complex!?" Remember back in Chapter 3, "Getting Started Writing Custom Controls," where we talked about thinking in layers — this might not seem like such a daunting task. Relax and take a few steps back and start to think about the various pieces of a ListBox and the different things you see in Figure 5.7.

We know that the ListBox, a subclass of ItemsControl, has a set of subparts that combine together to create its overall visual appearance. These include the template for the ListBox itself, the ItemsPanel for laying out the individual ListBoxItems, the ItemContainerStyle for controlling the appearance of each ListBoxItem, and finally an ItemTemplate for representing the bound data item. As we go through this sample, you see how we can customize each of these to contribute to our radar screen.

Moving Enemies in a **ListBox**

The center of a radar screen represents you or the craft that you are piloting. In our case, we are piloting a submarine. Scattered around the view are potential enemies including ships and planes.

Radar Versus Sonar

We realize that you wouldn't normally use the same device to search for airborne enemies as you would for underwater enemies. However, it's a really cool code sample so bear with us and pretend that we have really powerful radar-sonar combined devices powered by WPF!

The X and Y location of the enemies is constantly changing and doesn't follow a particular layout. This means that the `ItemsPanel` we pick for our control needs to make it simple for us to move the enemies around. The `Canvas` is an ideal choice here because it is the only panel that provides the ability to place items at absolute locations with the `Canvas.Left` and `Canvas.Top` attached properties. This is referred to as *absolute layout*. By binding the location of the enemies to these properties, we can easily place them and move them around within the `ListBox` without inhibiting any of the `ListBox`'s default behavior.

You might be thinking that we could probably use a `RenderTransform` to relocate the enemies throughout the radar screen. While technically possible, we'd have to attach the `RenderTransform` to each of the enemy instances. Later in the `ControlTemplate`, we would have to bind the `Enemy.Location` to the `TranslateTransform` of the `ListBoxItem`. All of this seems like a lot of extra work when we can just bind the enemy's coordinates to canvas coordinates. Here's a snippet of the style that sets the `ItemsPanel` of the `ListBox` to be a `Canvas`:

```
<Setter Property="ItemsPanel">
    <Setter.Value>
        <ItemsPanelTemplate>
            <Canvas IsItemsHost="True" />
        </ItemsPanelTemplate>
    </Setter.Value>
</Setter>
```

Concentric Circles and a Sweeping Cone

One of the most noticeable and memorable aspects of a radar screen is the set of concentric circles emanating from the "self" marker in the center. The idea is that your own vessel is sending out signals (pings) to detect nearby vessels. When the signal bounces off a nearby vessel (pong), you are able to figure out where the vessel is. This continuous search for nearby vessels is represented visually by a sweeping cone that continually scans in a circle around the center.

To show the concentric circles and the sweeping cone, we can leverage the drawing capabilities of WPF. If we know ahead of time how many circles we are going to show, we can simply use the `Ellipse` shape with increasing `Width` and `Height` properties; it's far easier to draw concentric circles in WPF than it is with a pencil! Similarly, we can use the `Path` shape to show the "spokes" that come out from the middle to segment the radar screen into four quadrants. Finally, we need a few `TextBlocks` to show the labels on each quadrant. In our sample, we're labeling the angles, but a video game might have different labels. Putting all of these `Shapes` and `TextBlocks` together will result in a lot of visual elements to manage and may become cumbersome if at a later date you want to add an extra circle or change the angle increments of the spokes or otherwise affect the radar screen.

To make things easier we encapsulate all of these visuals into a single `FrameworkElement` called `MarkersElement` and use the `OnRender` override to create the circles, segment spokes, and textual elements. Here we use the methods of the `DrawingContext` class to draw the visuals. The spokes and text labels don't need to be interactive, so we can opt for the lightweight alternatives here. There will be properties on the `MarkersElement` that allow the containing XAML to control some aspects of the drawing.

Regardless of how we draw the static background visuals, we still need to put them into the `ListBox` somehow. We know we can't use the `ItemContainerStyle` or `ItemTemplate` because those are specifically for item customizations. To tweak the `ListBox` itself and inject the `MarkersElement`, we need to use the `ControlTemplate`. In general, the `ControlTemplate` should be one of the first places you look for possibilities when trying to customize a control's visuals.

Fluorescent Green

Not soylent green (as in the 1973 movie on global warming effects), but fluorescent green, actually posed a bit of a problem. Picking the yellowish-green color for the circles and spokes was not immediately obvious. The standard green color looked bright on a dark background but lacked the fluorescent appeal. Adding a hint of yellow to the green made it look much brighter and gave the look of a real radar screen. The final color code was #42FF00 and thankfully no humans were consumed to generate that particular color.

To show the concentric circles, the spokes, and the text we use the `MarkersElement` with a property called `DeltaAngle` that is used to determine the spoke separation as well as the number of circles. The text along the circumference of the circle is also determined from increments of the angle. The `OnRender` method and a helper method called `GetPoint` are shown in the following code:

```
protected override void OnRender(DrawingContext dc)
{
    int steps = (int)(360 / DeltaAngle);
    Point center = new Point(RenderSize.Width / 2, RenderSize.Height / 2);

    dc.DrawEllipse(null, _pen, center, RenderSize.Width/2, RenderSize.Width/2);

    for (int i = 0; i < steps; i++)
    {
        double angle = i * DeltaAngle;
        Point p1 = GetPoint(angle, null);
        // Lines and Circles
        dc.DrawLine(_pen, center, p1);
        double radius = RenderSize.Width*0.5*i/steps;
        dc.DrawEllipse(null, _pen, center, radius, radius);

        // Text
        FormattedText text = new FormattedText("" + i * DeltaAngle,
                CultureInfo.InvariantCulture,
```

```
                    FlowDirection.LeftToRight, new Typeface("Verdana"), 12, Fore-
    ➥ground);
        Point p2 = GetPoint(angle, text);
        p2.X -= text.Width/2;
        p2.Y -= text.Height/2;
        dc.DrawText(text, p2);

    }
}
private Point GetPoint(double angle, FormattedText text)
{
    Point center = new Point(RenderSize.Width / 2, RenderSize.Height / 2);
    double radius = RenderSize.Width / 2;
    double radAngle = angle * Math.PI / 180;
    if (text != null)
    {
        radius += Math.Max(text.Width/2, text.Height/2);
    }
    double x = center.X + radius * Math.Cos(radAngle);
    double y = center.Y - radius * Math.Sin(radAngle);
    return new Point(x, y);
}
```

The number of circles and the number of angle increments are determined by the DeltaAngle property. The text along the circumference is positioned such that the center of the text lies along the spoke for that angle. GetPoint is a utility method that calculates the points along the outermost circle. If a FormattedText object is sent to this method, then the text is pushed an additional amount outward. This gives the text sufficient spacing and makes it more readable.

The use of the MarkersElement encapsulates all of the decoration logic for the radar screen and improves the readability of the ListBox's ControlTemplate (if all of that stuff was inside the template directly, it would be *very* hard to read). The next element to overlay on the template is the sweeping cone that rotates around the center. This is the representation of the signal scanner. We chose a fixed angle of 22.5 degrees to represent the cone. The cone itself is constructed using a Path element. Instead of using Expression Blend or Design to come up with the Path data we chose to use some simple trigonometric math to get the Path coordinates. We leave it as a reader exercise to determine these values using Figure 5.8 as a reference.

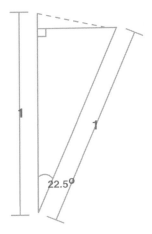

FIGURE 5.8   Reference figure for determining the sweeping cone coordinates.

Here is the `Path` for the cone:

```
<Path x:Name="SweepLine"
        Fill="{StaticResource SweepingLineBrush}"
        StrokeThickness="0"
        Stretch="Uniform"
        HorizontalAlignment="Left"
        Grid.Row="0"
        Grid.Column="1"
        RenderTransformOrigin="0,1"
        Data="M 0,0 L 0,1 L 0.382683432,0.0761204675 S 0.25,0 0,0 Z">
    <Path.RenderTransform>
        <RotateTransform />
    </Path.RenderTransform>
</Path>
```

Notice that there is also a `RotateTransform` attached to the `Path` since it will be rotating around the center of the radar screen. Both the `MarkersElement` and the `Path` segment will be placed inside the `ControlTemplate` of the `ListBox`. To start the continuous rotating animation of the sweeping cone, we added an `EventTrigger` in the `ControlTemplate.Triggers` section. The other elements in the `ControlTemplate` include the `ItemsPresenter` (which is a placeholder for the `ItemsPanel`) and an `Image` of the submarine at the center. Here is the complete control template:

```
<ControlTemplate x:Key="RadarTemplate"
        TargetType="ItemsControl">
    <Grid>
    <Grid.Resources>
        <RadialGradientBrush x:Key="SweepingLineBrush"
            GradientOrigin="0,1"
            RadiusX="1"
            RadiusY="1">
        <GradientStop Offset="0"
        Color="{Binding Color, Source={StaticResource FluoroGreen}}" />
        <GradientStop Offset="1"
        Color="Transparent" />
        </RadialGradientBrush>
    </Grid.Resources>
    <Grid.RowDefinitions>
    <RowDefinition />
    <RowDefinition />
    </Grid.RowDefinitions>
    <Grid.ColumnDefinitions>
    <ColumnDefinition />
    <ColumnDefinition />
```

```xml
        </Grid.ColumnDefinitions>
        <Image Width="64"
            Source="sub.png"
            Grid.Row="0"
            Grid.Column="0"
            Grid.RowSpan="2"
            Grid.ColumnSpan="2"
            Opacity="0.75" />
        <Chapter05:MarkersElement Foreground="{StaticResource FluoroGreen}"
            DeltaAngle="45"
            Grid.Row="0"
                        Grid.Column="0"
                        Grid.RowSpan="2"
                        Grid.ColumnSpan="2"
                        Opacity="0.75" />
        <Path x:Name="SweepLine"
                        Fill="{StaticResource SweepingLineBrush}"
                        StrokeThickness="0"
                        Stretch="Uniform"
                        HorizontalAlignment="Left"
                        Grid.Row="0"
                        Grid.Column="1"
                        RenderTransformOrigin="0,1"
                        Data="M 0,0 L 0,1 L 0.382683432,0.0761204675 S 0.25,0 0,0 Z">
        <Path.RenderTransform>
                        <RotateTransform />
        </Path.RenderTransform>
        </Path>

<ItemsPresenter Grid.Row="0"
                        Grid.Column="0"
                Grid.RowSpan="2"
                Grid.ColumnSpan="2" />
</Grid>
<ControlTemplate.Triggers>
    <EventTrigger RoutedEvent="FrameworkElement.Loaded">
    <BeginStoryboard>
                    <Storyboard>
                        <DoubleAnimation From="0"
                            To="359.99"
                            Duration="0:0:5"
                            Storyboard.TargetName="SweepLine"
                            Storyboard.TargetProperty=
                               "RenderTransform.(RotateTransform.Angle)"
```

```
                    RepeatBehavior="Forever" />
                    <DoubleAnimationUsingKeyFrames Duration="0:0:2.5"
                        Storyboard.TargetName="SweepLine"
                        Storyboard.TargetProperty="Opacity"
                        RepeatBehavior="Forever">
                    <LinearDoubleKeyFrame KeyTime="0%"
                        Value="0.1" />
                    <LinearDoubleKeyFrame KeyTime="50%"
                        Value="1" />
        <LinearDoubleKeyFrame KeyTime="100%" Value="0.1" />
    </DoubleAnimationUsingKeyFrames>
    </Storyboard>
    </BeginStoryboard>
    </EventTrigger>
    </ControlTemplate.Triggers>
    </ControlTemplate>
```

Now that we have the `ControlTemplate` and the `ItemsPanel` in place, we have to take care of the `ItemTemplate` and the `ItemContainerStyle`. The `ItemTemplate` is just a simple image that has its `Source` property bound to the `Type` property on the enemy vessel. We set the `Enemy.Type` to point to an image source, but you could easily use a converter (we've seen them several times so far in this book) to swap between enumerated data and image representations.

```
<DataTemplate x:Key="EnemyTemplate"
        DataType="Chapter05:Enemy">
        <Image Source="{Binding Type}"
            Stretch="Fill" />
</DataTemplate>
```

The `ItemContainerStyle` is a bit more involved since we have to show an information tip when the `ListBoxItem` is selected. We handle that in the `ControlTemplate` for the `ListBoxItem`. The `Visibility` of the entire information tip is initially set to `Collapsed`, and on item selection, it is set to `Visible`. Since the information tip is also part of the `ControlTemplate`, it moves as the enemy moves. The visuals are data bound to the `Location`, `Angle`, and `Direction` properties of the enemy object. The `ContentPresenter` has a `RenderTransform` of `RotateTransform` attached to it, which is data bound to `Enemy.Angle`. This ensures that only the enemy image is rotated and not the information tip.

There are a couple of other details about this `ControlTemplate` to note. In the trigger for the `IsSelected` property, we also set `Panel.ZIndex` and raise the stacking order of the enemy. This keeps the information tip visible and atop all others even when enemies cross paths. The talk bubble is a PNG image and not a vector graphic, but you could create your own entirely interactive bubble with a visual tree if you wanted to. When the ControlTemplate gets loaded, the nonstop sweeping cone animation is triggered using an EventTrigger.

An important thing to note about this sample is that a ListBox doesn't have to look like a rectangle with boring rectangular items contained within it. By creatively crafting the visuals for the ItemTemplate, ItemContainerStyle, ItemsPanel, and Template, the ListBox can be made to render any list-based data in just about any form, even a radar screen! A ListBox is after all a lookless control, which means you can have any visual appearance you want while keeping its core functionality the same.

Changing Templates at Runtime

If the template (DataTemplate or ControlTemplate) you want to use for item selection is complex, you could consider changing the template completely at runtime. This can't be done inside a ControlTemplate or a DataTemplate but is instead done at the Style level using Style.Triggers. You need a Trigger that listens to some property condition and responds by changing the Template or ContentTemplate of the ListBoxItem.

Summary

This chapter is all about not refabricating an entire wheel but instead taking off the parts you don't like and replacing them with your own fantastic customizations. We covered how to customize controls through the extensive use of properties, and we covered many examples of using templates to do everything from making small changes to completely changing the look and feel of a control.

The Power of Attached Properties

The concept of attached properties (AP) is one of the most innovative features of WPF and also one of the least utilized. This is because it usually takes several examinations of APs to really see their true benefit. At first glance, many developers may think that attached properties are nice and they let one configure controls using properties defined on a completely different control.

This is true, but it isn't the entire picture. After making the initial discovery about attached properties, a lot of people stop there. A second run through APs might make you think that *attached properties allow you to extend the functionality of existing controls without having the source code or using extension methods*. Now we're starting to get some idea of the true power of attached properties.

This chapter provides in-depth coverage of the purpose and implementation of attached properties. By the time you are done with this chapter, you should be fully convinced that, if only they were invented first, attached properties would indeed be better than sliced bread.

Overview of Attached Properties

You have seen a few instances of attached properties earlier in the book, but we've generally skipped over them until this point. Now we're ready to discuss APs in detail. One of the most common questions that bother developers new to the world of WPF is "What's the difference between a dependency property and an attached property?"

Regular dependency properties require that you set up the property on the class on which it will be used. In other words, the class that creates the dependency properties owns them. Dependency properties are best used within the context of the class and do not have much significance outside the class.

There may be many times when you find that you have a certain piece of functionality that you want to associate with a variety of classes. There are a couple of ways to do that today:

- ▶ If you have the source code to the base class of the set of classes you want to extend, you can add functionality to the base class and override it in the subclasses.

- ▶ You could use extension methods (introduced in the 3.5 version of the .NET Framework). However, with extension methods, you can only add new methods to a class and only have access to public members of the class being extended.

- ▶ Using dependency injection and using IOC (Inversion of Control) frameworks like Spring, Unity, Castle Windsor, and so on to inject the extension code.

Although these are all perfectly valid solutions, as UI developers we want something that is more flexible, works with third-party controls without requiring the source code, and is available in something we work with on a daily basis such as XAML. What we're really looking for is a way to add new behaviors into existing classes and do so using the XAML syntax just by associating properties on existing tags (classes). This is the exact purpose of attached properties—to provide a simple, declarative way to introduce new behavior into an underlying visual tree.

You can think of attached properties as dependency properties except that they are not tied to the class on which they are defined. They are a kind of "third-party" property. This means you can reuse an attached property on other classes by using the <classname>.<attached-property-name> syntax. This syntax provides a clear, concise, XAML-oriented way to inject third-party behaviors.

To use a namespace-qualified attached property, we use the following format:

```
<xml-namespace>:<classname>.<attached-property>
```

In the following code snippet, we added the HoverInteractor.UseHover attached property to a ListBox. Chapter06 is the namespace in which the HoverInteractor AP has been defined:

```
<ListBox x:Name="_listBox"
        Chapter06:HoverInteractor.UseHover="True"
        HorizontalContentAlignment="Stretch"
        ItemTemplate="{StaticResource ItemTemplate}"
        ScrollViewer.CanContentScroll="False"/>
```

When the code being represented by the XAML (remember, XAML is just a declarative way to instantiate your classes) is being instantiated and it encounters the setting of an attached property, the Property Changed callback for the attached property is called. The callback is then given a reference to the target instance on which the attached property is being used along with an instance of `DependencyPropertyChangedEventArgs`. This special type of event argument object contains the previous and new values of the AP. This is usually the place where you would inject your new functionality. Typical uses of APs here would include adding extra event handlers, invoking methods on the target instance, and modifying properties on the target instance.

Next we see an example of building and using an attached property to introduce new behavior.

Building the UseHover Attached Property

In this section of the chapter, we're going to explore how to introduce new functionality by creating a new attached property and then using it to inject new functionality on existing controls.

The first thing we need to do is create an attached property, which as we learned earlier, can be on any third-party class—it doesn't need to be on the class we're modifying. APs are created by invoking the `DependencyProperty.RegisterAttached` method, as shown here:

```
public static readonly DependencyProperty UseHoverProperty = DependencyProperty
    .RegisterAttached(
    "UseHover", typeof (bool), typeof (HoverInteractor),
    new PropertyMetadata(false, OnUseHoverChanged));
```

Here we create a Boolean attached property named `UseHover` on the `HoverInteractor` class. `HoverInteractor` is a `DependencyObject` that has been created (you can find the full source code for all of this in the code downloads for the book) that attaches a persistent `ToolTip` with the items in a `ListBox`. Unlike a regular `ToolTip` that fades away after a certain amount of time, the `HoverInteractor` keeps a hovering tip that stays as long as your mouse is on top of the `ListBoxItem`.

To use the AP in XAML, as in the previous example, we also need to set up a public static method that is invoked by the XAML parser. For the `UseHover` property, this method looks like this:

```
public static void SetUseHover(DependencyObject d, bool use)
{
    d.SetValue(UseHoverProperty, use);
}
```

All that is being done here is calling the `DependencyObject.SetValue` method to associate the attached property with the passed in object. Note how we have a `Boolean` parameter that matches the type of the `UseHover` property.

This is all great, but it doesn't actually do anything useful unless we respond to changes in the attached properties. This happens in the OnUseHoverChanged method, the property changed handler that was set up in the metadata for the AP:

```
private static void OnUseHoverChanged(DependencyObject d,
                                      DependencyPropertyChangedEventArgs e)
{
    ListBox lb = d as ListBox;
    if (lb != null)
    {
        if ((bool) e.NewValue)
        {
            lb.MouseMove += ListBox_MouseMove;
            lb.MouseLeave += ListBox_MouseLeave;
        }
        else
        {
            lb.MouseMove -= ListBox_MouseMove;
            lb.MouseLeave -= ListBox_MouseLeave;
        }
    }
}
```

Understanding how all this works is crucial to understanding the power of attached properties and their benefit to you as a WPF control developer. In the preceding code, if the UseHover attached property is set to true, then we attach our own handlers to the MouseMove and MouseLeave events for the ListBox in question. If UseHover gets set to false, we remove the event handler for MouseEnter and MouseLeave. Removing the mouse event handlers also removes the strong reference that is created between the HoverInteractor instance and the ListBox.

As you may be able to guess, we use the custom MouseEnter and MouseLeave event handlers to display and hide the ToolTip, respectively. Remember that we said that we have access to both the old *and* the new values of the property. In the simple case of our example, however, we only need the new value.

Also for the purposes of this sample, we're only adding this extension behavior to controls that are of type ListBox or its subclasses. To ensure this, we attempt to cast the DependencyObject to ListBox. If it fails, we ignore the event. Your attached properties can work to extend as few or as many controls as you see fit.

As the mouse moves over the ListBox item, we display the persistent ToolTip. When the mouse leaves that item, we remove the persistent ToolTip. Again, we can't stress enough how powerful this is: *We're adding this functionality to the ListBox* without having the source code to the ListBox class.

Figure 6.1 shows an example of the new UseHover property in action.

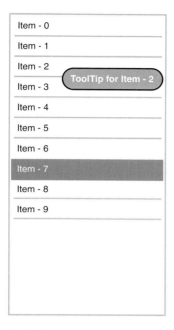

FIGURE 6.1   Using an attached property to create a persistent ToolTip.

The ToolTip is displayed using a custom adorner called HoverAdorner. It encapsulates a
ContentPresenter that acts as a container for the ToolTip visual. Since a
ContentPresenter exposes a ContentTemplate property, we can specify a DataTemplate to
customize the look of the ToolTip. The Content property of the ContentPresenter is set to
the item over which we are currently hovering.

For the screenshot in Figure 6.1, the DataTemplate for the ToolTip looks like this:

```
<DataTemplate x:Key="AdornerTemplate">
         <Border BorderBrush="Gray"
                 BorderThickness="1"
                 Background="#5F000000"
                 SnapsToDevicePixels="True"
                 CornerRadius="3"
                 Width="100"
                 Height="30">
            <TextBlock Text="{Binding}"
                       FontFamily="Times New Roman"
                       FontWeight="Bold"
                       FontSize="20"
                       VerticalAlignment="Center"
                       HorizontalAlignment="Center"
                       Foreground="White"/>
         </Border>
</DataTemplate>
```

Now that we've got our DataTemplate, we can create the hover adorner. The HoverAdorner class is instantiated inside the MouseMove event handler. This handler also removes any previous adorner (for a previously hovered-over item) and then creates the new one. We keep track of the adorner using a *private* dependency property called AttachedAdorner, as shown here:

```
private static readonly DependencyProperty AttachedAdornerProperty =
DependencyProperty
    .Register(
    "AttachedAdorner", typeof (AdornerInfo), typeof (HoverInteractor));
internal class AdornerInfo
{
    public HoverAdorner Adorner;
    public ListBoxItem ListItem;
}
```

You see this pattern of using private dependency properties more frequently as you experiment with more advanced WPF control creation. It is an effective way to store custom state on controls and its subparts without exposing it publicly. Here is the code for the HoverAdorner class:

```
public class HoverAdorner : Adorner
{
    public HoverAdorner(UIElement adornedElement) : base(adornedElement)
    {
        Container = new ContentPresenter();
    }

    protected override Size MeasureOverride(Size constraint)
    {
        Container.Measure(constraint);
        return Container.DesiredSize;
    }

    protected override Size ArrangeOverride(Size finalSize)
    {
        double left = AdornedElement.RenderSize.Width -
    ➥Container.DesiredSize.Width;
        Container.Arrange(new Rect(new Point(left,
    ➥AdornedElement.RenderSize.Height/2), finalSize));
        return finalSize;
    }

    protected override System.Windows.Media.Visual GetVisualChild(int index)
    {
        return Container;
```

```
    }

    protected override int VisualChildrenCount
    {
        get
        {
            return 1;
        }
    }

    internal ContentPresenter Container { get; set; }
}
```

At this point, we've got an attached property that we can refer to in XAML, and we have the property defined as a static property on a DependencyObject that we've written. The next step is to write the MouseMove event handler that deals with creating and removing the custom ToolTip adorner:

```
private static void ListBox_MouseMove(object sender, MouseEventArgs e)
    {
        // Check that we are hovering on a ListBoxItem
        ListBox lb = sender as ListBox;
        ListBoxItem item =
            lb.ContainerFromElement(e.OriginalSource as Visual) as ListBoxItem;
        if (item == null)
        {
            return;
        }

        // Remove any previous Adorners
        AdornerInfo prevInfo = lb.GetValue(AttachedAdornerProperty) as AdornerInfo;
        AdornerLayer layer = AdornerLayer.GetAdornerLayer(lb);
        if (prevInfo != null)
        {
            if (prevInfo.ListItem == item) return;
            layer.Remove(prevInfo.Adorner);
            lb.ClearValue(AttachedAdornerProperty);
        }

        // Attach new adorner to current ListBoxItem
        HoverAdorner adorner = new HoverAdorner(item);
        adorner.Container.Content =
➥lb.ItemContainerGenerator.ItemFromContainer(item);
        adorner.Container.ContentTemplate =
            item.FindResource("AdornerTemplate") as DataTemplate;
        layer.Add(adorner);
```

```
        AdornerInfo info = new AdornerInfo();
        info.Adorner = adorner;
        info.ListItem = item;
        lb.SetValue(AttachedAdornerProperty, info);
    }
}
```

In the `MouseLeave` event handler, we remove any existing `HoverAdorner` on the item that the mouse is leaving, as shown in the following code:

```
private static void ListBox_MouseLeave(object sender, MouseEventArgs e)
{
    ListBox lb = sender as ListBox;

    // Remove any previous Adorners
    AdornerInfo prevInfo = lb.GetValue(AttachedAdornerProperty) as AdornerInfo;
    AdornerLayer layer = AdornerLayer.GetAdornerLayer(lb);
    if (prevInfo != null)
    {
        if (layer != null)
        {
            layer.Remove(prevInfo.Adorner);
            lb.ClearValue(AttachedAdornerProperty);
        }
    }
}
```

To recap, we're using a private attached property (`AttachedAdornerProperty`) that we can use to keep track of whether an `Adorner` has been attached to an existing `ListBoxItem`. Using this property, we can query the value and then remove the adorner and clear the value when we encounter the `MouseLeave` event.

Using Attached Properties as Extension Points

The previous example showed you how attached properties can help in adding new functionality to existing controls. In fact, attached properties should be considered even before you attempt building a new control. We already covered this aspect in Chapter 3, "Getting Started Writing Custom Controls," where we talked about considering it in the elimination process before building a new control.

To use attached properties to extend a control, you need to make sure the control exposes appropriate public APIs (events, methods, properties) that will be useful for the functionality you want to add. Fortunately most of the controls in the WPF framework expose a wide variety of events, methods, and properties that can be used to attach additional functionality (behaviors). Thus, the controls that come out of the box have some core functionality, which is already part of the control, and other secondary features that have been associated via attached behaviors. If you are a control author, you would typically be concerned with the core functionality, but it is also helpful to think of exposing enough state information about the control. This helps users of your control to tweak it via attached properties. With judicious exposure of internal control state, you can create an ecosystem around the control, which looks like Figure 6.2. The central part is the core that is defined by you, the control author, and the surrounding plugs are attached behaviors written by users of your control.

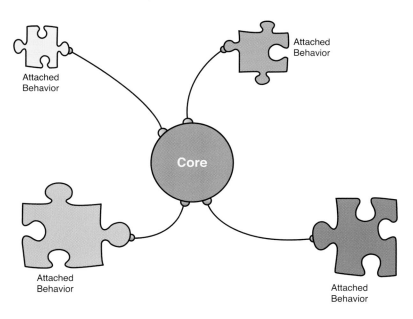

FIGURE 6.2   Designing core functionality and attached behavior.

Attached behaviors are such a useful feature of the WPF framework, that the Expression Blend team decided to take it a step further in standardizing it. In Microsoft Expression Blend 3, there is a new feature called attached behaviors that can be used to add functionality to existing controls along with design time support. If you think for a moment about the basic life cycle of an attached behavior, you will realize that you need a way to attach the behavior and some way to remove it at the appropriate time. Once you have attached a behavior to an element (FrameworkElements), you also want to have a reference to that element.

The abstract Behavior class that is part of the Microsoft.Expression.Interactivity namespace exposes this life cycle with convenient methods that can be overridden in subclasses. To attach a behavior, one needs to override the OnAttached method. The object on which the behavior is attached is available via the AssociatedObject property. You can use it to add event handlers, call methods, or set properties. When you are done with that behavior, you can dispose it by calling the public Detach method. This internally clears the behavior and also invokes the OnDetaching override. You would typically remove an event handler that you have set up or reset the internal state established on the `AssociatedObject`.

Before moving on to a more advanced example of the use of attached properties, let's take a look at a list of some of

NOTE

To learn more about the Behavior class, visit the Expression Gallery at http://gallery.expression.microsoft.com/site/items/behaviors.

the other ways in which APs can be used to make your life as a developer better (can you tell we *really* like attached properties?).

Data Templates

Attached properties can be used to add extra functionality into data templates. Let's say you want to execute some code when the visual tree of the data template has loaded. Instead of associating a code-behind class for the `ResourceDictionary`, you can create an attached property that gets notified when the template has loaded. In the property changed handler, you can then add the required functionality.

Property Abstraction

You can use attached properties to combine a group of properties and expose them as a more high-level abstraction. You saw an example of this in Chapter 3, "Getting Started Writing Custom Controls," when we took a range of values (0-20, 20-40, 40-60, 60-80, and 80-100) and exposed each interval as a `ProcessStage` value. This made it easier for us to apply a `Trigger` to show visual changes when the progress moved into one of the interval ranges.

Layout Animations

You can use attached properties to perform layout animations on a `Panel` for which you don't have the source code available. WPF exposes an event called `LayoutUpdated` (we saw this already in Chapter 4, "Building Custom Panels") that can be used to trigger the animations. Attached properties work great to expose functionality on a control that was not originally designed.

Constraining Panels

Constraining `Panels` is useful if you want to arrange the children in the panel based on some constraints. These constraints could be specified via attached properties. Default panels such as `Grid` and `DockPanel` utilize attached properties set on children to change the layout configuration. We have also seen an example in Chapter 4, "Building Custom Panels."

Application Services

Configuring application services is an interesting way of using attached properties. Imagine that you have UI components that rely on some applicationwide services that can be changed on a control-by-control basis. A good example of this is the `ToolTipService` available in WPF. You can configure these services to behave differently by using attached properties that are exposed on them. The next time you are designing a new application or control, consider exposing application services as attached properties.

UI Helper Objects

Attached properties can be considered helper objects for UI controls. For example, you can have a helper object that determines the currently visible rows and fires changes as new rows come into view and previous rows go out of view. This could be useful for virtualized list controls like `ListView`. Consider a sample `RowVisibilityService` that hooks into the `ScrollChanged` and `CollectionView.CollectionChanged` events to determine the currently visible rows. This service could be used by domain objects that need to subscribe to backend changes that happen on the rows. Instead of subscribing to all rows, the virtualized UI layer could only subscribe to the currently visible rows. It removes subscriptions for rows that go out of view and adds subscriptions for newly visible rows.

This brief list of some of the ways in which attached properties can be used to simplify your code and create new and powerful functionality is just a small sample of what is possible. As you get more familiar with the usage of APs, you will find even more ways to use them.

Implementing Drag and Drop with Attached Properties

With the preceding examples, you can see that attached properties can provide a good building block when designing applications and controls. In this next sample, we're going to take a look at a more realistic and practical example that shows how attached properties can dramatically decrease the amount of work a developer has to do. The example we're going to work with is drag and drop (DnD).

DnD is a common interaction paradigm that involves dragging an item with the mouse and dropping it into some other control or location within an application. DnD has become so commonplace that most users feel as though an application is broken or deficient if it doesn't support DnD in places where they would expect it. Drag and drop requires a drag source and a drop target. In WPF, DnD can be invoked by calling `System.Windows.DragDrop.DoDragDrop`. As you'll see, this is a fairly low-level method, and the mechanics of actually implementing a full drag and drop system can require a lot of boilerplate code if you're not using attached properties.

Because DnD is a mouse interaction, there are specific mouse events that you need to listen to before invoking the `DoDragDrop` method. For the *drag* part of DnD, the events you are interested in are `MouseDown`, `MouseMove`, and `MouseUp`. Once the `MouseDown` event is received, you have to make sure that the mouse has traveled a certain distance before initiating a drag operation. This can be checked by measuring the distance traveled in `MouseMove`. If you're wondering, *"how long do you have to travel before considering it a drag?,"* then fear not—WPF already has constants defined for this: `SystemParameters.MinimumHorizontalDragDistance` and `SystemParameters.MinimumVerticalDragDistance`. If a `MouseUp` is received before either of those distances has been traveled during the `MouseMove`, whatever state you are building for your DnD system needs to be reset and returned to waiting for a drag to occur.

After a legitimate drag has occurred, we can call the `DragDrop.DoDragDrop` method. Once this method is invoked, a set of events start firing on `UIElements` that have their `AllowDrop` property set to `True`. These are elements that can potentially become drop targets. As you move your mouse over potential drop targets, they are given a chance to change their visual appearance to indicate whether they will accept whatever it is you are trying to drop. The events that are sent to the potential drop target controls are `DragEnter`, `DragLeave`, `DragOver`, and `Drop`. By listening to these events, we can provide visual feedback about the effects of dropping the dragged element.

One of our favorite examples of allowing controls to respond before being dropped is in showing *what the state will look like after the drop takes place*. You can see this in many modern applications where dragging an item between two adjacent items causes them to separate, showing the user exactly where their dropped item will fit.

As a summary, here is quick listing of important events on the drag source and the drop target:

▶ **Drag source**—`MouseDown`, `MouseMove`, `MouseUp`

▶ **Drop target**—`DragEnter`, `DragLeave`, `DragOver`, `Drop`

An average-sized application window may have more than one drag-drop zone, and it could result in a tremendous amount of code to wire up events. To add to the complexity (and developer aggravation), many applications have drag-drop zones that are similar but not identical and can appear in multiple windows and change their behavior and rules depending on application state. Attached properties can come to the rescue here in simplifying the code required to set up drag and drop in your application. Through APs, we can hide all of the event wiring details and call some high-level methods on the drag source and drop targets. All of this will be managed by a single `DragDropManager` class.

The `DragDropManager` class exposes two dependency properties called `DragSourceAdvisor` and `DropTargetAdvisor`, each of which is required to implement an interface, `IDragSourceAdvisor` and `IDropTargetAdvisor`, respectively.

The following code shows the declaration and initialization of these dependency properties:

```
public static readonly DependencyProperty DragSourceAdvisorProperty =
    DependencyProperty.RegisterAttached("DragSourceAdvisor", typeof
(IDragSourceAdvisor),
typeof (DragDropManager),
                                    new FrameworkPropertyMetadata(
                                    new
PropertyChangedCallback(OnDragSourceAdvisorChanged)));
```

```
public static readonly DependencyProperty DropTargetAdvisorProperty =
    DependencyProperty.RegisterAttached("DropTargetAdvisor", typeof
(IDropTargetAdvisor),
typeof (DragDropManager),
                                    new FrameworkPropertyMetadata(
                                        new
PropertyChangedCallback(OnDropTargetAdvisorChanged)));
```

The DragSourceAdvisor attached property should be set on visual elements that you intend to be *dragged* as drag sources, and the DropTargetAdvisor property should be set on elements that are intended to be drop targets. Note that you can set both of these properties on elements that are both drag sources and drop targets.

The property changed event handlers for these properties do all of the event wiring and set up handlers for initiating the drag and calling the DoDragDrop method. During the drag and drop operation the DragDropManager class fires appropriate methods on the elements that allow clear, concise visibility into what exactly is happening.

The following code shows the code for the property changed event handlers for the DragSourceAdvisor and DropTargetAdvisor attached properties:

```
private static void OnDragSourceAdvisorChanged(DependencyObject depObj,
DependencyPropertyChangedEventArgs args)
{
    UIElement sourceElt = depObj as UIElement;
    if (args.NewValue != null && args.OldValue == null)
    {
        sourceElt.PreviewMouseLeftButtonDown += DragSource_PreviewMouseLeftButton
    ➥Down;
        sourceElt.PreviewMouseMove += DragSource_PreviewMouseMove;
        sourceElt.PreviewMouseUp += DragSource_PreviewMouseUp;

        // Set the Drag source UI
        IDragSourceAdvisor advisor = args.NewValue as IDragSourceAdvisor;
        advisor.SourceUI = sourceElt;
    }
    else if (args.NewValue == null && args.OldValue != null)
    {
        sourceElt.PreviewMouseLeftButtonDown -= DragSource_PreviewMouseLeftButton
    ➥Down;
        sourceElt.PreviewMouseMove -= DragSource_PreviewMouseMove;
        sourceElt.PreviewMouseUp -= DragSource_PreviewMouseUp;
    }
}

private static void OnDropTargetAdvisorChanged(DependencyObject depObj,
DependencyPropertyChangedEventArgs args)
```

```
{
    UIElement targetElt = depObj as UIElement;
    if (args.NewValue != null && args.OldValue == null)
    {
        targetElt.PreviewDragEnter += DropTarget_PreviewDragEnter;
        targetElt.PreviewDragOver += DropTarget_PreviewDragOver;
        targetElt.PreviewDragLeave += DropTarget_PreviewDragLeave;
        targetElt.PreviewDrop += DropTarget_PreviewDrop;
        targetElt.AllowDrop = true;

        // Set the Drag source UI
        IDropTargetAdvisor advisor = args.NewValue as IDropTargetAdvisor;
        advisor.TargetUI = targetElt;
    }
    else if (args.NewValue == null && args.OldValue != null)
    {
        targetElt.PreviewDragEnter -= DropTarget_PreviewDragEnter;
        targetElt.PreviewDragOver -= DropTarget_PreviewDragOver;
        targetElt.PreviewDragLeave -= DropTarget_PreviewDragLeave;
        targetElt.PreviewDrop -= DropTarget_PreviewDrop;
        targetElt.AllowDrop = false;
    }
}
```

In the preceding code, we set up preview events since we want to be the first to intercept the mouse events. If we weren't doing the preview events, then the events already defined by the underlying controls would take precedence and could interfere with our drag and drop implementation.

We set up the PreviewMouseDown, PreviewMouseMove, and PreviewMouseUp events on the DragSource since we detect drag operations happening on that control. Once a drag has been detected in the PreviewMouseMove event handler, we invoke the DragDrop.DoDragDrop method. Before calling that method, however, we need to ask the DragSourceAdvisor to give us the data that needs to be sent over to the drop target.

When drag and drop operations occur, a piece of data is sent from the drag source to the drop target. This allows the drop target to appropriately respond to the drop. For example, when dropping a file into a new folder, the piece of data might be the fully qualified path and filename of the file, allowing the folder (the drop target) to copy the file into that location and then visually update itself to include the new file.

Once the drag and drop operation has started, we keep asking the DropTargetAdvisor whether it accepts the drop data by calling the method IsValidDataObject. If it does accept it, we ask for a feedback visual that can be shown as the user drags the source over the target. If a real drop action occurs, we call the OnDropCompleted method on the DropTargetAdvisor. This is one of the many methods that we implemented to simplify and abstract the building of drag and drop interfaces. The call to OnDropCompleted is followed by the call to `FinishDrag` on the `DragSourceAdvisor`. Keep in mind that `DoDragDrop` is a *synchronous* and *blocking* call. This means while the DnD operation is being performed, no other mouse interaction is possible on the desktop.

The following code shows the interfaces for the source advisor and target advisor:

```
public interface IDragSourceAdvisor
{
    UIElement SourceUI { get; set; }

    DragDropEffects SupportedEffects { get; }

    DataObject GetDataObject(UIElement draggedElt);
    void FinishDrag(UIElement draggedElt, DragDropEffects finalEffects);
    bool IsDraggable(UIElement dragElt);
    UIElement GetTopContainer();
}
public interface IDropTargetAdvisor
{
    UIElement TargetUI { get; set; }

    bool ApplyMouseOffset { get; }
    bool IsValidDataObject(IDataObject obj);
    void OnDropCompleted(IDataObject obj, Point dropPoint);
    UIElement GetVisualFeedback(IDataObject obj);
    UIElement GetTopContainer();
}
```

Through these interfaces, we hide all of the low-level details of how a drag and drop interaction actually works without losing the ability to control all aspects of dragging and dropping. The developer only needs to be concerned with the actual data that gets transferred from the source to the target rather than worrying about the "plumbing" of hooking up all of the various DnD-related events. For an application that might have multiple drag and drop zones per window, multiple windows, and many different kinds of drag sources, this kind of abstraction is necessary to keep the application functional and maintainable.

As an example usage of the `DragDropManager` (remember you can see all of the source code for this in the book's code downloads), we consider a simple `Canvas` on which we want to move elements. Instead of setting up events explicitly we do it via our new attached properties on the `DragDropManager`. As the drag and drop operations happen, appropriate methods are called on the classes implementing `IDragSourceAdvisor` and `IDropTargetAdvisor`. In our case, the `Canvas` is both a drag source and a drop target; hence, we set up both attached properties to point to the same instance of the advisor. `CanvasDragDropAdvisor` is the class that implements these key interfaces.

```
<UserControl.Resources>
    <Chapter06:CanvasDragDropAdvisor x:Key="advisor" />
</UserControl.Resources>
<Grid>
    <Canvas Background="White"
Chapter06:DragDropManager.DragSourceAdvisor="{StaticResource advisor}"
Chapter06:DragDropManager.DropTargetAdvisor="{StaticResource advisor}">
...
...
...
    </Canvas>
</Grid>
</UserControl>
```

The most important thing to remember about the preceding XAML code is that it is *simple*. With the declaration of two attached properties, we allowed the child elements within this Canvas to be dragged around and dropped in new locations. Even better is that the code we wrote to enable DnD operations on this Canvas is completely reusable for *all* of our other controls because we implemented it using attached properties. You can see that the child elements have been dragged into various positions, and one of the buttons is dimmed (by reducing the opacity) to indicate that it is currently being dragged.

Figure 6.3 shows the drag and drop control in action.

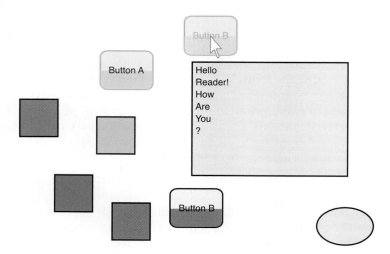

FIGURE 6.3   Drag and drop with attached properties.

All of the drag and drop logic is contained in the CanvasDragDropAdvisor, which implements both of the interfaces in our extension. When the drag operation is triggered, the

IDragSourceAdvisor.GetDataObject method is called. Here the advisor serializes the currently dragged element and puts it into a DataObject (but you can use any arbitrary data you like for your own applications and controls). When the drag completes, FinishDrag is called where the element is moved to the new location. The remaining methods in the interface are query methods that ensure that the drag and drop operation works correctly and flows smoothly. These include SourceUI, SupportedEffects, IsDraggable, and GetTopContainer. The SourceUI property is set by the DragDropManager and points to the element on which you set up the DragDropManager.DragSourceAdvisor attached property. In our case, we use it to move the children after the drag completes, but the action could be anything from initiating a file copy to storing a new record in a remote web service:

```
public UIElement SourceUI
    {
        get { return _sourceAndTargetElt; }
        set { _sourceAndTargetElt = value; }
    }

public DragDropEffects SupportedEffects
    {
        get { return DragDropEffects.Move; }
    }

public DataObject GetDataObject(UIElement draggedElt)
    {
        string serializedElt = XamlWriter.Save(draggedElt);
        DataObject obj = new DataObject("CanvasExample", serializedElt);

        return obj;
    }

public void FinishDrag(UIElement draggedElt, DragDropEffects finalEffects)
    {
        if ((finalEffects & DragDropEffects.Move) == DragDropEffects.Move)
        {
            (_sourceAndTargetElt as Canvas).Children.Remove(draggedElt);
        }
    }

public bool IsDraggable(UIElement dragElt)
    {
        return (!(dragElt is Canvas));
    }

public UIElement GetTopContainer()
    {
```

```
        return _sourceAndTargetElt;
    }
```

The `IDropTargetAdvisor` method implementations (shown in the following code) follow a similar pattern. As we move over the drop target area, the `IsValidDataObject` method gets called to check whether the drop zone accepts this data. If it does, we request for visual feedback by calling `GetVisualFeedback`. When the drop happens, we call the `OnDropCompleted` method. The two other properties that are part of the interface include the `TargetUI` and the `ApplyMouseOffset` properties. `TargetUI` in our case is again the `Canvas` element since we set up the `DragDropManager.DropTargetAdvisor` property on it. The `ApplyMouseOffset` property is used to offset the visual feedback by some X and Y coordinate values. This is the offset inside the dragged element at which the drag operation was invoked. The complete `IDropTargetAdvisor` implementation for our sample is shown here:

```
public UIElement TargetUI
{
    get { return _sourceAndTargetElt; }
    set { _sourceAndTargetElt = value; }
}

public bool ApplyMouseOffset
{
    get { return true; }
}

public bool IsValidDataObject(IDataObject obj)
{
    return (obj.GetDataPresent("CanvasExample"));
}

public UIElement GetVisualFeedback(IDataObject obj)
{
    UIElement elt = ExtractElement(obj);

    Type t = elt.GetType();

    Rectangle rect = new Rectangle();
    rect.Width = (double) t.GetProperty("Width").GetValue(elt, null);
    rect.Height = (double) t.GetProperty("Height").GetValue(elt, null);
    rect.Fill = new VisualBrush(elt);
    rect.Opacity = 0.5;
    rect.IsHitTestVisible = false;

    return rect;
}
```

```
public void OnDropCompleted(IDataObject obj, Point dropPoint)
{
    Canvas canvas = _sourceAndTargetElt as Canvas;

    UIElement elt = ExtractElement(obj);
    canvas.Children.Add(elt);
    Canvas.SetLeft(elt, dropPoint.X);
    Canvas.SetTop(elt, dropPoint.Y);
}


private UIElement ExtractElement(IDataObject obj)
{
    string xamlString = obj.GetData("CanvasExample") as string;
    XmlReader reader = XmlReader.Create(new StringReader(xamlString));
    UIElement elt = XamlReader.Load(reader) as UIElement;

    return elt;
}
```

The ExtractElement method is a helper method that we use inside OnDropCompleted to deserialize the UIElement from the passed in DataObject.

With the preceding example, you can see that attached properties can be used to provide a high-level abstraction around an otherwise complicated and code-intensive operation like drag and drop. By thinking in terms of drag and drop *advisors* (attached properties), we have raised the level of abstraction and simplified the task of adding DnD functionality to our application and, more importantly, to any application or control we build in the future.

If the DnD operations are similar for two different parts of the application, we can just make the advisor a little more generic and flexible to take care of the new possibilities and functionality. Note that we don't have to worry about associating event handlers or clogging up an ugly code-behind. All of the logic is neatly tucked away into an advisor class. Another bonus of the advisor class is that it can be independently *unit tested*.

Summary

In this chapter, we went through the basics of working with attached properties and illustrated some of the amazing things you can do with them. By thinking about controls as core behavior and attached behavior, additional features can be added easily and cleanly and still adhere to the Open Closed Principle. Extensions to the controls can leverage the publicly exposed API of a control to add more functionality. Developers can then add features that the original control creators never considered during the control's initial design.

The bottom line here is that attached properties are one of the most powerful and *least utilized* features of WPF. As a professional WPF developer, the use of attached properties should be in your daily arsenal.

When you couple attached properties with the techniques learned so far and all of the techniques yet to come, you will be able to create some absolutely amazing controls and applications.

CHAPTER 7

Advanced Scrolling

Users have been scrolling in some fashion since the earliest days of computer interfaces. Back in the days of the "green screen," our main vehicle for scrolling was the Unix pipe recipient *more*, which let us see 24 lines of text on the screen at a time and then hit the space bar when we were ready for more.

As the complexity of our interfaces grew, so too did the need for a more complex and powerful way of scrolling. Horizontal scrolling was introduced to accommodate the needs of people working with large horizontal sets of data such as spreadsheets.

Modern computer users almost instinctively recognize the presence of a scrollbar and what it means for the data they are viewing. Rather than thinking about the low-level interface concept of a scrollbar, if you think about the *intent* of a user who created the need for the scrollbar, we can take scrolling to a new level and use it in exciting, powerful new ways. This is the goal of this chapter.

The Anatomy of a Scrollbar

Using horizontal and vertical scrollbars is something that most users of modern software applications and operating systems know how to do. In addition, these users generally take for granted the purpose and functionality of these scrollbars; they expect them all to function a certain way regardless of what application or OS they are using. As a result, the fundamental components of a scrollbar have been made fairly standard and uniform across most graphical operating systems. Figure 7.1 illustrates these standard components as implemented by WPF.

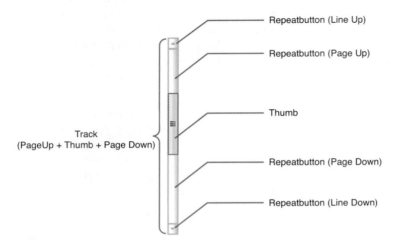

FIGURE 7.1   The anatomy of a scrollbar.

The scrollbar is made up of two RepeatButtons (Line Up and Line Down) and a Track. The Track is composed of two RepeatButtons (Page Up and Page Down) and a Thumb. The standard scrolling interaction involves dragging the Thumb on the Track (up/down or left/right depending on the orientation of the scrollbar). Additionally, you can also click on the Line Up/Line Down buttons to cause a scroll by a small amount (typically one line or one row of data). Clicking on the Page Up/Down buttons scrolls the data being displayed by a page.

Although the scrollbar is a standard component, the internal mechanism to actually scroll a page or control is not standardized. This means that two different controls may respond very differently to the user clicking the Line Up or Line Down buttons. On the Windows platform itself, UI technologies have varying internal scrolling mechanisms that differ mostly in terms of the effort required on the part of the programmer to implement custom scrolling.

In WPF, the ScrollViewer component provides a seamless scrolling behavior by encapsulating the vertical and horizontal ScrollBars and a scrollable region. The scrollable region is typically a Panel but can be any element that implements the IScrollInfo interface. The ScrollViewer supports two kinds of scrolling: physical (pixel-based) and logical (item-based). By default, the scrolling behavior is pixel-based, physical scrolling. This default behavior can often result in items being partially obscured "below the fold" during the scrolling process.

In the case of panels like the StackPanel and VirtualizingStackPanel, special support is built in to enable logical scrolling. Incidentally these panels are also the defaults for controls like the ListBox and ListView, which can be scrolled by an item (ListBoxItem or ListViewItem).

We mentioned that the ScrollViewer consists of the two ScrollBars and a scrollable region. The scrollable region is represented by the ScrollContentPresenter, which is a container for the scrolling area. Any component that needs to be scrolled is contained inside the ScrollContentPresenter. It acts as a proxy between the ScrollViewer and the actual scrolling content and routes the user interactions to the scrolling component. Therefore, it is the ScrollContentPresenter that makes the actual calls on a class that implements the IScrollInfo interface.

When creating a ControlTemplate for the ScrollViewer, you should ensure that the ScrollContentPresenter is present somewhere in the visual tree. The ScrollViewer maintains a close relationship with the ScrollContentPresenter, and its presence is important for the scrolling behavior to work correctly. The ScrollContentPresenter also implements the IScrollInfo interface and is therefore able to converse with the ScrollViewer.

The Magic of IScrollInfo

The IScrollInfo interface is an abstraction of the conversation between a user and a region of scrollable data. It defines the methods and properties for querying and manipulating the state of that scrollable region. It is defined in the System.Windows.Controls.Primitives namespace. The following code snippet shows the definition of IScrollInfo in its entirety:

```
public interface IScrollInfo
{
    // Methods
    void LineDown();
    void LineLeft();
    void LineRight();
    void LineUp();
    Rect MakeVisible(Visual visual, Rect rectangle);
    void MouseWheelDown();
    void MouseWheelLeft();
    void MouseWheelRight();
    void MouseWheelUp();
    void PageDown();
    void PageLeft();
    void PageRight();
    void PageUp();
    void SetHorizontalOffset(double offset);
    void SetVerticalOffset(double offset);

    // Properties
    bool CanHorizontallyScroll { get; set; }
    bool CanVerticallyScroll { get; set; }
```

```
    double ExtentHeight { get; }
    double ExtentWidth { get; }
    double HorizontalOffset { get; }
    ScrollViewer ScrollOwner { get; set; }
    double VerticalOffset { get; }
    double ViewportHeight { get; }
    double ViewportWidth { get; }
}
```

The next few sections describe these properties and methods by categorizing their purpose and functionality.

Responding to User-Requested Horizontal and Vertical Scrolling

The ability to respond to user-requested horizontal and vertical scrolling is handled by the following methods: LineDown, LineLeft, LineRight, LineUp, MouseWheelDown, MouseWheelLeft, MouseWheelRight, MouseWheelUp, PageDown, PageLeft, PageRight, and PageUp.

These methods are called when the user interacts with the different parts of the ScrollBar and the scrollable region. The Line*** methods are called when the user clicks on the single-line repeat buttons. Predictably, the Page*** methods are called when the user clicks on the large-block repeat buttons that typically advance or retreat the scrollable region by "pages."

The MouseWheel*** methods are called when the mouse wheel is used within the context of a ScrollViewer. Typically these methods call into the SetVerticalOffset and SetHorizontalOffset methods by passing the relevant change values. The offsets for the line button clicks are the smallest while the offsets for the page button clicks are the largest.

Controlling the Bounds for the Track and Thumb

The following properties determine the bounds of the scrollable region and are also used to proportionally size the Thumb: ExtentHeight, ExtentWidth, ViewportHeight, and ViewportWidth. In fact, the size of the Thumb is the ratio of ViewportWidth to ExtentWidth and ViewportHeight to ExtentHeight. The viewport size is always smaller than the extent size.

Managing the Location of the Thumb

The following properties and methods are used to manage the location of the Thumb: HorizontalOffset, VerticalOffset, SetHorizontalOffset, and SetVerticalOffset. The current location of the Thumb can be obtained by looking at the value of HorizontalOffset or VerticalOffset. These offsets are always between 0 and (ExtentWidth-ViewportWidth) or 0 and (ExtentHeight-ViewportHeight), respectively. The scrollbars are data bound to these offsets and use them to correctly size the `Thumb`. The `SetHorizontalOffset` and `SetVerticalOffset` methods are called when the user drags the `Thumb`. The implementations of these methods update the `HorizontalOffset` and `VerticalOffset` properties.

Logical Scrolling

Logical scrolling is managed through the `CanHorizontallyScroll` and `CanVerticallyScroll` properties and the `MakeVisible` method. Setting the `CanHorizontallyScroll` and `CanVerticallyScroll` properties to `True` allows the control to provide logical scrolling. The default, as we mentioned, is to do physical, pixel-based scrolling. `MakeVisible` is useful for bringing a particular visual child into view. Typically this would be called when you invoke `BringIntoView` on any of the contained children in the panel. It is also invoked when any of the children is clicked or receives focus.

Building a Custom Panel with Custom Scrolling

Now that we have a decent understanding of the building blocks that make up WPF's scrolling behavior and default controls, we can put that knowledge into action by implementing a custom panel that can be scrolled using a `ScrollViewer`. Our custom panel will be called `RowsPanel`, a panel that displays a set of fixed-height rows. A panel such as this might be used in table-based controls that display rows and columns of data. The `RowsPanel` in particular would be used to display rows of data and allow for those rows to be scrolled.

Creating the Layout Logic

First let's take a look at how `RowsPanel` will lay out its children. `RowsPanel` has a single `DependencyProperty` called `RowHeight` with a default value of 30.0. This property is used for all layout calculations. Here is the definition of this property:

```
public static readonly DependencyProperty RowHeightProperty =
DependencyProperty.Register(
                "RowHeight",
                typeof(double),
                typeof(RowsPanel),
                new PropertyMetadata(30.0D));
public double RowHeight
{
    get { return (double)GetValue(RowHeightProperty); }
    set { SetValue(RowHeightProperty, value); }
}
```

The layout logic for the panel is pretty straightforward. It sizes all of the rows to their available width and keeps their height fixed at the value of the `RowHeight` property. Figure 7.2 shows what `RowsPanel` looks like with a few rows displayed. Note that each row spans the entire width and has a fixed height.

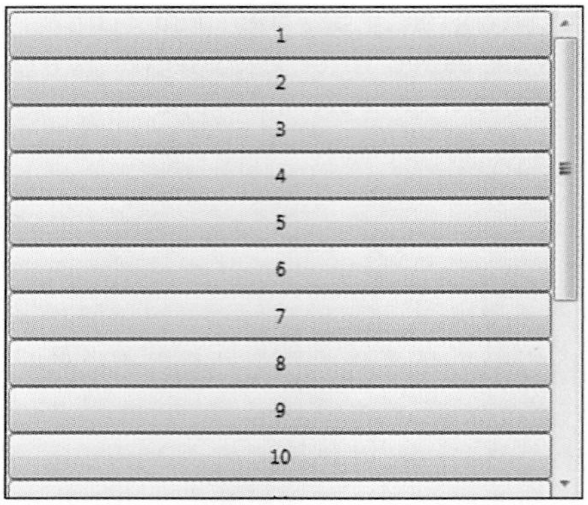

FIGURE 7.2   The **RowsPanel** control.

Here is the XAML that creates what you see in Figure 7.2:

```
<ScrollViewer CanContentScroll="True">
    <Chapter7:RowsPanel>
        <Button />
        <Button />
        <Button />
        <Button />
    </Chapter7:RowsPanel>
</ScrollViewer>
```

In the preceding XAML, you'll notice that the CanContentScroll property of the ScrollViewer is set to True. This informs the ScrollViewer that the embedded control knows how to scroll and has implemented the IScrollInfo interface. Without this setting, the ScrollViewer would assume that the control does not know how to scroll and would send Infinity as the bounds.

The MeasureOverride and ArrangeOverride (you should be familiar with these methods by now) methods of the RowsPanel class should make the layout logic clear:

```
protected override Size MeasureOverride(Size availableSize)
{
    UpdateScrollInfo(availableSize);

    int childCount = InternalChildren.Count;
    for (int i = 0; i < childCount; i++)
    {
        InternalChildren[i].Measure(
            new Size(availableSize.Width, RowHeight));
    }

    return availableSize;
}
```

```
protected override Size ArrangeOverride(Size finalSize)
{
    UpdateScrollInfo(finalSize);

    int childCount = InternalChildren.Count;
    for (int i = 0; i < childCount; i++)
    {
        UIElement child = InternalChildren[i];

        child.Arrange(new Rect(0, i * RowHeight,
            finalSize.Width, RowHeight));
    }

    return finalSize;
}
```

The call to UpdateScrollInfo is something that hasn't been discussed before. It is a precursor to the scrolling logic that we're going to add in the next section. UpdateScrollInfo does the bounds calculation for the Panel (which gets you viewport and extent sizes) and also invalidates the ScrollViewer if the bounds have changed. This allows us to return to the actual size of the panel in the MeasureOverride.

We also make a call to UpdateScrollInfo in the ArrangeOverride method to be on the safe side. The bounds of the panel could be different than the requested size if additional margins or alignments are associated with the panel.

Adding the Scrolling Functionality

Now that we have the layout logic in place, we can work on adding our custom scrolling functionality by implementing IScrollInfo. This is a key step that needs to be performed every time you create a custom control that you want to respond in a specific way to scroll events.

The logic for vertical scrolling is similar to the logic for horizontal scrolling. To keep things simple we concentrate on the code for vertical scrolling for now.

The core of the logic is inside SetVerticalOffset. It receives a parameter, called offset, which is the offset by which the panel should be scrolled. SetVerticalOffset is called by LineUp, LineDown, PageUp, PageDown, MouseWheelUp, and MouseWheelDown.

```
public void SetVerticalOffset(double offset)
{
    offset = CalculateVerticalOffset(offset);

    _offset.Y = offset;

    if (_scrollOwner != null)
        _scrollOwner.InvalidateScrollInfo();
```

```
    Scroll_Internal(HorizontalOffset, offset);
}

private double CalculateVerticalOffset(double offset)
{
    if (offset < 0 || _viewport.Height >= _extent.Height)
    {
        offset = 0;
    }
    else
    {
        if (offset + _viewport.Height >= _extent.Height)
        {
            offset = _extent.Height - _viewport.Height;
        }
    }
    return offset;
}
```

CalculateVerticalOffset ensures that the offset stays within the appropriate bounds. Here are all the methods that invoke SetVerticalOffset:

```
public void LineUp()
{
    SetVerticalOffset(VerticalOffset - 10);
}

public void LineDown()
{
    SetVerticalOffset(VerticalOffset + 10);
}

public void PageUp()
{
    SetVerticalOffset(VerticalOffset - ViewportHeight);
}

public void PageDown()
{
    SetVerticalOffset(VerticalOffset + ViewportHeight);
}

public void MouseWheelUp()
{
    SetVerticalOffset(VerticalOffset - 10);
}
```

```
public void MouseWheelDown()
{
    SetVerticalOffset(VerticalOffset + 10);
}
```

Note that each method passes in a different delta offset. Once the final `VerticalOffset` has been established, we are now ready to do the actual scrolling. Scrolling the panel equates to applying a `TranslateTransform` and modifying the transform's Y value. You can see this in the last statement of the `SetVerticalOffset` method, which is the call to `Scroll`. That method looks like this:

```
private void Scroll(double xOffset, double yOffset)
{
    _trans.X = -xOffset;
    _trans.Y = -yOffset;
}
```

The private field `_trans` is an instance of `TranslateTransform` that is initialized in the `RowsPanel`'s constructor:

```
public RowsPanel()
{
    // For use in the IScrollInfo implementation
    _trans = new TranslateTransform();
    this.RenderTransform = _trans;
}
```

The `UpdateScrollInfo` method is called only from `MeasureOverride` and `ArrangeOverride`. It does the job of calculating the viewport and extent sizes and invalidating the `ScrollViewer`'s scroll data. The invalidation happens only when the viewport or extent sizes change. The `UpdateScrollInfo` method is shown here:

```
private void UpdateScrollInfo(Size availableSize)
{
    // See how many items there are
    int itemCount = InternalChildren.Count;
    bool viewportChanged = false;
    bool extentChanged = false;

    Size extent = CalculateExtent(availableSize, itemCount);
    // Update extent
    if (extent != _extent)
    {
        _extent = extent;
        extentChanged = true;
    }
```

```
    // Update viewport
    if (availableSize != _viewport)
    {
        _viewport = availableSize;
        viewportChanged = true;
    }

    if ((extentChanged || viewportChanged) && _scrollOwner != null)
    {
        _offset.Y = CalculateVerticalOffset(VerticalOffset);
        _offset.X = CalculateHorizontalOffset(HorizontalOffset);
        _scrollOwner.InvalidateScrollInfo();
    }
}
```

The end result of this coding is that you should now feel confident that you can grab hold of the scrolling subsystem and make it do your bidding when creating your own custom controls that could potentially be visualizing enough data that they require custom scrolling capabilities.

Animated Scrolling

One of the biggest complaints that users have about scrolling is that it feels unnatural, jumpy, or just plain uncomfortable. A lot of really good applications have solved this problem by making the scrollbar gradually "slide" from its current position to the new position indicated by the user. This has the end effect of animating the transition from the current position to the end position. An example of animated scrolling that virtually everyone may be familiar with at this point is the "flip scroll" that made the iPhone UI so famous.

The good news is that you can make judicious use of WPF animations and implement animated scrolling in your own application!

The following code provides a replacement implementation of the Scroll method introduced previously:

```
private void Scroll(double xOffset, double yOffset)
{
    if (AnimateScroll)
    {
        DoubleAnimation anim = new DoubleAnimation(-yOffset,
            new Duration(TimeSpan.FromMilliseconds(500)));
        PropertyPath p = new PropertyPath("(0).(1)",
        RenderTransformProperty, TranslateTransform.YProperty);
        Storyboard.SetTargetProperty(anim, p);

        Storyboard sb = new Storyboard();
```

```
            sb.Children.Add(anim);
            EventHandler handler = null;
            handler = delegate
                    {
                        sb.Completed -= handler;
                        sb.Remove(this);

                        _trans.X = -xOffset;
                        _trans.Y = -yOffset;
            };
            sb.Completed += handler;
            sb.Begin(this, true);
                }
            else
            {
                // Translate
                _trans.X = -xOffset;
                _trans.Y = -yOffset;
            }
}
```

Here we're using a Boolean property called `AnimateScroll` to switch between the animated and nonanimated versions to allow the user to easily see the difference. Note how we are clearing the `Storyboard` after its completion. This has to be done since animations have higher precedence in setting the `DependencyProperty` and will override any local setting of the property. Clearing the storyboard is also helpful when you want to switch to the nonanimated version, where you set the translation values directly.

Taking Scrolling to the Next Step

What is `IScrollInfo`, really? On the one hand, it is a simple interface that controls the interaction between a scroll control (such as a `Scrollbar`) and a scrollable region of content. This is the way most programmers see `IScrollInfo`, but it has so much more potential.

Take a moment to think about the purpose of a scrollbar. Really it provides a visualization of your current progress between some minimum and maximum value. It allows you to control your current position between that minimum and maximum value. What that actual value does to the underlying scrollable region is really someone else's concern. When you think about `IScrollInfo` in this manner, more exciting and interesting possibilities start to crop up.

If you figure that the horizontal and vertical scrolling action can control two different values, you might allow the mouse wheel values to control a third value. If you figure a 3D model has three different dimensions that can be controlled, you could actually use `IScrollInfo` to manipulate the rotation of a 3D model. The combination of `ScrollViewer` and `IScrollInfo` is really just providing manipulation of three properties of the embedded control. These three properties could be anything that your application needs—an (X,Y,Z) tuple or any other set of three values that make sense for your application.

We've already guessed that you could use custom scrolling to manipulate the rotation of a 3D model. By styling the `ControlTemplate` for the `ScrollViewer` and `ScrollBar`, you could (within the bounds of good taste, of course) create an interface that behaves like a scroll viewer but looks nothing like one.

You could make the user experience more interesting by introducing overlays in the form of adorners. These could pop out (or fade in) at specific times giving more contextual information. Think of how Microsoft Office products like Word or PowerPoint show overlays when you scroll quickly on the document, or how the iPhone only shows a tiny scrollbar when you're actually scrolling.

By thinking of the `ScrollViewer` and the `IScrollInfo` interface as a means to manipulate a trio of values between some minimum and maximum value, you can create features and functionality that you might not otherwise have thought possible.

Scrolling Without `IScrollInfo`

The `ScrollViewer` is definitely the first control to think of when adding scrolling functionality to a `Panel`. However, when you do this you're going to have to implement the `IScrollInfo` interface in your `Panel`. As we've seen, this is an incredibly powerful interface that has a lot of potential but can also potentially be overkill for small projects.

Consider, for example, a `Panel` that only scrolls horizontally. It would be easier to hook up a horizontal `ScrollBar` with the Panel and bind the `ScrollBar` properties to those exposed by the `Panel`. This is a quick and easy way around a full-blown implementation of `IScrollInfo`.

As shown in Figure 7.3 a horizontal scrollbar needs three important properties to work: `Maximum`, `ViewportSize`, and `Value`. Maximum is similar to the `ExtentSize` property on the `IScrollInfo` interface, and `Value` is roughly the same as the `HorizontalOffset` property on `IScrollInfo`. The `Minimum` property defaults to 0.

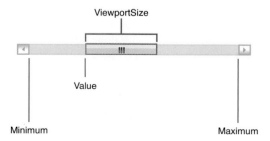

FIGURE 7.3   A horizontal scrollbar and its properties.

Horizontal scrolling for this panel works by exposing some dependency properties to which the ScrollBar can bind. Once the ScrollBar gets the required values for Value, ViewportSize, and Maximum, it comes to life by sizing the Thumb proportionately and allowing manipulation of the current value. Note that the bindings on the ScrollBar need to be TwoWay since the user can interact with the ScrollBar to change the properties. Internally the Panel uses a TranslateTransform as its RenderTransform and scrolls horizontally as the Thumb is moved.

Let us put all of these ideas to work with a custom panel called HScroll Panel. The first thing we need to do in the code is set up the dependency properties:

```
public static readonly DependencyProperty ViewportSizeProperty =
DependencyProperty.Register(
    "ViewportSize", typeof (double), typeof (HScrollingPanel));

public static readonly DependencyProperty ExtentSizeProperty =
DependencyProperty.Register(
    "ExtentSize", typeof (double), typeof (HScrollingPanel));

public static readonly DependencyProperty HorizontalOffsetProperty =
DependencyProperty.Register(
    "HorizontalOffset", typeof (double), typeof (HScrollingPanel), new
PropertyMetadata(0.0, OnHorizontalOffsetChanged));

private static void OnHorizontalOffsetChanged(DependencyObject d,
DependencyPropertyChangedEventArgs e)
{
    HScrollingPanel panel = d as HScrollingPanel;
    double x = (double) e.NewValue;
    panel._trans.X = -1 * x;
}
```

Next, we update the ViewportSize and ExtentSize properties inside the MeasureOverride and ArrangeOverride methods of the Panel:

```
protected override Size MeasureOverride(Size availableSize)
{
    UpdateScrollInfo(availableSize);

    foreach (UIElement child in InternalChildren)
    {
        child.Measure(ChildSize);
    }

    return availableSize;
}
```

```csharp
protected override Size ArrangeOverride(Size finalSize)
{
    UpdateScrollInfo(finalSize);
    for (int i = 0; i < InternalChildren.Count; i++)
    {
        InternalChildren[i].Arrange(new Rect(new Point(i * ChildSize.Width, 0),
ChildSize));
    }
    return finalSize;
}

private void UpdateScrollInfo(Size size)
{
    // Adjust ViewportSize
    if (size.Width != ViewportSize)
    {
        ViewportSize = size.Width;
    }

    // Adjust ExtentSize
    double extent = InternalChildren.Count*ChildSize.Width - ViewportSize;
    if (extent != ExtentSize)
    {
        ExtentSize = extent;
    }
}
```

Finally, we bind the ScrollBar to the Panel in the XAML:

```xml
<DockPanel>
    <ScrollBar DockPanel.Dock="Bottom"
               Minimum="0"
               Maximum="{Binding ExtentSize, ElementName=_panel}"
 ViewportSize="{Binding ViewportSize, ElementName=_panel}"
 Value="{Binding HorizontalOffset, ElementName=Panel, Mode=TwoWay}"
               Orientation="Horizontal" />
    <Chapter7:HScrollingPanel x:Name="Panel">
        <Button />
        <Button />
        <Button />
        <Button />
        <Button />
        <Button />
        <Button />
```

```
        <Button />
        <Button />
        <Button />
    </Chapter7:HScrollingPanel>
  </DockPanel>
```

Summary

This chapter was all about scrolling. We started the chapter with a look at the innards and components that make up the `ScrollBar` control. Then we took a look at how a component can be scrolled using the `ScrollViewer`, which can be done by implementing the `IScrollInfo` interface—a powerful abstraction that allows the manipulation of values between a minimum and a maximum. `IScrollInfo` is a contract maintained between the `ScrollViewer` and the scrolling component. We saw how this contract can be used to implement custom scrolling logic, even animating the transition between values. At the end of the chapter, we looked at how you can implement partial scrolling behavior by binding the `Minimum`, `ViewportSize`, and `Value` properties.

For more helpful information on scrolling and optimizing the performance of scrolling behavior in your application, check out this article by Cedric Dussud: http://blogs.msdn.com/jgoldb/archive/2007/12/14/improve-wpf-scrolling-performance.aspx.

7

Virtualization

In the last couple of years, hardware advancements have exponentially increased the hard drive and RAM capacity of the average, everyday consumer PC. Processing power and capacity that used to be considered a premium now ships out of the box for less than $500. This rapid increase in capacity has unfortunately led to the development of software by unseasoned developers that don't concern themselves with capacities or limits, creating slow and inefficient applications. Worse, most people have grown accustomed to blaming the operating system when the applications become slow or unresponsive.

This chapter focuses on how virtualization can increase the performance, responsiveness, and stability of your WPF applications as well as how virtualization works under the hood within WPF.

Virtualization Distilled

The idea of virtualization comes from developers embracing the fact that there are both physical and practical limits on what can be rendered in a modern GUI, despite whatever hardware might be supporting the application at the time. Only a certain number of items can be displayed on the screen at one time. If you try to stuff too many items onto the screen, you not only run the risk of needing to change your interaction model (for example, switch from a list to a tree or from a list to a search-driven combo list), but also you run the risk of bogging down the application processing items that aren't even on the screen.

Let's look at an example of attempting to display a really large map to your users. You may not be able to show all of the details in a single view, especially if the map is many times larger than the size of the user's monitor. Using a virtualization technique, you can choose to tile the map and only display those map tiles that fall into the user's view. Virtual Earth uses this approach to allow you to move around and navigate the maps without having to load the entire world into memory at once. Applications that function on the scale of Virtual Earth wouldn't even be physically possible without the concept of virtualization.

Managing too many visual items also increases the working set, and the application's performance may be degraded as a result. To circumvent these problems, you can use virtualization to allow an application to work with incredibly large data sets and only consume small amounts of resources and still remain responsive.

Building Blocks of UI Virtualization

The catalyst for UI virtualization is the fact that we are only interested in displaying a small subset of a larger data set at any given time. Thus, the view window represents a small area of the larger container that houses all of the items, as shown in Figure 8.1. The reason why virtualization works at all is because in-memory objects such as business objects, data models, and so on are relatively cheap to store, instantiate, and manipulate. On the other hand, fully rendered WPF objects with a logical and visual tree are significantly more expensive, and you should only be creating visual objects if they can *actually be seen by the user or will be seen by the user shortly.*

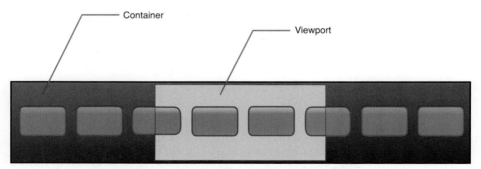

FIGURE 8.1   Diagram of a small viewport moving over a large container.

Before launching into a more in-depth discussion of virtualization, we should get a few terms out of the way so that you'll know exactly what we're talking about throughout the rest of the chapter. When we refer to the *container,* we are talking about the larger container in which all of the items reside. The view window that will be moving over this container is called the *viewport.*

In fact, the container and viewport are the key pieces that enable virtualization. In addition to the viewport and container, there is also a navigational element that allows you to manipulate the viewport's relative position within the container. This can be done by scrolling, zooming, or panning. As the viewport is moved over the container, items that resided in memory in raw form (nonvisual) are converted into visual items through a process called *realization*. When a previously nonvisual item has come into view and become visual, we call that item *realized*. An item is *virtually present* without any UI representation and is realized when it comes into view. So, in summary: Items within the viewport are realized, and items outside the viewport are virtualized.

Another common virtualization technique is to create a buffer zone around the outside edges of the viewport. Anything in this buffer zone is not visible to the user but has been realized. This allows the application to prerealize items that are *about to become visible* before they actually become visible. This can dramatically increase performance and also provides for a much smoother scrolling experience.

So, to recap, the following four items are the building blocks that make up UI virtualization:

▶ A large collection of items

▶ A container in which all of these items reside

▶ A viewport through which the user realizes the virtualized items

▶ A navigational element that allows the user to manipulate the viewport's relative position within the container

UI Virtualization in WPF

In taking the generic concepts of virtualization and applying them to WPF, a few classes immediately come to mind as ones that would benefit from virtualization: ItemsControl and its various subclasses including ListBox, ListView, TreeView, and so on. We saw in earlier chapters that the ItemsControl contains many parts that are necessary for rendering the final view. These parts include the ItemsPanel that arranges the items (layout), the ItemTemplate that is the visual representation for the data items in the list, and the ItemContainerStyle that is used to style the UI container for each item.

Since the final arrangement or layout of items happens on the ItemsPanel, it plays a vital role in how WPF virtualizes items. The ItemTemplate and ItemContainerStyle come into play only when the UI container is ready to be shown on the screen.

So far we've seen how WPF deals with the first two of the four key components of UI virtualization: the large collection of items (ItemsSource) and a container for those items (ItemsPanel). Now let's take a look at how WPF deals with the remaining two items. Both of these are generally provided by the ScrollViewer component. It has a viewport that shows a portion of the larger area and a scrolling mechanism that is provided using the vertical and horizontal scrollbars. The ScrollViewer is generally present in the ControlTemplate for the ItemsControl, and it contains the ItemsPanel as its child (through the ItemsPresenter). With that, we have all the required components for carrying out virtualization in the ItemsControl.

For the `ScrollViewer` to work correctly, there is a contract that allows it to communicate virtualization details with its child components. From the previous chapter, you may recall that this is the `IScrollInfo` interface. By implementing this interface, the `ScrollViewer` and the `ItemsPanel` can talk to each other and provide a seamless scrolling experience. As the scrollbars are moved, the viewport of the `ScrollViewer` changes, and this gets communicated back to the contained panel. For UI virtualization to work well, it is the interaction between the `ScrollViewer` and the `ItemsPanel` that brings everything together.

Component Interaction

Although the `ItemsPanel` has the knowledge of the viewport and the extent, it doesn't apply it directly to generate the items in the view or virtualize the items outside the view. This is the job of the `ItemContainerGenerator`, a helper class of the `ItemsControl`. Let's see how each of these components interact with each other to enable the complete UI virtualization process.

So far we've identified that UI virtualization in WPF requires a few key components:

- ▶ An `ItemsControl`
- ▶ An `ItemsPanel`
- ▶ A `ScrollViewer`
- ▶ An `ItemContainerGenerator`

Since we are targeting a large collection of items provided via the `ItemsSource` property, an `ItemsControl` becomes the prime candidate for UI virtualization. As such, it's no surprise that in WPF, the only classes that support virtualization are those that derive from `ItemsControl`. To help out the `ItemsControl` class, there are a few other components that take up core virtualization responsibilities. Since the UI items are being laid out inside the `ItemsPanel`, it becomes the container upon which the viewport is moved. The `ControlTemplate` for the `ItemsControl` needs to include a `ScrollViewer` that contains the `ItemsPresenter`. Basically what that really means is that you need to make sure that the items are presented within the context of a scroll viewer so that the viewport can move over them within their `ItemsPanel`.

The `ScrollViewer` is the navigating component that allows us to navigate from the first item in the collection to the last item, ensuring that items outside the viewport are *virtualized* and items within the viewport are *realized*. The `ScrollViewer` is the owner of the viewport and as such allows the `ItemsPanel` to determine the right set of items that fall inside the viewport. This is done using the layout logic of the `ItemsPanel`. Once the set of items that need to be realized are known, the `ItemContainerGenerator` can be fired up to generate the UI items from the underlying raw data.

In common virtualization scenarios, the `ItemsPanel` is a subclass of the `VirtualizingPanel`, an abstract panel-derived class that knows how to handle virtualization and also has direct access to the `ItemControl`'s `ItemContainerGenerator`.

For every data item, a UI container is created and managed by the `ItemContainerGenerator`. The `ItemContainerGenerator` is responsible for keeping track of which containers are already generated and also does the mapping from the item to the container.

Inside the virtualizing panel, the total extent of the container area, the size of the viewport, and the current offset of the viewport inside the extent are determined. These values are obtained by implementing the `IScrollInfo` interface on the virtualizing panel. We saw in the previous chapter how the `IScrollInfo` can be used to make the `ScrollViewer` work with the panel. In this case, we fetch the `ViewportSize`, `ExtentSize`, `HorizontalOffset`, and `VerticalOffset` from the `ScrollViewer`. Note that all of these properties help the panel determine the viewport within the container (ScrollViewer). The size of the viewport is then used inside the virtualizing panel to calculate the set of items that need to be displayed.

When any of these values change, the set of items in view will be recalculated. Items that are new to the viewport are generated (realized) using the `ItemContainerGenerator`. Items that fall outside the viewport are virtualized. This is done by removing the UI containers associated with those items from the panel. The set of items that should be displayed is determined by using the layout logic of the panel in addition to the position and size of the viewport.

A Deeper Look at the `ItemContainerGenerator`

Since the `ItemsPanel` implements the `IScrollInfo` interface, it can know the sizes of the viewport and the container, two things essential for virtualization. Additionally, it also knows about the scrollbar offsets within the `ScrollViewer`. When any of these values change, it effectively means that the viewport has been invalidated and the set of visible items needs to be recalculated. Typically the set of visible items is stored as an index range from the first visible index to the last visible index. This assumes that the `ItemsPanel` lays out the items sequentially. If the panel is laying out items using other schemes, you can adopt other ways of storing the list of visible items to accommodate those. After the `ItemsPanel` has determined this range, the `ItemContainerGenerator` can be called upon to generate the respective items. It will also be used to remove any items that fall outside the view.

The `ItemContainerGenerator` uses the `GeneratorPosition` class to keep track of which items it needs to generate. The generation process is kicked off by starting at a particular index. From there, the process can continue forward or backward (using the `GeneratorDirection` enum). The `GeneratorPosition` uses an `Index` and an `Offset` property to determine its exact location. The offsets are relative to this index. An `Index` of -1 indicates that the position is before the first element or after the last element ("last" is determined by the `GeneratorDirection` setting). The `Index` property corresponds to the item's index within the `ItemsControl`'s `Items` collection.

An offset of 0 indicates the current ungenerated item. An offset of 1 is the next ungenerated item, an offset of 2 is the item after that, and so on. An offset of -1 indicates the previous ungenerated item.

Using the `ItemContainerGenerator.StartAt` method, the generation process can start creating the UI containers. The method is overloaded and has the following signatures:

```
IDisposable StartAt(
    GeneratorPosition position,
    GeneratorDirection direction)

IDisposable StartAt(
    GeneratorPosition position,
    GeneratorDirection direction,
    bool allowStartAtRealizedItem)
```

From what you've read so far, the first two parameters should be fairly self-explanatory. The third parameter is useful if you want to restart generation at a realized item. Note how the `StartAt` method returns an `IDisposable`. This means that all of the item generation code should be enclosed within a `using` statement. The items are typically generated in a loop starting at the first visible index in the viewport and stopping at the last visible index.

The `GenerateNext` method is used to request a new UI container based on the current `GeneratorPosition` in the item-generation loop.

```
DependencyObject GenerateNext(    out bool isNewlyRealized)
```

When using the `GenerateNext` method, you can pass in a Boolean flag that can be used to track whether the item was newly created or was already present. It is common to have a combination of the `StartAt` and `GenerateNext` methods with the Boolean flags set to `True`. If the `StartAt` method does not have this flag set, an exception will be thrown if the generator tries to generate an already realized item. Note that the `GenerateNext` method also has a no-parameter overload. However, by passing this *out* flag, you can know whether you need to add this item to the panel. You add to the panel only when the flag is returned as `True`.

Once the UI container for the item has been generated, you definitely want to add it to your panel. But before doing that, you need to prepare it using the generator's `PrepareItemContainer` method. This internally calls into the `GetContainerForItemOverride` method and the `PrepareItemContainerOverride()` method of `ItemsControl`. Once the container is ready, you can add it to the panel. This is done using the `AddInternalChild` method. You cannot directly manipulate the panel's children collection and doing so will cause an exception. You need to use the protected internal methods to do that. These include the `AddInternalChild`, `InsertInternalChild`, and `RemoveInternalChildRange` methods.

So you can see that the `ItemContainerGenerator` has complete knowledge of the mapping between items and their associated UI containers. If you had to get to the container from an item or an index, you would have to query the `ItemContainerGenerator` rather than the `ItemsControl`. We saw in Chapter 5, "Using Existing Controls," how to use the

`ItemsControl.ItemContainerGenerator` property to get the associated container for an item. Now hopefully you know more about the mechanics of what is going on under the hood when dealing with item containers and the item container generator.

> **NOTE**
>
> At the time of this writing, the `ItemContainerGenerator` is a read-only property and cannot be overridden with a custom `ItemContainerGenerator` implementation. This may change with a future version of the framework.

Making Our Own Virtualized Control: The `StaggeredPanel`

So far we've talked a lot about how things work but haven't applied any of that knowledge to anything practical. For that reason, we're going to build a virtualization sample called a `StaggeredPanel`. This is a panel that implements virtualization and the `IScrollInfo` interface. The `StaggeredPanel` lays out a set of items as if a deck of cards had been fanned out from left to right. The first card is at the bottom of the pile and is also the leftmost. The top card of the deck stays on top of all others and is to the far right. The layout of these cards looks like the one shown in Figure 8.2.

FIGURE 8.2   The **StaggeredPanel** virtualizing panel.

You can see that the layout is purely a left-right horizontal layout. This means that the `IScrollInfo` methods that pertain to vertical movement will not be implemented and all the layout calculations are restricted to the horizontal direction. The real use of the `IScrollInfo` is to get the dimensions of the container, the dimensions of the viewport, and the position of the viewport over the container. For the virtualization to work, we need to know what part of the view is currently visible, and `IScrollInfo` does a great job giving those exact values.

Using the `ExtendWidth`, `ViewportWidth`, and the `HorizontalOffset` properties, we can determine the range of items that fall into the view. As has been mentioned many times during this chapter, items within the view are realized, and items without are virtualized. There are two scenarios in which these properties can be forced to change. One is when the panel is resized causing a layout pass to be triggered. The other is during scrolling caused by interacting with the scrollbars. If we make the scrolling action trigger the layout pass, we have only one place where we need to write the virtualization logic: in one of the layout overrides. Typically this is done in the `MeasureOverride` method of the panel, which is the first overridden method to be invoked during the layout pass.

Since we receive the new size in the `MeasureOverride` pass, we have a chance to update the `ExtentWidth` and the `ViewportWidth`. The `MeasureOverride` for the `StaggeredPanel` looks like this:

```
protected override Size MeasureOverride(Size availableSize)
    {
        UpdateScrollInfo(availableSize);

        // Virtualize items
        VirtualizeItems();

        // Measure
        foreach (UIElement child in InternalChildren)
          {
              child.Measure(new Size(ItemWidth, ItemHeight));
          }

        // Cleanup
        CleanupItems();

        return availableSize;
    }
```

It has been written in such a way that you can take this code and use it as a pattern and just provide your own implementations of the various methods called in the preceding listing.

The first step here is to update the IScrollInfo properties, ExtentWidth and ViewportWidth, since these two are essential to calculate the range of visible items.

Once the dimensions of the container and viewport are known we can perform the virtualization. The VirtualizeItems call updates the panel to include those children that fall into the view. That is followed by the Measure method being called on each of the children. Finally we have the CleanupItems call, which removes those items that are outside the view.

The UpdateScrollInfo method is similar to the one we saw in the earlier chapter. It checks to see whether the current values of ExtentWidth and ViewportWidth are different from the new size. If there is any change, these values are updated.

During VirtualizeItems, we use these values to figure out the visible items and realize them. This can be seen in the following snippet:

```
private void VirtualizeItems()
    {
        UpdateIndexRange();

        IItemContainerGenerator generator = ItemsOwner.ItemContainerGenerator;

        GeneratorPosition startPos =
generator.GeneratorPositionFromIndex(StartIndex);
```

```
        int childIndex = startPos.Offset == 0 ? startPos.Index : startPos.Index
➥+ 1;
        using (generator.StartAt(startPos, GeneratorDirection.Forward, true))
        {
            for (int i = StartIndex; i <= EndIndex; i++, childIndex++)
            {
                bool isNewlyRealized;
                UIElement child = generator.GenerateNext(out isNewlyRealized)
➥as UIElement;
                if (isNewlyRealized)
                {
                    if (childIndex >= InternalChildren.Count)
                    {
                        AddInternalChild(child);
                    }
                    else
                    {
                        InsertInternalChild(childIndex, child);
                    }
                    generator.PrepareItemContainer(child);
                }
            }
        }
    }
```

UpdateIndexRange is where we do the real calculations to figure out the visible items. It sets the StartIndex and EndIndex properties of the panel. These two properties are used during the virtualization process and keep track of the current index range. You can also see the first usage of the ItemContainerGenerator for realizing the children in the index range. We kick off the process by creating a GeneratorPosition for the StartIndex and invoking the StartAt call. Since StartAt returns an IDisposable, we surround our generation code with a using statement.

The actual container generation happens with the call to the GenerateNext method. Here we pass in a Boolean flag to know whether the container is a new one. Only newly generated containers are inserted into the panel. This makes sense because if the flag returned false, then the item container is already in the panel's Children collection.

The childIndex variable helps us determine the index where the generated item should be inserted. We initialize this value based on the GeneratorPosition returned by the call to GeneratorPositionFromIndex(). If the GeneratorPosition.Offset is 0, then we are already at the correct insertion index, if not we move forward by 1. We are incrementing our index because our generation process is going to be in the forward direction (GeneratorDirection.Forward).

If the childIndex is >= InternalChildren.Count, we know that we are at the end, so we simply append the child to the panel's Children collection. If not, we insert it at the index given by the childIndex value. Note the use of the protected methods AddInternalChild and InsertInternalChild to add the child to the panel's Children collection. Adding it directly to InternalChildren is not allowed and will result in an exception. These protected methods are provided because the VirtualizingPanel needs to do some housekeeping activities whenever a child is added.

After the virtualization process, we have the final set of children ready to be measured. This is then followed by the call to clean up any items that fall out of the view. Since cleanup only operates on items currently in the Children collection, our loop will run through the items and check whether any of their item's index is outside the StartIndex-EndIndex range.

It is important to understand that the GeneratorPosition is always relative to the generated items. Thus, GeneratorPosition's Index and Offset together point at the index of the item in the panel's Children collection. By generating the items sequentially we can afford a simple loop through the items at the time of cleanup. This can be seen in the following snippet:

```
private void CleanupItems()
{
    IItemContainerGenerator generator = ItemsOwner.ItemContainerGenerator;
    for (int i = InternalChildren.Count - 1; i >= 0; i—)
    {
        GeneratorPosition position = new GeneratorPosition(i, 0);
        int itemIndex = generator.IndexFromGeneratorPosition(position);
        if (itemIndex < StartIndex || itemIndex > EndIndex)
        {
            generator.Remove(position, 1);
            RemoveInternalChildRange(i, 1);
        }
    }
}
```

Since the ItemContainerGenerator maintains the mapping from the containers to the item indexes, we request the real index using the IndexFromGeneratorPosition method. Note that the GeneratorPosition is given by the index in the Children's collection and an Offset of 0. The ItemContainerGenerator automatically does the mapping from this position to the actual item index.

When any of the item indexes fall out of the range, we remove them from the panel's Children's collection using the protected RemoveInternalChildRange. At the same time, we also remove that GeneratorPosition from the ItemContainerGenerator.

With the cleanup operation, we have completed one cycle of virtualization—that is, starting with the VirtualizeItems, followed by Measure, and then with the CleanupItems. The only operation we have missed is the calculation of the index range (StartIndex – EndIndex). This is based on the layout strategy of the panel; in our case, it behaves like a fanned-out deck of cards. `UpdateIndexRange` is called before the realization process in the `VirtualizeItems` method:

```
private void UpdateIndexRange()
{
    double left = HorizontalOffset;
    double right = Math.Min(ExtentWidth, HorizontalOffset + View-
portWidth);
    StartIndex = CalculateIndexFromOffset(left);
    EndIndex = CalculateIndexFromOffset(right);

    Debug.WriteLine("Index Range : [ " + StartIndex + ", " + EndIndex + "
]");
}

private int CalculateIndexFromOffset(double offset)
{
    if (offset >= ExtentWidth - ItemWidth && offset <= ExtentWidth)
        return ItemsOwner.Items.Count - 1;

    double visibleArea = ItemWidth*StaggerValue;
    int index = (int)Math.Floor(offset/visibleArea);

    return index;
}
```

The virtualization principles we have seen so far have only been applicable in one direction, namely the X-direction. However, the same ideas can also be carried over to higher dimensions: 2D and 3D. 2D virtualization is easy to visualize for cases where we are viewing a large map that can be panned in both X and Y directions. The Virtual Earth application uses the technique of breaking up the map into a grid of tiles and displaying only those tiles that are currently in the view. As the user pans or zooms into the map, these tiles update to reflect the changed view.

On the same note, virtualization ideas can also be applied in 3D. We cover a few ideas related to this topic in a later section of this chapter.

Deferred Scrolling

Deferred scrolling is a feature added in the SP1 release of .NET Framework 3.5. It accommodates a scenario where live scrolling could be expensive. Instead of scrolling the items as soon as the scroll thumb is moved, the scrolling action is deferred until the user leaves the thumb. Microsoft Outlook uses this technique when scrolling email items. Deferred scrolling causes some loss in fidelity since the user is kept in the unknown about the items that will come into view. This can, however, lead to a perceived improvement in performance.

Deferred scrolling can be enabled on the `ScrollViewer` using its Boolean attached property: `ScrollViewer.IsDeferredScrollingEnabled`. Note that this is not turned on by default and is an opt-in feature.

```
<ScrollViewer CanContentScroll="True"
HorizontalScrollBarVisibility="Visible"
IsDeferredScrollingEnabled="True">
              <ItemsPresenter />
          </ScrollViewer>
```

Container Recycling

When a container is generated, its `DataContext` is set to the data item, and its `DataTemplate` is created with all of the bindings in it. This happens each time a new data item comes into the view. If the viewport is constantly moving and many new containers are being generated, a lot of overhead can be involved in just disposing of the previous containers and generating the new ones. To improve performance, the concept of container recycling was introduced in the SP1 release of .NET Framework 3.5.

With this technique, a pool of containers is used for each of the data items that come into the view. These containers are only generated the first time and reused again when a new a container needs to be used. When a data item goes out of the view, its container is put back into the container pool. By reusing the container, the `DataTemplate` does not have to be regenerated and neither do the bindings have to be associated again. The only thing that changes is the content associated with the container. This can give you a big jump in performance.

Container recycling is not used by default and is an opt-in feature. In the current release it is only available on the `VirtualizingStackPanel` with the attached property `VirtualizationMode`. This property is an enum of type `VirtualizationMode`, taking either of the following values: `Standard`, `Recycling`. By default `ListBox`, `ListView`, and `TreeView` use the `VirtualizingStackPanel`:

```
<ListBox VirtualizingStackPanel.IsVirtualizing="True"
VirtualizingStackPanel.VirtualizationMode="Recycling"
          ItemsSource="{StaticResource DataSource}"
          ItemTemplate="{StaticResource StringTemplate}" />
```

The preceding code snippet shows a `ListBox` that opts into the `Recycling` virtualization mode. Note that we have also set the attached property `VirtualizingStackPanel.IsVirtualizing` to `True` just for completeness. It is not mandatory, and `ListBox` by default uses a `VirtualizingStackPanel` that has this property set to `True`.

Virtualization in 3D

Virtualized 2D controls will account for a majority of your needs, but there are a few cases where you may have to go the route of applying the techniques to 3D. Although we don't cover all the different techniques and implementation details of how you can achieve this, we certainly go over a few important ideas. The 3D world definitely stands out as being separate and different from the way things work in 2D, but frankly it's still 2D. We are viewing the 3D world on a flat 2D screen, so essentially we are tricking our eyes to believe the sense of depth. This is cleverly done by projecting 3D objects onto 2D planes, a technique known as *perspective projection*. By determining the rectangular bounds of this flattened 2D shape, we can get back to the familiar Rect bounds and reuse our knowledge from the 2D world (see Figure 8.3).

FIGURE 8.3   2D bounding rectangles on 3D items.

WPF simplifies the part where you have to get the flat 2D rectangle from a 3D object. This can be obtained using the `GeneralTransform3DTo2D` class. Using the overloaded `Visual3D.TransformToAncestor`, which takes either a `Visual3D` or a `Visual` as a parameter, an instance of the `GeneralTransform3D` or `GeneralTransform3DTo2D` can be obtained, respectively. In our case, we are interested in the overloaded method that takes the `Visual` as parameter. Since the `Viewport3D` is a `FrameworkElement`, you can use that to fetch the 2D bounds of the 3D visual. Now that we have the transform to help us get the 2D bounds of a 3D object, you can leverage this fact and create a virtualized 3D control.

If you are planning on virtualizing a 3D layout of items that flow from left to right or top to bottom, you can think in terms of flattened 2D bounding Rects for each of the 3D items. The bounding Rect can be obtained using the `General3DTo2DTransform`. With that we are back to dealing with 2D rectangles, just that they are of different sizes because of the perspective projection. For a 3D layout with items flowing from left to right or top to bottom, we are really dealing with a list of 2D rectangles. The added responsibility is to map these 2D Rects to 3D objects and update the mappings as the viewport is scrolled or resized. You can also optimize by creating a limited set of 3D objects and reusing them. This is similar in principle to container recycling where you maintain a pool of 3D models and reuse them when the viewport is scrolled or resized. The models for the items that go out of the view are put back into the pool. Newly visible items are created using the models allocated from the pool. The model pool can grow adaptively based on the change in Viewport3D size, a change in the Camera, or other related parameters.

A slightly different strategy is to fix the number of items that you want to show in the viewport. With a fixed number of items, you don't have to worry about recalculating the visible objects when the viewport size changes or when it is scrolled. But you may have to create extra objects on the edges just to make it more seamless and keep a continuous animation. You can also apply the container recycling technique since your 3D container list is pretty much fixed.

There are certainly many other ways to add virtualization capability to 3D layouts. Hopefully the previous two techniques will spur you to come up with your own. Remember that virtualization works on some simple building blocks that we discussed early in the chapter. The shape and form of the layouts and UI items might change, but the underlying principles are still the same.

Summary

Everybody wants their application to work smoothly and respond quickly. In addition, there are many times where your application needs to deal with huge data sets and has only a small amount of screen real estate in which to render.

Virtualization is a technique that you can use as a developer to build a WPF application that can have highly responsive, fast displays that operate on massive data sets.

We strongly encourage you to take the code that accompanies this chapter, as well as the code you see in the book and experiment with it. Create your own virtualizing control and experiment with ways in which you can build rich, fast, *virtualized* GUIs.

CHAPTER 9

Creating Advanced Controls and Visual Effects

This chapter extends your knowledge of control creation in WPF by showing you how to create some advanced controls as well as implement some popular visual effects such as reflection, drop shadows, opacity masks, and gloss effects.

This chapter provides samples and background technical information on creating controls that implement lasso selection, a dock slide presenter, and even a generic container for implementing PowerPoint-like slide transitions.

Lasso Selection Using the InkCanvas

The `InkCanvas` is one of those controls that doesn't get nearly as much attention as the more common controls like `ListBox`, `TreeView`, or the classic `Button`. This control is, as you might expect, a Canvas layer that allows for pen, stylus, or touch-screen input for creating digital ink. If you have ever used a Tablet PC where you were able to annotate a Word document by circling words with the light pen, then you are familiar with the kind of functionality that the `InkCanvas` provides.

Interestingly enough, the `InkCanvas` can be used without a pen or a stylus and responds perfectly fine to the mouse. With a little bit of creative thinking, it isn't difficult to come up with some clever scenarios for using this control. The scenario we're going to look at in this sample is using digital ink to create a lasso selection tool, as shown in Figure 9.1.

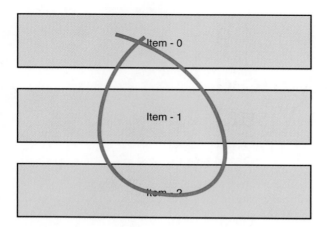

FIGURE 9.1   Lasso selection tool for selecting items in a **ListBox**.

By default, the InkCanvas gives you a black tip that can be used to create ink strokes on the canvas. These strokes are all recorded by the control and displayed in real-time. Each stroke is represented internally as a collection of StylusPoint objects from the time you put the ink device down until the time you lift it. Once a stroke is completed, a StrokeCollected event is fired. This event returns an InkCanvasStrokeCollectedEventArgs object that contains the captured stroke. If you are building a Tablet PC-aware application, there is a tremendous amount of useful information in this object. However, for this example, all we need are the rectangular bounds (which often are an approximation, given the typically nonrectangular nature of hand-drawn regions) of the stroke.

You're probably thinking something like, *"Oh great, now I have to figure out how to turn a collection of stroke points into a bounding region and do clipping and detection..."* Thankfully, WPF takes care of all that for us, and all we have to do is call the Stroke.GetBounds method. It almost seems too easy, but we won't complain too loudly. Using the geometry returned by this method call, we can perform the relatively simple operation of hit testing on the ListBox.

The following code snippet shows the code that is executed in response to a stroke collection event. In the following code, we get the bounds of the stroke, which set up a RectangleGeometry object that can then be used to perform a hit test using VisualTreeHelper:

```
        private void OnStrokeCollection(object sender,
InkCanvasStrokeCollectedEventArgs args)
        {
            _selections.Clear();

            RectangleGeometry geom = new
RectangleGeometry(args.Stroke.GetBounds());
                VisualTreeHelper.HitTest(ItemsListBox, OnFilter, OnResult, new
```

```
GeometryHitTestParameters(geom));

        foreach (ListBoxItem item in _selections)
        {
            item.IsSelected = !item.IsSelected;
        }

        OverlayInkCanvas.Strokes.Remove(args.Stroke);
        EndLassoSelection();
        LassoCheckBox.IsChecked = false;
    }

    private HitTestFilterBehavior OnFilter(DependencyObject potentialHitTest-
Target)
    {
        ListBoxItem item = potentialHitTestTarget as ListBoxItem;
        if (item != null)
        {
            _selections.Add(item);
          return HitTestFilterBehavior.ContinueSkipSelfAndChildren;
        }

        return HitTestFilterBehavior.ContinueSkipSelf;
    }

    private HitTestResultBehavior OnResult(HitTestResult result)
    {
        return HitTestResultBehavior.Continue;
    }
```

The purpose of this hit test is to find all of the ListBoxItems that fall within the rectangular region represented by the Lasso (which is, as we've seen, nothing more than a collected stroke on an InkCanvas). VisualTreeHelper gives us a convenient method, HitTest, which takes an instance of HitTestParameters. This parameter is used with a RectangleGeometry that is made from the bounding rectangle of the stroke. The HitTest method fires a callback each time a visual is encountered that *passes* the hit test criteria (within the stroke bounds). A HitTestFilterCallback and HitTestResultCallback are fired for each visual. The filter callback is used to return results in top-down fashion going from the parent to the child. Since we are only interested in ListBoxItems we stop when one is found and prevent the hit test firing to go into any further detail. This allows us to not fire redundant hit test passes for controls nested within the ListBoxItem, but the mechanism is there in case we need it for other applications.

The following is the complete signature for the HitTest() method. The hitTestParameters parameter can be either a PointHitTestParameters or a GeometryHitTestParameters instance. We are using the latter for our example.

```
public static void HitTest(
    Visual reference,
    HitTestFilterCallback filterCallback,
    HitTestResultCallback resultCallback,
    HitTestParameters hitTestParameters
)
```

Each time a `ListBoxItem` is found, we add it to the selection list. Once the hit testing is complete, we toggle the `IsSelected` property of each of the items to `true`. Note that `VisualTreeHelper.HitTest()` is a synchronous call so it is safe for us to keep the `ListBoxItem` selection loop after the call to `HitTest`.

A few other things in this sample are worth mentioning. The `InkCanvas` is overlaid on the `ListBox` but is hidden by default. When the Toggle Lasso Selection check box is clicked, the `InkCanvas` is made visible and ready to capture all mouse/stylus strokes. When a stroke is completed the `StrokeCollected` event is fired, which does the job of selecting the `ListBoxItems`. Unchecking the check box or completing a lasso selection hides the `InkCanvas` again.

> **NOTE**
>
> **Reader Challenge**
>
> You can use the concepts that you saw in this sample as well as concepts illustrated by earlier chapters to encapsulate ink-based functionality as attached properties. This allows you to set up lasso selection on any `ListBox` or its subclasses. `InkCanvas` also supports gestures, editing modes, and many other features. Using attached properties and some creativity, you can create some amazing functionality for any of your controls and position yourself ahead of the curve for programming against touch devices like the surface table or touch-screen monitors.

Building a Dock Slide Presenter

This control takes an interesting idea and combines the use of 3D and 2D perspectives and views in the same control to display two different screens at the same time, but where one has more temporary prominence than the other, as you can see in Figure 9.2.

The primary screen occupies the entire allocated space by default. When you want to proceed to the second screen, the primary screen is docked to the side and the secondary screen slides in. This docking and sliding behavior gives the control its name: `DockSlidePresenter`.

Before continuing with the rest of this section, we strongly recommend that you open up the code samples from the book and run the demo for the dock slide presenter a few times to get a feel for how the animation looks and works. There is only so much we can do using words to describe the animation, but seeing it actually happen before continuing makes this section much easier to follow and understand.

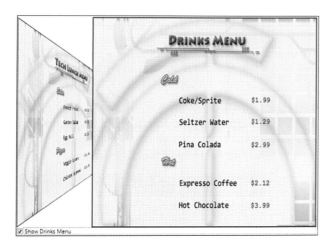

FIGURE 9.2   The **DockSlidePresenter** control in action.

At first glance, you might think that this is just a clever trick of perspective-based 2D transforms, but this time we're actually using a 3D view. As a result, we need to embed a Viewport3D into our control. This technique becomes handy for subtle use of 3D in an otherwise 2D UI. We can perform this embedding by making DockSlidePresenter derive from a FrameworkElement and then building our custom visual tree. This tree is built partly in XAML and partly within the code. We cover this in a later section in this chapter.

When the primary control (called the FrontChild) is docked, an animated 3D rotation occurs that puts the FrontChild control to the side. At the same time, the secondary child (called the BackChild) slides into view from the left. The docking and sliding mechanism is completely encapsulated within the control and exposed as a Boolean-valued DependencyProperty, as shown here:

```
public static readonly DependencyProperty IsChildDockedProperty =
        DependencyProperty.Register(
    "IsChildDocked", typeof(bool), typeof(DockSlidePresenter),
    new PropertyMetadata(false, OnIsChildDockedChanged));

private static void OnIsChildDockedChanged(DependencyObject d,
                    DependencyPropertyChangedEventArgs e)
{
    DockSlidePresenter presenter = d as DockSlidePresenter;
    bool docked = (bool)e.NewValue;
    if (docked) presenter.DockFrontChild();
    else presenter.UndockFrontChild();
}
```

Before the docking 3D rotation happens, we need to hide the 2D `FrontChild` element and bring in the `Viewport3D` that contains a texture-mapped 3D mesh (`MeshGeometry3D`). The texture of this 3D mesh comes from the `VisualBrush` of the `FrontChild`. When the 3D rotation happens, we want to hide the `FrontChild` and only keep the texture mapped 3D mesh on top.

The pitfall here that a lot of people fall into is that if you hide the `FrontChild`, it results in a blank `VisualBrush`, which means the 3D surface will be blank as well. To get around this we wrap the `FrontChild` in a `Decorator` and then hide the `Decorator`. This enables us to have a rendered `VisualBrush` of the `FrontChild` but also keep it hidden.

The `Viewport3D` gets overlaid on top of the `FrontChild` control such that the bounds and position match exactly. This is essential so that when the 3D rotation begins, the user doesn't experience a jarring "break" or "rip" effect when switching from a 2D view to a 3D animation.

Matching bounds and position is only part of it. We also need to ensure that the texture-mapped `MeshGeometry3D` is

> ### TIP
>
> It is interesting to note that hiding the parent of a control doesn't make the child's visibility hidden. This is what allows us to maintain a rendered `VisualBrush` of a child even though the parent is hidden. This technique can be repeated in any scenario where you need to "paint" something onto the surface of a 3D object but you don't want to show the source of the painting.

the same size as the `Viewport3D`. In other words, the camera of the `Viewport3D` has to be positioned in a spot so that the 3D mesh appears to be occupying the same space as the `FrontChild` control. This gives us a seamless switch to the 3D viewport when the 2D front control is hidden.

To determine the exact position of the perspective camera used in the viewport, we have to dust off some of those trigonometry skills we told our teachers we would never need to use. Don't worry, the pain only lasts a short while, and there is a big payoff when we get the control finished.

In Figure 9.3, **d** is the distance of the camera from the 3D mesh, and the angle **A** represents the `FieldOfView` property of the `PerspectiveCamera`. The marked angle is a horizontally described angle in the XZ-plane. Thus, the Figure 9.3 represents a top-down view where the base of the triangle is the top edge of the `MeshGeometry3D`. The positions of the `MeshGeometry3D` have to be defined such that its bounds are the same as the aspect ratio of the `Viewport3D`. Thus, *width / height = aspect*, where *aspect* is the aspect ratio of the `Viewport3D`. If we set the height to 1.0, then the width becomes equal to *aspect*. This makes it easy to set the positions of the mesh vertices. Since the mesh is located at the 3D origin of (0,0,0) with the center of the mesh coinciding with the origin, the four vertices of the mesh are shown in Figure 9.4.

Now if we refer back to the trigonometry illustrated in Figure 9.3, we can see why the left and right edges of the mesh (the base vertices of the triangle) are set as (*+aspect/2, +0.5*) and (*-aspect/2, +0.5*), respectively.

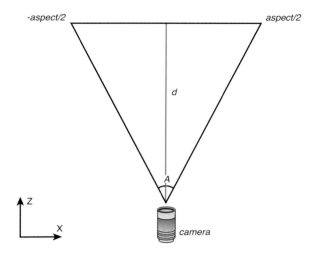

FIGURE 9.3   A perspective camera viewing a 2D plane in a 3D scene.

Fixing the FieldOfView to 60° (angle A = 60), we can use some trig skills (we promise, this is *almost* the last of it!), as illustrated in Figure 9.5.

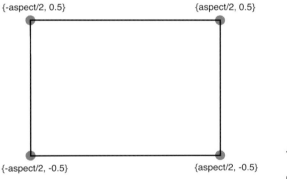

$$\tan\left(\frac{A}{2}\right) = \frac{aspect\;/2}{d}$$

$$\therefore d = \left(\frac{aspect}{2 * \tan 30}\right)$$

$$\therefore d = aspect * 0.866$$

FIGURE 9.4   Mesh vertices.

FIGURE 9.5   Trigonometry solving for d with an angle of 60°.

This value of **d**, which is along the +Z axis, is the distance at which the PerspectiveCamera must be positioned from the 3D mesh to exactly fit the size of the Viewport3D.

Docking and Undocking Controls

Now that we know how to set up the Viewport3D, the MeshGeometry3D, and the PerspectiveCamera (the three basic requirements for any 3D scene in WPF), we can now go about building the visual tree and the animations that do the docking and sliding actions. Let's start with the visual tree.

The visual tree for the DockSlidePresenter can be shown more easily with the following XAML snippet. This is a much easier way to create a visual tree than by doing it the "hard way" in code:

```xaml
<Grid xmlns="http://schemas.microsoft.com/winfx/2006/xaml/presentation"
    xmlns:x="http://schemas.microsoft.com/winfx/2006/xaml">
    <Grid.ColumnDefinitions>
        <ColumnDefinition Width="0.25*" />
        <ColumnDefinition Width="0.75*" />
    </Grid.ColumnDefinitions>

    <Decorator x:Name="BackChildContainer"
               Grid.Column="1"
               Grid.ColumnSpan="1">
        <Decorator.RenderTransform>
            <TranslateTransform />
        </Decorator.RenderTransform>
    </Decorator>
    <Decorator x:Name="FrontChildContainer"
               Grid.Column="0"
               Grid.ColumnSpan="2" />
    <Viewport3D x:Name="Viewport"
                Grid.Column="0"
                Grid.ColumnSpan="2"
                Visibility="Hidden">

    </Viewport3D>
</Grid>
```

For brevity, the contents of the Viewport3D element were omitted, but you can find it in its entirety in this chapter's code samples. Note the use of the decorators for wrapping the FrontChild and the BackChild. When the OnInitialized() method is called on the DockSlidePresenter, we build the visual tree and store references to the FrontChildContainer, BackChildContainer, and the Viewport3D. Now let's see how these are used during the docking and undocking actions.

When the IsChildDocked property changes, the DockFrontChild() or UndockFrontChild() method is called. Docking involves unhiding the Viewport3D, rotating the 3D mesh, and sliding the BackChild into view. Undocking does these operations in reverse: sliding the back child control out of the view and then rotating the mesh back to its original position. The Viewport3D is hidden, and the FrontChild control is then revealed. Since they both have the exact same bounds and the camera was adjusted properly and they are both displaying the same contents, the user never knows that there are two controls in play. The following code shows these two methods:

```
private void DockFrontChild()
{
```

```
    // Hide the front child container
    _frontChildContainer.Visibility = Visibility.Hidden;

    _viewport.Visibility = Visibility.Visible;

    Storyboard dockAnim = PrepareStoryboard(new AnimationParameters
    {
        DockDirection = "Dock",
        AnimationType = "Dock"
    });
    dockAnim.Begin(_viewport, true);

    // show the back child
    Panel.SetZIndex(_backChildContainer, 1);
    Storyboard slideAnim = PrepareStoryboard(new AnimationParameters
    {
        DockDirection = "Dock",
        AnimationType = "Slide"
    });

    slideAnim.Begin(_backChildContainer, true);
}

private void UndockFrontChild()
{
    Storyboard dockAnim = PrepareStoryboard(new AnimationParameters
    {
        DockDirection = "Undock",
        AnimationType = "Dock"
    });
    EventHandler handler = null;
    handler = delegate
    {
        // Hide the Viewport3D
        _viewport.Visibility = Visibility.Hidden;
        Panel.SetZIndex(_backChildContainer, 0);

        // show the FrontChild
                frontChildContainer.Visibility = Visibility.Visible;
        dockAnim.Completed -= handler;
    };
    dockAnim.Completed += handler;
    dockAnim.Begin(_viewport, true);
```

```
    // show the back child
Storyboard slideAnim = PrepareStoryboard(new AnimationParameters
{
    DockDirection = "Undock",
    AnimationType = "Slide"
});

slideAnim.Begin(_backChildContainer, true);
}
```

The PrepareStoryboard() method is used to set the proper values for the DoubleAnimation's From and To properties:

```
private Storyboard PrepareStoryboard(AnimationParameters ap)
{
    Storyboard anim = GetBaseStoryboard(ap.AnimationType == "Dock" ?
"DockAnimation" : "SlideAnimation");

    double from = 0;
    double to = 0;
    if (ap.AnimationType == "Dock")
    {
        from = ap.DockDirection == "Dock" ? 0 : 90;
        to = ap.DockDirection == "Dock" ? 90 : 0;
    }
    else if (ap.AnimationType == "Slide")
    {
        from = ap.DockDirection == "Dock" ? -ActualWidth : 0;
        to = ap.DockDirection == "Dock" ? 0 : -ActualWidth;

        double opacity = ap.DockDirection == "Dock" ? 1 : 0;
        (anim.Children[1] as DoubleAnimation).To = opacity;
    }

    (anim.Children[0] as DoubleAnimation).From = from;
    (anim.Children[0] as DoubleAnimation).To = to;

    return anim;
}
```

The storyboards for the animating between the docked and undocked modes come from a private ResourceDictionary, which is used to store the animations. The DockSlidePresenter expects this private dictionary to be present in the containing assembly and loads it up in its static constructor. This is a useful way of keeping resources private. Since storyboards are far easier to edit in XAML than in code, we chose to use this approach. Here is the static constructor and the GetBaseStoryboard() method that is used in PrepareStoryboard():

```
static DockSlidePresenter()
{
    ClipToBoundsProperty.OverrideMetadata(typeof(DockSlidePresenter), new
PropertyMetadata(true));
    _dictionary = Application.LoadComponent(new
Uri("/Chapters;component/Chapter09/InternalResources.xaml", UriKind.Relative)) as
ResourceDictionary;

}

private Storyboard GetBaseStoryboard(string animationName)
{
    return _dictionary[animationName] as Storyboard;
}
```

Expecting Storyboards from Outside

You can also allow the users of your control to provide their own storyboards for animating between the docked and undocked modes. You can do that by expecting storyboards with specific names somewhere higher up in the visual tree and using the FrameworkElement. FindResource() method. For example, you can keep a contract that if you find a storyboard named DockAnimation using the FindResource() method, you would use that, or resort to using the default storyboard instead.

To make this scheme robust, you can also do some checks on the storyboard to see whether it has the right kind of child animations.

The DockSlidePresenter control shows an interesting mix of 3D and 2D controls that are controlled via simple dependency properties like IsChildDocked. In addition to showing the blend of 2D and 3D, it shows a *tasteful* blend that has real value and purpose for a user. All too often we see 3D horribly abused in applications to do things like make buttons into 3D rotating cubes just for the sake of doing so. Controls like the DockSlidePresenter hopefully provide some prescriptive guidance for how to make subtle use of 3D blended with 2D to create compelling, useful user interactions and experiences.

By creating a simple façade that exposes properties for controlling internal components, you can create some amazing effects in your controls. The DockSlidePresenter touches on some useful concepts that you will be able to reuse again and again in your own applications and controls. Some of these concepts include techniques for auto-positioning a perspective camera for a full view of a 3D model, use of a private XAML file that contains the skeleton visual tree, and much more.

9

> **NOTE**
>
> **Extra Examples**
>
> The source code for this chapter includes two other examples that use techniques discussed in the chapters thus far. As shown in Figure 9.6, these include the magnifying glass, which uses an adorner for displaying the magnifier and a Parallax view, which is achieved using a layering of different sized images, each moving with different speed.

Magnifying Glass

Parallax View

FIGURE 9.6   Magnifying glass and Parallax view controls.

If you want to customize certain parts of the control specifically, you can expose additional properties externally that control the internal customizations.

Don't worry if some of the 3D work done for this sample seemed a little overwhelming. Chapter 11, "Bridging 2D and 3D Worlds," goes into plenty of detail on how this effect and many others work.

Building a Transition Abstraction: The `TransitionContainer`

There are few people who haven't watched a PowerPoint presentation where the presenter utilized a transition effect. These effects allow slides to fade out while new ones fade in, or they can be used to move one slide out while another one moves in from another direction. PowerPoint also allows you to get creative and make a variety of other transitions.

We are going to take this concept of using a transition between two slides and apply it to two WPF views. Transitions applied to views in an application can help guide users and give them visual feedback as to what is happening rather than instantaneously switching an entire screen full of data to something completely different. Using transitions not only shows users that something important is happening, but it gives their eyes (and more importantly, their brains) time to adjust to the new information being revealed by the transition. That doesn't mean all transitions are good—as with all things in WPF, at a certain point, transitions can become intrusive and annoying to users. The sweet spot is to find those subtle transitions that are informative, pleasing to the user, and unobtrusive.

Transitions like the ones we all know and love in PowerPoint are typically accomplished by playing a storyboard that animates between the current and the next view.

However, if you have a lot of views that you want to do this for, especially if you don't know at design time which view to which you are transitioning, you probably need a better way of organizing the views and the transitions between them. The TransitionContainer, a control that we build for this sample, provides this abstraction and makes it easy to play transitions between views. In addition to making it easy to play a transition, the TransitionContainer also makes the concept of transitions pluggable so that you can create your own and change them dynamically at runtime. Figure 9.7 shows this control performing a transition

FIGURE 9.7   The **TransitionContainer** control in action.

The TransitionContainer, as the name suggests, is first and foremost a container that keeps a stack of children. This stack starts at the foreground facing the user and recedes backward so that only the topmost child on the stack is visible.

The transition that will be used when shifting between views is held within the Transition property, which is of type TransitionBase (an abstract class). The pluggable aspect comes from the fact that you can create your own subclasses of TransitionBase and implement a variety of transitions. For example, if you were feeling creative, you could create a transition that splits the current view into a jigsaw puzzle, and as pieces of the puzzle are removed, the underlying view is revealed.

When the transition is playing (typically a short period of time like 0.5 seconds), the user does not interact with the views. The key thing that makes this all work is the VisualBrush of the view that will be utilized by the current Transition. A transition may use its own set of visuals to create the effect that it needs. For example, if you are creating a rotating cube effect, the transition itself would supply the Viewport3D and the

GeometryModel3D that represents the cube, and would paint the surfaces of the cube with the VisualBrush of the current and next views.

To allow a transition to have whatever visuals it needs to play the effect, the TransitionContainer control follows a particular visual tree structure. The root of the visual tree is a 1x1 grid panel that contains two other grids as its children. One of the grids contains all of the views, and the other contains the visuals that may be needed for a transition. In effect, this visual tree isolates the children and the transition's visuals.

The TransitionContainer derives from a ContentControl and sets its Content property to the root grid panel. The following code snippet from the TransitionContainer's constructor shows how this visual tree is created:

```
public TransitionContainer()
{
    _childContainer = new Grid();
    _transitionContainer = new Grid();

    _rootContainer = new Grid();
    _rootContainer.Children.Add(_transitionContainer);
    _rootContainer.Children.Add(_childContainer);

    Content = _rootContainer;
}
```

Why Does the TransitionContainer Derive from a ContentControl?

You may be wondering why we chose a ContentControl as the base class instead of a FrameworkElement. In the earlier chapters, we saw cases where a custom visual tree was built up in code, and for those controls, we chose to derive from a FrameworkElement. But doing so also requires us to implement the protected methods: MeasureOverride, ArrangeOverride, GetVisualChild, and VisualChildrenCount. Deriving from a FrameworkElement is a great choice if you intend to keep your visual lightweight and do not care about the templating aspect.

Since a ContentControl derives from a Control, you get the power of templates and also the concrete implementations for the previously mentioned protected methods. This simplifies the TransitionContainer, allowing us to focus more on the features like pluggable transitions.

When using the TransitionContainer in XAML, we want to have an easy way to add children (the views between which we are transitioning). It should be as easy as adding children to any Panel. As such, we want something like this:

```
<Chapter09:TransitionContainer x:Name="_trans">
    <Rectangle x:Name="_red" Fill="Red" />
    <Button x:Name="_blue" />
</Chapter09:TransitionContainer>
```

Whenever we're making controls, we want to make sure that the syntax for defining the properties of our controls is as easy as possible, *especially* in XAML. The more XAML-friendly our controls are, the more easily our controls can be used by designers and developers alike. This kind of syntax can be made possible by setting the `ContentPropertyAttribute` on the `TransitionContainer`. The following code snippet shows how to do this:

```
[ContentProperty("Children")]
public class TransitionContainer : ContentControl
{
    ...
    private readonly Grid _childContainer;
    public UIElementCollection Children
    {
        get { return _childContainer.Children; }
    }
...
...
}
```

Note that the string parameter to the `ContentPropertyAttribute` indicates the name of the property that will hold the children. When you define child elements in XAML, the compiler parsing the XAML attempts to locate a property that contains children. If such a property can be located, each child element of the control is instantiated from XAML and added as an element to the `UIElementCollection` property. A lot of really powerful things can be accomplished by using the `ContentPropertyAttribute` attribute. In our case, the Children property points to an instance of the Grid's (stored in the field *_childContainer*) Children collection. This is the Grid that holds the child controls.

Handling Transitions

Because we want to make transitions pluggable, we need to provide enough flexibility for a transition to use whatever visuals it needs. This is done by providing a separate grid panel that hosts any such transition visuals. However, the transition implementation itself need not know anything about these details. Think of this grid panel as a kind of off-stage setup area. Hiding these details from the transition is made possible through the `TransitionBase` class, which contains an abstract method called `SetupVisuals` that is used by transitions to ready the visuals needed during the transition.

```
public abstract class TransitionBase
{
    private Duration _duration = new Duration(TimeSpan.FromSeconds(1));

    public Duration Duration
    {
        get { return _duration; }
        set { _duration = value; }
```

6

```
    }

    public abstract Storyboard PrepareStoryboard(TransitionContainer container);
    public abstract FrameworkElement SetupVisuals(VisualBrush prevBrush,
                                VisualBrush nextBrush);
}
```

The SetupVisuals() method takes the VisualBrush of the current and next views and uses them in whatever way it sees fit. The transition need not know about where the individual brushes reside in the visual tree of the transition container. The transition must return the root FrameworkElement that hosts all of the visuals needed by the transition. The PrepareStoryboard() method gathers up all of the animations in the transition and returns a Storyboard instance. These could be any animations that would be applied to the visuals contained in the transition.

As an example, consider the SlideTransition that derives from TransitionBase and implements the two required abstract methods. The following snippet just contains the two overridden methods:

```
public override FrameworkElement SetupVisuals(VisualBrush prevBrush,
                                                VisualBrush nextBrush)
{
    _prevRect = new Rectangle();
    _prevRect.Fill = prevBrush;
    _prevRect.RenderTransform = new TranslateTransform();

    _nextRect = new Rectangle();
    _nextRect.Fill = nextBrush;
    _nextRect.RenderTransform = new TranslateTransform();

    _rectContainer = new Grid();
    _rectContainer.ClipToBounds = true;
    _rectContainer.Children.Add(_nextRect);
    _rectContainer.Children.Add(_prevRect);

    return _rectContainer;
}

public override Storyboard PrepareStoryboard(TransitionContainer container)
{
    Storyboard animator = new Storyboard();

    DoubleAnimation prevAnim = new DoubleAnimation();
    Storyboard.SetTarget(prevAnim, _prevRect);
    Storyboard.SetTargetProperty(prevAnim, new PropertyPath("(0).(1)",
        UIElement.RenderTransformProperty, TranslateTransform.XProperty));
```

```
    prevAnim.Duration = Duration;
    prevAnim.From = 0;
    prevAnim.To = Direction == Direction.RightToLeft ? -1 *
            container.ActualWidth : container.ActualWidth;

    DoubleAnimation nextAnim = new DoubleAnimation();
    Storyboard.SetTarget(nextAnim, _nextRect);
    Storyboard.SetTargetProperty(nextAnim, new PropertyPath("(0).(1)",
            UIElement.RenderTransformProperty, TranslateTransform.XProperty));
    nextAnim.Duration = Duration;
    nextAnim.From = Direction == Direction.RightToLeft ?
            container.ActualWidth : -1 * container.ActualWidth;
    nextAnim.To = 0;

    animator.Children.Add(prevAnim);
    animator.Children.Add(nextAnim);

    return animator;
}
```

The SlideTransition uses two Rectangle instances whose Fill is set to the VisualBrush of the views. You will see time and time again that clever uses of VisualBrush make the difference between plain ordinary user interfaces and fantastic, memorable user interfaces. The Storyboard consists of two DoubleAnimations that translate the rectangles in the x direction, resulting in a smooth animated slide.

Applying a Transition

The two methods SetupVisuals and PrepareStoryboard are invoked by the TransitionContainer whenever its ApplyTransition method is called. As mentioned earlier, during the transition there is no interactivity needed (in fact, it is strongly discouraged because the state of either view during a transition is indeterminate). This means that we can hide the grid that holds the children and keep only the transition-grid visible. We can then call the first of the two methods, SetupVisuals, and ask the transition instance to get ready to play the animations. SetupVisuals gives back the root element that hosts all the visuals that may be needed to by the transition.

Once the transition is all set up, the Storyboard is requested by calling the PrepareStoryboard method. We now play the storyboard on the transition grid. But before starting the animation, we hook into the Storyboard's Completed event to get notified when the animation completes. We need this to switch back to the nontransition mode where the children are visible and interactive.

You can see this logic in the following code snippet. Note that the ApplyTransition method is overloaded. One version takes the string names of the children, and the other accepts the actual child control instances:

```csharp
public void ApplyTransition(string prevChildName, string nextChildName)
{
    // Check if the named children exist
    FrameworkElement prevChild = (FrameworkElement)FindName(prevChildName);
    FrameworkElement nextChild = (FrameworkElement)FindName(nextChildName);

    ApplyTransition(prevChild, nextChild);
}

public void ApplyTransition(UIElement prevChild, UIElement nextChild)
{
    if (prevChild == null || nextChild == null)
    {
        throw new Exception("prevChild or nextChild cannot be null");
    }

    _prevChild = prevChild;
    _nextChild = nextChild;

    StartTransition();
}

private void StartTransition()
{
    // Make the children Visible, so that the VisualBrush will not be blank
    _prevChild.Visibility = Visibility.Visible;
    _nextChild.Visibility = Visibility.Visible;

    // Switch to transition-mode
    FrameworkElement root = Transition.SetupVisuals(
            CreateBrush(_prevChild), CreateBrush(_nextChild));
    _transitionContainer.Children.Add(root);
    _transitionContainer.Visibility = Visibility.Visible;
    _childContainer.Visibility = Visibility.Hidden;

    // Get Storyboard to play
    Storyboard sb = Transition.PrepareStoryboard(this);
    EventHandler handler = null;
    handler = delegate
{
        sb.Completed -= handler;
        FinishTransition();
};
    sb.Completed += handler;
    sb.Begin(_transitionContainer);
}
```

The `FinishTransition()` method that gets called at the end of the animation completes the whole process of playing the transition. In addition to hiding the transition grid and making the children grid visible, it also surfaces the next view on top of all others and fires the `TransitionCompleted` event:

```
public void FinishTransition()
{
    // Bring the next-child on top
    ChangeChildrenStackOrder();

    _transitionContainer.Visibility = Visibility.Hidden;
    _childContainer.Visibility = Visibility.Visible;
    _transitionContainer.Children.Clear();

    NotifyTransitionCompleted();
}
```

The `TransitionContainer` is a useful control that abstracts the process of playing transitions (animations) to switch between different views. You can use it for a variety of scenarios such as a photo viewer, a wizard that guides you through a series of steps, or just a simple way to switch between different data-bound views. You can even use transitions to flip views over to make it look like you're switching from a front view to a back view.

FluidKit Project

The open-source *FluidKit* project, hosted at http://fluidkit.codeplex.com, contains a control called *TransitionPresenter* that builds on the concepts discussed in this section. It provides many interesting transition effects such as: GenieTransition, CubeTransition, FlipTransition, etc. These transitions also expose properties to control the runtime behavior.

Implementing Popular Visual Effects

In this section of the chapter, we take a look at some popular visual effects that are simple to implement but create a lot of extra fit and finish to any application. Many of these effects, especially reflection and drop shadows, are commonly associated with modern, Web 2.0-style applications.

Reflection

The reflection effect is deceptively simple. Remember earlier when we mentioned that clever uses of `VisualBrushes` can result in some amazing effects? Reflection is one such effect. It works by flipping the `VisualBrush` of a target along the X-axis. The `VisualBrush` is applied as a fill on a rectangle that is placed below the target being reflected. The flipped `VisualBrush` of the target visual acts as the reflection. This can be seen in Figure 9.8

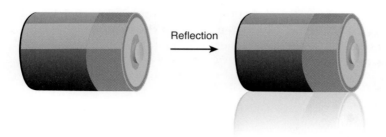

FIGURE 9.8   Reflection visual brush effect.

Now we all know that real reflections aren't perfect mirror images. In a classic reflection effect, the reflection fades away slowly as the image moves farther away from the source of the reflection. This is accomplished by using an OpacityMask on the rectangle. The mask is just a LinearGradientBrush that goes from a semitransparent white to fully transparent. The following XAML snippet illustrates how to create this fade-away reflection brush:

```xml
<LinearGradientBrush x:Key="ReflectionBrush"
            StartPoint="0,0"
            EndPoint="0,1">
    <LinearGradientBrush.GradientStops>
        <GradientStop Offset="0"
        Color="#7FFFFFFF" />
        <GradientStop Offset=".5"
        Color="Transparent" />
        <GradientStop Offset="1"
        Color="Transparent" />
    </LinearGradientBrush.GradientStops>
</LinearGradientBrush>

<Grid Width="232"
    Height="290">
    <Grid.RowDefinitions>
        <RowDefinition />
        <RowDefinition />
    </Grid.RowDefinitions>

    <Image x:Name="ElementVisual"
        Source="pack://siteoforigin:,,,/Resources/Chapter09/battery.png"
            Stretch="Fill"
            Grid.Row="0" />
    <Rectangle OpacityMask="{StaticResource ReflectionBrush}"
            Grid.Row="1"
```

```
            Width="{Binding ActualWidth, ElementName=ElementVisual}"
            Height="{Binding ActualHeight, ElementName=ElementVisual}">
        <Rectangle.Fill>
        <VisualBrush Visual="{Binding ElementName=ElementVisual}">
            <VisualBrush.RelativeTransform>
            <ScaleTransform ScaleX="1"
                    ScaleY="-1"
                    CenterX="0.5"
                    CenterY="0.5" />
            </VisualBrush.RelativeTransform>
        </VisualBrush>
        </Rectangle.Fill>
        </Rectangle>

</Grid>
```

Drop Shadows

Drop shadows are a common visual effect and, used judiciously, can provide a quick and easy way to add a bit more polish to a finished application, as shown in Figure 9.9. WPF makes this effect simple by providing a `DropShadowEffect`, a subclass of `Effect`. You can configure the `BlurRadius` and the `ShadowDepth` and `Direction` properties to change the look of the shadow. You can also change the color and opacity of the drop shadow.

```
<Image Source="pack://siteoforigin:,,,/Resources/Chapter09/battery.png"
        Stretch="Uniform"
        Width="232">
    <Image.Effect>
        <DropShadowEffect BlurRadius="15"
                ShadowDepth="5"
                Opacity="0.75" />
    </Image.Effect>
</Image>
```

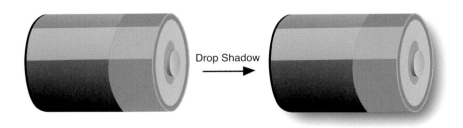

FIGURE 9.9   The drop shadow effect.

Opacity Masks

You have already seen how an opacity mask controls the fading of the reflection. The use of the `UIElement.OpacityMask` property can be put to a nearly infinite number of interesting uses since it gives you a quick pixel-perfect technique to mask out areas of the element itself. The `OpacityMask` only works on the alpha channel, which means the Red, Green, and Blue values of the element being masked will remain unaltered. By varying the alpha channel value from 0x00 to 0xFF (0 to 255), you can have gradually fading elements. For example, to create a soft-edged mask (also known as a feathered edge), you can use a PNG image (with an ImageBrush) that has a gradient transparency on the edges. Since you are dealing with a bitmap PNG image, you would generally keep your target visual the same size as the opacity mask image to avoid any bizarre or unexpected effects. The following XAML shows how to obtain the opacity mask shown in Figure 9.10:

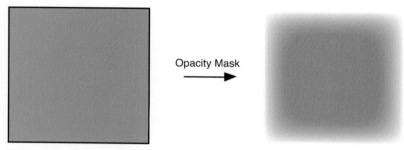

Opacity Mask

FIGURE 9.10   Using an opacity mask.

```
<ImageBrush x:Key="SoftEdgeBrush"
ImageSource="pack://siteoforigin:,,,/Resources/Chapter09/SoftEdgeMask.png" />

    <Rectangle Fill="IndianRed"
            Width="200"
            Height="200"
            StrokeThickness="2"
            Stroke="Black"
            OpacityMask="{StaticResource SoftEdgeBrush}" />
```

Gloss Effects

Gloss effects, as shown in Figure 9.11, are often subtle but can mean the difference between a professional application and an unpolished application to the average user.

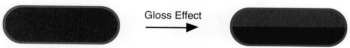

Gloss Effect

FIGURE 9.11   A gloss effect in action.

Typically a gloss effect is achieved by adding a highlight effect to the top half of a visual. This can be done with a vertical `LinearGradientBrush` that has a semitransparent white for the first half and a completely transparent portion on the bottom. In XAML, it looks something like this:

```xaml
<LinearGradientBrush x:Key="HilightBrush"
         StartPoint="0,0"
         EndPoint="0,1">
    <GradientStop Offset="0"
          Color="#3FFFFFFF" />
    <GradientStop Offset="0.5"
          Color="#3FFFFFFF" />
    <GradientStop Offset="0.5"
          Color="Transparent" />
    <GradientStop Offset="1"
          Color="Transparent" />
</LinearGradientBrush>
```

You wouldn't use a brush like this directly; instead you would apply this brush as a fill or a background to an overlay visual and place it on top of the target. Since the brush is mostly transparent, the underlying target will be seen with a gloss effect on its top half. The following XAML shows this in action:

```xaml
<Grid Width="200"
    Height="80">
    <Border BorderBrush="#AF000000"
        BorderThickness="3"
          CornerRadius="30">
        <Border.Background>
            <LinearGradientBrush StartPoint="0,0"
                    EndPoint="0,1">
            <GradientStop Offset="0"
                Color="Black" />
            <GradientStop Offset="1"
                Color="DarkRed" />
            </LinearGradientBrush>
        </Border.Background>
        </Border>
        <Border Background="{StaticResource HilightBrush}"
            BorderThickness="0"
            CornerRadius="30"
            Margin="3" />
</Grid>
```

You can experiment with different ways to create a gloss effect. You could create a clipping path so that the gloss effect actually has a semirounded shape so that it isn't just a straight line. You can also create a smaller gloss effect circle within a larger square gloss effect on your control, which can often create the resemblance of a specular highlight without having to deal with 3D or actual lighting.

Summary

In this chapter, we discussed a variety of advanced controls and visual effects that can be developed by mixing in creative ways some of the foundational building blocks you have already learned. These examples show that there is far more to WPF than first meets the eye. When developers new to the platform first see WPF, they often overlook some of the power hidden just beneath the surface. There is a massive breadth as well as depth just waiting to be tapped by any developer who takes the time to look underneath the surface. By using some of the techniques in this chapter, you can create controls that go far beyond traditional user interfaces and build applications that your users will be thrilled to use.

CHAPTER 10

Control Skinning and Themes

Before the advent of Windows Presentation Foundation (WPF) and the declarative GUI that XAML enables, a visit from designers would often send developers into a frenzy and looking for a hiding place. The reason for this was the huge disparity between the environment in which designers worked and the environment in which developers worked.

The problem was that previous GUI frameworks like Windows Forms required a massive amount of effort to make customizations to window shapes, glassy orblike buttons, and even things we take for granted like gradients.

The designers wanted to give users a beautiful experience and so did the developers, but the amount of effort to perform even the simplest of customizations to appearance and behavior was typically too much to justify the cost.

Fortunately with WPF, the skinning of interfaces is an integral part of the framework. More importantly, it makes the process of creating a skin fairly simple and can even be done without writing any code. Design and development teams can once again work toward the common goal of creating beautiful interfaces without slamming into artificial barriers imposed by limited technology.

In this chapter, we look at some of the options available to developers for skinning controls. We also consider some advanced use cases where you might need that extra bit of control within your skin.

Introduction to Skins and Themes

People use the terms *skin* and *theme* so often that it has become difficult to tell the difference between the two terms. Within the world of WPF, they have precise meanings to make the designer-developer workflow more seamless and to ensure that everyone is using the same set of terms. The term *theme* refers to the system/desktop theme and is usually specified by the desktop user. For example, the Aero theme in Vista is a system-level theme, and its various options can be configured with the desktop personalization panel.

WPF applications are aware of changes made to the desktop theme and can react accordingly by changing their look and feel at runtime. The default styles for all of the WPF controls in Vista, with the Aero theme, are packaged under the `PresentationFramework.Aero` library. When you run your application without applying custom styles to any of the standard controls, the default style information is loaded from this library. In addition, there are other system themes such as `Royale`, `Luna`, and `Classic` for which there are prepackaged WPF styles. Later in this chapter, we look at how you can create styles for your custom controls for each of these themes.

The term *skin* refers to the default look and feel of a control. The set of default styles (the *skin*) for the control can be specified either in the same assembly in which they are implemented or in a separate assembly. Skins can be changed independently of the system theme and may or may not respect the user change to the desktop theme. In other words, skins are more application-specific and can be changed dynamically without relying on any system theme changes.

To summarize, *skins* are *application*-specific, whereas *themes* are *system*-specific. Applications that use skins will generally not respect any theme settings.

One thing that both themes and skins in WPF have in common is the fact that they use styles and resource dictionaries to describe their look and feel. Every control has an associated style, which can get its value from a number of sources. This is based on a lookup policy that is adopted by the framework. The direction of lookup is always from local to global and starts at the bottom of the visual tree and works its way up.

Resource Lookups in WPF

When WPF is looking for styles or any other referenced resource, the first place it looks is at the element level. Every FrameworkElement has a property called `Resources` of type `ResourceDictionary` that can be used to store local resources. If no local resources are defined at the element level, the lookup continues up the parent chain. Any parent in the path to the root can provide a style in its `Resources` collection. If none of the parents have a style defined for the element, the lookup continues up the chain to the `Window` level and finally to the `Application` level. If it cannot find any resource by this point, the system-theme-specific `ResourceDictionary` is queried. As a final resort, the default style (generic theme) defined for the element is looked up in its containing assembly. This is usually defined in a file called `Generic.xaml` under the /Themes folder in the assembly. A failed attempt to load resources at this late stage can result in a blank representation for the element (it's in the logical tree but has no visual representation).

If the lookup succeeded, the final style for the element would be an accumulation of all property values from the root of the style tree to the element. The property values set at the child override any of the values set at the parent level (think of this as leaf-level precedence). Therefore, you can have a multilevel override of properties for an element as the lookup traverses the element hierarchy from leaf to root. This process becomes much clearer as we go through the process of working with themes and skins.

Building Default Styles

If you are defining a new custom control, you should always create a default style for it. As we saw in the earlier section on resource lookups, without a default style for your custom control, there is no visual representation. This happens because WPF has nowhere to look for a default style.

By creating a default style, you also provide a starting point for users of your control. They can then probe into the style to understand the structure and make any custom changes.

Creating a default style involves setting up a `<Style>` resource in the `Generic.xaml` file under the /Themes folder of the control's assembly. The key for the style is set to the type of the control. This is shown in the following bit of XAML:

```xaml
<Style x:Key="{x:Type Chapter10:SkinThemeControl}"
       TargetType="Chapter10:SkinThemeControl">
    <Setter Property="Template">
    <Setter.Value>
        <ControlTemplate
          TargetType="Chapter10:SkinThemeControl">
          <Border Background="{TemplateBinding Background}">
           <ContentPresenter Content="{TemplateBinding Content}"
              ContentTemplate="{TemplateBinding ContentTemplate}" />
          </Border>
        </ControlTemplate>
    </Setter.Value>
    </Setter>
</Style>
```

There are two more things you need to do to ensure that this style is picked up for the `SkinThemeControl` (the control that is being styled in the preceding example). First, you need to override the metadata for the `DefaultStyleKeyProperty`, which is usually done in the static constructor for the control, as shown here:

```csharp
public class SkinThemeControl : Control
{
    static SkinThemeControl()
    {
        DefaultStyleKeyProperty.OverrideMetadata(typeof(SkinThemeControl),
            new FrameworkPropertyMetadata(typeof(SkinThemeControl)));
    }
}
```

The `DefaultStyleKeyProperty`, as the name suggests, is used to tell WPF about the key that should be used to perform the style lookup. By overriding this property as shown in the preceding example, you are telling WPF to use the control's type as the key for its default style. If you skip this step, WPF will have no way to discover the default style of the control (defined in generic.xaml in the control's assembly).

The second thing that you need to do to ensure that the default style is used correctly by WPF is to set the `ThemeInfo` attribute for the control's containing assembly:

```
[assembly: ThemeInfo(
        ResourceDictionaryLocation.None,
        ResourceDictionaryLocation.SourceAssembly
)]
```

The first parameter is the value for the `ThemeDictionaryLocation` property, and the second parameter is the `GenericDictionaryLocation`. Both of these parameters take an enumerated value of type `ResourceDictionaryLocation`, which could be one of `None`, `SourceAssembly`, or `ExternalAssembly`.

Since we are not providing any theme-related styles, we are setting the theme dictionary location to `ResourceDictionaryLocation.None`. Remember, here "theme" means system-specific themes like Aero, Luna, Royale, and so on. The generic dictionary (the `Generic.xaml` file we discussed earlier) is in the control's containing assembly, and therefore we set the value to `ResourceDictionaryLocation.SourceAssembly`. The enumerated value `ExternalAssembly` is generally used for loading theme-specific resources. WPF automatically does the lookup in an assembly that is named as *<control assembly name>.<theme-name>*. For example, `PresentationFramework.dll`, the main assembly containing WPF controls, sets the `ThemeInfoAttribute` value as follows:

```
[assembly: ThemeInfo(
        ResourceDictionaryLocation.ExternalAssembly,
        ResourceDictionaryLocation.None
)]
```

Note that the `ThemeDictionaryLocation` is set to `ExternalAssembly`. For the Aero theme on Vista, WPF loads the appropriate resources from `PresentationFramework.Aero.dll`, which follows the naming convention mentioned in the preceding paragraph. In a later section in this chapter, we talk about how you can create your own theme-specific resources and styles.

Using Resources in Default Styles

When you define the default `ControlTemplates` for your custom controls, you will most likely use additional resources inside your template. These resources could include brushes, images, or additional templates. You should be careful not to define resources at the element level (for example, the root visual of your template). This is important because doing so limits the usage to only within the template or style. Unless you have a very special case where the resource will be used only once, try to put the resources at a level where it could be shared amongst many controls.

The recommended approach is to define resources in a separate `ResourceDictionary` and then include them inside the `Generic.xaml` file using the `ResourceDictionary.MergedDictionaries` property. The use of the `MergedDictionaries` property is a good practice to refactor the usage of resources. If you have a set of brushes that are being used at multiple places, you could extract them and keep in a separate `ResourceDictionary`. Later in the XAML where you use the brush, you could include it using the `MergedDictionaries` property. Here is how you would use it in `Generic.xaml`:

```
<ResourceDictionary
xmlns="http://schemas.microsoft.com/winfx/2006/xaml/presentation"
xmlns:x="http://schemas.microsoft.com/winfx/2006/xaml">
                <ResourceDictionary.MergedDictionaries>
                        <ResourceDictionary Source="Brushes.xaml" />
                </ResourceDictionary.MergedDictionaries>


        ...
</ResourceDictionary>
```

Refactoring with MergedDictionaries

`ResourceDictionary.MergedDictionaries` is a great way to categorize and keep related resources together. You can even make use of nested `ResourceDictionaries` if it provides better organization for your resources. For example, consider the previous `Brushes.xaml`. It can have its own `MergedDictionaries` consisting of brushes for the normal state of the controls (`NormalBrushes.xaml`), brushes for the disabled state of the controls (`DisabledBrushes.xaml`), and so on. The ultimate goal of such refactoring and categorization is to help you in your development process and provide an easy way to look up the `ResourceDictionary` for making changes. Never underestimate the productivity gains you can reap by having readable, organized code.

Using `MergedDictionaries` instead of keeping the resources at the `Style`, `ControlTemplate`, or element level avoids duplication of resources at runtime. But there is also an extra precaution you should take when setting the key (`x:Key`) for the resources. Usually you would just assign some arbitrary string key to the resource, but in the case of resources defined in themes, you should use the `ComponentResourceKey` to set the resource key. A `ComponentResourceKey` is actually a combination of a `System.Type` (`TypeInTargetAssembly` property) and a string `ResourceId`. Because of this, it behaves more like a composite key (fully qualified name) consisting of the `Type` in the theme's containing assembly and a string identifier.

The composite nature of the key helps in avoiding name collisions with string-based resources defined in the rest of the application (and from other control vendors!). It also ensures that the resource references always resolve to the ones defined in the theme dictionary. To create a `ComponentResourceKey` in XAML, use the `{ComponentResourceKey}` markup extension and set the `TypeInTargetAssembly` and `ResourceId` properties, as shown in the following code sample:

```
<SolidColorBrush x:Key="{ComponentResourceKey TypeInTargetAssembly={x:Type
Chapters:CustomControl}, ResourceId=BackgroundBrush}"
                    Color="GreenYellow" />


<Style x:Key="{x:Type Chapters:CustomControl}"
     TargetType="Chapters:CustomControl">
     <Setter Property="Template">
          <Setter.Value>
              <ControlTemplate TargetType="Chapters:CustomControl">
                    <Border Width="100"
                            Height="100"
     Background="{StaticResource {ComponentResourceKey
TypeInTargetAssembly={x:Type Chapters:CustomControl}, ResourceId=BackgroundBrush}}"
/>
                    </ControlTemplate>
              </Setter.Value>
     </Setter>
</Style>
```

The `TypeInTargetAssembly` property refers to any type defined in the theme's containing assembly. `ResourceId` is just a string value. The combination of the `TypeInTargetAssembly` + `ResourceId` results in a fully qualified component resource, which can be looked up faithfully inside a theme dictionary. The preceding markup shows you the use of a `ComponentResourceKey` and its reference in the `ControlTemplate` for the custom control.

> **NOTE**
>
> ComponentResourceKey allows you to keep resources in a separate assembly and faithfully retrieve them using a globally unique key: TypeInTargetAssembly + ResourceId. Note that you can use any Type in that assembly to retrieve the resource.

Creating Theme-Specific Styles

We saw in the previous section that the resource lookup process first checks whether there is a theme-specific resource before looking up the generic style. If you are planning to respect the user's desktop theme, you can set the `ThemeInfoAttribute`'s `ThemeDictionaryLocation` property. You can set it to either `ResourceDictionary-Location.SourceAssembly` or `ResourceDictionaryLocation.ExternalAssembly`. Setting it to `ResourceDictionaryLocation.None` indicates that you are not going to support styles specific to desktop themes. What you choose for these attributes is entirely dependent on the type of controls you are delivering and how you expect them to be styled and skinned.

Once you set the theme dictionary location to a value other than None, WPF looks for the theme-specific ResourceDictionaries either in the source assembly or external assembly, depending on your setting. These resource dictionaries have to be named in a specific format for the resource lookup to succeed, as shown here:

```
<Theme-Name>.<Color-Scheme>.xaml
```

Table 10.1 shows the names of some theme-specific resource dictionaries. All of these XAML files should be stored under the same /Themes folder of the control's containing assembly or an external assembly. When the user changes the desktop theme, WPF detects the change and automatically looks up control styles from these ResourceDictionaries. What this boils down to is if the user changes her desktop theme from Aero to Royale and if you have resources defined using the following conventions, your application automatically changes its own look and feel to correspond to the new desktop theme selection. This is an incredibly powerful feature that has not been readily available to developers prior to the release of WPF.

TABLE 10.1   Theme-Specific Resource Dictionaries

Theme	XAML Filename
Aero	Aero.NormalColor.xaml
Royale	Royale.NormalColor.xaml
Classic	Classic.xaml

If we have to support styles for the Aero and Classic themes for our custom SkinThemeControl that we've been building, we have to create the theme-specific resource dictionaries and put them under the /Themes folder, as shown in Figure 10.1.

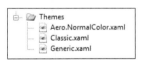

FIGURE 10.1   The Themes folder.

Inside each of those resource dictionaries, we have styles with their keys set to the control's Type.

To summarize, the following is a list of the steps necessary to enable skins and themes for your custom controls:

1. Create a ResourceDictionary named Generic.xaml under /Themes. This is in the control's containing assembly. This contains the default style that gets applied if no theme-specific resource dictionary is present.

2. Override the metadata for the DefaultStyleKeyProperty in the custom control's static constructor. Set the value to the Type of the control.

3. Create a `<Style />` element in `Generic.xaml` for the custom control. The key for the style is the control's `Type`.

4. If you want to enable theme-specific styles, create resource dictionaries named `<Theme-Name>.<Color-Scheme>.xaml` and put them under /Themes. You would also need to set the assembly-level `ThemeInfoAttribute` to either `ResourceDictionaryLocation.SourceAssembly` or `ResourceDictionaryLocation.ExternalAssembly`. WPF automatically loads the theme-specific resource dictionary whenever the system theme changes.

Enabling Runtime Skinning

The first time that either of the authors saw an application that was able to change its appearance on the fly was when we first used the Winamp program for listening to music. It had a great feature where you could go to its preferences settings and change its skin on the fly. In fact it even showed you a live preview before switching the skin. Skinning media players became a widely popular activity for professionals and hobbyists alike, and many companies even made custom media player skins to get "product placement" onto the desktop or to hype upcoming events or movies.

The ability to skin the application dynamically at runtime was a great feature, and we were used to seeing applications require a full restart to apply a new skin (if they even supported skinning in the first place!). Many of us are used to changing the Windows desktop themes on the fly, but few people get to see this same functionality in an application and adding it to your application may be a way to add unique value.

Fortunately WPF makes it pretty easy to enable runtime skinning in an application. Before we get into the details, we should spend some time understanding what it means to have runtime skinning from the WPF point of view.

We know that skinning really boils down to choosing a particular style for a control either at build-time or during runtime. Styles are basically just resources that are defined in a `ResourceDictionary` and then included in the application's context either automatically (for example, /Themes/Generic.xaml) or by populating the `Resources` property of the `Application` class. A `ResourceDictionary` can either contain a flat listing of resources or a set of nested resource dictionaries using the `MergedDictionaries` property. Effectively a single `ResourceDictionary` can represent a skin for the application or a window. These resources (styles) are referenced by controls either via the `StaticResourceExtension` (load-time) or the `DynamicResourceExtension` (runtime). For runtime skinning, it makes sense that we need to use a `DynamicResourceExtension` since we want the ability to switch the style *dynamically*. So to summarize, a `ResourceDictionary` describes the appearance of the skin, and the use of `DynamicResourceExtension` keeps the resource references dynamic and enables runtime changes.

Now we need a way to change the skin on the fly. This is made possible by flushing the current `Application.Resources` (remember, this is just a resource dictionary) and replacing it with the new skin (again, just another resource dictionary).

When we define the resources in the skin, we need to make sure the resource keys (indicated in XAML by x:Key) stay the same for all of the skins. The dynamic resource reference always points to the same key, and this particular fact ensures that resources from the new skin are not just applied but are applied *to the right controls*. During the planning stages of application skinning, you can define the vocabulary and conventions for the resource keys and make sure that you stick with that convention for all of your skins. Thus, the three key components to runtime skinning involve the ResourceDictionary, DynamicResourceExtension, and common style names (see Figure 10.2).

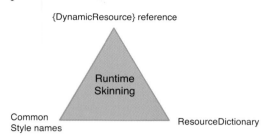

FIGURE 10.2   Triangle of components for dynamic skinning.

Let's consider an example where we have to skin a contact form on the fly. The form consists of four fields: Name, E-mail Address, Website, and Message. Each field is represented as a Label plus a TextBox. Figure 10.3 shows the form without any skin applied.

FIGURE 10.3   An unskinned contact form.

We'll skin this form in three different ways with skins stored in three different files: BlueSkin.xaml, GreenSkin.xaml, and RedSkin.xaml. Figure 10.4 shows what the contact form looks like after having been styled according to these skins.

Labels, TextBoxes, and a Button make up the controls in the contact form while the form itself is inside a container element like Border. Each of them gets their style by making a {DynamicResource ...} reference to a predefined resource key. These keys are shown in Table 10.2. Each skin uses the same key for defining the styles, as shown in Table 10.2.

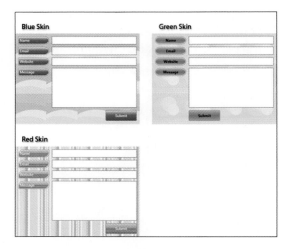

FIGURE 10.4   The contact forms skinned in three different ways.

TABLE 10.2   Resource Keys Used for Dynamic Skinning

Control	Resource Key
Label	LabelSkin
TextBox	TextBoxSkin
Button	ButtonSkin
Border	FormSkin

When the time comes to switch the skin, we clear the Resources and the MergedDictionaries of the top-level element (which, in our case, is a Grid named _contactForm) and repopulate it with the new skin's ResourceDictionary. This process is shown in the following code:

```
private void OnSkinChanged(object sender, RoutedEventArgs e)
{
        string name = (e.OriginalSource as RadioButton).Name;
        _contactForm.Resources.Clear();
        _contactForm.Resources.MergedDictionaries.Clear();

        if (name == "None") return;

        ResourceDictionary skin =
        Application.LoadComponent(new Uri("/Chapters;component/Chapter10/Skins/" +
    ➥name +
".xaml", UriKind.Relative)) as ResourceDictionary;
```

```
    _contactForm.Resources.MergedDictionaries.Add(skin);

    e.Handled = true;
}
```

The OnSkinChanged event handler is
called when any of the four
RadioButtons in the demo interface is
clicked, indicating the skin that we want
to apply, as shown in Figure 10.5. If the
RadioButton named "None" is clicked,
we default to the unskinned appearance.
Note that the example is changing the
resources for the form's container
element (_contactForm), but the same

FIGURE 10.5   Radio buttons for switching
between skins.

principles apply even at the Application level. In other words, you can choose whether
you dynamically change skins for your entire application or only for a small subset of
visual elements. This fact is both powerful and potentially confusing, so it is worth trying
to remember this point. Whenever you are troubleshooting skinning problems, always
make sure you double-check which element is getting the new skin before trying
anything else.

NOTE

Even if you don't want to support application skinning for users, it is still a good feature to
have since it allows you to try out new skins during testing. Don't underestimate the productivity gains you can get by allowing easy skin swapping. This also forces you to come up with
some semantic markups for your views, which maintain a common structure across all skins.
In many ways, you can think of application skinning as the WPF equivalent of optimizing your
old HTML to operate with divs, spans, and elegant CSS styles.

Using the ApplyTemplate Override

At this point in the book, you have probably begun to appreciate the role of the
ControlTemplate in enabling the concept of a lookless control. The concept of the
control only really applies to its properties and behavior. The visuals within the
ControlTemplate add the required "look" to the control. However, a control is not just
about appearance but also carries an implied requirement in terms of behavior. The
behavior is usually the source of interaction, which can come from anything from a
mouse to a keyboard or even a multitouch surface. If the control that you are developing
expects a certain kind of input, there may also be a certain set of visuals that you require
to be present to facilitate that interaction. If these visuals are present, you can activate the
behavior associated with the visual or leave out the behavior entirely. For some controls,
the presence of these visuals may be mandatory to facilitate the appropriate behavior, and
in those cases, you could throw an exception when those visuals are not present.

10

How do you go about checking for the presence of those required visuals? How do you ensure that your control template contains the necessary items to produce the functionality and behavior associated with your control? By default, WPF doesn't enforce any strict constraints on the control. However, it does provide a way to specify metadata for a control, which could then be used within the control's code to enforce constraints programmatically at runtime. This metadata can be specified with an attribute called `TemplatePartAttribute` affixed to the control's class. The following code snippet shows the use of `TemplatePartAttribute` on the stock `ComboBox` control:

```
[TemplatePart(Name = "PART_EditableTextBox", Type = typeof(TextBox))]
[TemplatePart(Name = "PART_Popup", Type = typeof(Popup))]
public class ComboBox : Selector
{
...
}
```

The `Name` property is a string value used to specify the expected name of the control inside the `ControlTemplate`. The convention is to have a prefix of `PART_` followed by the actual name with the first letter capitalized. For example, `PART_Minimize`, `PART_Maximize`, `PART_Close`, and so on. The `Type` property is the type of the visual. By specifying the `TemplatePartAttribute`, you are publishing an informal expectation about the required parts in the `ControlTemplate`. It is a good practice to include this attribute because tools like Expression Blend can discover this metadata and provide some kind of feedback when designing the `ControlTemplate`.

The information about the subparts comes into play when a new `ControlTemplate` is set for the control. After the framework does its job of setting up the visual tree, the `OnApplyTemplate()` override is called on the control. It is in this method where the lookup of the subparts happens followed by additional housekeeping activities. The subpart is looked up based on the information in the `TemplatePartAttribute` value. If these subparts exist, additional behavior can be injected by setting properties or attaching event handlers. The protected method `GetTemplateChild()` is used to retrieve the subpart in the `ControlTemplate`.

In the following example, we're going to consider a custom `Window` control that can be styled to our heart's content, including the title bar. One of the most common things that people want to learn when first encountering WPF is how to make custom-skinnable windows. The `Window` control provided by WPF only allows us to skin the client area, which is the area outside the title bar. This limits us to a window-chrome that is based on the current desktop theme. For an application that needs a complete branded appearance, you want to have a window that can be styled completely from edge to edge. Figure 10.6 shows the default style for the `CustomChromeWindow` class. We develop this control and the style in the following discussion.

Since we want to provide our own title bar, we need to get rid of the default one that comes with the `Window` control. This can be done by setting the `WindowStyle` property to None. If we also want an irregularly shaped window, we can set the `AllowsTransparency`

FIGURE 10.6   Custom Chrome window default appearance.

property to `True`. These two properties can be set in the default style for the window in
`Generic.xaml`. We can now put up our own title bar with the minimize, maximize, and
close buttons. Since our custom window needs to respond to these button clicks, we have
to discover the presence of these buttons in the `CustomChromeWindow`'s `ControlTemplate`.
If any of these buttons are present, we can attach the corresponding event handlers to
provide the standard minimize, maximize, and close functions. The expectation for these
buttons (subparts) can be set by adding the `TemplatePartAttributes` to the
`CustomChromeWindow` class:

```
[TemplatePart(Name = "PART_Close", Type = typeof(Button))]
[TemplatePart(Name = "PART_Minimize", Type = typeof(Button))]
[TemplatePart(Name = "PART_Maximize", Type = typeof(Button))]
public class CustomChromeWindow : Window
{
...
}
```

Note the use of the `PART_` convention for prefixing the subpart names. We discover these
parts in `OnApplyTemplate` and then attach the corresponding event handlers if any of
them are present:

```
public override void OnApplyTemplate()

{
        base.OnApplyTemplate();
        AttachToVisualTree();
}

private void AttachToVisualTree()
```

```
{
        // Close Button
        Button closeButton = GetChildControl<Button>("PART_Close");
        if (closeButton != null)
        {
            closeButton.Click += OnCloseButtonClick;
        }

        // Minimize Button
        Button minimizeButton = GetChildControl<Button>("PART_Minimize");
        if (minimizeButton != null)
        {
            minimizeButton.Click += OnMinimizeButtonClick;
        }
        // Maximize Button
        Button maximizeButton = GetChildControl<Button>("PART_Maximize");
        if (maximizeButton != null)
        {
            maximizeButton.Click += OnMaximizeButtonClick;
        }
        // Title Bar
        Panel titleBar = GetChildControl<Panel>("PART_TitleBar");
                if (titleBar != null)
        {
            titleBar.MouseLeftButtonDown += OnTitleBarMouseDown;
        }
}
```

The GetChildControl<T> is a custom method that internally calls the GetTemplateChild and also performs the type-casting as a convenience:

```
protected T GetChildControl<T>(string ctrlName) where T : DependencyObject
{
        T ctrl = GetTemplateChild(ctrlName) as T;
        return ctrl;
}
```

The buttons are defined in the ControlTemplate for the CustomChromeWindow with the same names as the ones in the TemplatePartAttributes (that is, PART_Minimize, PART_Maximize, PART_Close), as shown in the following XAML. Note that we have omitted parts of the template for readability:

```
        <ControlTemplate x:Key="{ComponentResourceKey
TypeInTargetAssembly=Chapter10:CustomChromeWindow, ResourceId=WindowTemplate}"
                        TargetType="Chapter10:CustomChromeWindow">
...
...
```

```
        <DockPanel x:Name="PART_TitleBar"
                    Grid.Row="0"
                    Background="{StaticResource TitleBrush}">
            <UniformGrid Rows="1"
                            Margin="0,2,10,0"
                            DockPanel.Dock="Right">
                <Button x:Name="PART_Minimize"
    Chapter10:CustomChromeWindow.NormalImage="WindowDecoration/min_normal.png"
    Chapter10:CustomChromeWindow.HoverImage="WindowDecoration/min_hover.png"

Chapter10:CustomChromeWindow.PressedImage="WindowDecoration/min_pressed.png"
                            Style="{StaticResource
{ComponentResourceKey TypeInTargetAssembly=Chapter10:CustomChromeWindow,
ResourceId=WindowButtonStyle}}" />
                <Button x:Name="PART_Maximize"
    Chapter10:CustomChromeWindow.NormalImage="WindowDecoration/max_normal.png"
    Chapter10:CustomChromeWindow.HoverImage="WindowDecoration/max_hover.png"

Chapter10:CustomChromeWindow.PressedImage="WindowDecoration/max_pressed.png"
                            Style="{StaticResource
{ComponentResourceKey TypeInTargetAssembly=Chapter10:CustomChromeWindow,
ResourceId=WindowButtonStyle}}" />
                <Button x:Name="PART_Close"

Chapter10:CustomChromeWindow.NormalImage="WindowDecoration/close_normal.png"
    Chapter10:CustomChromeWindow.HoverImage="WindowDecoration/close_hover.png"

Chapter10:CustomChromeWindow.PressedImage="WindowDecoration/close_pressed.png"
                            Style="{StaticResource
{ComponentResourceKey TypeInTargetAssembly=Chapter10:CustomChromeWindow,
ResourceId=WindowButtonStyle}}" />
            </UniformGrid>
...
...
        </ControlTemplate>
```

For this particular example, we don't really need references to the buttons after we attach the event handlers. However, for some controls, you may want to keep references to subparts if you plan to do work later. In the preceding template, you will notice the use of some attached properties on the button controls. These attached properties specify the images to use for the mouse-hover, mouse-press, and normal states of the button. Refer to the sample code to learn more about how these properties are used inside the ControlTemplate for the button. This is yet another application of the powerful attached properties.

10

Reader Exercise

As an astute reader, you may have caught a small problem with the `AttachToVisualTree` method. This relates to the case where the user changes the window's `ControlTemplate` on the fly. Since we are not detaching the event handlers of the buttons from the previous template, we have a memory leak waiting to happen. Fortunately, the fix is fairly straightforward and we leave that as a reader exercise.

For a control that contains subparts, you can think of the `ControlTemplate` as the visual structure that describes where the subparts are located. The `OnApplyTemplate` override is the part where you associate behavior with these subparts.

When designing the `ControlTemplates` for certain controls, it is a good idea to look up their `TemplatePartAttributes` and understand the required subparts. Sometimes if a control is not functioning as expected after applying a custom `ControlTemplate` it probably has to do with a missing name on a subpart causing behavior to be skipped or improperly applied.

NOTE

`GetTemplateChild` is a protected method and only useful inside the control's code. If you wanted to look up subparts in client code, you should use the `FrameworkTemplate.FindName` method. Note that `ControlTemplate` and `DataTemplate`, derive from `FrameworkTemplate`, so the `FindName` method works on both of them.

Control Customization Through Property Exposure

The `Template` property on the `Control` is the standard way to dynamically adjust the visual appearance of the control. However, there is one drawback to it: You need to change the complete visual tree, even if you want to adjust only a few properties on a subpart of the template. For some scenarios, this is definitely not acceptable.

A recommended way is to expose `Style`-based properties on the custom control that specifically target different subparts of the control. For example, the `GridView` (one of the default views for a `ListView`) exposes a property called `ColumnHeaderContainerStyle` to adjust the appearance of the column header, which is a subpart appearing at the top of the `GridView`. A more classical example would be of the `ItemsControl`, which exposes the `ItemContainerStyle` property to specifically style the UI containers that are generated for each data item. You may argue that one could just expose a `ControlTemplate`-based property for the subparts instead of a Style. However, you should note that a `Style` allows you to customize additional properties of the subpart in addition to the template. In most cases, the styling of a subpart does not end at just the `Template`, and having a `Style` greatly helps in encapsulating the complete customization.

In addition to the `Style`-based properties, you can also expose `DataTemplate`-based properties for customizing the data that gets put into the UI containers. For example, the

ItemsControl class exposes the ItemTemplate property to customize the data that gets put into the ItemContainer. Similarly the GridView class uses the ColumnHeaderTemplate property (of type DataTemplate) to customize the column header content.

Depending on the subparts that you want to target, you can expose appropriate Style- or DataTemplate-based properties to make them customizable outside the ControlTemplate for the control. A careful choice of such properties improves the development experience with that control.

Template Selectors

Some controls also expose a property to dynamically select a DataTemplate based on runtime criteria. Such properties are of the DataTemplateSelector type. For example, the ItemsControl exposes an ItemTemplateSelector property to dynamically pick a DataTemplate to be applied to the contained items. To create your own selectors, derive from DataTemplateSelector and override the SelectTemplate method. Note that in the ItemsControl only one of ItemTemplate or ItemTemplateSelector can be specified. Setting both of them will result in a runtime exception.

Summary

Skins and themes are great ways to add visual variety to your application and make it conform more to the particular tastes and desires of your users. However, there is more to skinning than just presenting the user with customized user interfaces. By building your application so that it is skinnable, you will actually find that your GUI is more testable, better organized, and more flexible to changes and adaptations as they are required by new designs and requirements.

This chapter provided an overview of how to skin your application and make your GUI aware of themes and theme changes. Adding this knowledge to your repertoire will make the products you build even more appealing.

10

CHAPTER 11

Bridging the 2D and 3D Worlds

So far in this book, all of the examples that we've seen have been controls restricted to the flat, two-dimensional world. The main reason for this is because the vast majority of UIs presented to users are two-dimensional unless you happen to be creating a full 3D game (in which case, you might be using XNA instead of WPF). In this chapter, we explore how your application can benefit from borrowing a few concepts from 3D worlds and joining them with a 2D user interface.

3D definitely has a charm of its own and can add a lot of excitement. Let's face it, people react very well to immersive, 3D environments. The trick is using enough 3D to add beautiful and useful elements to your application without assaulting your users with needless 3D graphics and effects.

We start this journey from 2D to 3D by illustrating how you can blend the 2D and 3D worlds and create interfaces that seamlessly (and tastefully!) combine the best of both.

A Brief Introduction to 3D Worlds

Many of you probably already know the basics of how 3D engines work and how all of the different pieces of a 3D world come together to create the games we play and the interfaces in which we immerse ourselves. If so, feel free to skip this section. Before continuing on with the rest of this chapter, we want to provide a quick overview of how 3D worlds become 2D graphics on a 2D monitor. Knowing these basic concepts helps you understand what WPF is doing under the hood and also makes clear why we do some of the things we do throughout this chapter.

As you (hopefully) already know, your computer is only ever displaying 2D graphics to you. No matter how good the 3D game is that you're playing, the end result is still nothing more than a single flat rectangle of colored pixels that change between 30 and 60 times per second (called the *frame rate* or *frames-per-second*). This creates the illusion of animation, and a whole lot of clever mathematics creates the illusion of 3D worlds, even though we're still only working with a flat rectangle.

The simplest way to think about it is to imagine that the coordinates for a whole bunch of 3D shapes are stored in memory. In addition to those shapes are materials that are associated with a *face* of that shape. (For a plane, there would be two faces, front and back, a cube would have six faces, and so on.) Then you place light sources in the scene, which are in the scene at 3D coordinates emitting light of some kind (modern 3D engines have hundreds of different kinds of light sources). Up until this point, all you really have are in-memory representations of the things that you would like to see, but you've still got no way to see your wonderful 3D scene.

What you need now is a camera. The camera is *also* in the 3D scene at a set of coordinates (3D coordinates have an x, y, and z value and are usually stored in *world units*; in other words, they have nothing to do with pixels in their raw form). Basically, the camera "looks" at the 3D scene by calculating the effect of all lights on all visible surfaces in the scene and then, using things like clipping planes and the area of view called a *frustum*, it performs more calculations that "flatten" all of the 3D elements into what amounts to a "window on the (3D) world." This window represents a single, frozen frame of time. To make your 3D world move, this same process is repeated over and over again, and the window is regenerated over and over again. When the human eye sees these frames changing rapidly, the brain compensates for the small gaps between the frames and the world appears to animate smoothly.

Obviously this is an oversimplification, and modern 3D engines do far more than what we've described. However, if you have a firm grasp on the concepts of how models, materials, lighting, and the camera all work together to produce a 2D image that appears to be a 3D world, then you will have very little trouble understanding the code samples for the rest of this chapter.

Using the `Viewport3D` Element

The `Viewport3D` element is basically a container for an entire 3D world, and it derives from `FrameworkElement`. Since it does not have a `Background` property (the control is transparent, essentially), you could have 3D models floating on top of your 2D interface. This is an important concept to remember and something that we will leverage inside our custom controls.

A `Viewport3D` element requires three things to produce something that the user can see. As mentioned in the brief introduction to 3D worlds, three things are required to go from a 3D world to a visible, flat image the user can see: models, lights, and a camera, as shown in Figure 11.1. Models refer to the actual geometry of the 3D models in the world (as well as associated textures, materials, and so on). Lights are needed to illuminate the world. Without lights, everything in the world would essentially render as a black pixel.

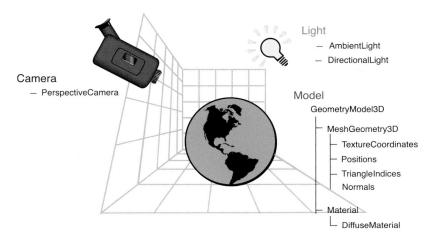

FIGURE 11.1   Models, lights, and the camera in a 3D world.

The camera is the lens through which the user looks at our 3D world, and the position and properties of the camera are what dictate how the 3D models are converted into a 2D image for rendering. We generally use an instance of the `PerspectiveCamera` to give us depth of field for a realistic-looking scene.

Even if you have your camera pointed in the right direction and you have sufficient lighting in your scene, you still might not see anything. This could happen because the surfaces of 3D models need a material. A material determines how the surface responds to light. Think about the difference between glass, water, and brick. When you shine light through glass, you illuminate the materials *behind* it (depending on the properties of the glass, obviously). When you shine light through water, the image of what is underneath the water is distorted by *refraction*. And when you shine light on a brick wall, the brick wall simply becomes brighter or simply visible.

Models are created using instances of the `GeometryModel3D`, which represents a surface geometry wireframe with a material applied to it. The surface geometry (an instance of `MeshGeometry3D`) is the wireframe for the model. To make the material nicely wrap the wireframe, you need to correctly specify the `TextureCoordinates`, `Positions`, and `TriangleIndices` for the `MeshGeometry3D`. With all those pieces in place along with lights and a camera, you finally have a 3D world that can be rendered by WPF.

The following XAML shows all of these concepts in action followed by the rendered output in Figure 11.2.

FIGURE 11.2   Rendered output of a 3D world defined by XAML.

```xml
<Viewport3D>
    <Viewport3D.Camera>
        <PerspectiveCamera FieldOfView="60"
                            Position="-0.5,2,3"
                            LookDirection="0.5,-2,-3"
                            UpDirection="0,1,0" />
    </Viewport3D.Camera>

    <ModelVisual3D>
        <ModelVisual3D.Content>
            <Model3DGroup>
                <AmbientLight Color="White" />
                <GeometryModel3D>
                    <GeometryModel3D.Geometry>
                        <MeshGeometry3D Positions="-0.625,0.5,0 0.625,0.5,0
0.625,-0.5,0 -0.625,-0.5,0."

                                        TriangleIndices="0,3,2 0,2,1"
                                        TextureCoordinates="0,0 1,0 1,1
0,1"

                                        Normals="0,0,1 0,0,1 0,0,1 0,0,1"
/>
                    </GeometryModel3D.Geometry>

                    <GeometryModel3D.Material>
                        <DiffuseMaterial Brush="IndianRed" />
                    </GeometryModel3D.Material>

                </GeometryModel3D>
            </Model3DGroup>
        </ModelVisual3D.Content>
    </ModelVisual3D>
</Viewport3D>
```

Don't worry if some of the preceding XAML looks a little confusing. Building 3D worlds is a complicated process, and most people use tools like Blender, Maya, or any number of commercial applications for building 3D models.

The Positions property refers to the X,Y,Z coordinates *of each vertex* in the 3D model. The TriangleIndices property specifies the triangulation of the model. The order (clockwise, anticlockwise) in which you specify these indices is crucial. You should make sure that the order is consistently maintained for all triangles in the model. The Normals property is essentially a list of 3D vectors that indicate the *direction in which the Normal is pointing for each vertex*. This allows the 3D rendering pipeline to do lighting calculations and shade the model. Finally, the TextureCoordinates property refers to a mapping that controls what pieces of the texture/material show up and where they show up on the 3D model. Again, few people ever do this by hand for anything other than super-simple shapes such as planes, pyramids, and cubes. For texture-mapping anything more complicated, people tend to use 3D modeling tools. Can you imagine mentally trying to figure out the normals, positions, and texture coordinates for a 3D model of a human being or even something relatively "blocky" like a space ship or a truck? Neither can we.

Embedding a `Viewport3D` Element

Now that you have a basic understanding of how the `Viewport3D` element works, we can take the next step to embedding this element inside a custom control. Before going much further, let's think about what kind of control we want to use as a base class for embedding a `Viewport3D`. Remembering Chapter 2, "The Diverse Visual Class Structure," we are looking for a control that can contain another visual element. In other words, what we're doing is composing our own visual tree. There are a couple of options for composing our own custom visual tree:

1. Subclass `Control` and then embed the `Viewport3D` inside its control template.

2. Subclass `UserControl` and embed the `Viewport3D` directly inside it.

3. Subclass a `FrameworkElement` and embed the `Viewport3D` programmatically.

Option 1 gives us maximum flexibility as we can have different `ControlTemplates` that embed `Viewport3D` differently. By giving the `Viewport3D` instance a name like `PART_Viewport`, we can locate it inside our template. We can then store a reference to this `Viewport3D` and do whatever we need to do afterward.

For more information about the `PART_*` naming convention and locating child templates, see Chapter 10, "Control Skinning and Themes."

Option 2 is useful if we were just wrapping a group of related controls and keeping them together. Remember that a `UserControl` is best used as a wrapper for related controls and for treating a group of controls as a single control. It is essentially a black box abstraction layer to encapsulate and hide the child controls from the rest of the controls.

Option 3 gives us minimal flexibility to design our `Viewport3D`-laden visual tree in XAML. However, it is well suited for composing visual trees using procedural code. Defining the visual tree programmatically rather than declaratively allows us to make hard assumptions about the tree structure and optimize lookups and other processing.

For the purpose of our samples, we adopt the third approach for composing the visual tree. Thus, our choice of base class becomes the `FrameworkElement`. Since the `Viewport3D` element is our only child, we can instantiate it in the constructor of our custom control. To make it appear in the visual tree, we need to remember to override the `MeasureOverride()`, `ArrangeOverrride()`, and `GetVisualChild()` methods, as well as the `VisualChildrenCount` property. Doing so makes our `Viewport3D` element appear on the screen. The following code puts these ideas into practice:

```
public class View3DElement : FrameworkElement
{
    private Viewport3D _viewport;
```

```csharp
    private Model3DGroup _modelGroup;

    public View3DElement()
    {
        CreateViewport();
    }

    private void CreateViewport()
    {
        _viewport = new Viewport3D();
    }

    #region Layout Overrides

    protected override Size MeasureOverride(Size availableSize)
    {
        if (availableSize.Width == double.PositiveInfinity ||
    availableSize.Height == double.PositiveInfinity)
            return Size.Empty;

        _viewport.Measure(availableSize);
        return _viewport.DesiredSize;
    }

    protected override Size ArrangeOverride(Size finalSize)
    {
        _viewport.Arrange(new Rect(finalSize));
        return finalSize;
    }

    protected override Visual GetVisualChild(int index)
    {
        if (index == 0) return _viewport;
        else throw new Exception("Bad Index");
    }

    protected override int VisualChildrenCount
    {
        get { return 1; }
    }

    #endregion
}
```

Using the preceding code, you only see a blank 3D world because we are instantiating and rendering the Viewport3D, but we don't have any models, lights, or a camera. We can easily modify the CreateViewport() method to incorporate these items as shown here:

```
private void CreateViewport()
{
    _viewport = new Viewport3D();
    _viewport = ResourceManager.Get<Viewport3D>("3DViewport");
    _modelGroup = LocateModelGroup();

    GeometryModel3D model = ResourceManager.Get<GeometryModel3D>("PlaneModel");
    _modelGroup.Children.Add(model);
}

private Model3DGroup LocateModelGroup()
{
    Model3DGroup group =
    ((_viewport.Children[0] as ModelVisual3D).Content as Model3DGroup).Children[1]
as
Model3DGroup;
    return group;
}
```

After adding the preceding code to our custom control, we can see that we're rendering a nice 3D plane, as shown in Figure 11.3.

FIGURE 11.3   3D plane rendered in a **Viewport3D**.

We are using a custom `ResourceManager` class to do the lookup of the resources from our private resource dictionary (in the code sample, you find this in `InternalResources.xaml`). `ResourceManager` has a generic `Get<T>` method that also does the casting to the right type. The resource `PlaneModel` is a `GeometryModel3D` that contains a simple plane mesh. We retrieve this instance and insert it into our `Viewport3D`. Here is how we define the `PlaneModel` resource with a `MeshGeometry3D` representing the plane geometry:

```
<GeometryModel3D x:Key="PlaneModel">
    <GeometryModel3D.Geometry>
        <MeshGeometry3D Positions="-0.625,0.5,0 0.625,0.5,0 0.625,-0.5,0 -
➥0.625,-0.5,0."
                        Normals="0,0,1 0,0,1 0,0,1 0,0,1"
                        TriangleIndices="0,3,2 0,2,1"
                        TextureCoordinates="0,0 1,0 1,1 0,1" />
    </GeometryModel3D.Geometry>

    <GeometryModel3D.Material>
        <DiffuseMaterial Brush="IndianRed" />
    </GeometryModel3D.Material>

    <GeometryModel3D.Transform>
        <TranslateTransform3D />
    </GeometryModel3D.Transform>
</GeometryModel3D>
```

The `View3DElement` contains the building blocks for embedding a `Viewport3D` inside a custom control. We can now add more features into our custom control and do something interesting like mapping 2D `DataTemplates` to their 3D counterparts! All of the 3D-related code can be nicely abstracted inside the custom control to provide a simple programming model for someone using your control. For a user of the `View3DElement`, it boils down to something as simple as a `View3DElement` tag:

```
<Grid>
    <Chapter11:View3DElement />
</Grid>
```

In the next section, we bridge the gap between 2D and 3D by making extensive use of the concepts explored so far.

Mapping 2D Visuals on 3D Surfaces

A plain `Viewport3D` embedded control isn't all that useful in the real world, but it illustrates the core concept of obscuring the use of a 3D world from the surrounding 2D environment. This is what we explore further in this section.

Let's make the control more interesting by creating a `Panel` element that does layout in 3D! Besides doing the 3D layout, our control maps the 2D visuals as a texture on the 3D plane. We have a panel that lays out 3D planes whose material is the `VisualBrush` from a 2D `UIElement`. But why use a `Panel`?

We saw in earlier chapters that a `Panel` is one of the key elements for an `ItemsControl` to work. `ItemsControl` does the job of creating UI containers for each of the data items in the list, and the `ItemsPanel` does the job of laying out these containers. Therefore, if we create a `Panel` that can lay out items in 3D, it could even work with an `ItemsControl`, resulting in a pretty awesome combination! We also leverage the framework capabilities such as data binding, data-to-UI mapping using the `DataTemplate` (`ItemsControl.ItemTemplate`), and other styling features provided by the control. WPF is inherently powerful, and it is wise to reuse functionality already provided by WPF whenever possible instead of rolling your own.

So let's get started building a `Panel` that gives the semblance of a regular 2D panel but actually hosts the items in a world populated by 3D planes floating in a `Viewport3D`. We reuse many of the ideas from the preceding section of this chapter, so instead of repeating them in code, we only talk about the additions we make.

Our panel is called `GardenViewPanel3D`. Carrying over some knowledge from Chapter 4, "Building Custom Panels," we know that for a custom `Panel`, we need to implement a few overrides to make the panel work within the WPF layout system. These include `MeasureOverride()`, `ArrangeOverride()`, `GetVisualChild()`, and `VisualChildrenCount`. The measure and arrange overrides should be familiar to you by now. Since we are laying out elements in 3D, we only need to call `Measure()` and `Arrange()` on the `Viewport3D` instance. It occupies the entire layout space for this panel:

```
protected override Size MeasureOverride(Size availableSize)
{
    if (availableSize.Width == double.PositiveInfinity ||
availableSize.Height == double.PositiveInfinity)
        return Size.Empty;

    _viewport.Measure(availableSize);

    foreach (UIElement child in Children)
    {
        child.Measure(new Size(ElementWidth, ElementHeight));
    }
    return availableSize;
}

protected override Size ArrangeOverride(Size finalSize)
{
_viewport.Arrange(new Rect(finalSize));
```

```
        foreach (UIElement child in Children)
        {
            child.Arrange(new Rect(new Size(ElementWidth, ElementHeight)));
        }
        return finalSize;
    }
```

In the preceding code, we call `Measure` and `Arrange` on each of the child elements. We do that because later in our code, we create a `VisualBrush` out of these elements and apply the brush as a material for the 3D plane. If we don't call `Measure()` and `Arrange()` on these elements, they have a size of (0,0) and the visual brush would not be able to pick up any texture. To size the elements consistently (for example, not using their `DesiredSize` property), we set a size of `ElementWidth` by `ElementHeight` on each of them. These are dependency properties that we expose on the `GardenViewPanel3D`.

Since we are modifying the default visual tree for the panel, we also have to override the `GetVisualChild()` and `VisualChildrenCount` members to make things work within WPF:

```
protected override Visual GetVisualChild(int index)
{
    if (index == 0) return _viewport;
    else throw new Exception("Bad Index");
}

protected override int VisualChildrenCount
{
    get
    {
        int count = base.VisualChildrenCount == 0 ? 0 : 1;
        return count;
    }
}
```

The `GetVisualChild()` method looks pretty straightforward, but the getter for `VisualChildrenCount` is something worth highlighting. Since we only have one child (the `Viewport3D`), we could have just returned 1 from the getter. However, you should remember that this `Panel` also needs to work well with an `ItemsControl`, which expects the panel to have zero elements in its visual tree when it first starts out. In our getter, we handle this scenario by querying the base implementation for the `VisualChildrenCount` and returning 1 only when the count is not 0. If you avoid this code and always return 1, you get an exception.

With these overrides in place, our panel is now ready to talk to an `ItemsControl` and lay out elements in a three-dimensional space. The `ItemsControl` can work with both a data-bound `IEnumerable` source and also with `UIElement`s that are directly added to its items collection. In our case, we take the former approach and populate the control from a data-bound ObservableCollection since this scenario is far more common than directly manipulating the items in an items control. Each time we add a data item in the ObservableCollection, the items control generates a corresponding UI container and adds it to the panel's Children collection. Since we want to show a 3D plane for each of the UI containers, we need a way to monitor changes happening to the Panel's Children collection. This can be achieved by overriding the OnVisualChildrenChanged() method of the panel. This method conveniently gives us the UI container that was added or removed:

```
protected override void OnVisualChildrenChanged(DependencyObject
          visualAdded,DependencyObject visualRemoved)
```

When a child gets added, we create a 3D plane and add it to our viewport. We also need to add some housekeeping information to keep track of the link between the model and container. We do that with a private DependencyProperty called LinkedModelProperty that we set on the UI container. When the container is removed, we retrieve the linked model and remove that from the viewport. This is illustrated by the following code:

```
private static readonly DependencyProperty LinkedModelProperty =
       DependencyProperty.Register("LinkedModel", typeof(ModelUIElement3D),
       typeof(GardenViewPanel3D));

protected override void OnVisualChildrenChanged(DependencyObject visualAdded,
DependencyObject visualRemoved)
{
       base.OnVisualChildrenChanged(visualAdded, visualRemoved);

       if (visualAdded != null && visualAdded != _viewport)
       {
              ModelUIElement3D model = CreateModel(visualAdded);
              visualAdded.SetValue(LinkedModelProperty, model);
              _modelContainer.Children.Add(model);
       }
       if (visualRemoved != null)
       {
              ModelUIElement3D model = visualRemoved.GetValue(LinkedModelProperty) as
ModelUIElement3D;
              model.Model = null;
              visualRemoved.ClearValue(LinkedModelProperty);
              _modelContainer.Children.Remove(model);
       }
}
```

The check to see whether the visualAdded is not our own viewport is required because the overridden method operates at the level of the visual tree, so *any* changes to the visual tree cause this method to be called. This means it is also called when we add the

Viewport3D to the panel's visual tree. We add it using `AddVisualChild()` in the panel's `OnInitialized()` override.

The only detail so far in the discussion has been the creation of the 3D planes for each UI container, implemented in the `CreateModel()` method. Here we instantiate a new 3D plane and set its material to the `VisualBrush` of the UI container. We also add some extra code to randomly place the 3D plane in 3D space.

```
private ModelUIElement3D CreateModel(DependencyObject visualAdded)
{
    int index = Math.Max(0, InternalChildren.Count - 1);
    ModelUIElement3D model = new ModelUIElement3D();
    model.Transform = new TranslateTransform3D();

    // Prepare the GeometryModel
    GeometryModel3D geomModel =
ResourceManager.Get<GeometryModel3D>("PlaneModel").Clone();
    (geomModel.Material as DiffuseMaterial).Brush = (new VisualBrush(visualAdded as
Visual));
    double zPos = -1 * index;
    double xPos = -index/2 + _random.NextDouble() * index;

    TranslateTransform3D trans =
    ((geomModel.Transform as Transform3DGroup).Children[1] as
TranslateTransform3D);
    trans.OffsetX = xPos;
    trans.OffsetZ = zPos;

    model.Model = geomModel;
    return model;
}
```

Now we have a custom control that can automatically show a 3D surface for each child added to the panel. The end users of the `GardenViewpanel3D` do not have to worry about configuring the `Viewport3D` or even worry about 3D or 3D models. From their point of view, it is just like using any other panel. Figure 11.4 shows the `GardenViewPanel3D` in action.

Getting Interactive with `ModelUIElement3D` and `ContainerUIElement3D`

In a real-world scenario, you want to do more than just display 3D planes that don't do anything interesting. You are going to want to add some interactivity. In this section, we add some mouse interactivity and make the 3D models respond to mouse clicks.

In previous versions of WPF, interacting with 3D models required a lot of effort because there was no way to attach event handlers to the `Viewport3D` or to its contained models.

FIGURE 11.4   GardenViewPanel3D in action.

To get around this, you had to manually write your own hit-testing code every time you wanted to create an interactive 3D model. So, to do what we're trying to do now, we would have had to cast a ray into the 3D world from the 2D mouse point where the click occurred and retrieve a list of models that intersect with that ray. Then you would have had to figure out whether the hit test actually applied to all models or just some or one.

With the .NET Framework version 3.5, the Viewport3D control has been extended to incorporate event handling on 3D models. Now if you want to listen to mouse events, all you need to do is attach event handlers to the models just like you would do for a 2D control. To enable this feature, some new 3D classes have been introduced that contain this event-handling wrapping code:

- **UIElement3D**—Abstract class that provides event handling and focus for a 3D model.

- **ModelUIElement3D**—Derives from UIElement3D. This is a wrapper class for a Model3D.

- **ContainerUIElement3D**—Derives from UIElement3D. This is a container element for zero or more UIElement3Ds.

We already saw the use of ModelUIElement3D and the ContainerUIElement3D in the preceding section. In CreateModel(), we wrapped each GeometryModel3D with a ModelUIElement3D. This model was then placed inside a ContainerUIElement3D in the OnVisualChildrenChanged() override.

The next step is to attach the event handler for the MouseDown event. Instead of attaching this handler for each ModelUIElement3D, we do it once for the ContainerUIElement3D. A good place to attach this handler is the `CreateViewport()` method that is called inside our panel's constructor:

```
private void CreateViewport()
{
    _viewport = ResourceManager.Get<Viewport3D>("3DViewport_Interactive");
    _modelContainer = LocateModelContainer();
    _modelContainer.MouseLeftButtonDown += ModelContainer_MouseLeftButtonDown;
}


private void ModelContainer_MouseLeftButtonDown(object sender, MouseButtonEventArgs
    ➥e)
{
    if (_prevHitModel != null)
    {
        int prevIndex = _modelContainer.Children.IndexOf(_prevHitModel);

        Storyboard anim = ConstructStoryboard(prevIndex);
        (anim.Children[0] as DoubleAnimation).To = 0;
        anim.Begin(_viewport);
    }

    ModelUIElement3D hitModel = e.Source as ModelUIElement3D;
    int index = _modelContainer.Children.IndexOf(hitModel);
    ConstructStoryboard(index).Begin(_viewport);

    _prevHitModel = hitModel;
}
```

Inside the event handler, we apply a quick little animation that makes the model jump up and down in its current location (see Figure 11.5). This gives immediate visual feedback to the user when she clicks on the item. Never underestimate the power that small, subtle, animated cues can provide when providing the user with context or feedback.

2D Bounds of a 3D Object

Embedding a `Viewport3D` inside a panel definitely gives us a great way to bridge the 2D and 3D worlds for the benefit of the user, but it also comes at a cost. For a regular 2D panel, you can add features like virtualization, custom layouts, scrolling, exposing events, and commands. Performing those activities on a 2D control are fairly well-known activities and standardized. To enable these features in a full 3D world would require quite a bit of effort, and there is also very little (if any) real documentation on doing this.

However, if we apply some of the principles from the previous chapters, it is possible to carry forward some of these concepts from 2D to 3D.

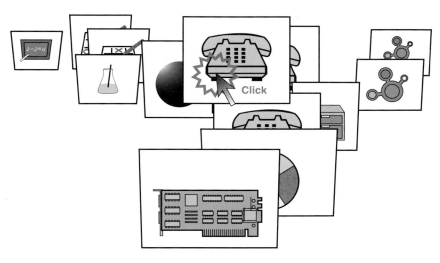

FIGURE 11.5   Jumping items in an interactive **GardenViewpanel3D**.

Even though we are dealing with 3D objects, it is ultimately flattened out on the rectangular 2D screen. By inverse mapping the 3D coordinates to 2D, we can add in most of the features that we're used to adding to our controls. WPF provides a class called GeneralTransform3DTo2D to help you in this mapping with the methods Transform(Point3D) and TransformBounds(Rect3D). The following line of code shows how you can map the ModelUIElement3D's bounds to a 2D rectangle:

```
Rect rect = hitModel.TransformToAncestor(this).TransformBounds(hitModel.Model.Bounds);
```

In this case, hitModel is an instance of ModelUIElement3D, and this points to the GardenViewPanel3D. Using this API, we can now refer to the various aspects of this control on the 2D world, and almost all of the concepts from previous chapters can be applied. There is also a GeneralTransform2DTo3D that can be used to do the process in the other direction. Using these transforms, you could overlay a 2D control on the 3D surface and make it interactive. This 2D control occupies the same area as the 3D object, giving a sense of interacting with the 3D object itself. You could also make this part of the custom control by embedding the logic to show and hide the 2D control on top of the 3D object.

As a reader exercise, you should try and come up with some ways that you might be able to (tastefully!) make use of a 2D overlay for a 3D model. For reference, you could take a look at Chapter 8, "Virtualization," where we discussed the notion of virtualization in 3D and overlaid Rectangle instances on 3D models.

Hints on Layout in 3D

3D really shows its power when it comes to laying out objects in a vast, 3D world within the confines of a `Viewport3D`. This is completely different from the 2D world and the two bear no resemblance whatsoever. In a 3D world, you don't have the `MeasureOverride()` and `ArrangeOverride()` calls, and you receive no information regarding the bounds of the 3D world. In fact, the `Viewport3D` gives you an infinitely sized world, and it is up to you how you want to segment it and use it for your purposes.

For most UI controls, you would not be using a freeform camera floating in the 3D space of a huge world nor would you need large geometries. When building interactive GUIs the camera is generally fixed and looking in one direction and used to produce specific effects. The 3D model used to represent the item is typically simple and probably a plane, sphere, or cube. Trying to limit your use of 3D to these scenarios simplifies your development and results in faster development time. Some of the most compelling user interfaces make subtle use of 3D and 3D perspectives and are not fully realized 3D interactive worlds such as those found in First-Person Shooter (FPS) games.

For a real-world example of layout in 3D, refer to the `ElementFlow` panel from the Open Source FluidKit project, which can be found at http://www.codeplex.com/fluidkit. Pavan Podila is the original author of FluidKit.

Interactive 2D-on-3D Surfaces

A new feature introduced in .NET 3.5 is the ability to interact with a 2D visual that has been texture-mapped onto the surface of a 3D model. This is an exciting feature that can be pretty useful for enabling some scenarios with little to no effort. `Viewport2DVisual3D` is the class that handles this interaction. It is similar to the `GeometryModel3D` with the addition of a `Visual` property. This property corresponds to the 2D visual, which will be mapped onto the 3D geometry. Note that the 2D visual becomes a logical child of `Viewport2DVisual3D`, which means it cannot be a child of a regular 2D control at the same time.

To enable this interaction you need to set the `Viewport2DVisual3D.IsVisualHostMaterial` attached property to `True` on the material. For example, if you are using a `DiffuseMaterial` as the material for the 3D surface, you would have to do the following:

```
<Viewport2DVisual3D.Material>
    <DiffuseMaterial Brush="White"
Viewport2DVisual3D.IsVisualHostMaterial="True" />
    </Viewport2DVisual3D.Material>
```

Figure 11.6 shows a simple `ListBox`, containing few `TextBlocks` and a `Button`, which has been mapped onto a 3D plane.

All of the standard mouse and keyboard interactions continue to work as expected. Just like any other feature in WPF, you need to be judicious in deciding to what extent this feature should be used. Features like these make an impact when they are used in subtle ways without assaulting the user with too much 3D and actually hampering the usability. A good use case would be an application that provides interactive

FIGURE 11.6   An interactive ListBox on a 3D model.

visualization of demographic data around the world. This could involve an interactive globe whose material is a 2D panel. The panel contains the event handling logic to place markers and color different parts of the globe. This is a much better approach than doing the event-handling inside the `Viewport3D`. If the user wants to switch to a 2D view, you can nicely animate the globe to become a plane. In the next chapter, we will show an example of morphing a sphere (globe) into a plane.

Summary

This chapter provided an introduction to the world of 3D while keeping our feet firmly grounded in the world of 2D controls and visual elements. WPF isn't a framework for building 3D Xbox 360 games, but if you want 3D and 3D-style interfaces for your WPF applications, this chapter provided the basics to get you started.

We started with an overview of the `View3DElement`, which showed the technique to embed a `Viewport3D` object for representing each child in a panel. We also added interactivity so you could click a 3D object and make it jump up and down in its own spot within a 3D world while still looking and behaving like a regular GUI control. Later we also demonstrated the use of `Viewport2DVisual3D` for mapping interactive 2D visuals onto 3D surfaces. With these concepts, you should be well positioned to create fascinating controls that blend the eye-popping power of 3D with the practicality and rapid development of the 2D world.

CHAPTER 12

Custom Animations

Animations are some of the best things that you can add to your application and at the same time some of the worst. Tastefully placed animations can provide visual cues to the user that something meaningful is taking place within the application and can even increase the density of information being conveyed without consuming additional screen real estate. The flip side, of course, is that animations can be used abusively. Animations that take too long, are obtrusive, or otherwise prevent the user from accomplishing his goals can positively ruin an otherwise fantastic application.

Animations such as fades, translations, rotations, zooms, blinks, and other interesting movements can add a bit of flare and class to an application. They have the power to transform a dull-looking interface into something that is full of life. Animations can even give users a positive emotional response to interacting with an application.

Procedural Animations

Animations within WPF are time-bound. By this we mean that they have a defined duration within which they complete. This makes sense for a user interface since most animations that happen in a UI are short and really meant for visual cues and not for cutscene-length animations like you would find in a video game. These visual cues aid the user in making decisions while working with the UI. For example, if you have a transition animation between two views, you would find it easier to specify that as a 0.5 second animation. The hard work of figuring out how the animated values change is left to the framework.

Animating Using the `DispatcherTimer`

In the past, one of the only ways to perform animations within an application's user interface was to rig up a timer that fired events at fixed intervals. At each interval, the application would then figure out a new value for the property being animated and perform the property change. This was pretty much the only way to do UI animations using Windows Forms.

WPF doesn't require you to perform your applications this way, but it is still good to know that it is possible. `DispatcherTimer` runs on the UI thread, and the events are also fired on the UI thread. This means you don't have to switch threads to make visual changes. If you've ever spent an entire day reworking GUI code to make sure that your visual changes all fire on the main thread, this aspect of the dispatcher timer should make you pretty happy.

Using a `DispatcherTimer` is useful for special types of animations that involve physics-based effects. In such effects, you need granular control over time and the interval between each timer event. Such types of animations are generally not time-bound and usually complete when particular values reach their final destination.

For example, if you want to perform a physics-grade downward acceleration of a ball dropping, you need precise control over how long the animation is running, as well as how frequently the timer fires.

Animating Using `CompositionTarget.Rendering`

`CompositionTarget.Rendering` is an event that is fired every time a frame is ready to be rendered. Each rendering pass is packaged as a frame that contains all of the information for dumping the visuals to the screen. The frame rate for the application determines the frequency with which these frames are rendered. This is generally governed by the computing resources available to the application at the time of execution such as memory, CPU, GPU, the current power management plan on a laptop, and so on. A high frame rate means that this event fires more often.

Some readers may recognize a similarity between this approach and higher-end graphics subsystems like DirectX. Do not mistake `CompositionTarget.Rendering` for a good injection point to create a WPF-based gaming graphics engine. High-end graphics and ultra-high frame rates are not the goal of this particular aspect of WPF animation.

Similar to the `DispatcherTimer` approach, animations based on `CompositionTarget.Rendering` are also not time-bound. However, these events are synced with the render thread resulting in smoother animations than the `DispatcherTimer`. Also there is no need to start and stop a timer, although you may have to detach and attach the event handler to improve performance.

Let's consider an example where a bunch of objects fall down based on gravity, as shown in Figure 12.1. Here we are not forcing the animation to complete in a specific time, but it would rather follow a natural duration. If additional forces act on these objects, they would take a longer time to come to rest. A time-bound animation cannot really capture these physical effects. `CompositionTarget.Rendering` or `DispatcherTimer` are better options for these kinds of animations.

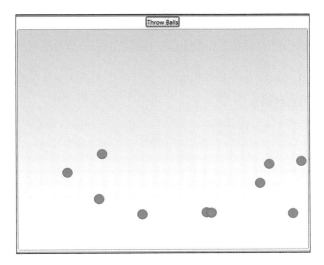

FIGURE 12.1   Animating physics-managed balls.

The animations are set up by subscribing to the `CompositionTarget.Rendering` event (CTR) in the `Window.Loaded` event handler.

```
void Window1_Loaded(object sender, RoutedEventArgs e)
{
    CreateBalls();
    CompositionTarget.Rendering += CompositionTarget_Rendering;
}

void CompositionTarget_Rendering(object sender, EventArgs e)
{
    for (int i = 0; i < TotalBalls; i++)
    {
        Ellipse ball = _container.Children[i] as Ellipse;

        PhysicsInfo info = ball.Tag as PhysicsInfo;
        UpdateBall(info);
        SetConstraints(ball, info);

        ball.SetValue(Canvas.LeftProperty, info.X);
        ball.SetValue(Canvas.TopProperty, info.Y);
    }
}
```

Inside the event handler, we loop through all of the ball objects, update their positions, and make sure they bounce against the sides of the window. When we create the balls, we assign them random accelerations so that each of them come to rest at different times. We also have the option to throw the balls into the air, which can again set them in motion. Thus, we can see that it is difficult to describe and animate the motion of balls in air and rebounding against the walls in terms of a time-bound animation. `CompositionTarget.Rendering` is ideally suited for this kind of scenario.

Animating with Storyboards

Both the `DispatcherTimer` and `CompositionTarget.Rendering` animation methods require you to write some procedural code to invoke and control the animation. Also note that these are not time-bound (unless your procedural code creates an artificial time binding). This may not be an ideal method when building a complex UI with many subtle animations. You would rather use a declaratively controlled, time-bound animation that completes after a defined duration. Storyboards are the perfect candidates for such animations. In fact, it is highly recommended that you make all your UI animations as storyboards. This allows a separate team of designers to create these animations, using tools such as Expression Blend.

Storyboards can be completely defined in XAML (although you can also define them procedurally if you must). This makes it easier to tweak the animation parameters without going down to the code level. Storyboards can nest multiple levels of animations, giving you enormous power in creating complex animations.

Animations in WPF are generally identified as one of the following: type-based animations, type-based animations using keyframes, path-based animations, and parallel timelines. We address each of these in turn.

> **NOTE**
>
> It is important to remember that animations work only on dependency properties. Dependency properties can be set from multiple places, and an animation is one such source. Dependency property values follow a precedence order, in which animations have a higher precedence compared to locally set values (that is, using `DependencyObject.SetValue()` API). When an animation starts, it changes the values of the dependency property from the start to the end. This overrides any of the locally set dependency property values. If you want to revert to the locally set value, you have to manually remove the animation.

Simple Type-Based Animations (From, To, and By)

All of the animation classes in WPF animate properties of a particular type. For example, the `DoubleAnimation` class animates only double values. `ColorAnimation` animates color values, giving you a smoothly animated change of colors. You may feel that such type-based animations may be limiting, but in reality they account for a majority of properties in the WPF system. For those few outlier cases, WPF gives us the power to create our own custom animations. We look into custom animations in a later section.

These type-based animations can be defined using some standard parameters such as From, To, By, Duration, `Storyboard.TargetName`, and `Storyboard.TargetProperty`. The From, To, and By values specify the start and end values for the animation. You can do with explicit start and end values like From-To or use the By to make the end value relative to the current From value. All type-based animations require an object that exposes dependency properties of that type. This is the target to which the animation gets applied.

```
<ColorAnimation From="Violet"
                         To="Red"
                         Duration="0:0:3"
                         Storyboard.TargetName="FromToEllipse"
          Storyboard.TargetProperty="Fill.(SolidColorBrush.Color)" />
```

In the preceding example, we are animating the `Color` dependency property of a `SolidColorBrush` from Violet to Red. The snapshot of the output is shown in Figure 12.2. Note the ease with which we can declaratively define this animation.

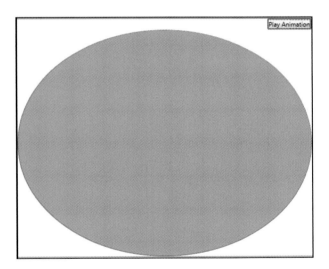

FIGURE 12.2   Simple animation example.

Keyframe Animations

If the animation you are defining has a single start and end value, a simple type-based animation as we already discussed would work best. However, if the property you are animating needs to go through a series of changes and you need to define the state of the property at each of those stages, you are talking about a keyframe animation.

Keyframes are specific snapshots of your property at different times during the length of the animation. The following snippet shows the definition of a `LinearDoubleKeyFrame`, which has a value of `"Blue"`, 3 seconds after the start of the animation.

```
<LinearColorKeyFrame KeyTime="0:0:3" Value="Blue" />
```

Keyframes can either be linear or spline-based. A linear keyframe changes value at a constant rate whereas a spline-based keyframe changes value along a Bézier curve. The KeySpline property provides this Bézier curve. By tweaking the KeySpline (which actually represents two control points that describe the shape of the curve), effects such as acceleration, deceleration, ease-in, and ease-out can be created.

```
<SplineColorKeyFrame KeyTime="0:0:3"
                     KeySpline="0.25,0.25 0.75,0.75"
                     Value="Blue" />
```

The following example shows the usage of a keyframe-based animation. Here we use the ColorAnimationUsingKeyFrames element to animate the Color property of the SolidColorBrush through various colors of the rainbow:

```
<ColorAnimationUsingKeyFrames Duration="0:0:7"
                              Storyboard.TargetName="KeyFrameEllipse"
             Storyboard.TargetProperty="Fill.(SolidColorBrush.Color)">
             <LinearColorKeyFrame KeyTime="0:0:0"
                                  Value="White" />
             <LinearColorKeyFrame KeyTime="0:0:1"
                                  Value="Violet" />
             <LinearColorKeyFrame KeyTime="0:0:2"
                                  Value="Indigo" />
             <LinearColorKeyFrame KeyTime="0:0:3"
                                  Value="Blue" />
             <LinearColorKeyFrame KeyTime="0:0:4"
                                  Value="Green" />
             <LinearColorKeyFrame KeyTime="0:0:5"
                                  Value="Yellow" />
             <LinearColorKeyFrame KeyTime="0:0:6"
                                  Value="Orange" />
             <LinearColorKeyFrame KeyTime="0:0:7"
                                  Value="Red" />
</ColorAnimationUsingKeyFrames>
```

Using Storyboards with Parallel Timelines

Keyframe-based animation allows you to animate a single property through a sequence of clearly defined states (appropriately enough, these interim states are called *keyframes*). If you want to change multiple properties on multiple objects but you want the same granular control over keyframes, you need to use a storyboard. Storyboards are a type of animation that allow nesting of other, subservient animations.

Storyboards do, however, have a limitation. They cannot nest other storyboards. You can easily remedy this limitation using the ParallelTimeline, which can be nested inside a storyboard. `ParallelTimeline` can contain animations and other `ParallelTimelines`. Thus, you can create a complex storyboard with multiple levels of nested animations. You should be careful not to create a deeply nested storyboard because that can affect both the readability of your code and the ease of maintenance.

In the following example, we continue expanding our rainbow color animation by adding a horizontal bar that shows the current color change (see Figure 12.3). The bar is split up into seven sections (one for each color), and each of these sections is animated independently. By using storyboards and `ParallelTimelines`, this is easily achieved.

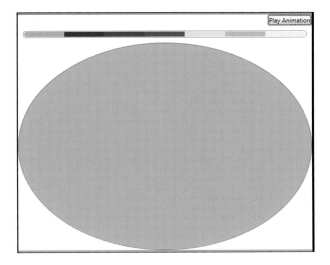

FIGURE 12.3   Keyframe animation with parallel timelines.

```
<Storyboard x:Key="NestedAnimation" FillBehavior="Stop">
        <ParallelTimeline>
        <DoubleAnimation To="1" From="0"
                    Duration="0:0:1"
                    Storyboard.TargetName="_violetRect"
                    Storyboard.TargetProperty="Opacity" />
            <DoubleAnimation To="1"
                From="0"
                Duration="0:0:1"
                BeginTime="0:0:1"
                Storyboard.TargetName="_indigoRect"
                Storyboard.TargetProperty="Opacity" />
            <DoubleAnimation To="1"
                From="0"
                Duration="0:0:1"
                BeginTime="0:0:2"
                Storyboard.TargetName="_blueRect"
```

```xml
                            Storyboard.TargetProperty="Opacity" />
                <DoubleAnimation To="1"
                From="0"
                Duration="0:0:1"
                BeginTime="0:0:3"
                Storyboard.TargetName="_greenRect"
                Storyboard.TargetProperty="Opacity" />
                <DoubleAnimation To="1"
                From="0"
                Duration="0:0:1"
                BeginTime="0:0:4"
            Storyboard.TargetName="_yellowRect"
            Storyboard.TargetProperty="Opacity" />
                <DoubleAnimation To="1"
            From="0"
            Duration="0:0:1"
            BeginTime="0:0:5"
            Storyboard.TargetName="_orangeRect"
            Storyboard.TargetProperty="Opacity" />
                <DoubleAnimation To="1"
            From="0"
            Duration="0:0:1"
            BeginTime="0:0:6"
            Storyboard.TargetName="_redRect"
            Storyboard.TargetProperty="Opacity" />
        </ParallelTimeline>
        <ColorAnimationUsingKeyFrames Duration="0:0:7"
                        Storyboard.TargetName="NestedStoryboardEllipse"
                        Storyboard.TargetProperty="Fill.(SolidColorBrush.Color)">
            <LinearColorKeyFrame KeyTime="0:0:0"
                        Value="White" />
            <LinearColorKeyFrame KeyTime="0:0:1"
Value="Violet" />
            <LinearColorKeyFrame KeyTime="0:0:2"
Value="Indigo" />
            <LinearColorKeyFrame KeyTime="0:0:3"
Value="Blue" />
            <LinearColorKeyFrame KeyTime="0:0:4"
Value="Green" />
            <LinearColorKeyFrame KeyTime="0:0:5"
Value="Yellow" />
            <LinearColorKeyFrame KeyTime="0:0:6"
Value="Orange" />
            <LinearColorKeyFrame KeyTime="0:0:7"
Value="Red" />
```

```
    </ColorAnimationUsingKeyFrames>
</Storyboard>
```

Using Path-Based Animations

Sometimes the movement that you want to illustrate with your animation can't be
defined by simply changing a single property of an object over the course of a fixed time
interval or extrapolated between keyframes. As we just illustrated, you can use
ParallelTimelines to affect multiple properties of multiple objects in the same coordi-
nated animation.

But what do you do if you want to animate something so that it moves in an ellipse?
Sure, you could do some math and figure out the keyframes of an ellipse, but what if the
animation path is mostly an ellipse but then the object does a rollercoaster-style loop
between two otherwise elliptical keyframes? Again, if you really and truly enjoy punish-
ment, you could manually plot out all of the individual keyframes required to produce
that animation, but thankfully there is a better, simpler way: the path animation.

The path animation is a special class of animation that animates visual objects along a
path. The most popular animation of this type is the DoubleAnimationUsingPath.
Conceptually this animation is similar to the DoubleAnimation but adds the extra capability of moving the object along a PathGeometry. A PathGeometry can be described using
one or more lines, curves, and arcs. This means that a path animation uses the regular
"From/To/By" values and also a path that describes the object's motion. It also has a
Source property, which is an enumeration of type PathAnimationSource. The source property indicates what aspect of the path is considered for the motion: X, Y, or a tangential
angle along the path.

Other animations in this category include MatrixAnimationUsingPath and
PointAnimationUsingPath operating on Matrix and Point data types, respectively.

The following code is a simple example of the path-based animation. It shows the Earth
following an elliptical path around the Sun (see Figure 12.4):

```
<Storyboard x:Key="EarthAroundSunAnimation"
    RepeatBehavior="Forever">
<DoubleAnimationUsingPath BeginTime="00:00:00"
    Duration="00:00:02"
    Storyboard.TargetName="Earth"
    Storyboard.TargetProperty="(UIElement.RenderTransform).(TranslateTransform.X)"
    Source="X">
<DoubleAnimationUsingPath.PathGeometry>
    <PathGeometry Figures="M385,-107.6665 C385,-79.77612 295.68081,-57.1665
185.5,-57.1665 C75.319192,-57.1665 -14,-79.77612 -14,-107.6665 C-14,-135.55688
75.319192,-158.1665 185.5,-158.1665 C295.68081,-158.1665 385,-135.55688 385,-
107.6665 z" />
</DoubleAnimationUsingPath.PathGeometry>
```

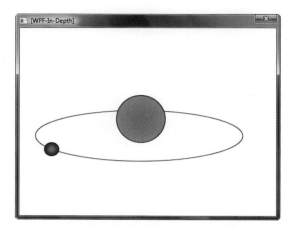

FIGURE 12.4   The Earth revolving around the sun using a path-based animation.

```
</DoubleAnimationUsingPath>
<DoubleAnimationUsingPath BeginTime="00:00:00"
      Duration="00:00:02"
      Storyboard.TargetName="Earth"

Storyboard.TargetProperty="(UIElement.RenderTransform).(TranslateTransform.Y)"
      Source="Y">
<DoubleAnimationUsingPath.PathGeometry>
      <PathGeometry Figures="M385,-107.6665 C385,-79.77612 295.68081,-57.1665
   ➥185.5,-57.1665 C75.319192,-57.1665 -14,-79.77612 -14,-107.6665 C-14,-135.55688
75.319192,-158.1665 185.5,-158.1665 C295.68081,-158.1665 385,-135.55688 385,
-107.6665 z" />
</DoubleAnimationUsingPath.PathGeometry>
</DoubleAnimationUsingPath>
</Storyboard>
```

Creating Custom Animations

As shown in Figure 12.5, so far we have seen many different kinds of animations, including the following:

- ▶ Animation using the DispatcherTimer
- ▶ Animation using CompositionTarget.Rendering
- ▶ Linear type-based animation (for example, int, double, and so on)
- ▶ Keyframe animations
- ▶ Nested animations using storyboards and ParallelTimeline
- ▶ Path-based animation

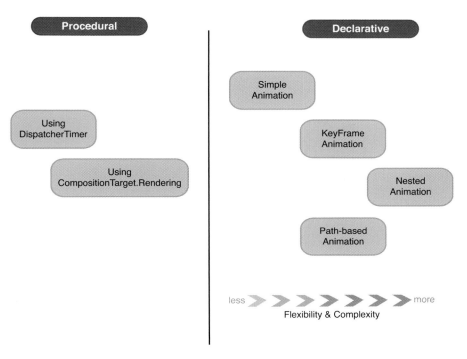

FIGURE 12.5   The complexity of various animation types.

Of the types in the preceding list, the procedural techniques are probably the least frequently used. The use of these two techniques requires a lot more effort and in most cases can be substituted by a storyboard animation. The thing to keep in mind about storyboard animations is that they work on specific types. WPF already provides a set of animations that take care of most of the types.

What do you do if you want to animate a property of a custom type? Can you still do it? Thankfully, the answer is yes. WPF's animation system is built to be extensible at all levels. In fact, the stock animations that come with WPF are built using the same framework you might use to create custom animations.

These animations all follow a standard naming convention. Regular animations are named `<Type>Animation`. Keyframe-based animations are named `<Type>AnimationUsingKeyFrames`. The keyframes contained within such an animation are named `<Type>KeyFrame`. Path animations are generally named as `<Type>AnimationUsingPath`.

Some of the common types that you will animate most often include the following:

▶ `Double`

▶ `Color`

▶ `Rect`

▶ Size

▶ Rotation3D

▶ Point3D

▶ Point

▶ Matrix

▶ Quaternion

In this section, we venture into creating our own custom type-based animations. When we are animating a property between two values, we are really producing an interpolated value between the two end values at specific points in time. At the beginning of the animation, we are at the beginning of the value range, and when the animation completes, we are at the end of the value range. The actual interpolation can be linear, or it can change along a Bézier curve, producing well-known effects like an "ease-in" or an "ease-out" animation, as shown in Figure 12.6.

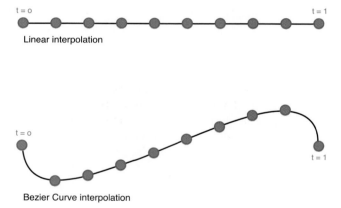

FIGURE 12.6   Illustrating linear and Bézier interpolation.

These values can be of various data types, and there is no single standard way to animate (interpolate) all of them. Only a custom type-specific animation can have the complete knowledge of how to interpolate the values over time between a start and end point. Therefore, in WPF, the primary responsibility of a custom animation is to provide interpolated values for its data type. Additionally other housekeeping details are required to make the animation a well-behaved citizen and cooperate with all of the other controls and subsystems within WPF.

To start exploring custom animations, let's take an example of animating 3D mesh geometries. Don't worry if you're not an expert in 3D graphics, WPF makes a lot of this easy, and there is a very good book on WPF and 3D written by Charles Petzold [*3D*

Programming for Windows, ISBN: 978-0735623941]. A 3D mesh geometry can be defined in WPF using a `Point3DCollection` that specifies the different vertex positions of the mesh. We also need to define the `Normals` (a direction indicating "up" for a particular shape), `TriangleIndices`, and `TextureCoordinates`, but again, we don't need to worry about these details right now. For our example, we are only concerned with the animation of vertex positions: `Point3DCollection`. It turns out that there is no built-in animation for the `Point3DCollection` type, so we're going to write our own.

The animation classes in WPF follow a particular convention when implementing a type-specific animation. For every type-specific animation, there is an abstract base class by the name of `<Type>AnimationBase`. Thus `DoubleAnimation` actually derives from `DoubleAnimationBase`, which in turn derives from `AnimationTimeline`. For our `Point3DCollection` type animation, we are going to need a `Point3DCollectionAnimation` class, which derives from `Point3DCollectionAnimationBase`, which in turn derives from `AnimationTimeline`.

Without further delay, here is the code for the `Point3DCollectionAnimationBase` class:

```
public abstract class Point3DCollectionAnimationBase : AnimationTimeline
{
    public override sealed Type TargetPropertyType
    {
        get { return typeof (Point3DCollection); }
    }

    public override sealed object GetCurrentValue(object defaultOriginValue,
                                     object defaultDestinationValue,
                                      AnimationClock animationClock)
    {
        if (defaultOriginValue == null)
        {
                throw new ArgumentNullException("defaultOriginValue");
         }
        if (defaultDestinationValue == null)
        {
                throw new ArgumentNullException("defaultDestinationValue");
        }
        return GetCurrentValue((Point3DCollection) defaultOriginValue,
                        (Point3DCollection) defaultDestinationValue,
                        animationClock);
    }
public Point3DCollection GetCurrentValue(
Point3DCollection defaultOriginValue,
                        Point3DCollection defaultDestinationValue,
                                 AnimationClock animationClock)
    {
            if (animationClock == null)
```

```
        {
                throw new ArgumentException("animationClock");
        }

return GetCurrentValueCore(defaultOriginValue,
        defaultDestinationValue, animationClock);
        }

protected abstract Point3DCollection
GetCurrentValueCore(Point3DCollection defaultOriginValue,
                    Point3DCollection defaultDestinationValue,
                    AnimationClock animationClock);
```

As you can see, the primary responsibilities of the <Type>AnimationBase class are as follows:

▶ Set the TargetPropertyType property.

▶ Ensure that the animation is working on the correct types.

▶ Create a more type-safe GetCurrentValueCore() method. This method is implemented in the derived class. GetCurrentValue() internally invokes this method.

With the base animation class defined, we can now concentrate on implementing the interpolation logic. Since we are animating mesh positions, we are really morphing one mesh surface into another. For example, we can consider four common 3D surfaces: plane, sphere, cylinder, and cone. All of the interpolation logic is captured in the MeshMorphAnimation class that derives from Point3DCollectionAnimationBase. To make it easier for specifying a mesh surface to animate, we expose two properties on the animation class: StartSurface and EndSurface; each is an enum of type SurfaceType.

MeshMorphAnimation assumes that both the starting and ending surfaces have the same number of vertices. Each surface is defined by a grid of points, each point (Point3D) located according to the SurfaceType. The grid itself is defined using the HorizontalPoints and VerticalPoints properties on the MeshMorphAnimation. With this assumption, the interpolation logic boils down to translating the vertices from the StartSurface to the EndSurface. As the vertices translate to their new positions, the surface morphs itself into the new shape. Remember that this only works on surfaces that contain the same number of vertices. Logic to figure out when to add and remove vertices to accommodate new shapes is beyond the scope of this book. Figure 12.7 shows an example of morphing the cylinder into a sphere.

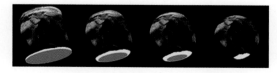

FIGURE 12.7   Interpolation from a cylinder to a sphere.

We know that the heart of any custom animation is the interpolation logic for the particular type. This interpolation depends on the `CurrentProgress` of the `AnimationClock`, which is specified as a value between 0 and 1. The framework fires the `GetCurrentValue()` on the `Point3DCollectionAnimationBase`, which in turn calls the type-safe `GetCurrentValueCore()` method. The parameters to this method include the starting `Point3DCollection`, ending `Point3DCollection`, and the `AnimationClock`.

In our example, `GetCurrentValueCore()` internally calls the private `Interpolate()` method passing the current animation progress, as shown in the following code:

```
protected override Point3DCollection GetCurrentValueCore(Point3DCollection src
Point3DCollection dest, AnimationClock clock)
{
        if (!_collectionsCreated)
        {
                _startPoints = StartSurface.HasValue
                                              ?
MeshCreator.CreatePositions(StartSurface.Value, HorizontalPoints, VerticalPoints)
                                        : src;
                _endPoints = EndSurface.HasValue
                                              ?
MeshCreator.CreatePositions(EndSurface.Value, HorizontalPoints, VerticalPoints)
                                        : dest;
                _collectionsCreated = true;
                return _startPoints;
        }
        if (clock.CurrentProgress >= 1)
                return _endPoints;

        return Interpolate(clock.CurrentProgress.Value);
}

private Point3DCollection Interpolate(double progress)
{
        Point3DCollection points = new Point3DCollection();
        for (int i = 0; i < _startPoints.Count; i++)
        {
double x = _startPoints[i].X + (_endPoints[i].X -
_startPoints[i].X)*progress;
                double y = _startPoints[i].Y + (_endPoints[i].Y -
_startPoints[i].Y)*progress;
                double z = _startPoints[i].Z + (_endPoints[i].Z -
_startPoints[i].Z)*progress;

                Point3D p = new Point3D(x, y, z);
                points.Add(p);
```

```
        }

        return points;
}
```

At the start of the animation, we cache the starting and ending `Point3DCollections` using the `_startPoints` and `_endPoints` members. The core of the method is the linear interpolation that happens between the starting and ending points.

Linear Interpolation

Linear interpolation, or lerp, between two points A and B is defined by the parametric equation:

`lerp(t) = A + (B - A) * t`

where t is the parametric variable whose value changes between 0 and 1. Putting these values into the equation, we can see that at the start of the animation (t=0), lerp(t) = A. At the end of the animation (t=1), lerp(t) = B.

We mentioned earlier that `Point3DCollectionAnimationBase` derives from `AnimationTimeline`. `AnimationTimeline` in turn is a descendant of `Freezable`. A `Freezable` derives from `DependencyObject` and supports a read-only frozen state and a writeable state. If all the properties in a `Freezable` are `DependencyProperties`, then the only other thing that the class needs to do is implement `CreateInstanceCore()`, which is responsible for spawning a new instance. In our case, all of the properties in `MeshMorphAnimation` are `DependencyProperties`, which leaves us with only one other method to override:

```
protected override Freezable CreateInstanceCore()
{
        return new MeshMorphAnimation();
}
```

To summarize, a custom animation class needs to do the following:

▶ Create an abstract `<Type>AnimationBase` class, which derives from `AnimationTimeline`.

▶ Override the `TargetPropertyType` property in `<Type>AnimationBase` to return the associated type.

▶ Override the `GetCurrentValue()` method in `<Type>AnimationBase` class and invoke a more type-safe `GetCurrentValueCore()` method. Note that `GetCurrentValueCore()` is a custom method and not something provided by the framework.

▶ Create a custom `<Type>Animation` class that derives from `<Type>AnimationBase`.

▶ Override the protected `GetCurrentValueCore()` method and provide the interpolation values for the associated type.

▶ Override the `CreateInstanceCore()` method in the `<Type>Animation` class to return an instance of `<Type>Animation`.

Creating the 3D Surfaces

One aspect that we kind of skimmed over in our previous discussion of custom animations was the logic to create the different surfaces. In our case, we have four different types: plane, sphere, cylinder, and cone. To maintain consistency and also to simplify the interpolation logic, we defined these surfaces as a grid of points (vertices). These vertices are located in 3D space in such a way that they describe the appropriate surface.

In Figure 12.8, you can see how the grid of vertices wraps around the surface. Thinking of our surface in terms of a vertex grid makes it easier to identify the mesh `Positions`, `TextureCoordinates`, and `TriangleIndices`. The following code shows the creation of the vertex positions in a `Point3DCollection` for the plane and sphere.

```
private static Point3DCollection CreatePlane(int hPoints, int vPoints)
{
        Point3DCollection points = new Point3DCollection();
        for (int i = 0; i < vPoints; i++)
        {
                double vStep = (double) i/(vPoints - 1);
                double y = 1 - 2*vStep;
                for (int j = 0; j < hPoints; j++)
                {
                        double hStep = (double) j/(hPoints - 1);
                        double x = -1 + 2*hStep;
                        double z = 0;
                        Point3D point = new Point3D(x, y, z);
                        points.Add(point);
                }
        }
}
```

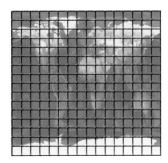

FIGURE 12.8   Vertices of different mesh surfaces.

```
        return points;
}

private static Point3DCollection CreateSphere(int hPoints, int vPoints)
{
        // Generate the vertices
        Point3DCollection points = new Point3DCollection();
        for (int i = 0; i < vPoints; i++)
        {
                double s = (double) i/(vPoints - 1);
                for (int j = 0; j < hPoints; j++)
                {
                        double t = (double) j/(hPoints - 1);

                        double z = -Math.Cos(t*2*Math.PI)*Math.Sin(s*Math.PI);
                        double x = -Math.Sin(t*2*Math.PI)*Math.Sin(s*Math.PI);
                        double y = Math.Cos(s*Math.PI);

                        points.Add(new Point3D(x, y, z));
                }
        }

        return points;
}
```

Using the preceding as an example, we can create the cylinder and the cone as well.

> **Performance Tip**
>
> You can use the `Timeline.DesiredFramerate` attached property to control the quality of the animation and also improve performance. By default, WPF renders animations at 60 FPS, which may be too high for your application. Changing it to a lower value can greatly improve the CPU usage and improve performance.

Animating Within the `DrawingContext`

The general use of animations in WPF is mostly applied to the logical tree and done using the declarative markup or in the code-behind. A lesser-known fact about animations is that you can also apply them at the level of the `DrawingContext`. Some of the methods on `DrawingContext` are overloaded to accept an `AnimationClock`, which can be used to trigger animations. The methods are mostly related to drawing shapes like `DrawEllipse()`, `DrawLine()`, `DrawRectangle()`, `DrawRoundedRectangle()`, and miscellaneous methods like `DrawVideo()`, `DrawImage()`, and `PushOpacity()`. For these animations to work, you need to create compatible `AnimationClocks`. For example, the `DrawEllipse()` overload that accepts an `AnimationClock` has the following signature:

```
DrawingContext.DrawEllipse(Brush, Pen, Point, AnimationClock, Double, Animation-
Clock, Double, AnimationClock)
```

The three animation clocks correspond to the Center, RadiusX, and RadiusY parameters of the ellipse. To animate the center of the ellipse on each OnRender() call, you need to provide an AnimationClock of PointAnimation. This can be done using the CreateClock() method of the PointAnimation, as shown in the following code:

```
PointAnimation anim = new PointAnimation(new Point(300, 400), new
Duration(TimeSpan.FromSeconds(1)));
AnimationClock clock = anim.CreateClock();
```

Although you may not use this kind of animation as much as the storyboard animations, it is good to know that such a possibility also exists.

Summary

Animation is one of those tricky aspects of UI development that developers cannot afford to ignore. These days, if an application doesn't animate anything at all, users will think that something is "off" about the application and may not want to use it. On the other hand, if everything in the application is bouncing, jiggling, and rotating out of control then the users will be even more irritated.

The trick is finding the balance of subtlety and helpful animation that conveys meaning to the user and gives them a sense of immersion in the application. With the tools and tips provided in this chapter, you should be well on your way to being able to provide compelling animations that are subtle, beautiful, and useful to the users of your application.

CHAPTER 13

Pixel Shader Effects

Despite being referred to merely as a "service pack," the .NET Framework 3.5 SP1 has actually introduced some incredibly powerful new features and functionality. Among these new features is the concept of **pixel shaders**.

This chapter provides an introduction to shaders, including how they work and what they do. In addition, we cover plenty of code samples illustrating a host of powerful effects that can be produced using shaders, and we also introduce the language in which shaders are written: High Level Shading Language (HLSL).

Pixel shaders have been an integral part of DirectX for some time now, and with the release of .NET Framework 3.5 SP1, they are now available in WPF. Pixel shaders provide the ability to post-process the rendered (rasterized) output from WPF directly on the GPU (Graphics Processing Unit, the specialized CPU residing on the video card). In the world of graphics programming, pixel shaders represent an important step in the graphics pipeline.

Post-processing of output on the GPU is generally referred to as a **shader**. Typically there are two kinds of shaders: **vertex shaders** and **pixel shaders**. A vertex shader operates on every visible vertex in the scene, whereas pixel shaders process the color applied to each visible pixel after the vertex shading stage. Thus, the output of the vertex shader becomes the input to the pixel shader, and the output of the pixel shader goes to the monitor.

At the time of this writing, WPF only supports pixel shaders. So throughout this chapter as we refer to **shaders**, keep in mind that we are actually referring to pixel shaders.

In WPF, shaders are written using HLSL, a C-like language that provides a high-level abstraction to the GPU assembly instructions.

New and Improved Bitmap Effects

In previous versions of the .NET Framework, bitmap effects were the main way in which rendered output was modified. However, bitmap effects were software-only and could not take advantage of hardware acceleration from the GPU. Animation of a bitmap effect, although possible, was not at all a recommended practice as it would bring the application to a standstill. In fact, in future versions of the WPF framework, these effects will be made obsolete and their usage will result in a no-op.

With shaders, this limitation has been removed, giving way to high-performance GPU-accelerated pixel post-processing. Some of the earlier (slow!) bitmap effects, like `BlurBitmapEffect`, `DropShadowBitmapEffect`, have been changed so that they take advantage of shaders and are now called `BlurEffect`, `DropShadowEffect`, and so on. In short, the term "bitmap" has been dropped from the names of these effects. The new pixel shader related classes are part of the `System.Windows.Media.Effects` namespace and include `Effect`, `ShaderEffect`, and `PixelShader`. We take an in-depth look at these classes throughout this chapter.

Working with Shaders

In this section of the chapter, we walk you through setting up your development environment so that you can reuse existing shaders as well as create your own. We walk through getting what you need for Visual Studio as well as provide an overview of the HLSL.

Setting Up the Environment

Since HLSL is a language specific to DirectX, we are going to need to install the DirectX SDK to gain access to the HLSL compiler. Even though you can customize the DirectX installation so that you just install utilities, make sure you have sufficient disk space before the install. The tool that we use throughout this chapter is `fxc.exe`, the HLSL compiler. Fxc compiles the HLSL source code to pixel shader byte code.

Fxc is a command-line utility and provides the options shown in Table 13.1. Note that this is not an exhaustive listing of options, but rather a list of options most important to us for the purposes of this chapter.

TABLE 13.1   Fxc Command-Line Options

Switch	Description
/T	Picks a shader profile. We use ps_2_0, which is the Shader 2.0 profile.
/E	Used to specify the entry point for the shader. This is equivalent to the Main() function in a C# program.
/Fo	Filename of the compiled output. The convention is to name the file with a .ps extension.

Suppose our HLSL code is defined in the `MyEffect.fx` file, with a `MainPS()` entry point. We can compile this into `MyEffect.ps` using the following command line:

```
Fxc.exe /T ps_2_0 /E MainPS /Fo MyEffect.ps MyEffect.fx
```

Once you have compiled a `.ps` file, you need to include it in your project and set its build action to Resource, as shown in Figure 13.1.

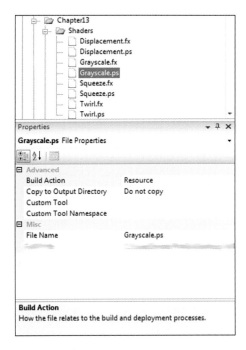

FIGURE 13.1   Build as Resource.

An Overview of HLSL

As mentioned earlier, shaders are written using a domain-specific language called HLSL, which stands for High Level Shading Language. It is a C-like language that provides an abstraction of the GPU instructions and gives developers the added benefit of writing GPU-accelerated code in a language that is GPU-agnostic. This means that, provided the video card is powerful enough, your shader effect will work on any video card without having to alter your source code.

HLSL is a language specific to the DirectX graphics pipeline. In case you're not familiar with it, DirectX is the graphics framework that powers the vast majority of Windows games as well as Xbox 360 games. In this section, we take a tour of the HLSL syntax and highlight some important differences between HLSL and C. For a thorough understanding of the language, refer to the MSDN documentation on HLSL (http://msdn.microsoft.com/en-us/library/bb509561(VS.85).aspx).

HLSL Keywords

Being similar to C, HLSL uses most of the keywords that you might already be familiar with as a C, C++, or C# developer. The following is a set of some of the keywords used by HLSL:

do	While	If	else
return	In	Out	inout
for	Const	True	false
float	sampler	Struct	typedef
void			

HLSL Data Types

HLSL supports most of the standard C data types, like `bool`, `int`, `float`, and `double`, and additional types like vectors and matrices that come in especially handy for manipulating graphics output. For pixel shaders in WPF, the float type is used extensively and is also the best supported. If you need to use Boolean values or integers, you can represent those as a `float` (for example, `0.0` could be `"false"` and `1.0` will be `"true"`). Vectors are special types that represent **tuples** of floats. Shader authors generally use a form of vectors that involve post-fixing `float` with either the digit 2, 3, or 4, as in `float2`, `float3`, and so on. `float2` is a common vector type used to represent a 2D texture coordinate while `float4` represents a color value consisting of an RGB (red, green, blue) value as well as an alpha (transparency) value. `float3` is used to represent an RGB vector with no alpha component.

Vector types have an additional feature called **swizzling**. Swizzling allows you to select the vector components in any order. For example, a `float4` consists of four components (r, g, b, a). However, if you want to only pick the 'r' and 'g' components, you could write it as:

```
float4 color = (1,0,0,1);
float2 comp2 = color.rg;
```

Swizzling provides an interesting capability and can be used to save a lot of time and code. For example, if you want to swap the x and y components of a `float2`, you can write something like this:

```
float2 coord = (0,1);
coord.xy = coord.yx;
```

As with any domain-specific language, you sacrifice the ability to do everything for the ability to do domain-specific things (like swizzling) with greater efficiency.

Samplers

Textures (the brush that is applied to a visual) inside HLSL are accessed via samplers. The effect framework within WPF automatically makes the texture of a visual control available inside HLSL by storing it in the s0 register. Don't worry if this sounds a little confusing now; the code samples will help clear things up, as will some extra reading on MSDN about HLSL. The s0 register can be referenced using the sampler2D construct.

Semantics

Semantics are strings attached to shader inputs and outputs and convey the intended usage of the parameter. They are used for passing information between shader stages. In our case, we are only concerned about the pixel shader stage, and our use of the semantics is limited to this stage.

The common pixel shader semantics are listed in Table 13.2.

TABLE 13.2   Commonly Used Shader Semantics

Semantic	Description	Data Type
COLOR	Diffuse or specular color.	Float4
TEXCOORD	Texture co-ordinate. A 2D point that lies between (0.0,0.0) and (1.0,1.0). +X is to the left, -X to the right. +Y is up, -Y is down.	Float2

Flow Control

HLSL supports most of the standard C flow control constructs, and they behave the way you would expect them to behave:

▶ Looping and conditional: if-else, do-while, for

▶ Standard operators including the "?:" ternary operator.

▶ Statements

▶ Functions

Intrinsic Functions

HLSL gives you a number of math-related functions to assist you in your shader development. These are standard functions that you might find in any mathematics library. The list presents some of the intrinsic HLSL functions. For a complete listing, refer to the MSDN documentation: http://msdn.microsoft.com/en-us/library/bb509611(VS.85).aspx.

- ▶ sin
- ▶ cos
- ▶ atan2
- ▶ lerp (linear interpolation)
- ▶ min
- ▶ max
- ▶ tex2D
- ▶ degrees
- ▶ radians

Writing Custom Shaders

Now that you've been briefly introduced to the world of HLSL, let's get to work on building some of our own custom pixel shaders. In this section, we cover the following types of shaders:

- ▶ Simple shaders with no parameters—The grayscale effect
- ▶ Linking shader parameters using DependencyProperty—The twirl effect

Grayscale Shader

For the first custom shader, let's start out by implementing a simple grayscale effect, as shown in Figure 13.2. The core of the effect involves averaging the red, green, and blue components and setting their values to that average. The alpha value (transparency) is left unchanged.

Here is the HLSL code that produces the grayscale effect:

```
sampler2D implicitInput : register(s0);

float4 MainPS(float2 uv : TEXCOORD) : COLOR
{
    float4 src = tex2D(implicitInput, uv);

    float4 dst;
    float average = (src.r + src.g + src.b)/3;
    dst.rgb = average;
    dst.a = src.a;

    return dst;
}
```

FIGURE 13.2   The grayscale effect.

There are a couple of things to note here. The first line of the preceding code shows the use of the `sampler2D` instance of the texture stored in register `s0`. WPF makes the rasterized texture of the visual control available in this register. To get the color value at the current output coordinate, we use the sampling function `tex2D()` by passing in the texture-map (`implicitInput`) and the texture coordinate.

`MainPS()` is the entry point into the pixel shader. This function is called in parallel by the GPU so it could be processing many output coordinates simultaneously in a massively parallel fashion. The variable `uv` of type `float2` represents the current output coordinate that is being processed. `MainPS` is responsible for giving the output color at that coordinate. This is returned as a `float4` value. `COLOR` and `TEXCOORD` are the semantics for the output color and the current output coordinate, respectively. Note that your HLSL code is applied on a single pixel at time but the GPU will process many pixels in a parallel fashion.

In the statement

```
dst.rgb = average;
```

you can see the use of **swizzling** to automatically replicate the average value into each of the vector components (r, g, and b). The alpha value (component "a") is left unchanged by just copying the value from the source color.

The next step is to compile this code using the `fxc` compiler, which produces the pixel shader byte code. HLSL code is generally stored in files with the `.fx` extension, with an ASCII file encoding. The compiled byte code is generally given the `.ps` extension.

```
Fxc.exe /T ps_2_o /E MainPS /Fo Grayscale.fx Grayscale.ps
```

The preceding command invokes the `fxc` compiler and compiles our HLSL to pixel shader byte code. The `/T` switch is used to pick a pixel shader profile—currently ps_2_0 (version

2.0 of the pixel shader). This is the only supported profile under WPF at the time of writing of this book. The /E switch is used to point at the pixel shader entry point, which in our case is MainPS. The /Fo switch is used to specify the output file (Grayscale.ps).

A compiled pixel shader is only part of the whole story. What we are really interested in is consuming this shader within our WPF application. This is done by subclassing the ShaderEffect class and setting the protected PixelShader property to point to this compiled Grayscale.ps file.

```
public class GrayscaleEffect : ShaderEffect
{
    private static PixelShader ShaderInstance = new PixelShader()
            {UriSource =
    ➥newUri(@"pack://application:,,,/Chapter_PixelShader;component/Shaders/
Grayscale.ps")};
    public static readonly DependencyProperty InputProperty =
    ShaderEffect.RegisterPixelShaderSamplerProperty("Input",
typeof(GrayscaleEffect), 0);

    public Brush Input
    {
        get { return (Brush)GetValue(InputProperty); }
        set { SetValue(InputProperty, value); }
    }


    public GrayscaleEffect()
    {
        PixelShader = ShaderInstance;
    }
}
```

The preceding code brings the grayscale pixel shader into our application. Note how we pass the rasterized output from WPF to the shader using the ShaderEffect. RegisterPixelShaderSamplerProperty. This rasterized output is stored in the shader register s0. WPF automatically populates this input Brush for each render cycle. The Grayscale.ps file is stored as a resource in the current assembly, as shown in Figure 13.3.

Essentially, the shader effect subclass acts as a wrapper around the compiled pixel shader. We can now use this effect in XAML, as shown here:

```
<Image Source="image.jpg"
    Stretch="Fill">
    <Image.Effect>
        <Chapter_PixelShader:GrayscaleEffect />
    </Image.Effect>
</Image>
```

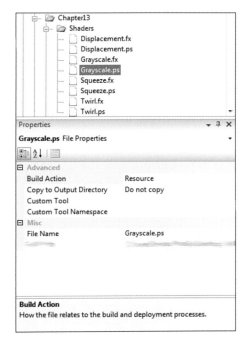

FIGURE 13.3   Grayscale.ps as a resource.

Building a Parameterized Shader: `TwirlEffect`

Now that we've seen the basic life cycle of going from HLSL code to a usable effect within WPF, let's make things a little more interesting and introduce the concept of parameters used to control the shader output. Parameters can be passed to shaders using registers (remember in the preceding example, the rasterized output is sent by WPF using register s0). There are, in all, 32 registers for the shader 2.0 profile (ps_2_0), which works pretty well for most of the shaders. In WPF, we can use a special callback function to pass information from a `DependencyProperty` to a shader register. However, you should note that the data transfer can only happen from the WPF application to the shader and not in reverse.

```
public static readonly DependencyProperty RadiusProperty =
DependencyProperty.Register("Radius", typeof(double),
typeof(TwirlEffect),
new UIPropertyMetadata(PixelShaderConstantCallback(0)));
```

In the preceding snippet, we are passing the value of the radius `DependencyProperty` to the shader register c0 (not to be mistaken with s0) using the `PixelShaderConstantCallback(0)`. The callback takes the index of the register to which the data needs to be passed. Note that the letter "c" in c0 stands for "constant register". Similarly, the letter "s" in s0 stands for "sampler register".

Inside the HLSL code, we can use the value from the c0 register by storing it in a variable:

```
float radius : register(c0);
```

The callback function is invoked each time you change the `DependencyProperty`. This means we can use regular data binding to tweak the shader output on the fly!

Let's put these ideas into action by creating a twirl effect. This effect distorts the image/texture by twisting it about the center, as shown in Figure 13.4. The amount of twist can be controlled by using two parameters: radius and angle. Both of these are dependency properties:

```
public class TwirlEffect : ShaderEffect
{
    private static PixelShader ShaderInstance = new PixelShader()
                                                {UriSource =
➡newUri(@pack"//application:,,,/Chapter_PixelShader;component/Shaders/Twirl.ps")};
    public static readonly DependencyProperty InputProperty =
ShaderEffect.RegisterPixelShaderSamplerProperty("Input",
typeof(GrayscaleEffect), 0);

    public Brush Input
    {
        get { return (Brush)GetValue(InputProperty); }
        set { SetValue(InputProperty, value); }
    }

public static readonly DependencyProperty RadiusProperty =
DependencyProperty.Register("Radius", typeof(double),
            typeof(TwirlEffect),
new UIPropertyMetadata(PixelShaderConstantCallback(0)));

public static readonly DependencyProperty AngleProperty =
DependencyProperty.Register("Angle", typeof(double),
            typeof(TwirlEffect),
new UIPropertyMetadata(PixelShaderConstantCallback(1)));

public double Radius
{
    get { return (double)GetValue(RadiusProperty); }
    set { SetValue(RadiusProperty, value); }
}
public double Angle
{
```

```
    get { return (double)GetValue(AngleProperty); }
    set { SetValue(AngleProperty, value); }
}

public TwirlEffect()
{
    PixelShader = ShaderInstance;
    UpdateShaderValue(InputProperty);
    UpdateShaderValue(RadiusProperty);
    UpdateShaderValue(AngleProperty);
}
```

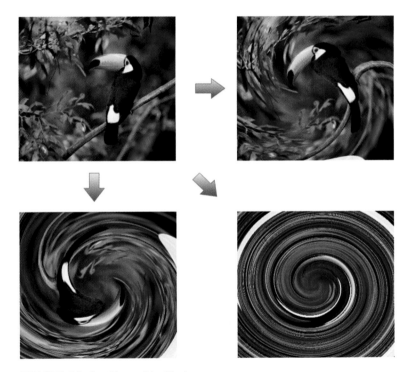

FIGURE 13.4   The twirl effect.

Most of the code is similar to the earlier grayscale effect. RadiusProperty and AngleProperty are the two dependency properties that we can tweak externally to control the shader output. They map to the registers c0 and c1, respectively. We are also calling the UpdateShaderValue() method for each of the dependency properties to force a refresh on the shader at load time. This ensures that you see the effect immediately after it is applied.

Now let's take a look at the HLSL code that is used to produce the twirl effect:

```
sampler2D implicitInput : register(s0);
float radius : register(c0);
float angle : register(c1);

float4 MainPS(float2 uv : TEXCOORD) : COLOR
{
    float2 center = (0.5, 0.5);
        float2 delta = uv - center;

    float distance = length(delta);
    float phi = atan2(delta.y, delta.x) + angle * ((radius - distance)/radius);

    float2 uv1 = center + float2(distance * cos(phi), distance * sin(phi));

    float4 src = tex2D(implicitInput, uv);
    float4 dst = tex2D(implicitInput, uv1);

    return (distance < radius) ? dst : src;
}
```

Note how we store the c0 and c1 register values in the radius and angle variables (lines 2-3). The twirling effect is obtained by calculating the distance of the input pixel from the center and rotating about the center by the given angle. The closer the point to the center, the more extreme the twirling effect. The last line shows that we only apply the twirl effect to points that lie within the given radius. For the points lying outside, we return back the original color value.

The preceding two examples give you a taste of what you can do with shaders. Using some of the intrinsic shader functions and adding a little bit of creativity, you can, come up with some truly amazing effects. Many of the cool effects you see in games (such as lighting, water, glass, etc.) are implemented as pixel shader effects, and some of them can now be used in a WPF application. As with all things in WPF, where you are limited only by your imagination, you should also limit things within the bounds of good taste and good UI design. Effects used purely for the sake of showing an effect generally do not impress anyone and run the risk of irritating your users.

To recap, the following is a list of steps that you need to take to create your own shaders:

1. Write your own shader in HLSL. Compile to a pixel shader byte code file (.ps) using the Fxc tool from the DirectX SDK.

2. Add the .ps file to your project and set the build action to Resource.

3. Subclass ShaderEffect and point its PixelShader property to the compiled .ps file.

4. Set up an `Input DependencyProperty` of type `Brush` and bind it to the shader register s0 using the `ShaderEffect.RegisterPixelShaderSamplerProperty` method.

5. If the shader has parameters, create dependency properties for each parameter and bind them to a shader register using the `PixelShaderConstantCallback`.

6. Call `UpdateShaderValue` for each `DependencyProperty` in the constructor for the shader to trigger the effect on first display.

Animating the Shader Effects

If you remember the topics from Chapter 12, "Custom Animations," and you've noticed how we send input parameters to pixel shaders in this chapter, you may have been wondering whether we can animate those DPs to animate the effect itself. If so, you're right. The effect can be animated over time by animating its input parameters over time. One really common use for animated shader effects is creating animated transitions between visual states in an application.

If you have a particular distortion effect or color-transform effect that you want to use for a transition, you can start by thinking about how it would look at a certain fixed point in time. Then you can go ahead and create a shader that can output such an effect. Next, parameterize the shader such that the output can be varied over time using animation. Connect the parameters to dependency properties and animate them using a `Storyboard`. Since most of the parameters are generally doubles, you can use a `DoubleAnimation` for each of the parameters.

As an example, consider an animation that we might use for the `TwirlEffect` from the previous section. We can use the `Angle` and `Radius` DPs to animate it over time. A simple `DoubleAnimation`-based `Storyboard` like the one shown in the following code can make this work. If you want fancier effects, you can also use a double animation with keyframes.

```
<Storyboard>
    <DoubleAnimation To="0"
        Duration="0:0:3"
Storyboard.TargetName="_twirlEffect"
Storyboard.TargetProperty="Radius" />
    <DoubleAnimation To="0"
        Duration="0:0:3"
Storyboard.TargetName="_twirlEffect"
Storyboard.TargetProperty="Angle" />
</Storyboard>
```

Effect Mapping for GUI Interaction and Eventing

The twirl effect that we presented earlier is an example of a shader effect that distorts the rasterized input from WPF. If you apply such effects to interactive controls like buttons, the mouse and stylus events will not work properly. The reason for this is that the location of the pixel your mouse is hovering over isn't the location of the pixel being used for hit testing on the control (because the pixels have been distorted via shaders). By default, WPF thinks that the bounds of the control are still rectangular and not the newly distorted output. If you try and click on an area outside the distorted shape, it will still be mapped to the control, which might not be the desired functionality.

What we really want is to make shaders cooperate nicely with interactive controls and help WPF in using the proper coordinates. Fortunately, this is exactly what the protected ShaderEffect property EffectMapping does. It acts as an intermediate helper for WPF that takes the raw mouse coordinates and maps them to the distorted effect coordinates. It also has the option to tell WPF whether the given coordinates are valid. This is useful if the mouse event happened outside the distorted shape and you don't want the mouse event to trigger any actions.

In this case, the EffectMapping stage can report that there is no valid transform for the given coordinate. Besides mapping mouse coordinates, the EffectMapping is also invoked when explicitly calling the TransformToAncestor(), TransformToVisual(), TransformToDescendant(), and TranslateToPoint() methods. Therefore, if a ShaderEffect is applied to a UIElement that distorts the shape, EffectMapping is the helper transform that can guide WPF in using the right coordinates.

EffectMapping is of type GeneralTransform, a transform object that does coordinate transformations. If you are building a shader effect that outputs a distorted shape, a GeneralTransform-derived class also needs to be implemented with a few overridden methods. Note that you need to provide the EffectMapping only if you want your users to interact with the shader-distorted visuals. This step can be skipped for non-interactive scenarios.

Let's take an example of a simple shader effect that distorts the sampler input (the rasterized WPF texture). In Figure 13.5, we consider a squeeze effect that squishes the texture along the x-axis.

The HLSL for the SqueezeEffect can be seen in the following snippet (Squeeze.fx):

```
sampler2D implicitInput : register(s0);
float left : register(c0);
float right : register(c1);


float2 GetTextureCoord(float2 uv)
{
    float tx = lerp(0, 1, (uv.x-left)/(right-left));
    float2 pos = float2(tx, uv.y);

    return pos;
}
```

```
float4 MainPS(float2 uv : TEXCOORD) : COLOR
{
    if (uv.x >= left && uv.x <= right)
    {
        float2 pos = GetTextureCoord(uv);
        return tex2D(implicitInput, pos);
    }
    else return float4(0,0,0,0);
}
```

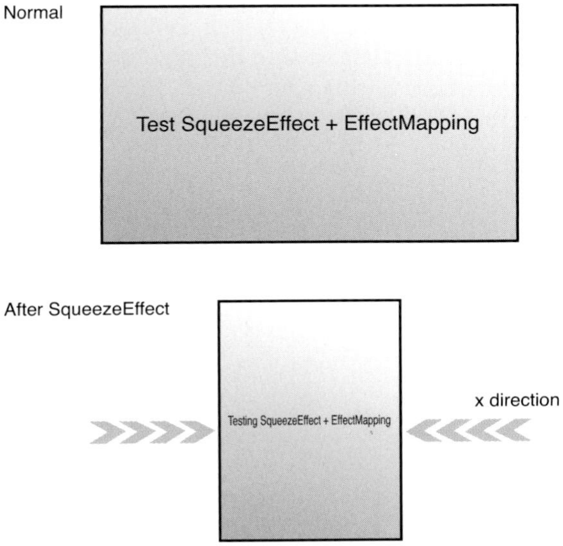

Normal

Test SqueezeEffect + EffectMapping

After SqueezeEffect

Testing SqueezeEffect + EffectMapping

x direction

FIGURE 13.5   Squeeze effect illustration.

Most of the HLSL code here should look familiar to you by now. The shader has two parameters to identify the left and right bounds for the squeeze. Note that we also use functions to divide the shader logic. The GetTextureCoord() function does the mapping of
the input texture coordinates to the squeezed output coordinates. Essentially we are
remapping the input coordinates to a new interval defined by the left and right parameters.

The backing C# class derives from ShaderEffect and sets up the dependency properties.
This is almost the same as the previous shader effect classes with one important difference. In SqueezeEffect, the EffectMapping property has been overridden to allow the
displayed and actual distorted coordinates to match:

```
private SqueezeTransform _transform = new SqueezeTransform();
protected override GeneralTransform EffectMapping
{
```

```
    get
    {
        _transform.Left = Left;
        _transform.Right = Right;
         return _transform;
    }
}
```

SqueezeTransform is our custom transform class that helps in properly mapping the mouse coordinates to the distorted coordinate space. In the get accessor, you can see that we are passing some information back to the transform to help in the calculations. Each time a mouse event occurs on the element, the EffectMapping is queried to find out the real position. SqueezeTransform derives from GeneralTransform and overrides the TryTransform() method that does the real work of converting coordinates. That code is shown here:

```
public override bool TryTransform(Point inPoint, out Point result)
{
    result = new Point();
    if (IsInverse)
    {
        if (inPoint.X < Left ¦¦ inPoint.X > Right)
            return false; // Transform does not exist


        double ratio = (inPoint.X - Left)/(Right - Left);
        result.X = inPoint.X* ratio;
        result.Y = inPoint.Y;
    }
    else
    {
        double ratio = inPoint.X;
        result.X = Left + (Right-Left) * ratio;
        result.Y = inPoint.Y;
    }

    return true;
}
```

IsInverse is a private property that we use to keep track of the direction of mapping. Its value is changed when the overridden Inverse property gets called:

```
public override GeneralTransform Inverse
{
    get
    {
```

```
    SqueezeTransform transform = this.Clone() as SqueezeTransform;
    transform.IsInverse = !IsInverse;

    return transform;
    }
}
```

When the mouse hovers on the button that has a `SqueezeEffect`, the `Inverse` property gets called to determine the actual effect coordinates. Here we're cloning the current instance of the `SqueezeTransform` and flipping its `IsInverse` flag. Since the inverse is again a `SqueezeTransform`, its `TryTransform()` method is called with the current mouse coordinates. If the point lies inside the squeezed texture, we return the mapped coordinates and mark it as a valid transform. If the point lies outside the squeezed texture, we report that there is no transform available by returning false from the method.

When you run the effect mapping sample that comes with the code for this chapter, you can see this in action by hovering on the squeezed button. The events only work when the mouse events happen inside the squeezed texture.

Multi-Input Shaders

In the examples so far, we have seen the use of only one input texture to the shader. The default behavior of a shader is to take the rendered output of the `UIElement` on which the effect has been set and present it to the shader. This is considered the "implicit input" to the shader. However, WPF also supports the notion of supplying multiple texture inputs to a single shader with each being set on a different sampler register (sampler registers all start with the letter s). By default, the implicit input to the shader is stored in sampler register s0. Additional inputs can be set on sampler registers s1 and up. There are in all correct, XX sampler registers for the pixel shader 2.0 profile.

Multiple inputs to the shader are useful when you want the default input image to be modified based on a secondary input. For certain shader effects that involve the blending of two or more images or textures, the additional sampler inputs are the only way to accomplish the task. With multiple shader inputs and parameters, you have tremendous power and flexibility in creating amazing effects.

Scaling of Shader Inputs

The inputs to the shader are always scaled to the size of the `UIElement` on which the shader effect was applied. For example, if you set a shader effect on a `Panel` that is 400x500, with an additional input image (ImageBrush) of size 100x100, the smaller image brush will be resized to 400x500 before the pixel shader is invoked. In other words, all additional sampler inputs will be the same size as the first, implicit input.

Using `DisplacementFilter` as a Multi-Input Shader Effect

To demonstrate the use of multiple inputs to the shader, let's consider a simple `DisplacementFilter` that distorts the implicit input image based on a grayscale gradient image (`LinearGradient` or `RadialGradient`). The idea is to displace the pixels in the input image by an amount proportional to the corresponding pixel value of the gradient image. Thus, the gradient image is our additional image to the `DisplacementShaderEffect`. Note that the secondary input to the DisplacementFilter can be any brush, not necessarily a gradient brush.

```
<Grid>
    <Rectangle x:Name="DisplacementVisual"
                Fill="{StaticResource GradientBrush}" />
    <Image Source="/Resources;component/Shared/toucan.jpg"
                Stretch="Fill">
        <Image.Effect>
            <ShaderLibrary:DisplacementEffect x:Name="Effect"
                                        ScaleX="{Binding Value,
ElementName=_scaleXSlider}"
                                        ScaleY="{Binding Value,
ElementName=_scaleYSlider}">
                <ShaderLibrary:DisplacementEffect.Input2>
                    <VisualBrush Visual="{Binding ElementName=DisplacementVisual}" />
                </ShaderLibrary:DisplacementEffect.Input2>
            </ShaderLibrary:DisplacementEffect>

        </Image.Effect>
    </Image>
</Grid>
```

`Input2` is a `DependencyProperty` defined on the `DisplacementshaderEffect` that stores the additional input in the sampler register s1.

```
public static readonly DependencyProperty Input2Property =
                ShaderEffect.RegisterPixelShaderSamplerProperty("Input2",
typeof(DisplacementShaderEffect), 1);
```

The parameter "1" to the `RegisterPixelShaderSamplerProperty()` method refers to the sampler register s1.

In the preceding XAML snippet, we set the gradient brush as a fill on the `Rectangle` and then use the `VisualBrush` of the rectangle as our `Input2`. You may be wondering why we went this roundabout way to accomplish what we wanted to do. This is because WPF only supports an `ImageBrush` or a `VisualBrush` as the sampler input. If you set the `GradientBrush` resource as the value for `Input2`, an exception will be thrown telling you that this is an unsupported operation.

The `.fx` file for the `DisplacementShaderEffect` is fairly straightforward and is shown here:

```
sampler2D input1 : register(S0);
sampler2D input2 : register(S1);
```

```
float scaleX : register(C0);
float scaleY : register(C1);

float4 MainPS(float2 uv : TEXCOORD) : COLOR
{
    float component = tex2D(input2, uv).r;
    float dispX = ((component - 0.5) * scaleX);
    float dispY = ((component - 0.5) * scaleY);

    float4 color = tex2D(input1, float2(uv.x + dispX, uv.y + dispY));
    return color;
}
```

Note the reference to the additional shader input in sampler register s1. scaleX and scaleY are two parameters set on the shader. The amount of displacement of the source pixel is based on the corresponding pixel value stored in input2. This difference is just a displacement from the midvalue of 0.5, scaled by a factor (scaleX or scaleY).

With a RadialGradientBrush and a SpreadMethod of Repeat, we can get a wavy effect on the input image, as shown in Figure 13.6.

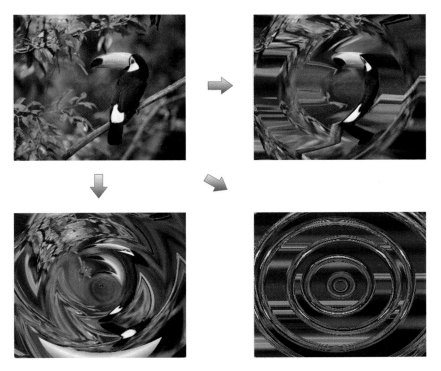

FIGURE 13.6   Displacement shader effect.

A Useful Tool

The development cycle of write-compile-test for authoring a pixel shader can be lengthy. For a much faster turnaround, you can use a tool called Shazzam by Walt Ritscher. In the author's very own words:

> The goal of Shazzam is to make it simple to edit and test WPF Pixel Shader Effects. Shazzam compiles HLSL code, auto-generates C#/VB classes, and creates a testing page for each effect. Plus it supports animations of the effect.

Figure 13.7 shows a screenshot of the tool in action.

You can download Shazzam from http://shazzam.codeplex.com/.

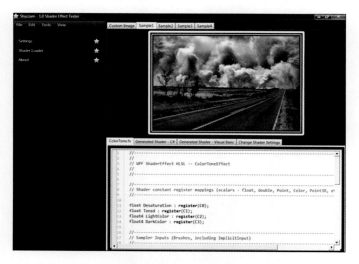

FIGURE 13.7   The Shazzam tool.

Summary

Pixel shaders are an incredibly powerful tool in the arsenal of a custom WPF control developer or any developer who wants to add extra flare to an application to make it stand out from the rest of the crowd. After reading this chapter, you should now be ready to start using pixel shaders in your own applications and even creating your own pixel shaders.

The following is a list of PDF files that were used as references in writing this chapter:

http://www2.imm.dtu.dk/visiondag/VD03/grafisk/WolfgangEngel.pdf

http://www.cs.uoi.gr/~fudos/grad-exer2/hlsl-intro.pdf

CHAPTER 14

Events, Commands, and Focus

This chapter provides detailed information on some advanced UI building concepts: routed events, commands, and focus. Each of the topics in this chapter is fairly isolated; you can skip to the section that interests you most, or you can read the chapter from start to finish. Reading the entire chapter, however, gives you a more thorough understanding of how to build responsive, well-architected applications that maximize the use and efficiency of routed events, commands, and control focus.

Routed Events

UI programming is generally event-driven. For example, a user performs some action that in turn causes a control to raise an event. Then actions are taken by code you write that handles the event through a subscription to that event. In this regard, WPF is no different from typical UI systems. But the kind of events that you deal with in WPF are usually more specialized, and they are built on top of the standard .NET CLR event system.

These WPF-specialized events are called *routed events,* and they form the core building blocks of the WPF event system. The biggest advantage of a routed event over a regular CLR event is that they can be propagated (routed) through the visual tree and raised on multiple nodes within the tree. The RoutedEvent class gets its name from the notion that it travels a specific route through the element tree. This route is defined by the RoutingStrategy, which can be one of Direct, Bubbling, or Tunneling.

The `Direct` strategy raises the event only on the source object. `Bubbling` routes the event from the source all the way up to the root. `Tunneling` follows the opposite path; the event travels from the root down to the source. `Tunneling` events, also called `Preview` events, occur before the `Bubbling` or `Direct` events. Most events in WPF have both a `Bubbling` and a `Tunneling` version. For example, a `MouseDown` event, which is a `Bubbling` event, has a `PreviewMouseDown` event as well that follows a `Tunneling` strategy. The use of the `Preview` prefix is a convention that allows developers to quickly and easily identify `Tunneling` events. Figure 14.1 shows the different routing strategies clearly.

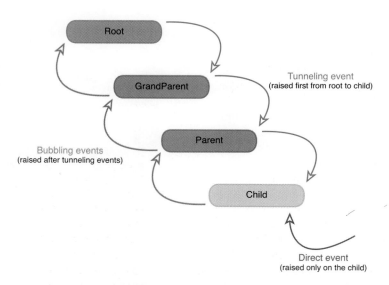

FIGURE 14.1   Routed events and their routes and orders.

`RoutedEvents` are created as `public static readonly` instances and are registered with the WPF event system through the `EventManager.RegisterRoutedEvent()` method. Here is code that shows how the `MouseLeftButtonDown` event is registered on the `UIElement`:

```
public static readonly RoutedEvent MouseLeftButtonDownEvent =
EventManager.RegisterRoutedEvent("MouseLeftButtonDown", RoutingStrategy.Direct,
typeof(MouseButtonEventHandler), typeof(UIElement));
```

The parameters are, in order: the event name, the routing strategy, the type of event handler, and finally the type of the event owner. In the preceding example, `UIElement` is set as the owner of the `MouseLeftButtonDown` event, which is a direct-strategy event.

To raise the routed event, one can use the `RaiseEvent` method defined on `UIElement`. For example, consider a simple `SearchBar` user control that defines a `SearchInvoked` routed event. This event is raised when the user presses the Enter key on the textbox or clicks the search-button. The following snippet shows the event definition as well as invoking this event. The `RaiseSearchInvoked` method is called from the event handlers for the `KeyDown` event on the textbox and the `Click` event on the search-button.

```
        public static readonly RoutedEvent SearchInvoked =
EventManager.RegisterRoutedEvent("SearchInvoked",
        RoutingStrategy.Bubble,
        typeof (RoutedEventHandler),
        typeof (SearchBar));

        private void RaiseSearchInvoked(string searchText)
        {
            var args = new SearchEventArgs()
                            {
                                SearchText = searchText,
                            RoutedEvent = SearchInvoked
                            };

            RaiseEvent(args);
        }
```

In the preceding examples, we have shown how you can create your own custom `RoutedEvents` in your own UI controls and classes. However, sometimes you may find that the event you want is already available on some other class. Instead of defining new `RoutedEvents`, the WPF event system allows you to reuse and repurpose existing events. For example, let's say you wanted your control to have a `SelectedEvent`. Instead of registering a new event for the same purpose, you can reuse the existing event on the `System.Windows.Primitives.Selector` class. This can be done by marking your custom control (in this case `MyCustomControl`) as an additional owner of this event. `RoutedEvent` exposes a static method called `AddOwner()` that can be used for exactly this purpose.

```
public static readonly RoutedEvent SelectedEvent =
Selector.SelectedEvent.AddOwner(typeof(MyCustomControl));
```

Routed Events, Event Triggers, and Property Mirrors

It is a good practice to expose the right set of `RoutedEvents` for external consumption on your control. With a careful choice, many of the visual changes in your interface can be controlled by `EventTriggers` that listen to `RoutedEvents`. `EventTriggers`, when used in a `ControlTemplate` or a style, can be used to start or stop a `Storyboard` when a particular `RoutedEvent` is raised. For example, a popular usage of this technique is to start an animation as soon as a control is loaded. This can be done with an `EventTrigger` that starts the storyboard when the `FrameworkElement.Loaded` routed event is fired.

However, `EventTrigger` only supports `TriggerActions` and no property setters. This means that you cannot change individual properties of a control inside an `EventTrigger`. This has to be done using the standard triggers (Trigger or DataTrigger). But these triggers do not support `RoutedEvents` and rely on property changes. In other words, we need to expose a `RoutedEvent` as a `DependencyProperty`. WPF uses this technique of mirroring `RoutedEvents` as properties throughout the framework. For example, `UIElement.MouseEnter` and `UIElement.MouseMove` are mirrored by `UIElement.IsMouseOver`. `ListBox.SelectedEvent` is mirrored by a `ListBoxItem.IsSelected` property. `UIElement.GetMouseCaptureEvent` is mirrored by `UIElement.IsMouseCaptured` and so on.

Property mirrors are usually set when the actual event occurs and cleared when some other event or state-change occurs in the control. For example, for the `SearchBar` user control we saw earlier, we can set a Boolean `IsSearchInvoked` property whenever the `SearchInvoked` event is raised. The property can be cleared when the user starts typing in the textbox or changes focus between the textbox and the search-button.

This capturing of event-driven state using the event-as-property technique is useful for scenarios where only simple property changes are needed rather than storyboards.

Source and OriginalSource in RoutedEventArgs

WPF sets the `OriginalSource` before any class handlers or instance handlers are invoked. It is based on pure hit testing and cannot be modified by any of the handlers. However, the class handler can choose to modify the `Source` property if the element on which the hit testing happened is too primitive for external consumption. For example, if you have a `Button` that has been styled, the `Click` event may have its `OriginalSource` pointed at a deeply nested visual (say inside a `ControlTemplate` or a `DataTemplate`). The `Source`, however, will be pointing to the `Button` instance. It is up to the custom control author to decide whether the `Source` property needs to be changed for the `RoutedEventArgs`.

Routed events also work well when you want to inform the outside world about changes in your control. A `UserControl` that wraps a set of related controls can expose `RoutedEvents` that abstract one or more events happening internal to the control. The SearchBar user control we saw earlier is a good example since it wraps a text box and a button and exposes the SearchInvoked event when you press the Enter key on the text box or click the button. Instead of burdening the consumers of your control with listening for both the Enter key and the mouse click they can now subscribe to a single SearchInvoked routed event. This neatly abstracts the inner controls, hides the consumer from the actual implementation of your control, and generally makes everything cleaner.

Attached Events

As the name suggests, attached events are similar in concept to attached properties. Just like you use attached properties on a class, which are not defined on the class itself, attached events allow you to associate event-handlers for routed events not defined on the class itself. This is a useful concept and allows a degree of separation between the source of the event and the target that handles the event. It is also interesting to note that neither the object raising the event (sender of the event) nor the target handling the event *"own"* that event. This should become clear in the following example.

Imagine you have a StackPanel that houses a set of buttons where each button causes a slightly different action on the UI. You could do that by listening to the Click event of each Button individually, or more simply use Attached Events and associate the Click event only once. We can add the attached event to the parent container, that is, the StackPanel, using the Button.Click syntax, as shown in the following code snippet:

```
<StackPanel Button.Click="OnButtonClick">
    <Button x:Name="first" Content="First" />
    <Button x:Name="second" Content="Second" />
    <Button x:Name="third" Content="Third" />
    <Button x:Name="fourth" Content="Fourth" />
    <Button x:Name="fifth" Content="Fifth" />
</StackPanel>
private void OnButtonClick(object sender, RoutedEventArgs e)
        {
    Button b = e.Source as Button;
    var message = string.Empty;
    switch (b.Name)
    {
        case "first":
            message = "You have clicked the First button";
            break;
        case "second":
            message = "You have clicked on the Second button";
            break;
        default:
            message = "You have clicked the Third, Fourth, or Fifth button";
            break;
    }
    MessageBox.Show(message);
}
```

In the OnButtonClick event handler, we differentiate between the controls using their names (x:Name property). You can also see that attached events require the use of a fully qualified event name (<Event-Owner>.<Event-Name>) that is associated with the parent element (in our case, the StackPanel). This is again similar to the use of attached properties, where you need to fully qualify the name of the property with the type that defines that property.

Within the event handler, the *sender* parameter points to the StackPanel and **not** the button instance, as one would expect. In other words, the event is raised on the StackPanel rather than the Button instance. To get to the button, we have to use the RoutedEventArgs.Source property. If you recall from our preceding discussion, where we

14

mentioned that neither the sender nor the target is the real "owner" of the event, we can now see why that is the case. The StackPanel, which is the sender and also the target of the event, is not the real "owner" of the Click event. This is certainly a thing to remember when working with attached events.

As seen so far, attached events clearly simplify the association of a common event handler for a set of controls. They are also useful if you want to handle an event originating deep in your visual tree, somewhere higher up in the hierarchy. Under the hood, attached events are just routed events and can propagate along the visual tree with the bubbling or tunneling strategy. The <Event-Owner>.<Event-Name> syntax that we saw earlier is just a convenient way to use them in XAML. If you would like to add/remove event-handlers for attached events in code, you can use the UIElement.AddHandler and UIElement.RemoveHandler methods respectively. In fact, the XAML syntax that we saw earlier gets compiled to the UIElement.AddHandler method call, as shown below:

```
((System.Windows.Controls.StackPanel)(target)).AddHandler(System.Windows.Controls.P
rimitiv
es.ButtonBase.ClickEvent, new
System.Windows.RoutedEventHandler(this.OnButtonClick));
```

Defining Your Own Attached Events

With a background in attached events, we can now take a look at how you can support attached events for your own RoutedEvents. To do that, two pattern methods need to be implemented in the class that defines the RoutedEvent: Add*Handler() and Remove*Handler(), where the * refers to the name of the RoutedEvent. For example, the System.Windows.Input.Mouse class defines the MouseDown event as an attached event by implementing the AddMouseDownHandler() and RemoveMouseDownHandler(). Note that the * is replaced by the string "MouseDown" in the event handlers.

```
public static void AddMouseDownHandler(DependencyObject element,
MouseButtonEventHandler
handler)
{
    UIElement.AddHandler(element, MouseDownEvent, handler);
}
public static void RemoveMouseDownHandler(DependencyObject element,
MouseButtonEventHandler handler)
{
    UIElement.RemoveHandler(element, MouseDownEvent, handler);
}
```

With that, you can use the Mouse.MouseDown="<event-handler>" syntax to associate a handler for the attached event, right within XAML.

Class Handlers

We saw earlier that RoutedEvents propagate on the visual tree with a route determined by the event's routing strategy. WPF gives us the ability to control the propagation of a RoutedEvent using the associated RoutedEventArg's Handled property. By setting the Handled property to true, the propagation of a RoutedEvent can be terminated for a bubbling or tunneling routing strategy. This may lead us to believe that we can never really see all the events that happen in an application. Fortunately, that is not the case, and WPF gives us a way out using the power of class handlers.

By registering a class handler for a certain kind of event, it is possible to see all instances of that event occurring in the application, including ones that have been handled.

> **A Case for Class Handlers**
>
> A practical use of registering class handlers is for UI Auditing. Say you wanted to record some metrics for how often users of your application are using different controls. To detect the usage of a control, you would want to know the RoutedEvents that originate from that control. It is possible that some of these events are getting handled at some parent or ancestor in your visual tree, because of which you won't see all the events that are getting raised. The only reliable way to detect all events is to register class handlers for the various RoutedEvents that you are interested in. This is also a non-intrusive way to detect events since you don't have to modify your control code specifically for UI Auditing.

EventManager.RegisterClassHandler() is the API to hook a class handler for a particular RoutedEvent. Its signature looks like so:

```
public static void RegisterClassHandler(Type classType, RoutedEvent routedEvent,
➥Delegate
handler, bool handledEventsToo)
```

The first parameter declares the System.Type on which class handler should be defined. This means that all events that surface up to this type get passed on to your handler. The RoutedEvent declares the event that is of interest to you and handler is the Delegate that handles this event. The last Boolean parameter can be set to true if you are interested in events that are already handled (RoutedEventArgs.Handled = True).

As an example, consider a class handler that listens to all MouseDown events:

```
static ClassHandlerExample()
{
    EventManager.RegisterClassHandler(typeof(ClassHandlerExample),
➥Mouse.MouseDownEvent,
        new RoutedEventHandler(OnMouseDownClassHandler), true);
}

private static void OnMouseDownClassHandler(object sender, RoutedEventArgs e1)
{
```

```
    Debug.WriteLine("MouseDownEvent Occurred");
}
```

As an extreme example, if you want to take a peek at all RoutedEvents that occur in your application, you can do the following:

```
private static void HandleAllRoutedEvents()
{
    var events = EventManager.GetRoutedEvents();
    foreach (RoutedEvent routedEvent in events)
    {
        EventManager.RegisterClassHandler(typeof(ClassHandlerExample), routedEvent,
        new RoutedEventHandler(AllEventsClassHandler), true);
    }
}


private static void AllEventsClassHandler(object sender, RoutedEventArgs e)
{
    // Handle the routed event
}
```

The key concept here is the use of the EventManager.GetRoutedEvents() method that gives you all the RoutedEvents registered with the WPF event system.

Weak Events Using Weak References

Associating event handlers with an event comes with an implicit responsibility to remove that handler when there is no need for the handler anymore. This is because subscribing to events causes the event-source to maintain a strong reference to the event listener. If the listener's lifetime is much shorter than the source, it will not get garbage collected at the right time, thus causing a memory leak. A typical scenario where the source outlives the listeners is in the case of data binding. When a control's property is data-bound to some long-living model object, it starts listening to the property change events on the model. If the control gets removed from the visual tree, the model object continues to maintain a strong reference to the control, resulting in a memory leak. This could be a serious problem in the case of a large application, where many data-bound controls are added and removed from the visual tree. Thankfully, WPF provides a design pattern, called *weak events*, to prevent this particular situation.

To generalize this further, weak events are useful if any of the following applies:

▶ The lifetime of the association between the event source and the event listener is not clear.

▶ The listener does not know when to detach itself from the event.

▶ The source of the event lives longer than the listener to the event.

The data-binding scenario that we considered previously falls under the last category where the source outlives the listener. Here the model object has no relationship with the WPF control. Since the control listens to the property-change events on the model, the model stores a strong reference to the control. When the control gets removed from the visual tree, there is no communication with the model, which is why weak events become relevant and help in avoiding a memory leak.

Implementing the Weak Event Pattern

Now that we understand the problem that the weak event pattern tries to solve, let's look at the WPF implementation that addresses it. Clearly we want to avoid having strong references between the source of the event# and the listener. Also the standard C# syntax of associating events: <source>.<event> += <listener-delegate> cannot be used anymore, since it implicitly creates a strong reference. What we are looking for is an alternate way to subscribe to events such that no strong references are created. Enter the WeakEventManager.

The System.Windows.WeakEventManager (WEM) is a class that provides the mechanism to avoid strong references between the source and listener. It does so by using a WeakReference to access the listener object. This allows the listener instance to be garbage collected if there is no strong reference pointing to it, which is certainly what we want. Additionally, the WEM also provides a way to register listeners for the event. Since the WEM is the one maintaining the weak reference to the listener, it only makes sense for it to also provide the event-registering mechanism.

You can think of the WEM as a wrapper around the event-source with no strong references to listeners and providing an alternate way for listeners to subscribe to the event. The WEM, however, is only one half of the weak event pattern. The other half is about actually delivering events to the listener. If there is an alternate means to subscribe there should also be an alternate way to receive events. This is exactly where the IWeakEventListener comes in. As the name suggests, it is an interface that the listener should implement in order to receive events. The WEM specifically checks for the presence of this interface when a listener subscribes. The IWeakEventListener interface, as shown in the snippet below, consists of only one method called ReceiveWeakEvent:

```
public interface IWeakEventListener
{
    bool ReceiveWeakEvent(Type managerType, object sender, EventArgs e);
}
```

Don't worry about the signature as of now. We will have an in-depth look at this interface and also the WeakEventManager in the following section.

Now that we understand what it means to implement the weak event pattern, let's look at a scenario where the pattern can be used. Through this example, we will show you how the WeakEventManager and the IWeakEventListener collaborate to handle events.

Imagine we have an object of type `DataSource`, a custom type that raises an event called `DataChanged`. The event is raised whenever some data of the `DataSource` instance changes. The signature of the `DataChanged` event looks like so:

```
public event EventHandler DataChanged;
```

Also we have custom controls that implicitly subscribe to this event whenever they are instantiated. These controls could be added and removed on the fly by the user. The `DataSource` instance is independent of these custom controls and is not related in any way. The controls have a much shorter lifetime than the `DataSource`, but their subscription to the `DataChanged` event causes the `DataSource` instance to maintain strong references to the controls. We know from our previous discussion that this is a breeding ground for memory leaks. Certainly we don't want the lifetime of the controls to be influenced by the `DataSource` instance. To remedy the situation, we implement the `WeakEvent` pattern, which as we know consists of the `WeakEventManager` and an implementation of the `IWeakEventListener` interface. Let's look at each of them in turn.

Subclassing the Weak Event Manager

The WEM is actually an abstract class and cannot be used directly. Thus, the first step to using a WEM is to subclass it. Also, a WEM has a one-to-one association with the event that is, you cannot use a single WEM subclass for more than one event. However if you have two events with the same signatures, you could piggy back on the same WEM.

For our example, we need a WEM-subclass for the `DataChanged` event, which we call `DataChangedEventManager`. This class overrides two abstract methods of the WEM: `StartListening` and `StopListening`, both of which take in the source object as a parameter. These methods are used to cast the source object to the actual type and then subscribe or unsubscribe to the event. This is a safe cast because the WEM is tied to a particular event signature and also knows the type of the source. The following code shows the complete implementation of the `DataChangedEventManager`:

```
public class DataChangedEventManager : WeakEventManager
{
    private static DataChangedEventManager _mgr;
    private DataChangedEventManager() {}

    public static void AddListener(DataSource source, IWeakEventListener
    ➥listener)
    {
        CurrentManager.ProtectedAddListener(source, listener);
    }

    public static void RemoveListener(DataSource source, IWeakEventListener
    ➥listener)
    {
        CurrentManager.ProtectedRemoveListener(source, listener);
    }
```

```csharp
protected override void StartListening(object source)
{
    DataSource evtSource = source as DataSource;
    evtSource.DataChanged += PrivateOnDataChanged;
}

protected override void StopListening(object source)
{
    DataSource evtSource = source as DataSource;
    evtSource.DataChanged -= PrivateOnDataChanged;
}

private void PrivateOnDataChanged(object sender, EventArgs e)
{
    DeliverEvent(sender, e);
}

private static DataChangedEventManager CurrentManager
{
    get
    {
        Type mgrType = typeof (DataChangedEventManager);
        _mgr = GetCurrentManager(mgrType) as DataChangedEventManager;
        if (_mgr == null)
        {
            _mgr = new DataChangedEventManager();
            SetCurrentManager(mgrType, _mgr);
        }

        return _mgr;
    }
}
        }
    }
}
```

You can see the casting of the passed-in source object in the StartListening and StopListening overrides. We also subscribe to the DataChanged event with a private method: PrivateOnDataChanged. This method internally calls the protected method DeliverEvent, which is defined on the WeakEventManager class. As the name suggests, DeliverEvent is the one responsible for forwarding the events happening on the DataSource to the listeners. Internally it checks whether the listener (an instance of IWeakEventListener) still exists and forwards the event if present. If not, it is removed from the list of listeners. This check is possible because the WEM uses a weak reference to access the listener.

You can also see two public methods: AddListener and RemoveListener. These methods provide the alternate means to subscribe to the DataChanged event. Since they are static methods, you don't have to create an instance of the DataChangedEventManager to use them. This works great because a listener should not be concerned with the mechanics of instantiating the DataChangedEventManager.

Internally we maintain a singleton instance of the DataChangedEventManager and use the private CurrentManager property to reference this singleton. Inside the getter for this method, we ensure the singleton nature of our class by creating only one instance. The WeakEventManager internally maintains a dictionary of all the different manager instances, keyed by their type. In the getter for the CurrentManager property, we check this dictionary using the protected GetCurrentManager method. If no instance is found, we create one and update the dictionary using SetCurrentManager.

The core functionality of the DataChangedEventManager can be distilled to two things:

1. *Providing the alternate means to register the event* with the AddListener, RemoveListener public methods and the StartListening and StopListening overrides.

2. *Delivering the event* using the PrivateOnDataChanged method, which internally calls the protected DeliverEvent method.

Delivering Events Via the IWeakEventListener

So far we have only one half of implementing the weak event pattern. The other half is about receiving the event on the listener. Toward the end of the previous section, we saw that the WEM subclass uses the protected DeliverEvent method to dispatch the event to the listener. The WEM works with the assumption that a listener that wants to subscribe to a weak event will implement the IWeakEventListener interface. In fact, the AddListener and RemoveListener methods take an IWeakEventListener as a parameter.

The interface contains only one method: ReceiveWeakEvent. A typical implementation might look like so:

```
public bool ReceiveWeakEvent(Type managerType, object sender, EventArgs e)
{
    if (managerType == typeof(DataChangedEventManager))
    {
        // Do some action
        return true;
    }

    return false;
}
```

Here, we check if the managerType parameter is of the right type since we are only interested in the DataChanged event. This is a common practice since you may be interested in receiving multiple weak events, in which case you will have a few more checks. The sender parameter, as expected, points to the event-source.

WPF provides a couple different implementations of the weak event pattern. There is one for the `INotifyPropertyChanged.PropertyChanged` event (provided by the `System.ComponentModel.PropertyChangedEventManager`), which of course is used for data-binding scenarios. There are also others for collection change events, focus change events, and so on. As a parting note before we move on to the next section, the name `WeakEventManager` comes from the fact that it uses `WeakReferences` to reference the listeners. If you explore this class using `Reflector`, you find the usage of `WeakReference` when a listener gets added to the list.

As an aside, Greg Schechter has a slightly different implementation of the weak events, which he calls Weak Delegates. Take a look at http://blogs.msdn.com/greg_schechter/archive/2004/05/27/143605.aspx.

Commands

The commanding infrastructure provides one more abstraction for performing actions whenever interesting changes happen in your application. Events and properties are two ways of informing the interesting changes happening in a control, but a command gives you a more loosely coupled abstraction that separates the source of the command and the target that finally handles the command.

If you have a common action that needs to be performed by multiple input gestures (keyboard presses or mouse clicks or a combination of mouse and keyboard hits, such as Ctrl + Click) or `RoutedEvents`, commands can handle that. So for example, a `Refresh` command in a browser can be tied to pressing the F5 key on the keyboard and also the mouse click on the toolbar button. Both of them raise a common `Refresh` command that gets handled at a common point.

Events are directed actions since they are specifically raised on a particular control. This is evident from the fact that the sender of the event is passed into the event-handler for that event. Commands on the other hand are open-ended actions, completely dissociating the source of the command from the target that handles it.

Commands in WPF implement the `ICommand` interface, which is shown in the snippet below:

```
public interface ICommand
{
    // Events
    event EventHandler CanExecuteChanged;

    // Methods
    bool CanExecute(object parameter);
    void Execute(object parameter);
}
```

The `CanExecute` method is a filter method that gets called before the `Execute`. Only when the `CanExecute` returns true does the `Execute` method get called. The `CanExecuteChanged` event is used to indicate the change in the command's ability to execute. This typically happens when the output of the CanExecute method changes. The following example demonstrates these concepts with a simple ICommand implementation:

```csharp
public class TestCommand : ICommand
{
    Random _random = new Random();
    public void Execute(object parameter)
    {
        Debug.WriteLine("TestCommand Executed");
    }

    public bool CanExecute(object parameter)
    {
        return (_random.NextDouble() < 0.5);
    }

    public event EventHandler CanExecuteChanged
    {
        add
        {
            CommandManager.RequerySuggested += value;
        }
        remove
        {
            CommandManager.RequerySuggested -= value;
        }
    }
}
```

The TestCommand randomly changes the status of its CanExecute method, which causes its ability to execute to fluctuate. Additionally, we are also tying the CanExecuteChanged event to the CommandManager's RequerySuggested event. We get to the CommandManager in a later section, but for now think of this event as WPF's mechanism to determine the execution status of a command.

Now, the TestCommand by itself is not so useful unless it is associated with a control. We do just that in the following snippet. Here we set up a new TestCommand instance and assign it to the button's Command property. We also set up a CommandBinding, which actually makes the command work. CommandBinding is discussed later. Note that the code below can also be written declaratively. We leave that as a reader exercise.

```csharp
public SimpleCommandingExample()
{
    InitializeComponent();

    var command = new TestCommand();
```

```
    this.CommandBindings.Add(new CommandBinding(command));
    CommandRaiserButton.Command = command;
}
```

A `Button` control automatically enables or disables itself depending on the output of its command's `CanExecute` method. If you run the `SimpleCommandingExample` in the `BookExplorer` app, you see the button instance fluctuating between the enabled/disabled states. This happens when you change focus or enter some keystrokes or click the mouse. The reason why the button's `IsEnabled` value changes so frequently is because of the tie-up we do with the `CommandManager.RequerySuggested` event inside the command's `CanExecuteChanged` event. When any of the actions mentioned previously (focus change, mouse clicks, keyboard presses) happens, WPF's commanding system does a requery over all its commands to check whether their `CanExecute` has changed. If it has changed, the associated control gets notified of the change. In case of the `Button`, it uses this notification to enable/disable itself.

> ### Reader Exercise
>
> As an exercise try commenting out the code for the `CanExecuteChanged` event's add/remove methods. When you run the example with this change, you see that the `Button` always stays enabled or disabled, depending on the load time call to `TestCommand`'s `CanExecute`. Any amount of typing on the keyboard or changing the focus or clicking on the mouse does not change the `IsEnabled` value of the `Button`.

The previous example touched on some interesting classes and concepts. Let's now dig into it in a little more detail.

For the commands to actually work, four components need to be present:

- ▶ **Command**—You need to have a command defined somewhere. This contains the action to be executed.

- ▶ **CommandSource**—A command source invokes the command. These are controls such as the `Button` we saw earlier, and they implement the `ICommandSource` interface. We discuss that later in the chapter.

- ▶ **CommandBinding**—This maps the command to the command logic. The `CommandBinding` is really the glue that binds the `CommandSource` and the command. Without it, there is only a mechanism to invoke a command but no way to execute the command logic. When a command is invoked, WPF walks the visual tree to find the nearest `CommandBinding` that contains a mapping for the invoked command. As an aside, when you create a new `CommandBinding` instance, you also have the option to specify the event handlers for the `Executed` and `CanExecute` `RoutedEvents`. This is useful if you are not embedding command logic directly inside your commands, as we saw earlier. The following snippet shows the signatures for the `CommandBinding`'s constructor. Note that it also takes event handlers for the `Executed` and `CanExecute` events:

```
public CommandBinding(ICommand command)
public CommandBinding(ICommand command, ExecutedRoutedEventHandler executed)
```

```
    public CommandBinding(ICommand command, ExecutedRoutedEventHandler executed,
CanExecuteRoutedEventHandler canExecute)
```

▶ **CommandTarget**—A command target is the object on which the command is raised. The `ICommandSource` interface contains a `CommandTarget` property that can be set to a specific object. By default, the command source itself is considered the command target.

Figure 14.2 clearly shows the relation between various parts of the WPF command system.

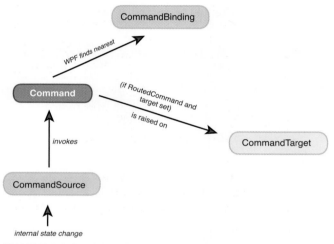

FIGURE 14.2   The WPF command system.

In addition to `CommandBindings`, WPF also gives you `InputBindings`, which is a way of binding an input gesture (mouse or keyboard) to a command instance. `InputBindings` provide a great way to associate keyboard shortcuts with the commands in your application. For example, consider the following `InputBinding` that binds the keyboard gesture Ctrl+Shift+T to our `TestCommand` instance:

```
var command = new TestCommand();
var inputBinding = new InputBinding(command, new KeyGesture(Key.T,
ModifierKeys.Control ¦
ModifierKeys.Shift));
InputBindings.Add(inputBinding);
```

With these basic components of the WPF commanding system, we are now in a position to explore the specialized WPF command: `RoutedCommand`.

Routed Commands

As we mentioned earlier, all commands must implement the ICommand interface. If you are defining custom commands, implementing this interface directly could be one option. However you can also consider using RoutedCommands, which are specialized WPF commands that also implement the ICommand interface and provide some additional functionality. As the name suggests, RoutedCommands provide some routing capabilities just like the RoutedEvents. When a command source invokes a regular ICommand, it gets handled by the nearest CommandBinding. This is also true for a RoutedCommand; that is, a RoutedCommand also looks for the nearest CommandBinding, but additionally it also raises two RoutedEvents. The bubbling versions are the Executed and CanExecute events, whereas the tunneling versions are PreviewExecuted and PreviewCanExecuted.

We saw earlier that a CommandBinding can be created with the ExecutedEventHandler and the CanExecuteEventHandler. These event handlers are invoked only when the Executed and CanExecute events are fired, which incidentally happens only when a RoutedCommand is invoked. Since these are routed events, they propagate up or down (bubbling/tunneling) the visual tree looking for an event handler. The propagation can be stopped if an event handler sets the RoutedEventArgs.Handled property to true. For a RoutedCommand, the command logic is implemented in these event handlers.

For a regular ICommand implementation, the ExecutedEventHandler and the CanExecuteEventHandler never get called, even if you specify them in the CommandBinding's constructor. This is something to remember when you implement your own custom commands.

WPF provides many built-in RoutedCommands that can be used in your applications. These commands are neatly categorized into static classes (also called a command library), making it easier to identify them. The following list gives a sampling of these commands:

- The ApplicationCommands class defines Cut, Copy, Paste, Delete, Print, and so on.
- The NavigationCommands class defines BrowseBack, BrowseForward, FirstPage, LastPage, Refresh, Search, and so on.
- The MediaCommands class defines Play, Pause, Rewind, Forward, Stop, and so on.
- The ComponentCommands class defines ScrollPageUp, ScrollPageDown, MoveToHome, MoveToEnd, and so on.

These classes are defined in the System.Windows.Input namespace. The commands in each of these classes are actually instances of RoutedUICommand, a subclass of RoutedCommand. RoutedUICommand provides a Text property that is used to display as header text for some controls—for example, MenuItem.

Commands Versus Events

The end result of a command and a routed event is some action that is performed by the application. However, there are some semantic differences between a command and an event that are important to understand. A routed event is a broadcast mechanism to indicate that something interesting happened in the control. For example, when you drag the thumb of a slider, a ValueChanged RoutedEvent is fired by the Slider control. A mouse click on a button fires its Click event; clicking on an item in a ListBox raises its SelectionChanged event. In other words, a routed event is just a way to inform the outside world that a state change happened in the control. It doesn't tell you what action should be taken. That is left up to someone who subscribes to the event.

On the other hand, a command is the action associated with a particular event. A command can be invoked based on a single event or based on multiple events. Earlier in the chapter, we gave an example of the Refresh command that is invoked by either pressing the F5 key or clicking on the toolbar. Commands are a great way to encapsulate an action that can be invoked in multiple ways. It is really a higher level abstraction compared to the routed event, where it is not concerned with the source of the event but rather the resulting action. In WPF, commands can be invoked by CommandSources (that is, controls that implement the ICommandSource interface), by input gestures (think InputBindings), or simply by calling the command's Execute method.

Commands also play a useful role inside ControlTemplates or DataTemplates. For example, a typical ControlTemplate for the ScrollBar consists of RepeatButtons, Track, and a Thumb. The Command property of the RepeatButtons can be set to scrollbar commands such as LineUpCommand, LineDownCommand, PageUpCommand, and PageDownCommand to invoke scrolling actions. When the RepeatButton is clicked, it invokes its associated command. The ScrollBar control sets up CommandBindings internally to handle the commands mentioned previously. Thus, when the RepeatButton is clicked, WPF will look for the nearest command-binding, which would be the one established on the ScrollBar. This subsequently causes the ScrollBar to respond by scrolling in a particular direction.

The following snippet shows the template for a vertical scrollbar. Note the use of the PageUpCommand and PageDownCommand on the RepeatButtons:

```
<ControlTemplate x:Key="VerticalScrollBarTemplate"
        TargetType="ScrollBar">
    <Grid>
        <Border CornerRadius="30,5,5,30"
            Background="{StaticResource TrackBrush}"
            BorderBrush="#999999"
            BorderThickness="1"
            Padding="1">
        <Track x:Name="PART_Track"
            IsDirectionReversed="True">
            <Track.DecreaseRepeatButton>
                <RepeatButton Command="ScrollBar.PageUpCommand"
                    Template="{StaticResource RBTemplate}" />
            </Track.DecreaseRepeatButton>
        <Track.Thumb>
```

```
        <Thumb Template="{StaticResource ThumbTemplate}"
                   Background="{TemplateBinding Background}"
                   BorderThickness="1"
                   BorderBrush="{TemplateBinding BorderBrush}" />
        </Track.Thumb>
        <Track.IncreaseRepeatButton>
            <RepeatButton Command="ScrollBar.PageDownCommand"
                       Template="{StaticResource RBTemplate}" />
        </Track.IncreaseRepeatButton>
    </Track>
</Border>
</Grid>
</ControlTemplate>
```

If you think of the previous scenario for a moment, you will understand a few things we discussed concerning commands versus events. The click on the RepeatButton is an event, which internally invokes its associated command. In the preceding example, this is either a PageUpCommand or PageDownCommand. The ScrollBar internally implements the command logic for these commands by scrolling up or down, respectively. Note that the commands are not concerned with the source that invokes it. In fact, if you want to be adventurous, you can put a few more RepeatButtons in there and set their Command property to PageUpCommand or PageDownCommand. The ScrollBar will continue to work properly and do the scrolling as expected!

Request Requery

We already saw that a command executes its logic only when its CanExecute returns True. The calls to CanExecute are automatically made by the CommandManager as a part of the commanding system. We saw an example in an earlier section on ICommand and the TestCommand implementation.

Certain conditions cause the commanding system to reevaluate all of its commands. These typically include change in keyboard focus, typing on the keyboard, mouse clicks, or change in the command target. If these conditions are not sufficient, you also have an option to provide additional conditions and invalidate the CommandManager as you see fit. This can be done by calling CommandManager.InvalidateRequerySuggested(). This internally calls CanExecute on all of the registered commands (remember, commands are registered with a CommandBinding) and also raises the RequerySuggested event. CommandSources typically use this event to change their enabled state based on the command's CanExecute output.

Recall the following snippet from the TestCommand implementation:

```
public event EventHandler CanExecuteChanged
{
    add
    {
```

```
            CommandManager.RequerySuggested += value;
    }
    remove
    {
            CommandManager.RequerySuggested -= value;
    }
}
```

See how we are associating the `CommandManager`'s `RequerySuggested` event to the `CanExecuteChanged` event. This is an important step since `CommandSources` typically register for the `CanExecuteChanged` event on the `ICommand`. If we add the event handler to `CommandManager.RequerySuggested`, the `CommandSource` gets notified automatically whenever the `CommandManager` does a requery on its commands. Without this code, the `CommandSource` cannot take any action (such as enabling/disabling itself) when the command's `CanExecute` changes.

This leads us nicely into the next section where we talk about how controls can become `CommandSources`.

The `ICommandSource` Interface

Some of the popular controls in WPF accept a command to be invoked when a particular event is triggered. `Button`, for example, triggers a command when its `Click` event happens. Similarly a `MenuItem` is an example of a control that triggers a command on its `Click` event. A control can expose a `Command` property and also invoke commands if it implements the `ICommandSource` interface. Let's take a look at the interface:

```
public interface ICommandSource
{
   // Properties
   ICommand Command { get; }
   object CommandParameter { get; }
   IInputElement CommandTarget { get; }
}
```

The `Command` property should be obvious, but the `CommandParameter` and the `CommandTarget` need some explanation. The `CommandTarget` is the object on which the `CanExecute` and `Execute` events are raised. It is only useful if the associated command is an instance of `RoutedCommand`. For instances that only implement the `ICommand` interface, the `CommandTarget` is ignored. By default, when the `CommandTarget` is not set, the element with the keyboard focus is used. The commanding system propagates the command from the command source all the way to the root of the visual tree until a `CommandBinding` for that command is found. It is recommended that the `CommandBindings` are set on a parent or ancestor of the command source. This is only to improve the readability of your XAML files and have a common location for all of your `CommandBindings`. Imagine setting up a `CommandBinding` individually on every control that raises a command. As your application grows in size, it is difficult to locate the various command bindings throughout your application. Defining the bindings at a common parent or ancestor improves readability, makes the bindings easily locatable and also gives you opportunities to refactor.

The CommandParameter is any parameter that is set on the command source. In case of the RoutedCommand, this parameter is passed in via the ExecutedEventArgs and CanExecuteEventArgs of the Execute and CanExecute events, respectively. For a simple ICommand that is not a RoutedCommand, the CommandParameter is passed in to its CanExecute and Execute methods.

A custom control can act as a CommandSource by implementing the ICommandSource interface. Typically the control would have some internal state change or event that invokes the command. Since you can bind only one command to the control, you would use the default event or state of the control as a trigger for the command. We saw earlier that, in the case of the button, the default is to use the Click event for invoking the command.

To make things clear and see how all this pans out, let's look at a custom control that implements ICommandSource. Our custom control, named SpikeControl, implements the ICommandSource interface and exposes the Command and CommandParameter properties as dependency properties:

```
public static readonly DependencyProperty CommandProperty =
DependencyProperty.Register(
    "Command", typeof(ICommand), typeof(SpikeControl), new PropertyMetadata(null,
OnCommandChanged));

public static readonly DependencyProperty CommandParameterProperty =
DependencyProperty.Register(
    "CommandParameter", typeof(object), typeof(SpikeControl));

public ICommand Command
{
    get { return (ICommand)GetValue(CommandProperty); }
    set { SetValue(CommandProperty, value); }
}

public object CommandParameter
{
    get { return (object)GetValue(CommandParameterProperty); }
    set { SetValue(CommandParameterProperty, value); }
}

public IInputElement CommandTarget
{
    get;
    set;
}
```

```
private static void OnCommandChanged(DependencyObject d,
DependencyPropertyChangedEventArgs e)
{
    SpikeControl control = d as SpikeControl;
    control.HookUpCommand(e.OldValue as ICommand, e.NewValue as ICommand);
}
```

When the command is set, its property changed handler OnCommandChanged gets called. We set up the command with the HookUpCommand() method:

```
private void HookUpCommand(ICommand oldCommand, ICommand newCommand)
{
    if (oldCommand != null)
    {
        oldCommand.CanExecuteChanged -= Command_CanExecuteChanged;
    }
    if (newCommand != null)
    {
        newCommand.CanExecuteChanged += Command_CanExecuteChanged;
    }
}
```

Inside HookUpCommand, we subscribe to the ICommand's CanExecuteChanged event and unsubscribe for the previous command. Subscribing to the CanExecuteChanged event allows the command source (SpikeControl) to enable or disable itself when the command's CanExecute changes. We saw how this works out in the section "Request Requery" earlier in the chapter. Next we have the event handler for the CanExecuteChanged event. This is the place where the command source enables or disables itself:

```
private void Command_CanExecuteChanged(object sender, EventArgs e)
{
    if (Command != null)
    {
        RoutedCommand command = Command as RoutedCommand;

        // RoutedCommand.
        if (command != null)
        {
            if (command.CanExecute(CommandParameter, CommandTarget))
            {
                IsEnabled = true;
            }
            else
            {
                IsEnabled = false;
```

```
        }
    }
    // Not a RoutedCommand.
    else
    {
        if (Command.CanExecute(CommandParameter))
        {
            IsEnabled = true;
        }
        else
        {
            IsEnabled = false;
        }
    }
    }
}
```

Since the command's CanExecute capability has changed, the command source queries for that and sets its IsEnabled property accordingly. Note how the command source specifically checks for a RoutedCommand. The CommandTarget and the CommandParameter are both passed to the RoutedCommand's CanExecute method. For a simple ICommand, only the CommandParameter is passed.

When the default event for the SpikeControl is raised, it invokes its associated command. This happens only when the control is enabled, which in turn happens if the command's CanExecute returned true. For the SpikeControl, this is handled by the private InvokeCommand method:

```
private void InvokeCommand()
{
    if (Command != null)
    {
        RoutedCommand command = Command as RoutedCommand;
        if (command != null)
        {
            command.Execute(CommandParameter, CommandTarget);
        }
        else
        {
            Command.Execute(CommandParameter);
        }
    }
}
```

Once again, you can check for RoutedCommand to pass the CommandTarget to the command's Execute method. The CommandParameter is passed in for both the

RoutedCommand and the plain ICommand. Finally you can also see what it means to invoke a command. Up to this point, we mentioned several times about invoking a command but never really showed the code for doing so. This is nothing more than calling the command's Execute method!

Input Binding is an ICommand Source

An interesting fact to note is that the InputBinding class we saw earlier also implements the ICommandSource interface. This is not surprising because an InputBinding also invokes commands when the user applies a key gesture or a mouse gesture. The keyboard gestures are handled by the KeyBinding class, a subclass of InputBinding, and the mouse gestures are handled by MouseBinding, again a subclass of InputBinding.

Focus Management

The primary purpose of focus within an application is to handle keyboard input. It allows you to navigate and interact with controls using various key combinations. In WPF, focus is managed using the Tab key and other variants such Ctrl+Tab, Shift+Tab, Ctrl+Shift+Tab, and mouse clicks.

Logical and Keyboard Focus

Focus management in WPF comes in two flavors, namely, *logical focus* and *keyboard focus*. Keyboard focus is probably easier to grasp. An element that has keyboard focus receives all the keyboard input that happens in the application. Only one element can have keyboard focus at any time on the entire desktop. For a UIElement to receive keyboard focus, it must have its Focusable and IsVisible properties set to true. Focus can be set on a UIElement by calling its Focus() method or using the static Keyboard.Focus() method. An element that has keyboard focus also has its IsFocused, IsKeyboardFocused, and IsKeyboardFocusWithin properties set to true. These properties can be used with Triggers to visually indicate focus on an element. Keyboard.FocusedElement refers to the element that last received focus. The recommended place to set keyboard focus is inside the Loaded event handler of the containing control.

Before we look at logical focus, we need to understand the notion of focus scopes. A *focus scope* is a container that keeps track of the element that has logical focus. Only one element in a focus scope can have logical focus. We can have multiple focus scopes in an application, and WPF by default provides the following focus scopes: Window, Menu, ContextMenu, and ToolBar. However, each scope can have only one logically focused element. This element is available through the FocusManager.FocusedElement, for a given focus scope.

When a focus scope receives keyboard focus, it is the FocusedElement inside that scope that receives the keyboard focus. Thus, an element that has keyboard focus automatically has logical focus in its contained scope. When the keyboard focus shifts to a different focus scope, the previous scope maintains its logically focused element through the FocusManager.FocusedElement. You can create a focus scope by setting the Boolean attached property FocusManager.IsFocusScope. You can retrieve the containing focus scope for an element using the `FocusManager.GetFocusScope()` method. A little known fact is that you can have nested focus scopes. In that case, the `FocusManager.FocusedElement` is maintained for both the parent and child focus scopes.

The diagram in Figure 14.3 shows three focus scopes and how the logical focus is maintained as the keyboard focus shifts between them. Only one control at any time can have keyboard focus (indicated by the red rectangle) but many controls can have logical focus at the same time (indicated by the blue rectangles).

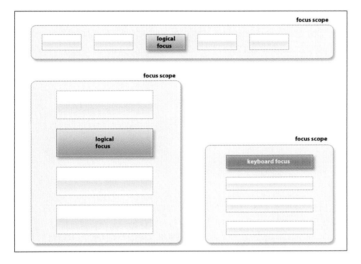

FIGURE 14.3   Focus scopes.

Focus-Related Events and Properties

As focus shifts within an application, WPF sets various properties and fires a set of events to notify the change in focus to controls that have subscribed to focus changes. To visually indicate focus through style or template triggers, properties such as `IsFocused`, `IsKeyboardFocused`, and `IsKeyboardFocusWithin` may be used. All of these properties are available on `UIElements`. The `IsFocused` property relates to logical focus, whereas the `IsKeyboard`-prefixed properties are for keyboard focus.

To handle change in focus programmatically, events such as `GotFocus`, `GotKeyboardFocus`, `LostFocus`, `LostKeyboardFocus`, `IsKeyboardFocusedChanged`, and `IsKeyboardFocusWithinChanged` may be used. Once again, `GotFocus` and `LostFocus` are for logical focus, and the remaining are for keyboard focus. As we saw earlier, having keyboard focus automatically implies logical focus. This means you can simply hook into events related to logical focus and safely manage change in focus. However, if you do need finer-grained control over keyboard focus, you also have specific events for that.

FocusVisualStyle

A little more useful property exposed on a control is the `FocusVisualStyle`, which is of type `Style` and consists mainly of a `ControlTemplate`. `FocusVisualStyle` is useful when you want to provide richer styling of focus. WPF creates a separate visual tree when using `FocusVisualStyle` and applies it as an adorner on top of the control. This makes it easier to reuse a common focus style across a range of controls. The default is to show a dashed rectangle around the focused control. `FocusVisualStyle` works exclusively with keyboard focus.

Figure 14.4 shows the default focus visual style and also a custom one. The source files for this example are provided with this book. The interesting-looking border for the custom focus style was originally created in Adobe Illustrator, which was then imported into Expression Blend and converted to a DrawingBrush.

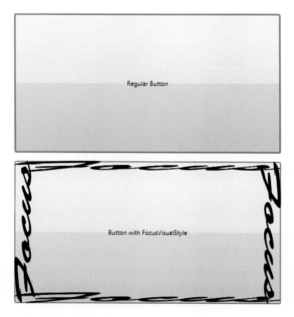

FIGURE 14.4   Focus visual styles.

Let's look at an example of using the `GotFocus` and `LostFocus` events in the context of a watermarked text box. When the text box has no focus, some help text is shown to indicate the kind of input it expects. When the text box receives focus, the help text goes away and instead shows a caret for keyboard input. On losing focus, the help text shows up again if the text box has no characters. Figure 14.5 shows the two states of a watermarked text box.

We implement this feature using attached properties. The class `TextBoxWatermarkHelper` exposes two attached properties, `IsWatermarkVisible` and `WatermarkText`, that can be used by text boxes to add the watermark behavior. The `Boolean` property

FIGURE 14.5   A watermarked text box.

IsWatermarkVisible is set if the text box has no focus. On receiving focus, it is reset. We can use these attached properties inside the text box's ControlTemplate to get the effect we need. The following snippet shows the custom ControlTemplate for the text box:

```
<ControlTemplate TargetType="TextBox">
    <Border BorderThickness="1"
        BorderBrush="{TemplateBinding BorderBrush}"
        Background="{TemplateBinding Background}"
        Padding="1"
        SnapsToDevicePixels="True">
        <Grid>
            <ScrollViewer x:Name="PART_ContentHost"
                    Margin="4,0,0,0" />
            <TextBlock x:Name="Watermark"
                    Margin="8,0,0,0"
                    Text="{TemplateBinding
Chapter14:TextBoxWatermarkHelper.WatermarkText}"
                    Focusable="False"
                    FontSize="14"
                    FontStyle="Italic"
                    FontFamily="{TemplateBinding FontFamily}"
                    VerticalAlignment="Center"
                    Cursor="IBeam"
                    ForceCursor="True"
                    Foreground="#AF000000" />
        </Grid>
    </Border>

    <ControlTemplate.Triggers>
        <Trigger Property="Chapter14:TextBoxWatermarkHelper.IsWatermarkVisible"
            Value="True">
            <Setter Property="Visibility"
                    Value="Visible"
                    TargetName="Watermark" />
            <Setter Property="Visibility"
                    Value="Hidden"
                    TargetName="PART_ContentHost" />
```

```
        </Trigger>
        <Trigger Property="Chapter14:TextBoxWatermarkHelper.IsWatermarkVisible"
                     Value="False">
            <Setter Property="Visibility"
                        Value="Hidden"
                        TargetName="Watermark" />
            <Setter Property="Visibility"
                        Value="Visible"
                        TargetName="PART_ContentHost" />
        </Trigger>
    </ControlTemplate.Triggers>
</ControlTemplate>
```

Note the use of the attached properties in the `Triggers` section and on the `TextBlock` named `WatermarkText`. It is also worth pointing out that the use of attached properties allows us complete control over the styling of the watermark help text. In our case, we are using a `TextBlock`, but this could be made even more interesting by using images and animations.

Now let's look at the `TextBoxWatermarkHelper` class that implements the attached properties. We set up a property changed handler for the `WatermarkText` attached property and in that hook into the `GotFocus` and `LostFocus` events of the `TextBox`. The `IsWatermarkVisible` attached property is set or reset depending on whether the `TextBox` lost focus or got focus, respectively.

```
    public class TextBoxWatermarkHelper : DependencyObject
    {
        public static readonly DependencyProperty IsWatermarkVisibleProperty =
DependencyProperty.RegisterAttached(
            "IsWatermarkVisible", typeof(bool), typeof(TextBoxWatermarkHelper));

        public static readonly DependencyProperty WatermarkTextProperty =
DependencyProperty.RegisterAttached(
            "WatermarkText", typeof(string), typeof(TextBoxWatermarkHelper),
new PropertyMetadata("Watermark", OnWatermarkTextChanged));

        public static string GetWatermarkText(TextBox control)
        {
            return (string)control.GetValue(WatermarkTextProperty);
        }

        public static bool GetIsWatermarkVisible(TextBox control)
        {
            return (bool)control.GetValue(IsWatermarkVisibleProperty);
        }

        public static void SetWatermarkText(TextBox control, string text)
```

```
        {
            control.SetValue(WatermarkTextProperty, text);
        }

        private static void OnWatermarkTextChanged(DependencyObject d,
DependencyPropertyChangedEventArgs e)
        {
            TextBox control = d as TextBox;
            if (control == null) return;

            control.SetValue(IsWatermarkVisibleProperty, true);
            control.LostFocus += OnControlLostFocus;
            control.GotFocus += OnControlGotFocus;
        }

        private static void OnControlGotFocus(object sender, RoutedEventArgs e)
        {
            (sender as TextBox).SetValue(IsWatermarkVisibleProperty, false);
        }

        private static void OnControlLostFocus(object sender, RoutedEventArgs e)
        {
            TextBox control = sender as TextBox;
            if (control != null)
            {
                    if (string.IsNullOrEmpty(control.Text))
                    control.SetValue(IsWatermarkVisibleProperty, true);
            }
        }
    }
```

Keyboard Navigation

We are all familiar with the registration forms that we see on websites. They consist of a few text boxes and some buttons to submit or cancel the registration. Once the form receives focus, you can navigate within it using the standard Tab key or the Shift+Tab keys. Tab shifts focus to the next control, whereas Shift+Tab moves focus to the previous control. The use of these keys to move focus between controls is called *keyboard navigation*, and the container within which this navigation happens is called the *navigation container*.

WPF not only allows this standard behavior but also gives you more control over navigating controls in a view. This is possible using the KeyboardNavigation class. The focus navigation keys include Tab, Shift+Tab, Ctrl+Tab, Ctrl+Shift+Tab, Up, Down, Left, and Right. The KeyboardNavigation class allows you to control the navigation behavior of these keys using the attached properties TabNavigation, ControlTabNavigation, and

DirectionalNavigation. Each of them point to an enum of type KeyboardNavigationMode with possible values of Continue, Local, Contained, Cycle, Once, and None. The default value of a navigation container is set to Continue. The meanings of these values are described in the Table 14.1.

TABLE 14.1   The KeyboardNavigationMode Enumeration

Value	Description
Continue	Each element inside the container receives focus as long as it is a navigation stop. Navigation leaves the container when an edge is reached (first or last control in the container).
Contained	The focus cycles within the container. If the TAB key is hit from the last control, focus moves to the first control of the same container instead of the first control in the next container.
Local	The KeyboardNavigation.TabIndex is considered only inside the local tree and behaves like Continue thereafter.
Cycle	The keyboard focus cycles through all the elements in order. When the first or last element is reached, the navigation wraps around and stays inside. Thus, it is not possible to leave the container using local keyboard navigation.
Once	The focus is received on the container and all of its children only once. It is received on either the first control or the last focused element.
None	No navigation is allowed within the container.

Although it may sound obvious, it is important to remember that the KeyboardNavigation properties only affect the focus navigation inside the container. This may bite you when you are designing nested forms where each child form has its own navigation behavior.

The TabNavigation property relies on KeyboardNavigation.IsTabStop and KeyboardNavigation.TabIndex to do its work. If the IsTabStop property is set to false, TabNavigation skips that control in the navigation container. The TabIndex property is of type int and is useful for ordering the flow of focus navigation. By default, the flow is based on the order in which the controls are declared.

ControlTabNavigation is useful when working with navigation containers like a TabControl. It allows you to switch between the different TabItems. The standard KeyboardNavigationMode used for this type of navigation is Cycle—that is, once you reach the last tab and press Tab again, it takes you back to the first tab. Ctrl+Tab takes to your previous tab and also allows you to alternate between the current and the previous tabs.

`DirectonalNavigation` is useful in the context of list-based controls such as `ListBox`, `ListView`, `TreeView`, and so on. It allows you to navigate between the different items using the Up, Down, Left, and Right arrow keys.

Summary

In this chapter, we saw how events, commands, and focus management allow you to add interactivity to your application. Understanding these three areas is crucial when designing your custom controls and managing the different input events that can occur in your application. By exposing routed events on your controls, you can make it easier to animate between different states of the control, via storyboards. Commands are yet another feature that you can expose on your custom controls to invoke actions on the control from command sources inside its control template. We saw an example where `RepeatButtons` were used inside the scrollbar's `ControlTemplate` to invoke scrolling commands such as `PageUpCommand`, `PageDownCommand`, and so on.

Finally, we concluded with a section on focus management and looked at various ways in which keyboard focus can be moved inside an application. WPF gives a great amount of control to fine-tune the flow of focus within your control as well as in your application.

14

CHAPTER 15

Advanced Data Binding

Data binding technologies have come a long way in the years that we have been building graphical desktop applications. In the early days, there was no such thing as data binding, and you had to use imperative programming techniques to manually create instances of visual objects and manually control their properties. In many cases, you couldn't even set "text" properties; you had to manually draw rendered text strings at specific coordinates.

Data binding was originally a double-edged sword. On the one hand, it allowed you to rapidly connect visual controls with an underlying source of data, resulting in huge increases in productivity. The problem was that early data binding technologies were so inefficient and resulted in so many unnecessary, redundant data re-fetches that most programmers at the time actually considered data binding an anti-pattern in production, commercial-grade applications.

Thankfully those days are behind us. WPF has an incredibly powerful data binding system that can work with whatever you use for your backing store: SQL database, XML files, objects fetched from a web service, or anything else that can be represented as a CLR (Common Language Runtime) object.

This chapter takes you through the mechanics of how data binding works within WPF and then shows you some advanced techniques that will not only help your own data binding use but also allow consumers of your custom controls to perform advanced data binding techniques themselves.

Dependency Properties

Dependency properties (or DPs as most people call them) are one of the cornerstones of WPF, and you have already seen them used extensively throughout this book. It is the existence of the DPs that enable features like data binding, property change notification, styling, and animation. DPs are typically defined on dependency objects as they provide convenient access to data via the `SetValue()` and `GetValue()` methods.

In this section, we cover some advanced aspects of DPs that should come in handy as you build applications and custom controls.

Dependency Property Precedence

DPs are used in multiple ways throughout the WPF framework, and there are multiple ways in which they could be set. For example, consider the following snippet of XAML that sets the width of the rectangle at two different places:

```
<UserControl xmlns="http://schemas.microsoft.com/winfx/2006/xaml/presentation"
             xmlns:x="http://schemas.microsoft.com/winfx/2006/xaml">
    <UserControl.Resources>
        <Storyboard x:Key="WidthAnimator">
        <DoubleAnimation From="0"
                                                To="400"
                                                Duration="0:0:1"
                                                Storyboard.TargetName="Rect"
Storyboard.TargetProperty="Width"/>
        </Storyboard>
    </UserControl.Resources>
    <Grid>
        <Rectangle x:Name="Rect"
                        Fill="Red"
                        Width="100"
                        Height="100"
                        Stroke="IndianRed"
                        StrokeThickness="1" />
    </Grid>
    <UserControl.Triggers>
        <EventTrigger RoutedEvent="UserControl.Loaded">
<BeginStoryboard Storyboard="{StaticResource WidthAnimator}" />
        </EventTrigger>
    </UserControl.Triggers>
</UserControl>
```

The first way the property is set is inside the `Rectangle` tag where the width is directly set to the value of 100. The second way the property is set is when the storyboard fires after the `UserControl` has loaded. At that time, the storyboard sets the `Width` property. While the storyboard plays, the width is steadily increased from 0 to 400, overriding the local value set on the rectangle. If we remove the storyboard after it completes, the width snaps immediately back to the local value (100). The fact that the storyboard can temporarily override the local value of the Width property is due to the precedence order of how dependency properties are resolved.

This precedence order is necessary because there can be (and usually are) multiple sources of input for any given DependencyProperty. Without knowing which value is the "real" current value and without knowing how to peel values off the stack in the appropriate order, the use of DPs would result in total chaos. Unfortunately, most developers who use DPs on a daily basis are completely unaware of the 11 different levels of precedence. These levels are listed in the descending order of precedence in Table 15.1.

Coercion for Checking Constraints

Property coercion is a great way to ensure that certain constraints are always maintained on a control. The slider control uses coercion to ensure that its Value property is always between the Minimum and Maximum whenever any of the three values change. By calling DependencyProperty.CoerceValue with a DP as a parameter, property coercion can be invoked on that property. The constraint checking can be carried out by associating a CoerceValueCallback in the DP's property metadata.

TABLE 15.1   Precedence Levels of Dependency Properties

Precedence Level	Description
Property Value Coercion	Coercion allows you to control the final value that is set on the DP via the CoerceValueCallback assigned in the DP's PropertyMetaData. It is a programmatic way of constraining the value of the DP. Coercion is performed as the last step before the value is assigned.
Storyboard Animations	Values set when the storyboard is playing, as described in the previous example.
Local Value	Local values are set using the SetValue() method or via the CLR property accessors.
TemplatedParent Template Properties	Properties set inside a ControlTemplate or DataTemplate. Elements inside a template have a TemplatedParent. Within the template, the triggers take precedence over local values set on the elements. Note that triggers can be used to set properties and/or play storyboards.
Implicit Style	This applies only to the Style property of a FrameworkElement. This style is looked up based on a key that matches the type of the element. The lookup does not go up to the themes but stops at the page or application.

TABLE 15.1   Precedence Levels of Dependency Properties

Precedence Level	Description
Style Triggers	These are triggers inside a `Style`.
Template Triggers	These are triggers defined on a template inside a `Style`. For example, via the setter for the `Template` property of a `Control`.
Style Setters	Value set using the `Style` property setter.
Default (Theme) Styles	These are the styles used when no custom themes/styles are defined inside an application or page. They default to the framework styles that are shipped with WPF. The styles are looked up based on the type of the element. Inside the style, triggers take precedence of property setters.
Inheritance	Some DPs inherit their values from the parent.
Default Value Defined in Property Metadata	This is the value that has been defined in the `PropertyMetaData` for the `DependencyProperty`.

WPF also gives you a way to determine which of these different sources was responsible for the current effective value of the `DependencyProperty`. The static class `DependencyPropertyHelper`'s `GetValueSource()` method can be used for this purpose. It's signature looks like this:

```
public static ValueSource GetValueSource(DependencyObject dependencyObject,
DependencyProperty dependencyProperty);
```

By passing in a `DependencyObject` and the associated `DependencyProperty`, you can retrieve the source of the DP value, the object responsible for the current effective value of the DP. The return type of this method is a struct of type `ValueSource` that contains all the information you need about the source. It has convenient Boolean properties to tell you if the source was a binding expression, animation, or coercion. These are `IsExpression`, `IsAnimated`, and `IsCoerced`, respectively. If none of these are true, you can query the `BaseValueSource` property, which gives you one of the 11 types of sources from Table 15.1. The `BaseValueSource` property is an enumeration of type `BaseValueSource` and has the following values:

- ▶ Unknown
- ▶ Default
- ▶ Inherited
- ▶ DefaultStyle
- ▶ DefaultStyleTrigger

- ▶ Style

- ▶ TemplateTrigger

- ▶ StyleTrigger

- ▶ ImplicitStyleReference

- ▶ ParentTemplate

- ▶ ParentTemplateTrigger

- ▶ Local

A standard scenario where the DependencyProperty precedence matters is when you remove a storyboard that was animating a property. As soon as you remove the storyboard, the DP value goes back to its value before the animation started. It should now be clear why this happens. The storyboard was responsible for the effective value during the animation, but as soon as it was removed, the value reverted to its previous base value. To retain the end value of the storyboard after it is removed, you have to manually set the DependencyProperty's value using the SetValue() method.

Using AddOwner Instead of Creating a New DependencyProperty

When you are authoring a custom control, it is common to define a set of dependency properties related to that control. Sometimes the properties are similar to the ones already available in the WPF framework or on some of your existing controls. It would be nice if you could reuse those properties without having to define your own new custom properties.

The AddOwner() method on the DependencyProperty class serves exactly this purpose. It allows you to add your control type as a new owner of this DP and also allows you to redefine the property metadata. There are two overrides of the AddOwner() method that you can use:

```
public DependencyProperty AddOwner(Type ownerType);
public DependencyProperty AddOwner(Type ownerType, PropertyMetadata typeMetadata);
```

Out of the two, the second override is more useful since it also allows you to specify your own property metadata. This is typically used to override the PropertyChanged handlers and also set a default value for the property. WPF makes good use of AddOwner() for many of its classes. For example, the Control class defines its Background property by calling AddOwner on the Panel's BackgroundProperty.

```
public static readonly DependencyProperty BackgroundProperty =
Panel.BackgroundProperty.AddOwner(typeof(Control), new
FrameworkPropertyMetadata(Panel.BackgroundProperty.DefaultMetadata.DefaultValue,
FrameworkPropertyMetadataOptions.None));
```

It is common for the properties defined using `AddOwner` to carry the same name as the original property along with CLR property wrappers around the `SetValue()` and `GetValue()` methods. In case of the `Control`, a CLR wrapper property called `Background` is defined like so:

```
public Brush Background
{
    get
    {
        return (Brush) base.GetValue(BackgroundProperty);
    }
    set
    {
        base.SetValue(BackgroundProperty, value);
    }
}
```

Framework Reuse

When creating your own custom control, try to look for an existing framework class that defines a similar `DependencyProperty`. Depending on the shape of the data that the custom control expects, you can look up similar controls in the framework. For example, if you are dealing with a range of values, look for properties defined on `RangeBase`. If you are creating a custom `ItemsControl` with selections, try looking at the `Selector` control for similarly defined properties, and so on.

Listening to Property Changed Events on Dependency Properties

When you are a custom control author, you have complete control over the property changes that happen on your DPs. This is because you have the option to provide the property changed handlers in the DP's metadata. However, as a consumer of a control, you have to rely on events fired from the control that send change notifications to the DPs. It is possible that the control author decided not to fire any events when changes happen to a DP (though this situation may cause you to reconsider your decision to use such a control). In cases like this, you have two options for getting notified on property changes. The first option is to check whether the control author has provided protected methods that get called when a property changes. If you have such methods, you can subclass the control and make use of them. This option adds a bit of overhead since you have to create a separate class just to listen to property changes.

A second, less intrusive option is to use the `AddValueChanged()` method on the `DependencyPropertyDescriptor`. `DependencyPropertyDescriptors` are wrappers around `PropertyDescriptors` that account for additional characteristics of a DP.

PropertyDescriptors

`PropertyDescriptors` are wrappers around regular CLR properties. They provide convenient access to the property's name, attributes, type, etc. You can obtain the property descriptors for an object using `System.ComponentModel.TypeDescriptor.GetProperties()`, passing in the object instance as a parameter. This call returns an array of property descritors for the type. `DependencyPropertyDescriptor`, which is a wrapper around the `PropertyDescriptor`, is more commonly used when working with WPF controls. It provides better performance over a `PropertyDescriptor` by caching the results obtained during reflection on the type's properties. `PropertyDescriptor` reflects on the type's properties on every call.

To retrieve a descriptor, you can call one of the two static methods of `DependencyPropertyDescriptor`:

```
public static DependencyPropertyDescriptor FromName(string name, Type ownerType,
Type targetType)
public static DependencyPropertyDescriptor FromProperty(DependencyProperty
dependencyProperty, Type targetType)
```

The second method is just a more type-safe version of the first method. Once you have the descriptor, you can call the `AddValueChanged()` method to set up a property changed handler:

```
public override void AddValueChanged(object component, EventHandler handler)
```

The parameter `component` is the instance on which the property changes happen. For example, suppose you wanted to listen to changes on the `ItemSource` property of a `ListBox`. By default, the `ListBox` control doesn't send notifications about changes happening on this property. However, with our newfound knowledge of DPs, we can listen to the changes using the `AddValueChanged()` method as follows:

```
ListBox lb = FindName("ContactsList") as ListBox;
var descriptor =
DependencyPropertyDescriptor.FromProperty(ItemsControl.ItemsSourceProperty, typeof
(IEnumerable));
descriptor.AddValueChanged(lb, (sender, e) =>
                    {
                            // Take action
                    });
```

Notice the use of the `AddValueChanged()` method on the last line. Our component instance is the `ListBox`, and the attached event handler (shown as a lambda function) is the place where we take action on the change notification.

Using this simple technique, we can listen for interesting changes throughout WPF that might not otherwise be broadcasted.

> ### Important Data Binding Fact
>
> If a source object does not implement `INotifyPropertyChanged` or derive from `DependencyObject`, WPF uses the `PropertyDescriptors'` `ValueChanged` event to notify changes to the UI. It listens to the property changes on the source by using the `PropertyDescriptor.AddValueChanged` method, the one we saw in the previous section. This is known to cause a memory leak, and the source and target objects never get garbage collected. A Knowledgebase Article on MSDN discusses this issue, along with some workarounds. You can view it here: http://support.microsoft.com/kb/938416.
>
> The suggested solution is to either implement the `INotifyPropertyChanged` interface on the source object or use a binding mode of `OneTime`.

Special Data Binding Scenarios

In this section, we take a look at a few important but unconventional data binding scenarios. We look at using the `RelativeSource.PreviousData` property as well as a few special properties of the `Binding` class.

Using `RelativeSource.PreviousData`

For a data-bound `ItemsControl`, each item in the source collection is the `DataContext` for the generated UI container. By default, the binding expressions used in the `ItemTemplate` are evaluated with respect to this `DataContext`. This is useful if all of the information that the template needs is contained in this context. This is actually the case in the vast majority of data binding expressions. However, there might be times when you also want to take a peek at the previous item to do some work. For example, say you are plotting a sales chart and you want to show the percentage change in market share over five years. Here the change can be calculated within the `ItemTemplate` and shown in red for a decrease and in green for an increase. In this case, it is necessary to have information about the previous item in the data-bound list. This is where the exact scenario that the `RelativeSource` class was designed for with its `PreviousData` property.

`RelativeSource.PreviousData` points to the previous item in the bound collection and can be used by setting the binding's `RelativeSource` property. Once the relative source property is set, it is considered the source for the binding expression.

```
<Binding Path="." RelativeSource="{RelativeSource PreviousData}" />
```

To demonstrate `RelativeSource.PreviousData`, let's build a line chart where each segment, of the graph is created as part of the `ItemTemplate` (see Figure 15.1). To build a line segment, we need the current data point and the previous data point. We fetch the previous data point using `RelativeSource.PreviousData`. The idea of building a line chart with separate segments is also useful from a practical standpoint. Say you wanted to color specific line segments differently based on specific criteria. This would be impossible without the ability to draw individual line segments. This can all be done inside the `ItemTemplate` using triggers. Note that you could also build this line chart by using a `PolyLine`, but you lose the ability to control the appearance of each individual line segment.

{Visual Instance}

Layout

Opacity

Opacity

FIGURE 15.1   Line chart using **RelativeSource.PreviousData**.

```
<ItemsControl ItemsSource="{Binding Path=DataPoints, Source={StaticResource
    ➥LineGraph}}"
                        ItemTemplate="{StaticResource LineSegmentTemplate}"
                        Template="{StaticResource GraphTemplate}" />
```

The ItemsControl, which represents our line chart, uses a custom ControlTemplate and an ItemTemplate, which are shown here:

```
<Chapter15:LineSegmentConverter x:Key="LineSegmentConverter" />

<DataTemplate x:Key="LineSegmentTemplate">
        <Path Stroke="Black"
                StrokeThickness="3"
                StrokeEndLineCap="Round"
                Stretch="None">
            <Path.Data>
                    <MultiBinding Converter="{StaticResource
➥LineSegmentConverter}">
                            <Binding Path="."
                                    RelativeSource="{RelativeSource
➥PreviousData}" />
                            <Binding Path="." />
                            <Binding Path="ActualWidth"
                                    RelativeSource="{RelativeSource
➥FindAncestor, AncestorType={x:Type Canvas}}" />
                            <Binding Path="ActualHeight"
                                    RelativeSource="{RelativeSource
➥FindAncestor, AncestorType={x:Type Canvas}}" />
                    </MultiBinding>
            </Path.Data>
        </Path>
</DataTemplate>

<ControlTemplate x:Key="GraphTemplate">
        <Canvas IsItemsHost="True">
```

```
                <Canvas.Background>
                        <ImageBrush
ImageSource="pack://siteoforigin:,,,/Resources/Chapter15/graph_background.png"
                                TileMode="Tile"
                                Viewport="0,0,50,50"
                                ViewportUnits="Absolute" />


                </Canvas.Background>
        </Canvas>
</ControlTemplate>
```

Notice how the ItemTemplate uses RelativeSource.PreviousData in the MultiBinding for Path.Data. A value converter is needed for the MultiBinding to use the bound values and generate a LineGeometry. Note that the Data property of Path is of type Geometry. Since we are building line segments, a LineGeometry works perfectly.

> ## Caveat for Virtualized ItemsControl
>
> There is a little caveat to remember when using RelativeSource.PreviousData for an ItemsControl that uses a virtualized panel. In those cases, it only works for generated item containers and returns null for any virtualized items. Say, you have a ListBox that uses a horizontal VirtualizingStackPanel and you have scrolled to item 30 of 100 with 10 visible items. Thus, there are only 10 ListBoxItems in the ListBox for items 30–39. Here the ItemTemplate for the 30th item gets a null for RelativeSource.PreviousData even though the data item is present in the collection. This happens because the 29th ListBoxItem has been virtualized.
>
> The workaround for this is to give up using RelativeSource.PreviousData and instead look up the previous item from the original collection. Note that you will now be using a MultiBinding that binds to the item as well as it's containing collection. You will also need a IMultiValueConverter whose Convert method will look up the index of the item within the collection. The previous item will be at [index - 1].

Using NotifyOnSourceUpdated and NotifyOnTargetUpdated

In the preceding section, we saw that it is possible to be notified of property changes on DPs that have no publicly exposed event from their parent element. This was possible with the AddValueChanged method of the DependencyPropertyDescriptor class. It turns out that for data-bound DPs, there is yet another way to be notified when the value changes. This is made possible through some interesting properties of the Binding class, specifically the NotifyOnSourceUpdated and NotifyOnTargetUpdated properties.

The Binding class fires a change notification whenever a bound DP has its value changed. By setting the Boolean property NotifyOnSourceUpdated or the Boolean property NotifyOnTargetUpdated, the corresponding events SourcedUpdated and TargetUpdated are fired on the UI element. You can attach the event handlers directly on the UI element that is data bound or somewhere higher up in the data context (parent or ancestor UI element). For example, consider the following XAML snippet that shows a `UserControl` with a `ListBox`:

```
<UserControl x:Class="Chapters.Chapter15.NotifySourceTargetExample"

                    xmlns="http://schemas.microsoft.com/winfx/2006/xaml/presentation"
                    xmlns:x="http://schemas.microsoft.com/winfx/2006/xaml"
                    xmlns:Chapter15="clr-namespace:Chapters.Chapter15"
                    TargetUpdated="OnItemsSourceChanged">
        <UserControl.Resources>
                <Chapter15:AddressBook x:Key="DataSource" />
        </UserControl.Resources>
        <Grid>
                <ListBox x:Name="ContactsList"
                        ItemsSource="{Binding ContactNames, Source={StaticResource
DataSource}, NotifyOnTargetUpdated=True}"
                                            />
        </Grid>
</UserControl>
```

The `ItemsSource` property of the `ListBox` is data bound, and the `NotifyOnTargetUpdated` property of the `Binding` has been set to true. This means that whenever the `ListBox.ItemsSource` property changes, a notification is fired. To listen to this notification, we need to set up an event handler for the `TargetUpdated` event. In our case, we attach the handler on the `UserControl` instead of the `ListBox`. When the `ItemsSource` changes, the `OnItemsSourceChanged` event handler (that we created) is invoked in the code-behind for the user control.

Similarly you could also handle changes made to the source when the binding updates the associated data source. This occurs when the user does something in the GUI that changes the underlying data value. You can handle the property change notification by setting the `NotifyOnSourceUpdated` property to true and setting up an event handler for the `SourceUpdated` event. Note that the `TargetUpdated` and `SourceUpdated` events are available only for `FrameworkElements` and `FrameworkContentElements`. The `Binding` class also exposes these events as attached events, namely, `Binding.SourceUpdated` and `Binding.TargetUpdated`.

The Dispatcher and DispatcherPriority

The UI operations in a WPF application mostly happen on a single UI thread. We say "mostly" because a few operations such as rendering and asynchronous data binding do happen on a different thread. The `Dispatcher` class is responsible for maintaining the single-threaded nature of the WPF application. Every UI operation is pushed as a `DispatcherOperation` on the dispatcher queue and processed based on a `DispatcherPriority`.

The priority is an enumeration that defines several levels of priority as detailed in Table 15.2, ordered from lowest priority to highest.

> **NOTE**
>
> For an in-depth coverage of the WPF threading model, refer to this MSDN article: http://msdn.microsoft.com/en-us/library/ms741870.aspx.

There are a few priorities that you really need to memorize and be familiar with, specifically `Background`, `Loaded`, `Render`, and `DataBind`. Operations carried out at these

TABLE 15.2   Dispatcher Priorities

Priority Level	Description
Invalid	This is not a valid priority.
Inactive	Operations are not processed.
SystemIdle	Operations are processed when system is idle.
ApplicationIdle	Operations are processed when application is idle.
ContextIdle	Operations are processed after all background operations are complete.
Background	Processed after all non-idle operations are completed.
Input	Processed at the same priority as input (keyboard, mouse, stylus).
Loaded	Processed after layout and render has completed but before input operations are processed. Also used to raise the Loaded event.
Render	Processed at the same priority as render.
DataBind	Processed at the same priority as data-binding operations.
Normal	Processed at normal application priority.
Send	Highest priority level. Processed before other asynchronous operations.

priorities can assume that higher level operations have already been completed and certain information about the UI elements is guaranteed to be available. For example, operations at the `Loaded` priority can assume that the sizes of UI elements are available since both layout and render have already occurred. Similarly, operations at the `Render` priority can assume that the data-bound properties have obtained their values since render occurs at a lower priority than `DataBind`.

The `Dispatcher` class allows us to post operations onto a queue using the `BeginInvoke` method. You pass in the delegate that should be invoked, the `DispatcherPriority`,

and the arguments to the delegate (if any). Following are some overloads for that
method:

```
public DispatcherOperation BeginInvoke(Delegate method, params object[] args);
public DispatcherOperation BeginInvoke(DispatcherPriority priority, Delegate
➡method);
public DispatcherOperation BeginInvoke(Delegate method, DispatcherPriority
➡priority,
params object[] args);
public DispatcherOperation BeginInvoke(DispatcherPriority priority, Delegate
➡method,
object arg);
public DispatcherOperation BeginInvoke(DispatcherPriority priority, Delegate
➡method,
object arg, params object[] args);
```

Deferring UI Operations

One of the practical uses of `Dispatcher.BeginInvoke` is to post a deferred UI operation on
the dispatcher queue. Since the operation is deferred, it is typically of a lower priority,
such as `DispatcherPriority.Background`. The WPF framework uses this technique to
carry out cleanup activities in case of a virtualized panel. We know from Chapter 8,
"Virtualization," that the virtualization process involves creating the UI containers when
items come into view and removing the containers (cleanup) when they go out of view.
This cleanup activity need not be carried out immediately and can be deferred until all
other non-idle tasks have been completed.

To perform cleanup as a deferred activity, you can post a delegate on the dispatcher queue
at a `Background` priority. The actual removal of the virtualized containers can now be
performed inside this delegate.

Consider a second example where you want to carry out an animation that depends on
the final width and height of a control. The only way to be sure that the control has been
sized is after the layout has been completed. Referring to Table 15.2, we can see that the
layout is completed at the `Loaded` priority. By posting a delegate on the `Dispatcher` queue
with a priority equal to or lower than `Loaded`, we can predictably animate the control.
Since many UI tasks require a completely sized and rendered control, in other words a
loaded control, WPF provides a convenient `Loaded` event on all `FrameworkElements`.

With the previous two examples, you can see that deferred UI operations are pretty useful
for certain kinds of scenarios. If at any time, you have to wait for certain UI tasks to
complete before you can do your work, think of using `Dispatcher.BeginInvoke` with a
lower `DispatcherPriority`.

Posting Messages from Worker Threads

With a single-threaded UI framework like WPF, it is only possible to do UI tasks on the
main thread (that is, the UI thread). If you have to carry out a long-running task like

connecting to a remote server, you cannot start it on the UI thread. Doing so blocks the UI from updating itself, giving the impression that the application has hung. To keep a responsive UI, you need to run these IO- or CPU-bound operations on a separate thread (called the *worker thread*) and post updates periodically on the UI thread.

`Dispatcher.BeginInvoke` is once again a useful method to post updates from a non-UI thread onto a UI thread. It is also a safe way to do so since the `Dispatcher` maintains complete control over the UI thread and ensures that the messages get onto the dispatcher queue. Since you need access to the dispatcher from a non-UI thread, you need to pass in the dispatcher instance at the time you create the thread. The worker thread is generally created on the UI thread, which means you can pass the dispatcher instance using the `Dispatcher.CurrentDispatcher` property.

When posting messages from the worker thread, a `Normal DispatcherPriority` is used. We pick the `Normal` priority because once the work is done, you want to inform the UI as soon as possible. Note that you can also use the `Send` priority, which is the highest, to inform the UI. The usage of the Normal priority is more of a convention.

The idea of posting messages from a worker thread to a UI thread is the building block for multithreaded data binding. You can collect all the data on a worker thread and post an update on the UI when the data is available. Once on the UI thread, you can update the data-bound properties with the new values.

Let's consider an example where we show progress on the UI of a long-running background task. The UI itself is fairly simple and provides buttons to start and stop the background task. When the Start button is clicked, we spawn a new thread for the task and also pass a reference to the `Dispatcher`. From within the task, we can now post UI updates using `Dispatcher.BeginInvoke`.

```
private void StartWork(object sender, RoutedEventArgs e)
{
        _cancelled = false;

        _bgThread = new Thread(new
ParameterizedThreadStart(PerformLongRunningOperation));
        _bgThread.IsBackground = true;

        StartButton.IsEnabled = false;
        CancelButton.IsEnabled = true;
        _bgThread.Start(Dispatcher);
}

private void PerformLongRunningOperation(object argument)
{
        Dispatcher dispatcher = argument as Dispatcher;
        for (int i = 0; i <= 100; i++)
        {
                if (_cancelled) break;
```

```
                Thread.Sleep(250);
                dispatcher.BeginInvoke(DispatcherPriority.Normal, new
Action<int>(ReportOperationProgress), i);
        }

        dispatcher.BeginInvoke(DispatcherPriority.Normal, new
Action(OnOperationComplete));
}

private void ReportOperationProgress(int progress)
{
        DataContext = progress;
}
```

As you can see in the `PerformLongRunningOperation` method, we post an update after each iteration and also after the loop completes. This allows us to do any cleanup activities on the UI. When the Stop button is clicked, we cancel the task by setting the _cancelled flag. Notice that we are checking this flag inside our loop.

```
private void CancelWork(object sender, RoutedEventArgs e)
{
        _cancelled = true;
}

private void OnOperationComplete()
{
        CancelButton.IsEnabled = false;
        StartButton.IsEnabled = true;
}
```

The BackgroundWorker Class

The `BackgroundWorker` class was first introduced in the .Net 2.0 time frame to aid in multithreaded operations on a Windows Forms UI. However, it is also useful in the context of WPF applications. `BackgroundWorker` provides a nice abstraction for updating the UI from a worker thread. All of the thread-switching is handled internally, and appropriate events are raised for doing the long-running task, showing progress on the UI, and doing any work when the long-running task completes.

To actually start the background work, we call the `RunWorkerAsync` method, which raises the `DoWork` event. Progress can be reported from the background task by setting the `WorkerReportsProgress` flag and calling the `ReportProgress()` method on `BackgroundWorker`. This raises the `ProgressChanged` event on the UI thread. To do any cleanup activities on the UI after the background work completes, you can listen to the `RunWorkererCompleted` event.

User cancellation is also supported by setting the `WorkerSupportsCancellation` flag. To respect user cancellations, we should check the `DoWorkEventArgs.CancellationPending` flag in the `DoWork` event handler periodically. If this flag is set, we quit our task, or if it is not, merrily continue until completion.

To demonstrate `BackgroundWorker`, let's convert the example from the previous section to use the `BackgroundWorker` instead of `Dispatcher.BeginInvoke()`. The creation of the `BackgroundWorker` happens when the Start button is clicked. This is the place where we hook up all the event handlers and then kick off the task using the `RunWorkerAsync()` method.

```csharp
private void StartWork(object sender, RoutedEventArgs e)
    {
        _worker = new BackgroundWorker();
        _worker.WorkerSupportsCancellation = true;
        _worker.WorkerReportsProgress = true;

        _worker.DoWork += PerformLongRunningOperation;
        _worker.ProgressChanged += ReportOperationProgress;
        _worker.RunWorkerCompleted += OnOperationCompleted;

        StartButton.IsEnabled = false;
        CancelButton.IsEnabled = true;

        _worker.RunWorkerAsync();
    }

private void PerformLongRunningOperation(object sender, DoWorkEventArgs e)
    {
        BackgroundWorker worker = sender as BackgroundWorker;

        for (int i = 0; i < 100; i++)
        {
            if (worker.CancellationPending)
            {
                break;
            }

            worker.ReportProgress(i);
            Thread.Sleep(1000);
        }
    }

private void CancelWork(object sender, RoutedEventArgs e)
    {
        if (_worker != null)
```

```
        {
            _worker.CancelAsync();
        }
    }
```

Notice the check on the `CancellationPending` flag in the `PerformLongRunningOperation` () method. If this flag is set, we break out of the loop and end the task. When the user clicks the Stop button, we cancel the task using `BackgroundWorker.CancelAsync()` method.

Introduction to Continuous LINQ (CLINQ)

So far in this chapter, we've covered the various things you can do to have your GUI continue to respond as changes occur within the data-bound objects, but what we haven't covered are the various ways that you can make changes to your data-bound objects.

In what most of us think as a traditional data-bound WPF application, we fetch data from some location, perhaps a file on disk, a SQL database, a web service, or even a high-speed messaging system. Once we have the data, we populate the data-bound objects and then the GUI automatically responds because we've been following the advice contained in this chapter up to this point.

This is great, but what do you do when your data changes frequently? What do you if your data changes frequently and you need to continually perform massaging or aggregation operations on that data?

A common solution is to create some kind of timer on a short interval. Each time the timer elapses, your code polls the data to see whether it has changed. If it has, it grabs the data, converts it into a format suitable for your view model, and then the GUI responds accordingly. Polling frequently to detect changes in an underlying data source simply to keep your UI up-to-date is inefficient, hard to maintain, and the code can get very ugly.

Wouldn't it be great if you could declaratively use LINQ (Language Integrated Query) to define a query over some streaming data source that produced view model quality objects that would *continuously update as data arrives, is deleted, or is modified?*

This is where Continuous LINQ (CLINQ) comes in. This is an open-source project that you can find on CodePlex at http://www.codeplex.com/clinq. In short, it takes advantage of the same language extensions that make LINQ over CLR objects possible and rigs up all the plumbing necessary to continually monitor the sources of all of your queries. Each time anything significant happens to an object in the source or the source collection itself, the query is smartly reevaluated and, if necessary, the output results are modified in real-time. This allows you to define, declaratively using familiar LINQ syntax, collection queries and aggregate values that will be continuously updated throughout the lifetime of your application as data is retrieved from remote sources.

Let's start with a simple example. Say that you have a master collection of messages coming from your enterprise called `AllMessages`. You have a WPF application responsible for displaying the messages that are destined for tech support in one list box and the messages destined for R&D in another list box.

Without a tool like CLINQ, you would have to write complicated, hard to read code that polls the contents of the AllMessages collection every few milliseconds and then splits it based on message type. This is horribly inefficient because during each polling cycle, you have to traverse the entire source collection, and even if only one item changed during the polling cycle, you could conceivably end up traversing the entire collection, which could have thousands upon thousands of messages in it.

With CLINQ, you could define your queries like this

```
using System.Linq;
supportMessages = from Message msg in AllMessages
    where msg.MessageType == MessageTypes.SupportMessage
    order by msg.MessageDate descending
    select msg;
devMessages = from Message msg in AllMessages
    where msg.MessageType == MessageTypes.ResearchAndDevelopment
    order by msg.MessageDate descending
    select msg;
```

and be guaranteed that a minimal amount of effort, CPU, and memory would be used to keep your binding-friendly output collections up-to-date and properly sorted in real-time. In addition, CLINQ supports a host of other features including continuous aggregation and even built-in continuous aggregates like sum, average, standard deviation, and much more. Simply manipulate the items within AllMessages from within a background thread (either by hitting a web service or receiving push messages or whatever) and CLINQ takes care of pushing all those changes to where they need to be, including notifying the GUI on the appropriate dispatcher thread.

Kevin Hoffman is the creator of the original version of CLINQ, but Andrew Kutruff has been doing a lot of work lately adding a host of features and performance enhancements, taking the original experiment and turning it into a world-class development library.

Anywhere in WPF that you can bind to a single value or a collection of values, you can bind to the output of a CLINQ query. We strongly urge you to go check out the CodePlex site, download the library, and experiment with it.

Summary

This chapter provided example of some powerful things that you can do to enhance and improve data-bound WPF applications—everything from working with dependency properties to adding notifications on DP changes to working closely with the dispatcher and performing background processing while still allowing your data to be bound smoothly.

By now you should be comfortable getting data from the lower tiers of your application up into the GUI tier, as well as taking events and user input from the GUI and propagating that throughout your objects and middle tiers.

Finally, we introduced you to CLINQ, a library that allows you to declaratively define LINQ queries that stay up-to-date in real-time without the use of a polling timer.

15

Control and Visual Design Tips

This chapter represents a grab bag of tips, tricks, practices, and other bits of knowledge that we have accumulated over the years of building desktop applications and implementing good visual designs in applications. We go through some tips for control design, cover a few useful design patterns, and finally offer some tips for visual design that can apply to many different platforms, not just WPF.

By the end of this chapter, you should feel as though you have even more tools in your tool belt for dealing with the complex, real-world design and implementation problems that arise on a daily basis for WPF developers.

Control Design Tips

Throughout this book, we covered dozens of different types of syntax, libraries, and APIs that you can use to make incredibly powerful and compelling controls. This section provides some tips and tricks that you can keep in mind while designing and building your custom controls that hopefully make those controls easier to build, maintain, and ultimately more powerful and extensible.

Use Internal Resource Dictionaries

Resource dictionaries are a great way to organize resources. WPF provides the `Resources` property that is available on all classes that descend from `FrameworkElement`. This allows us to look up resources defined at the current element, its parent, and all the way up to the root of the application. However, with the `Resources` property, you need to specify the resources external to the control's definition.

Sometimes you may want to keep some resources private to the control and not have them exposed publicly through the Resources property. For example, we saw in Chapter 11, "Bridging the 2D and 3D Worlds," that the Viewport3D definition was contained in an internal ResourceDictionary. This particular resource is only used inside the control and is not particularly useful outside it. Such resources can be organized using internal resource dictionaries. You can couple that with a custom ResourceManager class that can look up a resource generically.

Some of the more useful types of resources that you can embed are control-specific icons, ControlTemplates, DataTemplates, as well as visual trees and Brushes. Using resource dictionaries to define these visuals is far superior to hand-coding them.

Define Complex Controls as Partial Classes

If you are developing controls that have a variety of features and need to implement a set of interfaces, a good organization idea is to make the control a partial class and implement the interfaces in separate files. For example, if you are implementing a control that supports scrolling, virtualization, and custom selection modes you may have to implement interfaces such as IScrollInfo, IVirtualizer, and ISelectionMode (the last two might be interfaces you created that are not part of the core WPF). If the number of methods and properties to implement is really large (like with IScrollInfo), you should split the implementation into multiple files. The main file will be the name of the control, say MyControl.cs. The selection interface can be implemented in a partial class, stored in the MyControl.Selection.cs file. The virtualization logic could be in MyControl.Virtualizer.cs, and so on. Keeping partial classes neatly organized in separate files also keeps the control code maintainable.

You can also group these files inside Visual Studio, just like the Control.xaml and Control.xaml.cs files are grouped. This can be done by editing the .csproj file and using the <DependentUpon> element. Here is a snippet showing how to do the grouping:

```
<Compile Include="MyControl.Selection.cs">
    <DependentUpon>MyControl.cs</DependentUpon>
    <SubType>Code</SubType>
</Compile>
```

Here the partial class that contains the selection logic, defined in MyControl.Selection.cs is visually nested under the MyControl.cs file inside Visual Studio.

Use Scoped Dependency Properties for Internal State Management

For some of your controls, you may have to define additional state that you want to store pertaining to the control. You could be maintaining state either for that control or for the children contained in the control. A common approach is to use a Dictionary<T,S> as a map that stores state of type S against a UIElement of type T.

Another approach is to define protected DPs on the control and use them to set the state on the children using the `DependencyObject.SetValue()` method. Since the DP is protected, only your control or its derived controls can make use of it. This serves as a great way to store control-specific information. Since these are DPs, you can also listen to property changes and take action on state changes in the control. It also gives a way to abstract some of the functional parts of your control.

Use Attached Properties for Adding Functionality

Throughout this book, we've seen clear examples of the virtues of using attached properties, and they are definitely one of the many important arrows in your WPF quiver. They give you a XAML-oriented way to extend the functionality or runtime behavior of your control. Sometimes attached properties on existing controls can give you the extra functionality that you need. This can save you from implementing your own custom controls. The power of WPF really lies in the creative use of templates, attached properties, and styles to get the exact look and feel that you want.

Compose Graphics Using Simpler Building Blocks

Certain templates (for example, `DataTemplate`, `ControlTemplate`) are easier to build if you can identify the primitive visuals that can be used to compose the final look and feel. For example, in Chapter 3, "Getting Started Writing Custom Controls," you saw the use of the `Arc` shape with the `StartAngle` and `EndAngle` properties to define the curve. Later on, we build our `ProgressBar` template by overlaying arcs of various sizes to give it the desired look. Thinking of the template in terms of building blocks like the `Arc` allowed us to quickly compose the graphics.

Discovering the primitive building blocks in a complex visual may not always be straightforward. Thinking of the graphic in terms of its layers helps you understand the visual structure. Refer to Chapter 3 where we talked about thinking in layers.

At first this might be difficult for some people, but the more you use WPF, the easier it becomes. Eventually you will be able to look at a proof from a designer done in Photoshop or Illustrator and be able to pick out the primitive WPF controls that can be composed to create that exact look or effect. Even if you don't have an impending project, you might want to spend time practicing this workflow—taking a flat design mockup from a designer and figuring out how to build that same look using a composition of primitive WPF controls. You can then refactor those primitives into more efficient abstractions and custom controls.

Communicating Between a Control and Its Subparts

When your control has only a few simple parts, it can be easy to simply maintain strong references to the child elements. For example, if your control is a search control that consists of a text box and a search button, you can probably just create standard instances of those components without much worry. However, as the number of moving parts, children, and even descendants in a complicated tree structure increases, maintaining strong references to all of these objects becomes untenable.

Keeping these strong references to subparts and deeper components within a tree leads to messy code and quickly becomes complicated to code, maintain, and debug.

A better way to deal with this problem is to borrow a technique from composite application design and broadcast an internal message to the subparts. Each subpart (or descendant of a subpart) subscribes to these events and can take whatever specific action is necessary in response. Broadcasting events instead of maintaining strong references helps in decoupling the subpart from its containing control and also gives you the flexibility to modify the control hierarchy without breaking dozens of other related components. This particular strategy also fits in well with the development workflow of people who use Inversion of Control (IoC) containers like Unity or Castle Windsor.

For subparts to subscribe to the events, they need to have a reference to their containing parent. There are two ways in which the subparts can discover their parent control. In the first method, the parent is aware of all its children and specifically looks for them. It then passes its "self" reference to each of the children, usually by setting a publicly known property on the subpart. This is typically done in the OnApplyTemplate overridden method of the parent control where it discovers its subparts. This option is a little tricky in that you can easily fall back into the trap of giving the parent too much explicit knowledge (and dependency) on the control hierarchy.

The second method for discovering the parent control involves discovery from the bottom up. For example, each child is aware of its containing parent (aka owning control) and specifically looks it up in the visual tree when it gets loaded. Once it finds the parent, it maintains a reference to the parent. An example of this approach can be found in the case of VirtualizingPanel, which specifically looks for its containing ItemsControl. It needs the reference to its parent to take action whenever new items are added or removed. The panel looks up its parent using the ItemsControl.GetItemsOwner method.

While these two are the most common ways of allowing communication between the children and parent, you need to take a look at *why* you need the communication to take place. If the communication is simply to allow communication to lower tiers, you might want to consider a *service* approach. In this approach, the parent and all children maintain a reference to a service object. This object coordinates communication between children, descendants, and the parent and serves as a gateway to the lower, UI-less tiers. Another advantage to the service approach is that you can have your favorite DI (Dependency Injection) container inject the reference to the service for you automatically and maintain loose coupling between the control and the service. Some books and articles on patterns also refer to this type of service object as a *provider object*.

As an aside, if the subparts are likely to be swapped out without the knowledge of the containing parent, you can use the weak event pattern, discussed in Chapter 14, "Events, Commands, and Focus."

Use a State Machine to Handle Multiple Events and Property Changes

If your control code is becoming a spaghetti bowl of if/else blocks you might be in need of a state machine. A state machine works great to define clear states within the control and what actions need to be taken for different states. You could draw a simple state diagram to depict the flow of control. This technique is just an implementation of the state design pattern. The state transitions happen at a single place in your control, and the rest of the control code only looks at the current state to take state-specific action.

If you find yourself running up a huge number of states or you find that the complexity of describing the workflow within your application is so large that even a simple state machine doesn't seem to be enough, you might want to consider allowing the workflow foundation to take some of that burden off of your GUI and separate the workflow logic completely from the rendering and GUI logic.

Use Low-Priority Delegates for Noncritical Tasks

The `DispatcherPriority` is an enumeration that contains values that range from -1 to 10 with larger numbers indicating higher priority. The `Normal` priority is usually used for application-specific tasks like timers. By designating a callback at `SystemIdle` or `ApplicationIdle`, you can defer noncritical tasks such as cleaning up virtualized containers or doing some background processing on downloaded images, or any UI-specific task that doesn't require user intervention. This could lead to better responsiveness from the application since these tasks are not happening in real-time or blocking while they occur. Typically the cleanup of virtualized containers is done using this technique.

Use `x:Shared` for Cloning Resources

If the resources you use have to be cloned often, it is easier to do it via the Boolean `x:Shared` attribute on a resource. By default, `x:Shared` is set to true, which means that the same instance is returned for each resource lookup. By setting it to false, you can get new instances of the resource each time it is requested. A classic example of this is for the `Storyboard` resource, which may be used several times on a control that animates each of its items. Setting the `x:Shared` attribute to false on the storyboard results in a new instance each time the resource is referenced. The XAML for that looks something like this:

```
<Storyboard x:Key="PlaneJump_Animation"
                      x:Shared="False">
          <DoubleAnimation Duration="0:0:0.25"
                                        To="1" />
     </Storyboard>
```

It also helps for resources that don't have `ICloneable` implemented. In Chapter 11, we saw the usage of `x:Shared` with the `View3DElement` control where the `Viewport3D` had to be cloned for each instance. This was easily done via the `x:Shared` attribute on the `Viewport3D` tag. Note that `Viewport3D` does not implement `ICloneable`, which means there is no programmatic way to actually clone it. However, using the x:Shared attribute gives us this much needed ability.

Use Markup Extensions to Encapsulate Object Creation

Markup extensions provide a great declarative solution for encapsulating custom object creation code. You can think of them as implementations of the factory method pattern, which provides an abstraction over creating instances of a particular class. To create a MarkupExtension, we need to subclass the abstract class MarkupExtension and override the ProvideValue method.

For example, consider the LinearGradientBrushExtension class, which provides a simple way to create LinearGradientBrushes. The following code snippet shows that class in its entirety:

```
public class LinearGradientBrushExtension : MarkupExtension
{
        private static Regex GradientStopsRegex = new Regex(
                    @"(?<GradientStop>\( (?<Offset>\d (\.\d)?) \¦
(?<Color>\#([0-9a-
fA-F]{6} ¦ [0-9a-fA-F]{8}))\)))",
                    RegexOptions.Compiled ¦ RegexOptions.CultureInvariant ¦
RegexOptions.Singleline ¦ RegexOptions.IgnorePatternWhitespace ¦
RegexOptions.IgnoreCase);

        [ConstructorArgument("colors")]
        public string Colors { get; set; }
        public double Angle { get; set; }

        public LinearGradientBrushExtension()
        {

        }

        public LinearGradientBrushExtension(string colors)
        {
                Colors = colors;
        }

        public override object ProvideValue(IServiceProvider serviceProvider)
        {
                MatchCollection m = GradientStopsRegex.Matches(Colors);

                GradientStopCollection stops = new GradientStopCollection();

                foreach (Match match in m)
                {
```

```
            double offset = double.Parse(match.Groups["Offset"].Value);
            string hexColor = match.Groups["Color"].Value;
            Color color = (Color)
ColorConverter.ConvertFromString(hexColor);

            stops.Add(new GradientStop(color, offset));
        }
        return new LinearGradientBrush(stops, Angle);
    }
}
```

This extension defines two properties: Colors and Angle, which can be used to customize the linear gradient brush. We use a regular expression to parse the value of the Colors property. The default constructor allows the XAML parser to create the instance of LinearGradientBrushExtension and call its ProvideValue method. With all of that in place, we can now create a linear gradient brush inline as an attribute value instead of having to reference it as a resource:

```
<Grid Background="{Chapter16:LinearGradientBrush Angle=90,
Colors=(0¦#232323)(1¦#234567)}">
```

Useful Patterns for GUI Development

The following is a quick rundown of various design patterns and how they apply to GUI development, especially to WPF developers. For more information on the individual design patterns and their implementations, we strongly recommend the book *Design Patterns in C#* by Steven John Metsker, ISBN: 0321126971.

The Strategy Pattern

The strategy pattern is typically used to define a family of algorithms. Each algorithm within the family is encapsulated within a class, and, most importantly, the algorithms are interchangeable.

- ▶ Useful if you want dynamic runtime behaviors
- ▶ Can be defined by an interface and provide specific implementations for the different dynamic runtime behaviors
- ▶ Great for delegating functionality to a specific interface implementation
- ▶ Example: Change hover, selection behaviors, or dynamic panel layouts at runtime

The Builder Pattern

The builder pattern involves separating the process of creating a complex object from the object itself. This enables the same construction process to be used to build varying representations.

▶ The builder pattern is good for encapsulating the creation of visual trees and other visual objects like complex storyboards.

▶ The pattern generally is implemented with an abstract base class and supporting derived classes.

▶ The base class defines the skeleton of the creation process and calls more high-level methods on the derived classes.

▶ A strikingly similar pattern called the template is also useful for creating a base skeletal representation of a process. The individual steps of this process are defined in the subclasses, which are implemented as overrides.

Model-View-Controller

The MVC pattern is a classic pattern that enables clear separation of concerns. This pattern splits GUI functionality into three distinct responsibilities: the Model, the View, and the Controller.

▶ The Model and View do not have any knowledge of each other. The Controller establishes the relationship by wiring them together and managing the interactions (behaviors).

▶ If the Controller doesn't do the "wiring," a Dependency Injection (DI) container can perform that responsibility in its place.

▶ The MVC pattern is useful for managing the different moving parts of a custom control. The Controller becomes the central hub for delegating and managing functionality.

▶ Example: Building a list-based control that does selections, virtualization, different hover behaviors, changes of layout, and custom visual creation. These features are not completely independent of each other and require some mediating component. This is the job of the Controller. Each of the changing parts can be replaced with an interface (Inversion of Control principle).

Model-View-View Model

The MVVM pattern is a variation on the MVC pattern and is a popular pattern for building data-bound user interfaces.

▶ Instead of binding directly to the model, the bindings are established on a wrapper UI object called the ViewModel, which maintains a reference to the actual model.

▶ The ViewModel typically implements the INotifyPropertyChanged and/or INotifyCollectionChanged interfaces. Doing so makes the changes in the ViewModel immediately visible in the WPF GUI.

▶ The following article by Josh Smith on *MSDN Magazine* provides a good introduction to MVVM, explaining its benefits with several code samples. Refer to http://msdn.microsoft.com/en-us/magazine/dd419663.aspx.

Factory Method

The factory method pattern is where an interface is defined for creating an object, and subclasses/implementers are the ones that decide which concrete class is instantiated. A common approach is to have a static class that provides methods for creating various kinds of objects.

- ▶ Encapsulates the creation of a complex object with a simple high-level method
- ▶ Good for creating storyboards with some supplied parameters
- ▶ Useful when instantiating custom visual objects like a `ContentControl` used in list-based controls

Composed Method

This is more of an implementation pattern (see *Implementation Patterns* by Kent Beck, ISBN: 0321413091) than a design pattern.

- ▶ Break up long methods into shorter methods and name them such that comments are no longer required.
- ▶ Each statement in a method should be at the same level of abstraction. For example, if you have a method where most of the statements are calls to methods, having a simple statement like incrementing an internal counter variable makes the method unbalanced. This is because all of the statements are not at the same level of abstraction.
- ▶ Kent Beck's book mentioned previously also details several other implementation patterns, which are definitely worth reading.

State Pattern

In a pure implementation of the state pattern, an object's functionality is altered when its internal state has been modified. To external consumers, the object appears to be a different class after the state has changed.

- ▶ If a control supports a variety of views or has different modes of operation, encapsulate this behavior in a state and manage states instead of conditional logic inside each method.
- ▶ The easiest way to identify this is to check whether you are doing state-specific conditional checks in many of your core behavior-defining methods.
- ▶ The state pattern allows you to scale up the set of supported states and turn your control into an arbitrator of states.

Code Should be Idiomatic with Regard to "Framework Design Guidelines"

Even though we are talking about creating controls, we are still creating them in .NET. As such, your code should be, as much as possible, idiomatic .NET code. In other words, it should look like good .NET code and follow the guidelines and conventions set out by industry experts and the Microsoft .NET and C# teams.

The book *Framework Design Guidelines* by Brad Abrams and Krzysztof Cwalina outlines the do's and don'ts of good API design. It is important to organize and structure the code of your control, but it is equally important to make it easy for someone to discover the functionality of your control simply by glancing at the API. Good APIs help make it easy for other developers (in-house or paying customers) to consume your code.

Visual Design Tips

So far we looked at tips, techniques, and best practices for structuring and defining your controls and writing overall good .NET code. This section shifts the attention to the visual aspect of building WPF applications and provides a set of general visual design tips and practices that you will find useful when you have to "XAML-ify" that incredible-looking mockup made by the designer on your team.

Using Tile Brushes

Tile brushes such as `DrawingBrush`, `ImageBrush`, and `VisualBrush` (with viewports) can be used to create interesting background patterns for some controls. You can create a complex nesting of visuals to achieve some interesting and good-looking results. An example of this kind of composed background might be the "swirl" you see in the background of Word 2007.

It is not unusual for designers to create such artwork in Adobe Illustrator since it provides greater flexibility and productive tools for creating vector artwork. Fortunately, you can import an illustrator file into Expression Blend 3 or Expression Design and then export it as XAML. If you are using Expression Blend 3, you can import the AI file, select the root element of the vector artwork, and choose to convert it into a `DrawingBrush`. The `DrawingBrush` can then be used as a background for your elements. If you plan on animating some of the elements in the vector artwork, you can leave the imported artwork in its default XAML form, which is basically a `Canvas` tag with nested `Path` elements.

The following example shows the background swirl that you see in Word 2007, implemented without the use of rasterized graphics in native XAML. The original artwork was created in Adobe Illustrator and then imported into Expression Blend 3. Within Blend 3, we selected the root visual of the imported artwork and then converted that into a `DrawingBrush`. The result is shown in Figure 16.1.

The corresponding XAML code for the `DrawingBrush` is as follows:

FIGURE 16.1   A **DrawingBrush** used to emulate the Word 2007 "swirl."

```xml
<DrawingBrush x:Key="WordSwirlBrush"
                    Viewbox="0,0,624,444"
                    ViewboxUnits="Absolute">
        <DrawingBrush.Drawing>
            <DrawingGroup>
                <GeometryDrawing Geometry="M0,480L640,480 640,0 0,0z">
                    <GeometryDrawing.Brush>
                        <LinearGradientBrush EndPoint="0.5,0"
                                StartPoint="0.5,1">
                        <GradientStop Color="#FF000000"
                                Offset="0" />
                        <GradientStop Color="#FF656565"
                                Offset="1" />
                        </LinearGradientBrush>
                    </GeometryDrawing.Brush>
                </GeometryDrawing>
                <GeometryDrawing Brush="#FF7D7D7D"
                        Geometry="M321.09099,16.429
C354.92299,9.3469997 388.46199,3.8959999 421.33499,1.4242829E-11 L-5.0590639E-
12,1.4242829E-11 -5.0590639E- 12,146.941 C75.818998,91.880997 188.428,44.199999
321.09099,16.429" />
                <GeometryDrawing Brush="#FF636363"
                        Geometry="M314.52999,16.092999
C347.67099,9.1559997 380.52399,3.8159999 412.72699,-5.0413008E-12 L-5.0022209E-12,-
5.0413008E-12 -5.0022209E-
12,143.93799 C74.269999,90.003997 184.578,43.295998 314.52999,16.092999" />
                <DrawingGroup>
```

```
                        <DrawingGroup.Transform>
                    <MatrixTransform Matrix="1,0,0,1,2.8421709430404E-14,0" />
                        </DrawingGroup.Transform>
        <GeometryDrawing Brush="#FF7D7D7D"
                        Geometry="M358.671,12.268 C396.463,6.9799998
  433.928,2.9089999 470.649,-1.0089707E-11 L-2.5011104E-12,-1.0089707E-11 -
2.5011104E-12,109.723 C84.692001,68.608998 210.482,33.003999 358.671,12.268" />
                    </DrawingGroup>
                </DrawingGroup>
            </DrawingBrush.Drawing>
    </DrawingBrush>
```

Using Gradients with Relative Transforms

Gradient brushes in WPF are powerful and have a lot of interesting features.
SpreadMethod and RelativeTransform are two lesser-used properties that, when
combined, can create compelling effects. Take a look at the gradient shown in Figure 16.2,
which creates a nice candy cane effect. It has been created using LinearGradientBrush
with a SpreadMethod of Repeat.

FIGURE 16.2   Candy cane gradient bar.

The XAML for this brush is as follows:

```
<LinearGradientBrush SpreadMethod="Repeat"
                              EndPoint="0.939,-0.007"
                              StartPoint="0.821,0.49">
                <LinearGradientBrush.RelativeTransform>
                    <TranslateTransform X="0"
                                        Y="0" />
                </LinearGradientBrush.RelativeTransform>
                <GradientStop Color="#FFEAEAEA"
                            Offset="0" />
                <GradientStop Color="#FFFFFFFF"
                            Offset="0.522" />
                <GradientStop Color="#FFC30000"
                            Offset="0.526" />
                <GradientStop Color="#FFFF0000"
                            Offset="1" />
            </LinearGradientBrush>
```

The gradient brush definitely provides an interesting effect, but this is only the tip of the
iceberg. We can take this effect up a notch by animating it. You may have seen progress

animations on the Web, other applications, or other operating systems where the stripes (like the ones in Figure 16.2) move horizontally, giving you the impression of forward progress or motion. It represents a state where the web page or application is doing some work and showing some progress toward the completion of that work. This can be easily achieved by animating the `RelativeTransform` property of the `LinearGradientBrush`, specifically the `TranslateTransform.X` property. The storyboard for this animation looks like this:

```
<Storyboard x:Key="ProgressAnimation"
            RepeatBehavior="Forever">
    <DoubleAnimationUsingKeyFrames BeginTime="00:00:00"
                            Storyboard.TargetName="rectangle"
                            Storyboard.TargetProperty="(Shape.Fill).
Brush.RelativeTransform).(TranslateTransform.X)
">
            <SplineDoubleKeyFrame KeyTime="00:00:00"
                            Value="0" />
            <SplineDoubleKeyFrame KeyTime="00:00:03"
                            Value="0.715" />
    </DoubleAnimationUsingKeyFrames>
</Storyboard>
```

The actual values for the keyframes were tweaked in Expression Blend such that the start and end of the animation matched exactly. This is essential to get the continuously flowing stripes effect. Note that the storyboard has a `RepeatBehavior` set to `Forever`, which results in a nonstop animation. As you can see, a relatively complex-looking animation can be easily achieved with creative use of gradient brush relative transforms. Try playing with different values for the `StartPoint`, `EndPoint`, and `GradientStops` to get some other interesting effects.

XAML Coding Conventions

The following is a set of XAML coding conventions that you may choose to follow or set as standards for your development team. These are our personal opinions, and, should you choose to follow these guidelines, we are not responsible for damage that may occur to your machine or nearby small furry animals:

▶ Keep all of your brushes in a `Brushes.xaml` file.

▶ If you have more complex brushes, say `DrawingBrushes`, you can put them in their own XAML files and add into a `MergedDictionary` inside `Brushes.xaml`. The whole idea is to have organized files and resources that can be located easily.

▶ Have an `AppResources.xaml` file that contains the `MergedDictionary` of all the resources in your application. This is sometimes easier to manipulate than having the `MergedDictionary` inside `App.xaml`.

▶ Have a folder called StyleGuide that contains all the XAML files and design assets.

▶ Try to organize the files into separate folders if there are too many in number. For example, if you have a variety of templates for ContentControls, you can put them in separate XAML files named according to the context in which they are used.

▶ Use themes, skins, application-specific styles, and window-specific resources and refactor them all into separate assemblies.

▶ Use a separate ResourceDictionary to capture common sizes and values used throughout the application—for example, margins, fonts, text styles, converters, and anything else you may use repeatedly throughout an application.

▶ These guidelines are meant to improve the workflow between designers and developers, which is an integral part of building WPF applications. For an in-depth understanding of this topic, refer to this white paper: http://windowsclient.net/wpf/white-papers/thenewiteration.aspx.

Use the Vista Interface Guidelines

WPF gives you spectacular power to create highly stylized interfaces. It also gives you tremendous amounts of flexibility and choice. Having all of this power and flexibility can often lead you to create user interfaces that, although beautiful, might be so unfamiliar with the way users do their regular day-to-day work that the use of the application feels awkward and cumbersome to them.

To help steer you in the right direction, Microsoft has a set of UI design guidelines to which Windows Vista also adheres. By keeping these guidelines in mind when building your application, you can make informed choices in structuring your application to help make your users feel at home when using it. The online reference to the UX guidelines can be found at http://msdn.microsoft.com/en-us/library/aa511258.aspx.

Keep in mind that this does *not* mean that your application needs to look exactly like Windows Vista. It only means that there are common metaphors and paradigms that users of Windows Vista have come to expect, and if your application incorporates some of those common preconceptions, it may be easier for people to use and may seem more familiar them.

Using Nonstandard Fonts for Icons

Using embedded fonts for interesting visuals (think Dingbats and Wingdings, for example) has been a common technique for quite some time now and remains a valid technique for use in WPF applications.

Using these fonts at larger sizes can often be a good substitute for using certain kinds of rasterized visuals. For example, Figure 16.3 shows two buttons that use the Webdings font for the left/right arrows.

FIGURE 16.3   Using Webdings for left and right arrows.

The XAML for these buttons looks like this:

```
<Grid>
        <StackPanel Orientation="Horizontal"
                        VerticalAlignment="Center"
                        HorizontalAlignment="Center">
        <Button Width="100"
                        Height="100">
            <TextBlock Text="3"
                        FontFamily="Webdings"
                        FontSize="72" />
        </Button>
        <Button Width="100"
                        Height="100">
            <TextBlock Text="4"
                            FontFamily="Webdings"
                            FontSize="72" />
        </Button>
</StackPanel>
</Grid>
```

Using fonts like Webdings and Dingbats can be great for designing some of the icons in your application. If you think these default fonts (which should definitely be present on the average Windows installation) are not sufficient, you can search the Web for many more alternative fonts.

Using Transparent PNGs

The use of transparent PNGs is possibly one of the most underrated but powerful techniques you can adopt. They can be used to add seemingly complex effects to your application that are actually nothing more than carefully arranged layers of transparent PNGs.

One such technique is to use PNG sequences to play high-fidelity animations or any nonstandard animation that cannot be created using storyboards. The PNG sequence can be created in a motion-graphics editing tool and exported as a PNG sequence. Typically these sequences are numbered, and it becomes easier to loop through these images in your control code. The motion-graphics software also allows you to specify the numbering format. By authoring a simple control that displays these images at the same frame rate at which they were created, you can reproduce the animation within a WPF application.

Import from Photoshop and Illustrator

Another useful visual design tip is to use Adobe Illustrator to design complex vector graphics as it provides powerful tools for vector manipulation. You can then save it with the PDF Export option and import the .ai file into Expression Design or Expression Blend 3. With Blend 3, you can also import Photoshop PSD files. We already saw an example of this technique with the Word 2007 swirl in the previous section.

Opacity Masks

Opacity masks (which are a type of brush) come in handy when you want to mask or clip areas of a visual that cannot be easily described using a path element. For example, a mask that gradually fades off at the bottom is hard to describe with a path element. Instead, an opacity mask with a linear gradient brush can be used to achieve this effect. The reflection effect, which is a popular Web 2.0 style effect and already discussed in Chapter 9, "Creating Advanced Controls and Visual Effects," can be built using this approach.

The power of opacity masks becomes more apparent when used with images. A transparent PNG image, used as an `ImageBrush`, can be useful to create a soft-edged visual. Soft edges on a visual refer to edges that gradually fade off and create a nice blend with the visuals below it. This technique was also discussed in Chapter 9. Opacity masks give that extra creative flexibility, which is sometimes hard to achieve with discrete vectors. It might seem strange, but transparent bitmaps are incredibly useful in a vector world.

Using Clip Geometries

The `Clip` property on a `UIElement` is used to hide parts of the element. The geometry specified by the clip is the part that is actually revealed. In terms of behavior, the `Clip` is similar to an opacity mask in that it is used to conceal parts of the visual. However, unlike the opacity mask, which is a brush, `Clip` is of type `Geometry`, which means you get a vector to describe the clipped part of the visual. Figure 16.4, followed by the corresponding XAML, shows the difference between clipping and opacity masks. The opacity mask has been created using a `RadialGradientBrush`, whereas the `Clip` is an `EllipseGeometry`.

With OpacityMask   With Clip geometry

FIGURE 16.4   Opacity mask versus clipping geometry.

The corresponding XAML is as follows:

```
<Image Source="/Resources;;;component\Shared\toucan.jpg"
       Width="300">
    <Image.OpacityMask>
        <RadialGradientBrush RadiusX="75"
                             RadiusY="75"
                             MappingMode="Absolute"
```

```
                    GradientOrigin="150,100"
                    Center="150,100">
          <GradientStop Color="White"
                    Offset="0" />
          <GradientStop Color="Transparent"
                    Offset="1" />
        </RadialGradientBrush>
      </Image.OpacityMask>
    </Image>
    <Image Source="/Resources;;;component\Shared\toucan.jpg"
          Width="300">
      <Image.Clip>
        <EllipseGeometry RadiusX="75"
                    RadiusY="75"
                    Center="150,100" />
      </Image.Clip>
    </Image>
```

Instead of a fixed geometry, we can also animate the Clip, which leads us to interesting possibilities. You can use clip geometry animations to create transitions between visuals or progressively reveal a single visual. The following example shows an animation for progressively revealing a Path element. The animation makes the Path appear as if it is drawing itself slowly over time.

```
<Grid Width="400"
      Height="200">
  <Path Stretch="Fill"
        Stroke="#FF000000"
        Data="M125,207 C138.44886,207 147.60709,210.25003 159,203
174.39332,193.20425 163.45714,185.09285 186,202 190.96352,205.72264
187.26771,213.91536 196,203 200.4998,197.37525 198.61039,190.40559 209,196
228.27092,206.37665
213.29623,208.70377 234,188 239.05209,193.05209 242,206.72788 242,215
245.86032,209.8529 244.56681,205.57178 252,205 260.84815,204.31937
260.50858,200.10191&#xd;&#xa;266,212
268.05653,216.45582 266.90929,221.66652 276,215 279.40037,212.5064
281.81893,208.09463 284,219 293.09107,222.03036 295.49576,211.74788 304,216
310.93796,219.46898
322.62612,215.75074 329,220 333.19255,222.79503 329.97704,230.40897 333,232
334.91785,233.00939 335.32557,229.50233 337,229 339.92457,228.12263 343.86855,229
347,229 354.67657,229&#xd;&#xa;373.00576,221.03456 375,233 399.15241,233
400.94198,219.94198 423,242 427.06008,236.58656 425,231.26262 425,224 425,242.09143
431,259.89144 431,278
```

16

```
431,242.015 420.41503,195.75492 432,161 449.89521,178.89521 461.74977,218.74885
467,245 467,244 467,243 467,242 467,241.33333 467,240.66667
467,240&#xd;&#xa;467,244 467,248 467,252 473.40762,239.18476 467.32981,245 486,245
494.33333,245 502.66667,245 511,245 511,247.66667 511,250.33333 511,253
515.68677,250.18794 519.65275,246.18406 523,242
523,242.66667 523,243.33333 523,244"
                StrokeThickness="2" />


        <Grid.Clip>
            <RectangleGeometry x:Name="ClipRect"
                            Rect="0,0,0,0" />
        </Grid.Clip>
    </Grid>
```

We animate the `RectangleGeometry`'s `Rect` property with a `RectAnimation`. The animation starts out with a zero-width `Rect` and goes to the full-width of the graph.

```
        <Storyboard>
            <RectAnimation From="0,0,0,200"
                        To="0,0,400,200"
                        Duration="0:0:1"
                        Storyboard.TargetName="ClipRect"
                        Storyboard.TargetProperty="Rect" />
        </Storyboard>
```

To run this example, refer to the `Chapter16/ClipAnimationExample.xaml` in the sample code for the book.

Some Useful Tools

For most WPF developers, Visual Studio (and its rich plug-in ecosystem) is the world, but if you have a design bent of mind, styling controls for your interface, Expression Blend, Illustrator, and Photoshop occupy your desktop. Although the aforementioned tools are the main tools of trade, there are few others that we think will be useful in your WPF development.

Snoop

Snoop is a tool developed by Pete Blois that allows you to inspect the WPF UI at runtime. It gives you a complete picture of the visual tree, allowing you to monitor events happening in the application and also modify some properties to see live changes. It also serves as a great runtime debugging tool to check whether your UI is rendering the way you expect. Figure 16.5 shows how the Snoop tool looks when inspecting BookExplorer, the application containing all the examples in this book. To download this tool, visit http://blois.us/Snoop.

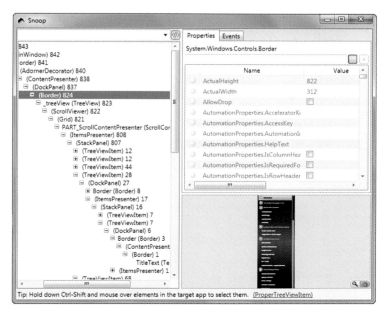

FIGURE 16.5   The Snoop window showing the visual tree, property pane, and the preview pane.

Mole

While Snoop allows you to inspect a running WPF app, Mole is an open-source tool that allows you to inspect the visual tree inside the Visual Studio Debugger. It is essentially a debugger visualizer for the WPF visual and logical trees. It is written by Karl Shifflett, Josh Smith, and Andrew Smith. The latest version along with rich documentation can be obtained from http://karlshifflett.wordpress.com/mole-for-visual-studio. Figure 16.6 shows a screenshot of the visualize window, which is launched when you hit a breakpoint and select the Mole visualizer on an instance of a visual object.

Kaxaml

Kaxaml is a handy (and great-looking) tool for experimenting with XAML. It gives you a live preview of the rendered XAML as you type and also has some IntelliSense to auto-complete the properties of a tag. It also has other useful features such as formatting XAML, storing XAML snippets, taking snapshots of visuals, and so on. Although Expression Blend is a commonly preferred tool for rapid prototyping, Kaxaml comes in handy when you want to quickly try out a few concepts in plain old XAML. This tool was developed by Robby Ingebretsen and can be downloaded from http://www.kazaml.com. Figure 16.7 illustrates Kaxaml in action.

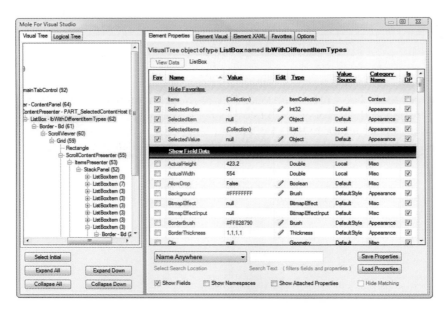

FIGURE 16.6   The Mole window showing various ways to explore the visual and logical tree.

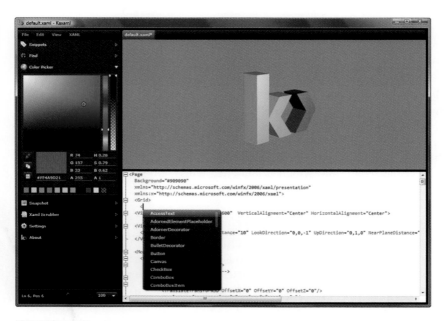

FIGURE 16.7   Kaxaml.

Summary

In this chapter, we discussed a large grab bag of tips, tricks, techniques, and patterns for working with WPF controls, designing the visuals, and building generally better WPF applications. We started with some important ideas for organizing and structuring your control code. Then we looked at some common and useful design patterns and how they apply to WPF application and control development. In the visual design section, we looked at a variety of techniques for making visually pleasing WPF applications. Finally, we wrapped up with a list of useful tools that make WPF development all the more fun.

16

CHAPTER 17

Performance

Improving the performance of WPF controls and applications is a large topic and could fill an entire book on its own. Many people think that performance tuning is really about taking a small section of a method and optimizing it to run faster. While that is certainly one type of performance tuning, it isn't the big picture. Performance tuning is a process of arriving at a global optimum.

Performance tweaks can be applied at multiple levels, the combination of which gives the user the perception of a faster application. In this chapter, we discuss some of the different ways in which performance can be improved and also leave you with some pointers to online resources for further study. Thinking early about performance is a sure-fire way to meet your performance goals, but you have to remember to stay away from premature optimization (the act of applying optimization techniques too early or without profiling the application)—which can cause other architectural problems for your application.

Performance is often a juggle between time and space trade-offs. Although this chapter talks specifically about improving the performance of a WPF application, we are still talking about a .NET application underneath. This means that many of the standard performance optimization techniques that people make at the lower levels of .NET applications can improve the performance of a WPF application as well.

The MSDN online reference offers in-depth coverage about improving the performance of a .NET application. We think that you will see the most dramatic performance improvement in your application by combining the strategies from the online references with the ones covered in this chapter.

Different Kinds of Performance

The WPF framework is rich and deep with a wide range of features. It's no wonder that there are many areas in which performance tweaks can be applied. With so much to think about when building a WPF application, it's easy to miss areas for improving performance. This section provides a brief overview of the various areas of WPF in which performance enhancements are typically applied, including the following:

- ▶ Choice of visuals

- ▶ Brushes and caching

- ▶ Resource management

- ▶ Reference handling

- ▶ Data binding

- ▶ Background threads

- ▶ Scrolling and virtualization

- ▶ Storyboard animations

- ▶ Pixel shaders

- ▶ `FrameworkPropertyMetadataOptions`

- ▶ `RenderCapability`: Hardware and software rendering

- ▶ Optimizing the render pipeline

- ▶ 3D visuals

Choice of Visuals

The graphic elements in WPF range from the simplest visual to the complex control. For getting the maximum performance from your control, you need to pick a visual class depending on the visual richness that is desired along with the total number of instances of the visual that would be present. For example, if you want to create a charting control with potentially tens of thousands of data points, you cannot afford to instantiate a control for each data point. That would drastically raise the working set, leading to a poorly performing application. A `DrawingVisual` would provide better performance since it has a much lower memory footprint and also has fewer services (that is, no layout, data binding, styles, and so on). You can refer to Chapter 2, "The Diverse Visual Class Structure," to refresh your memory on the different visual classes.

Panels, the layout champions of WPF, also provide varying levels of complexity. The simplest panel, `Canvas`, gives you the maximum performance but with the least amount of features. In fact, counter to the purpose of what most people use panels for, a `Canvas` hardly does any layout and only does absolute positioning of its children. On the other hand, panels like `Grid` and `DockPanel` provide many more features but come with additional CPU cost. The choice of a good panel plays an important role especially when rendering large visual trees.

Text is another area where you can squeeze out performance gains especially for cases where a lot of textual content is being rendered. Think of a data grid control that has a column of type string. By default, this column is rendered using a `TextBlock`. However, if you have a large number of rows, better options are available to you. Instead of a `TextBlock`, you could have a template defined using simple glyphs or a custom element that draws out a `GlyphRun` in the `OnRender` override with tighter constraints. If the primary purpose is to present large amounts of text, a `FlowDocument` or `FixedDocument` is ideal.

When you are looking for both high visual richness and something that is easy to manipulate, you want to use a `Control`, which has additional facilities like `ControlTemplates` and `DataTemplates`. A `Control` gives you the ability to define a visual entirely in XAML, including the interactive behaviors for the mouse and keyboard. If the number of instances that you might have on hand at any given time is relatively high, you might switch to a virtualized control that keeps the instance count low but still allows the user to access large numbers of controls.

Visual richness should always be scaled from low to high. Start the thinking process with plain visuals and scale them up as your needs become more crystallized. Once you make a large investment of both time and resources in your visual design, it becomes hard to throw it away (physically and emotionally!). This doesn't mean you can't build beautiful prototypes, but starting with the simplest control and gradually upgrading and adding features is usually more productive than aiming for the most complex visual tree first.

WPF uses what is called the *painter's algorithm*, which is just another way of saying that it paints from back to front. Visuals lower in the stack order are painted before higher-order visuals. If a higher-order visual completely obscures a lower-order visual, it is better to remove the lower-order visual. For example, if you have some background animation that is being obscured almost completely by some content overlaid on top, it is probably better to remove that animation completely as the user can't see it in the first place.

All modern graphics/game engines do this task automatically—polygons that the camera can't see are never rendered. Unfortunately, WPF won't do this for you. So if you find that your UI *appears* simple and uncluttered but is still running slowly and consuming a lot of CPU, check and see whether you have something complex in the tree that is just obscured by higher order controls.

Brushes and Caching

VisualBrush is a live brush, which means it is refreshed in each render cycle. This is unlike the behavior of brushes like SolidColorBrush, which have a fixed rendering and do not refresh during each render cycle. For a VisualBrush that is being refreshed from a complex and frequently changing visual tree, this could be a costly operation.

To minimize the refreshes on the VisualBrush, WPF provides caching hints that can help to improve the performance. By default, WPF does not cache a TileBrush (VisualBrush derives from this class) and caching needs to be specified explicitly. RenderOptions.CachingHint is one property that you can set to enable caching on the visual brush. This can be further controlled by setting the cache invalidation threshold. The invalidation threshold is a ratio by which the visual changes its size before a refresh is performed. For example, a value of 0.5 means that the size of the visual could drop by 50% before a refresh is called. Similarly, a value of 2.0 means that the size of the visual should scale up by 200% before causing a refresh. Two properties—CacheInvalidation.Thresholdminimum and CacheInvalidation.Thresholdmaximum—control the caching policy. They are typically set to values of 0.5 and 2.0, respectively. Here is a code snippet that shows how you can set the caching hints for a visual brush:

```
VisualBrush brush = new VisualBrush(elt);
RenderOptions.SetCacheInvalidationThresholdMinimum(brush, 0.5);
RenderOptions.SetCacheInvalidationThresholdMaximum(brush, 2.0);
```

If you are planning to make heavy use of opacities, it is recommended that you apply the opacity to brushes instead of the visuals. Opacities applied on a brush result in a faster blend with the visuals below than applying the opacity on the element directly.

If the sole purpose of using a VisualBrush is to show a static visual, you can use the RenderTargetBitmap class, which creates a static bitmap of the visual. The classic case for using VisualBrushes is for transitions. In those cases, you really don't care so much for a live visual because the transition is typically done quickly and you don't want people clicking the in-transit elements anyway. In this case, you want to take a static snapshot of the rendered control, and RenderTargetBitmap is the best tool for the job here.

The RenderTargetBitmap class, which is part of the System.Windows.Media.Imaging namespace, has a method called Render that takes in a visual as a parameter and generates a bitmap snapshot of the visual as it appeared at the time of the method call.

```
RenderTargetBitmap bitmap = new RenderTargetBitmap((int)_video.NaturalVideoWidth,
                  (int)_video.NaturalVideoHeight, 96, 96, PixelFormats.Pbgra32);
bitmap.Render(_video);
bitmap.Freeze();
```

In the preceding snippet, _video is an instance of MediaElement. We are also freezing the bitmap to improve performance. The use of freezable controls is discussed in the "Data Binding and Freezables" section later in the chapter.

Resource Management

Shared resources should always be at a level where they can be shared the most among all controls, pages, and windows. For example, if a `LinearGradientBrush` resource is being used by several `UserControls` in your application, you could put that in the `Application.Resources` dictionary, making it globally available. At the same time, avoid having resources directly in `DataTemplates` or `ControlTemplates` since those templates can be created multiple times, resulting in multiple copies of the same resource. Always be wary of the impact a resource might have on your overall working set.

`StaticResources` should be generally preferred over `DynamicResources` unless you need runtime skinning of your application (see Chapter 10, "Control Skinning and Themes," for a discussion of runtime skinning). For large applications, the difference between these two kinds of resources is not so noticeable, in which case you can adopt `DynamicResources` throughout the application.

Reference Handling

We are all aware that subscribing to events results in strong references being maintained by the event source. If the source lives longer than the subscribers, the subscriber instances are not garbage collected because of the strong references. When such a situation arises, you should resort to the use of weak events (as we saw in Chapter 14, "Events, Commands, and Focus"), or find an appropriate time to detach the handlers from the source, say the `Unloaded` event of a page, user control, or window.

There are also instances where implicit strong references are created, such as `DataBinding` scenarios. A binding established on a target that binds to a value on a source and where the source lives longer than the target could be the cause of an uncollected target. Make sure you remove these bindings when the visual is removed. Similarly, if you have continuously running animations on your page or window, make sure you remove the storyboard when you navigate away from the page or close the window. Storyboards can be removed using the `Remove` method.

The following article by Jossef Goldberg discusses a few more cases: http://blogs.msdn.com/jgoldb/archive/2008/02/04/finding-memory-leaks-in-wpf-based-applications.aspx.

Data Binding and Freezables

Data binding is one of the most powerful features of WPF and is used heavily within `DataTemplates`. The data binding engine in WPF works by listening to property changes on objects and ensuring that the GUI is updated accordingly. In addition, changes in the GUI can also be pushed onto data-bound objects. In the case of `DataTemplates`, whenever the source instance changes, the template is regenerated. If you expect the source to change often, the template that was instantiated only a few moments ago will be thrown away and a completely new one will be created. This could result in an undesirable spike in CPU usage for frequently changing data.

17

Instead of binding to the object, you can bind to a proxy that internally forwards requests to the real object. The proxy implements INotifyPropertyChanged and surfaces the property changes on its contained object. This way the DataTemplate is not regenerated each time the real object changes, since the template is only listening to changes on the proxy instance, which is fixed. This is a useful pattern to use whenever the DataContext associated with the DataTemplate changes often.

For more details on data binding proxies, refer to this article by Jossef Goldberg: http:/ /download.microsoft.com/download/2/d/b/2db72dcf-5ae0-445f-b709-7f34437d8b21/ Scrolling_in_WPF.doc.

Pretty much all of the visual changes in WPF are driven by property change notifications that are happening in the visual tree. WPF has a class called Freezable that provides the ability to turn off these property change notifications by freezing the instance. The kind of objects that can be frozen include animations, storyboards, brushes, styles, templates, and pretty much any resource that you define in your visual tree. Freezing these objects also allows you to use them in cross-thread scenarios.

A Freezable instance can be explicitly frozen by using the Freeze method. You can also freeze an object in markup using the PresentationOptions:Freeze attribute defined in the http://schemas.microsoft.com/winfx/2006/xaml/presentation/options namespace. The xmlns:PresentationOptions prefix is the recommended prefix when using this in XAML.

You should note that certain kinds of freezables cannot be frozen, including the following:

- ▶ Freezables that have animated or data-bound properties
- ▶ Freezables that contain subobjects that cannot be frozen
- ▶ Freezables that have properties that are set by a dynamic resource reference

For an in-depth overview of freezables, refer to this MSDN article: http://msdn.microsoft. com/en-us/library/ms750509.aspx.

Background Threads for Long-Running Operations

Long-running operations should always be carried out on a separate thread, and regular updates should be posted on the UI thread using the Dispatcher.BeginInvoke method. Doing any long-running operation on the UI thread blocks it from doing any UI updates, making your application appear hung. When a UI thread is blocked (waiting for something to happen) for long enough, some versions of Windows actually try to indicate to the user that the application is "Not Responding." We have already explored this concept in Chapter 15, "Advanced Data Binding," where we looked at the Dispatcher class and also the BackgroundWorker class that provides an abstraction over Dispatcher.BeginInvoke.

Scrolling and Virtualization

In Chapter 7, "Advanced Scrolling," when talking about IScrollInfo, we saw that there are two kinds of scrolling: logical and physical. Logical scrolling performs the scroll movement based on individual items, whereas physical scrolling is similar to pixel-based scrolling. Sometimes you might find logical scrolling to be a little more efficient because the visuals are rendered only when a new item falls *completely* into the view. Pixel-based scrolling requires more CPU resources since every pixel scroll requires the item to be rendered.

The .NET Framework v3.5 SP1 also introduces the notion of deferred scrolling. Deferred scrolling allows the user to move the scroll thumb without actually scrolling the panel. The panel is scrolled only when the user leaves (lets go of) the thumb. This really helps when you might have tens of thousands of rows and someone wants to scroll down to roughly the 75% point within the data set. Without deferred scrolling, thousands of individual scroll messages would be sent and individual scroll operations would take place, dramatically impacting performance. Logical scrolling and deferred scrolling are some of the ways in which you can improve your application's scrolling performance, especially for large data sets.

If you have a list with a large number of items but only a few visible at any given time, there is no need to create the visuals for all of the items. A way to make this more efficient would be to create visuals only for those items currently in the view. This is the premise for UI virtualization, as we saw in Chapter 8, "Virtualization." The .NET Framework v3.5 SP1 also introduced an additional optimization mechanism in virtualization scenarios called *container recycling*.

Container recycling optimizes the generation of containers by reusing existing ones. In the current version of the framework, only the `VirtualizingStackPanel` has the built-in capability to perform container recycling. This was covered in greater detail in Chapter 8.

Storyboard Animations

By default, WPF plays all animations at 60 frames per second. This frame rate might actually be too high for most applications and create an unnecessary rendering burden on the application. Fortunately, you can lower this frame rate with the `Timeline.DesiredFrameRateProperty`. Setting this to a lower value before an animation is started can give the animation a performance boost, especially if you have multiple animations going on simultaneously.

Pixel Shaders

Pixel shaders, as you have already seen in this book, work great on large areas. However, they do not work so well for many small areas. For each effect, a temporary composition surface is created, which is then pushed for rendering. If you have many small areas, these temporary composition surfaces increase and can cause the application to become sluggish and slow to respond. In short, you want to avoid scenarios where you have large numbers of small region pixel shader effects on the screen at any given time.

Framework Property Metadata Options

When defining a `DependencyProperty`, you have the option to specify metadata flags using `FrameworkMetadataOptions`. This metadata is evaluated each time the property changes. A few flags such as `AffectsRender`, `AffectsMeasure`, `AffectsArrange`, `AffectsParentMeasure`, and `AffectsParentArrange` should be used cautiously for cases where there might be frequent changes to the property value. Layout could be a costly operation when these flags cause cascading layout refreshes.

An alternative is to manually invoke `InvalidateMeasure`, `InvalidateArrange`, or `InvalidateVisual` in the DP's property changed handler. This can also be used to combine a bunch of visual updates into one single update. For example, if you have a custom control that is supposed to handle visual updates happening at a high frequency, you could group a set of updates into one by specifically calling `InvalidateVisual` when the batch of updates is ready to be displayed.

`FrameworkPropertyMetatadaOptions.Inherits` is yet another flag that should be used with caution. The `Inherits` flag is a convenient way to propagate DP values from the root to the descendants. When a value is set at the parent or root level, it is automatically propagated to all descendants who possess that property. This could have performance implications especially if a property change can cause side-effects such as layout updates, invoking property changed handlers, and so on. In WPF, the font-related properties, such as `FontFamily`, `FontStyle`, and `FontSize`, defined on `System.Windows.Documents.TextElement`, have their metadata set to `FrameworkPropertyMetadataOptions.Inherits`.

RenderCapability—Hardware and Software Rendering

WPF applications work on a variety of Windows systems from Windows XP to Windows 7 as well as many hardware and software configurations. If your graphics-intensive applications and controls need to run in varied environments, you might want a way to gradually scale the visual richness. In other words, you might want to disable certain animations or shaders on low-end systems but have them run with full richness on faster systems with better video cards. What you really need is an adaptable UI, and thankfully WPF gives you that ability out of the box.

WPF allows you to inspect the environment and make these rendering decisions. `RenderCapability.Tier` is one property that you can use to adjust the visual complexity to match the capabilities of the workstation. This property is of type `Integer` and can have values ranging from 0 to 2. Tier 0 has the least amount of capabilities. It has no hardware acceleration, and certain features such as `TileBrushes`, `RadialGradientBrush`, 3D lighting, layered windows, and so on are all software rendered. Tier 1 has partial hardware acceleration, while Tier 2 is the most powerful and tries to hardware accelerate most of the features of WPF. However, certain features such as `RadialGradientBrush`, `TileBrushes`, and 3D lighting when applied on *large* textures still result in software rendering as a fallback plan.

In addition to dynamically scaling the visual complexity and richness of your application based on the `Tier` property, you can also profile your application to determine the thresholds for RAM and CPU usage. Later in this chapter, we look at a few tools that can help you in profiling your application.

Optimizing the Render Pipeline

A visual in WPF goes through multiple stages of rendering before the rasterized output is sent to the video card for display. These stages are shown in Figure 17.1.

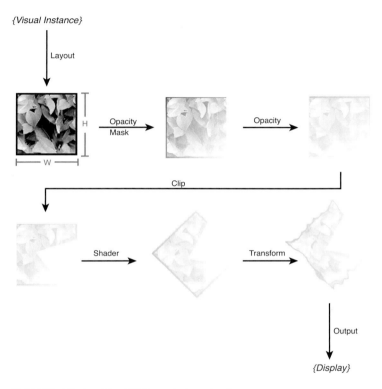

FIGURE 17.1   The WPF rendering pipeline.

If many elements are going through these stages, the rendering is going to take longer. Try to see whether some of these stages can be combined. For example, the opacity and opacity masks need not be separate. In other words, it may be possible to make do with a single opacity mask or only the opacity. In general, the more aware of this pipeline you are when building your templates and animations, the more likely you are to see opportunities for optimization.

3D

Although WPF does hardware acceleration of 3D, there are still some measures you need to take to ensure smooth rendering of your 3D worlds. These include the following:

▶ Minimize the number of `GeometryModel3D` objects or `ModelUIElement3D` objects in the scene. If the 3D models are purely for display, it should work fine, but if they are interactive, hit testing can become sluggish. Although rendering might be done in hardware, the hit-testing feature is software-based, which is why you often see the CPU usage spike when large numbers of clickable models are visible.

▶ MeshGeometry3D uses the Point3DCollection to store its mesh positions. If you try to modify these positions at runtime (as we did in Chapter 12, "Custom Animations"), each change (add, remove, or update) to the collection results in a "collection changed" event being fired. For large mesh geometries, this can result in an unwanted flood of events. The recommended practice is to detach the Point3DCollection instance before modifying it. You can plug it back in after the changes are done. The following snippet shows an example of doing this:

```
MeshGeometry3D mesh = _currentMesh;
mesh.Positions = null; // Detach collection
Point3DCollection newPoints = new Point3DCollection();
// Populate collection
mesh.Positions = newPoints; // Re-attach collection
```

▶ Try to keep the size of your meshes (MeshGeometry3D) on the smaller side. WPF is not the best technology for representing a million-polygon 3D character. Generally meshes up to a few hundred vertices perform relatively well. We cannot stress enough that even though WPF has 3D capabilities, it should never be used as a game engine for high-polygon-count 3D games.

▶ Use caching hints when using VisualBrush or in general a TileBrush as a material on the 3D model. We already discussed the use of caching hints with the RenderOptions class earlier in this chapter.

As mentioned earlier, the preceding section is only a subset of the different areas in which performance can be improved. A great article by Kiran Kumar covers many more areas, including the ones in this chapter: http://blogs.msdn.com/kiranku/attachment/904197.ashx. WPF, being a technology built on top of the .NET Framework, also benefits from the performance-tuning knowledge already available for .NET applications in general. The following MSDN article goes into great depths and covers a wide selection of topics for improving the performance of a .NET application: http://msdn.microsoft.com/en-us/library/aa970683.aspx.

A few blogs to which you can subscribe to obtain your daily dose of performance tips are the following:

▶ **Rico Mariani's blog**—http://blogs.msdn.com/ricom

▶ **Vance Morrison's blog**—http://blogs.msdn.com/vancem

▶ **Jossef Goldberg's blog**—http://blogs.msdn.com/jgoldb/default.aspx

Measuring Performance

So far, we have seen a variety of areas where performance can be improved. However, to squeeze out the maximum performance from your CPU and memory, you need good tools to help identify the bottlenecks. Additionally, if you can't reliably benchmark the performance of your application, you can't quantify the change in performance after making adjustments.

Microsoft provides a set of tools to help you identify and isolate the performance issues in your controls and application. The WPF Performance Suite, available from http:/ /windowsclient.net/wpf/perf/wpf-perf-tool.aspx, contains tools such as the Visual Profiler, Perforator, and ETW Trace Viewer, all of which help in identifying rendering bottlenecks. Visual Profiler and Perforator are by far the most commonly used tools in the suite, so we spend a little more time on those in this section. A complete description of each tool and its associated usage is beyond the scope of this book. If you want that information, you can refer to http://msdn.microsoft.com/en-us/library/aa969767.aspx for detailed usage.

Visual Profiler

Visual Profiler is a tool that shows how the WPF services such as layout, animation, rendering, and so on are being used by elements in the application. The tool shows the visual tree on the left-hand side, and selecting an element shows the allocation of the various services on the right in the form of a graph. The graph gives the usage breakdown for each of the services. Figure 17.2 (from the WindowsClient.net website) shows these features of the tool.

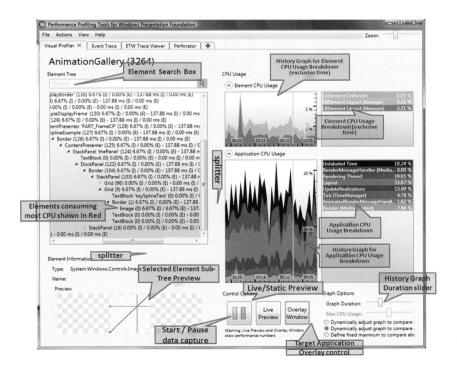

FIGURE 17.2   Visual Profiler features.

The Visual Profiler is particularly handy for identifying elements that take up a major portion of the CPU time as well as other WPF resources. You can right-click inside the visual tree and expand the element that is along the hot path (the one that consumes the most CPU in that subtree). Once the element is selected, you can also view its CPU usage breakdown. This is a much better way of identifying bottlenecks than looking at function call graphs, which is what a traditional profiler would provide. Once you have identified the troublesome element, a traditional profiler can be used to analyze the function call graph surrounding that one element.

Perforator

Perforator, shown in Figure 17.3, is a tool for analyzing the rendering behavior of your application.

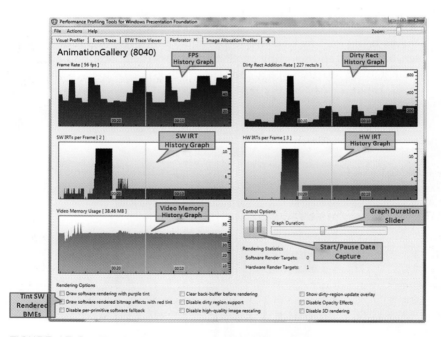

FIGURE 17.3   The Perforator view with the different graphs.

It gives you a real-time graph showing the performance of the application in different categories, such as the following:

▶ **Frame Rate**—The rate at which the application is rendering to the screen. This value should stay close to zero when there are no animations in the scene.

▶ **Dirty Rect Addition Rate**—Indicates how fast the updates are being triggered in your application. Generally this is higher when layout is happening, say, when resizing the window.

▶ **SW/HW IRTs per Frame**—This indicates the number of Intermediate Render Targets (IRT) being used to render a single frame of the application. IRTs are generally used for DrawingBrushes, VisualBrushes, opacity/opacity masks on a visual, Tile Modes on a TileBrush, and so on. A large number of these indicate that WPF is spending a lot of time in rendering the application.

▶ **Video Memory Usage**—Tracks the video memory allocation made exclusively by WPF, typically for textures and render targets. Exceeding the video memory results in a fallback to pure software rendering in the WPF application.

The tool also gives you a number of options to control the real-time rendering behavior, such as showing overlays of software rendered visuals, disabling dirty region support, disabling opacity effects, and disabling 3D rendering.

Third-Party Tools

Several third-party profiling tools are also available for measuring the performance of .NET applications. Many of these tools provide memory profiling capabilities, such as taking snapshots and identifying memory leaks. Some of the popular tools include the following:

▶ JetBrains DotTrace, http://www.jetbrains.com/profiler

▶ Red Gate Ants Profiler, http://www.red-gate.com/products/ants_performance_profiler/index.htm

▶ SciTech .NET Memory Profiler, http://www.memprofiler.com

Perceived Responsiveness

As we have seen so far, there are many areas for improving performance. However, certain activities are difficult to improve in terms of performance. The classic example is of network activity. When developing in a controlled environment, you may have the best network bandwidth and may not notice any lag. In a production environment, this may cause severe network lags and can cause your application to go into a "frozen" state. Accounting for such scenarios is important to let the user know that the application is alive and not overworked.

A common way to improve this is by showing progress either with a progress bar or with some repeating animation. If you know how long it is going to take, you can suggest the expected completion time. When the completion time is unknown, you can run a continuous animation to indicate activity. Since you have rich styling capabilities, you can brand the progress bar to blend with rest of the application.

Deferred scrolling, which allows the user to move the scroll thumb without actually scrolling the panel, is yet another perceived performance boost. The real panel scroll happens when the user lets go of the scroll thumb. Interaction mechanisms such as this can also aid in improving the overall application performance.

Many people lump the activities of keeping up perceived responsiveness (as opposed to actual performance improvement) into the categories of "hacks" or "tricks." This couldn't be further from the truth. The goal behind perceived responsiveness is to keep the user engaged during long-running operations. Some of the best examples come from games, where the character shows boredom if the user is not interacting with rest of the environment. Instead of just freezing on the screen, the character may resort to whistling, twiddling his thumbs, or just looking around. Adopting such ideas for a WPF application can make it lively and also tell the user that the application has not hung.

Summary

In this chapter, we covered some of the important areas of improving performance in your WPF applications and controls. Since the scope of this chapter is limited to touching on the different areas, it is strongly recommended that you also refer to the additional links included in the sections. WPF is after all a part of the .NET Framework, which means in addition to fine-tuning WPF features, you can also use the general principles applicable for any .NET application.

The tools mentioned in the previous sections should help you in identifying performance bottlenecks and also isolate the causes. In some cases, there is no easy way to speed up an application—for example, network delays or reading from the hard disk. These scenarios can be handled by presenting progress bars or performing background operations and allowing the user to continue with his work. Although this is subjective, the general idea is to convey activity to the user and show that the application is alive. This is the notion of perceived responsiveness.

Performance is a large topic, but hopefully with this chapter, you have gained enough background to attack your performance problems with some good tools, good knowledge, and a few tips and tricks, as well as all of the techniques you've learned throughout this book.

CHAPTER 18

Control Automation

So far throughout this book, you have seen a variety of features of WPF. We learned about the diverse class structure, customized existing controls, built our own custom controls, delved into the world of 3D, and looked at ways to improve performance and expose control state through events and commands. Our view of WPF so far has been from the inside looking out as a control author, looking at the techniques used to build and customize controls. In this final chapter of the book, we change our perspective and examine WPF from the outside-in and learn how to perform inspection on WPF UI. This outsider view is useful for discovering controls in an application, automating some UI actions, and also making it easier for assistive and accessibility technologies like screen readers and text-to-speech engines.

The UI automation framework is a relatively new introduction to the Windows platform and a successor to Microsoft Active Accessibility. The framework provides a unified way to discover UI controls in an application built using any of the desktop UI technologies: Win32, Windows Forms, or WPF. However, in this chapter, we focus solely on how this new framework works with WPF applications and controls.

The Need for UI Automation

Before we dig deeper into the automation support included in WPF, we need to first understand what we mean by *UI automation*. As a control author or someone building the UI for a WPF application, you know what controls you are using. You can see the control hierarchy laid out before you in XAML and in your Solution Explorer. You know the purpose of your controls and where they are located within the UI. You also know how to respond to different UI events and take action accordingly.

What if you wanted to make all of this information available to an external program that knows nothing about your application, an external application such as a screen reader? The screen reader has no clue about your application or your UI unless you go the extra mile and put in extra effort to communicate this information.

Similarly if you wanted to test your UI by automating tasks such as clicking buttons, entering text in text boxes, scrolling a list, or selecting an item, there has to be some kind of agreed-upon protocol through which the test harness and the WPF application communicate. Without some kind of mutual understanding (protocol), there is no way any external entity can communicate with and perform functions on your application.

This is where an automation framework comes in. A UI automation framework provides this common protocol for exchanging information between your WPF application and an external entity such as a screen reader or a test harness that programmatically communicates with your UI.

On the Windows platform, a unified automation framework works across all desktop UI technologies such as Win32, Windows Forms, and WPF. The automation framework provides a set of APIs for exposing information about the UI and also reading that information from an external application. It provides APIs to discover controls, navigate the visual tree, read the current state of controls, and perform control-specific actions. In the following section, we dig deeper into these APIs and look at the building blocks of the automation framework.

The Automation Object Model

We know that the WPF UI is represented as a tree of controls commonly called the visual tree. There is a root element, which could be a window, page, or frame, and all of the other controls are nested inside it. From an automation perspective, the situation is no different. The WPF UI is still represented in a tree structure, but instead of each node being a control, it is an instance of `System.Windows.Automation.AutomationElement`. The root element of the automation tree is the desktop whose children are the application windows.

There are other core differences between the visual tree and the automation tree. When the application window is loaded, the visual tree is completely built and rendered on the screen. In other words, every visible element on the screen is actually present in the visual tree. This may seem obvious, but this analogy is useful when we compare it with the automation tree. Every visible element on the screen may not have a corresponding automation element in the automation tree. This is because providing automation support in a control is an opt-in feature and in some cases, the control is such that an automation element does not make sense—for example, a border, shape, panel, or a visual that is purely for decorative purposes. By default, all of the standard WPF controls have built-in support for automation.

Assemblies and Namespaces

The automation support is divided into two distinct parts: the provider side, which is implemented by controls that want to expose themselves on the automation tree, and the client side, which interacts with the provider. The provider typically implements one or more interfaces defined in the `UIAutomationProvider.dll` under the `System.Windows.Automation.Provider` namespace and raises property change events. The interfaces in this assembly correspond to control patterns, which we discuss in the next section.

The client-side story is all about interacting with the automation providers. `UIAutomationClient.dll` contains the necessary APIs to interact with providers, listen to events, query information, send input, and so on. These APIs are defined under the `System.Windows.Automation` and `System.Windows.Automation.Text` namespaces. Additionally, clients also use the types in `UIAutomationTypes.dll`, under the `System.Windows.Automation` namespace, to query the provider for the interfaces and patterns that it supports.

AutomationElement, AutomationPeer, and Control Patterns

We know that every node in the automation tree is an instance of the UI-agnostic `AutomationElement` class. It contains a variety of information about its associated control that exposes the control's automation capabilities. However, an `AutomationElement` is a runtime representation of a control that supports automation. It extracts the information from a separate object that is provided by the control. In the case of WPF, this object is an instance of a class that derives from `AutomationPeer`. The control makes this instance available by overriding the protected method `OnCreateAutomationPeer`. Any control that provides its own `AutomationPeer` is said to support UI automation.

`AutomationPeer` is an abstract class, and you should not actually subclass it directly. Instead, the framework provides a number of derived classes that can serve as a base class for your own automation peer. Figure 18.1 gives a small subset of automation peers that you can use for your own controls.

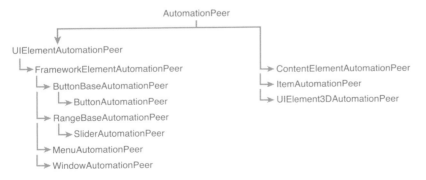

FIGURE 18.1   Automation peer hierarchy.

The main purpose of the automation peer is to expose capabilities that could be used by automation clients such as screen readers and test harnesses. These capabilities are specified in terms of control patterns. A control that supports UI automation typically exposes one or more control patterns. For example, the InvokePattern, which is a control pattern implemented by controls such as Button, Hyperlink, MenuItem, indicates to the automation client that the control is capable of invoking an action or being invoked. Automation peers for each of Button, Hyperlink, and MenuItem implement this pattern by raising the Click event. Similarly, controls that implement the ScrollPattern allow automation clients to perform scrolling actions programmatically. Not surprisingly, the ScrollViewer is one control that implements the ScrollPattern. You can think of UI automation control patterns as a kind of loose, high-level UI contract or interface. Rather than defining the methods that must be implemented by a control, these patterns define the behavior that the automation client can expect the control to implement.

Although you can have an infinite variety of controls, the control patterns are strictly limited. Limiting these patterns means that assistive technologies have complete knowledge about the controls and need not try to guess about custom patterns or the potentially unknown purpose and behavior of a given control. The complete set of patterns can be found within UIAutomationClient.dll. Figure 18.2 shows the complete list of all supported UI automation control patterns.

FIGURE 18.2   Complete list of control patterns.

As you can see from Figure 18.2, a control pattern is an instance of BasePattern. Although BasePattern is a public class, its constructor is internal, which means that developers cannot create instances of custom patterns. The premise of this restriction is that any control can be represented by combining one or more of these predefined patterns. Although the premise applies to a wide variety of controls, there will be times when we just can't find a set of patterns that match our control. We see an example of this scenario later in the chapter and some suggested approaches to handling this situation.

It is automation peer's responsibility to expose its supported control patterns. Interestingly enough, this is done without directly using the control pattern types seen earlier. Instead, each control pattern has a corresponding pattern interface, which, when implemented by the `AutomationPeer`, makes the peer automatically flagged as supporting that control pattern. The `InvokePattern` and `ScrollPattern` examples have corresponding pattern interfaces named `IInvokeProvider` and `IScrollProvider`. The automation peers for the `Button`, `Hyperlink`, and `MenuItem` controls implement the `IInvokeProvider`, and similarly the peer for `ScrollViewer` implements `IScrollProvider`.

Looking at the `-Provider` suffix of these interfaces may remind you of the provider APIs, and indeed these interfaces are part of the `UIAutomationProvider.dll` assembly that contains all of these interfaces. Controls that implement their `AutomationPeers` reference this assembly to implement their supported control patterns. Figure 18.3 shows all the pattern interfaces found in the `UIAutomationProvider.dll` assembly. It should be fairly straightforward to correlate the pattern interfaces with the control patterns from Figure 18.2. There are a few extra types and interfaces in Figure 18.3 that you can ignore for now.

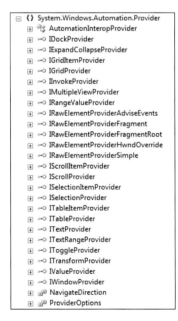

FIGURE 18.3   Pattern interfaces.

Automation Properties

The properties supported by the control are generally specified by the control's implementation of the `AutomationPeer` and the pattern interfaces. However, some properties can be overridden in XAML, at the point of specifying the control. These are defined as dependency properties inside `System.Windows.Automation.AutomationProperties` in the `PresentationCore.dll` assembly. The list of properties include the following:

- `AcceleratorKeyProperty`
- `AccessKeyProperty`
- `AutomationIdProperty`
- `HelpTextProperty`
- `IsColumnHeaderProperty`
- `IsRequiredForFormProperty`
- `IsRowHeaderProperty`
- `ItemStatusProperty`
- `ItemTypeProperty`
- `LabeledByProperty`
- `NameProperty`

For example, the following XAML snippet shows how you can set the automation properties on a `TextBox`—in this case, the `AutomationId` and `HelpText` properties:

```
<TextBox Text="{Binding CompanyName}"
         AutomationProperties.HelpText="The Company Name"
         AutomationProperties.AutomationId="ID_CompanyName" />
```

Navigating the Automation Tree

When an automation client tries to peek into the UI of your application, it sees a tree of `AutomationElements`, called the automation tree. One of the core activities of an automation client is to navigate the tree: Go to the parent node, drill into the child nodes, look at the sibling nodes, and so on. The `System.Windows.Automation.TreeWalker` class defined in `UIAutomationClient.dll` provides this exact functionality. In fact, the `TreeWalker` provides three different views of the automation tree, called the raw view, control view, and content view.

The raw view gives you the complete set of automation elements without applying any additional filtering criteria, which means it is the most detailed view of the automation tree. `TreeWalker.RawViewWalker` is handy for navigating the raw view of the automation tree.

The control view is a subset of the raw view such that it only contains `AutomationElements` that have their `IsControlElementProperty` set. The control view gives you all the interactive controls in the UI such as `Button`, `ListBox`, `ComboBox`, and `ScrollBar`. It thus matches the logical structure of the UI. `TreeWalker.ControlViewWalker` helps in traversing this view of the automation tree.

Finally, the content view is a subset of the control view and only contains elements that represent true information to the end user. A `ListBox` would be part of the content view since it would contain a list of data items, which is information for the user. Similarly a `ComboBox` would also be part of the content view since it is semantically a list of items but only one of them is visible at a time. The automation elements in a content view have their `IsContentElementProperty` set, and to navigate this view, we use the `TreeWalker.ContentViewWalker`.

But you are not limited to only these three views of the automation tree. You can also create custom views based on specific filter criteria, specified with `Condition` elements. A condition can be one of `PropertyCondition`, `AndCondition`, `OrCondition`, and `NotCondition`. A `PropertyCondition` can be used to filter the automation tree based on the value of a particular property. The control view and the content views are created using `PropertyConditions`, the former checking for the presence of `IsControlElementProperty` and the latter checking for `IsContentElementProperty`. `AndCondition`, `OrCondition`, and `NotCondition` work like Boolean operators and are used to compose more complex conditions.

To actually extract a custom view of the automation tree, we use the `AutomationElement`'s `FindFirst` or `FindAll` methods, each of which accepts a `TreeScope` and a `Condition`. The `TreeScope` is used to restrict the search to a particular part of the automation tree. It is an enumeration with the following values: `Ancestors`, `Descendants`, `Children`, `Element`, `Parent`, and `Subtree`. Since this enumeration has the `FlagsAttribute`, you can combine values using bitwise operators (|, &, ~, ^). Table 18.1 gives a description of each of these values.

TABLE 18.1   TreeScope Enumeration Values

Value	Description
`Element`	Search includes the element itself.
`Children`	Search includes the element's immediate children.
`Descendants`	Search includes the element's descendants, including children.
`Parent`	Search includes the element's parent. Not supported.
`Ancestors`	Search includes the element's ancestors, including the parent. Not supported.
`Subtree`	Search includes the root of the search and all descendants.

The `FindFirst` and `FindAll` methods are instance methods of `AutomationElement`, which means you need to have an instance of `AutomationElement` to actually create a custom

view. By default, we have the desktop, the root of the automation tree, available via the
`AutomationElement.RootElement` static property. We can create custom views starting
from the `RootElement`, but most often you would want to create a custom view starting
with your application window. To do so, we have the static method `AutomationElement.`
`FromHandle`, which takes an `IntPtr`, the handle to your application window. This can be
obtained by creating a `WindowInteropHelper` for your application window and accessing
the `Handle` property. The following code snippet shows how you can get an
`AutomationElement` from your application window:

```
IntPtr handle = new WindowInteropHelper(Application.Current.MainWindow).Handle;
AutomationElement elt = AutomationElement.FromHandle(handle);
```

In addition to obtaining specific views of the automation tree, you can also navigate the
tree using some of `TreeWalker`'s methods. These include `GetFirstChild`, `GetLastChild`,
`GetNextSibling`, `GetPreviousSibling`, and `GetParent`. Each of these accepts an
`AutomationElement` as input and returns an `AutomationElement` relative to the input
element.

This section discussed a variety of concepts, which may be little overwhelming. Figure
18.4 summarizes and simplifies the different concepts.

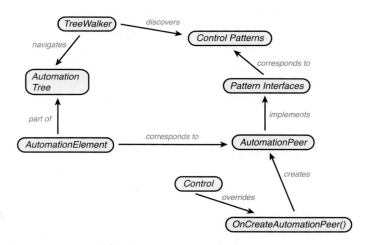

FIGURE 18.4   The UI automation process.

Using the Automation API

Now that we have a better understanding of the different things involved in using UI
automation, let's get to the actual APIs involved. In this section, we consider a few different scenarios and show what APIs can be used to tackle the situation. Taking this
scenario-based approach helps you understand the context in which the APIs are
supposed to be used. All of these cover the client-side usage of the APIs. We take up the
provider side story of automation in the following section.

Automation clients such as screen readers and UI test harnesses are the primary consumers of the client-side API. Generally the clients run in a separate process, but they can also be inside the same application window—that is, in-process. If you are planning to use the client-side APIs from within the application, it is recommended that you run them on a separate thread. This is because certain search and navigation scenarios can be CPU-intensive and may block the main UI. If your automation requirements are limited to querying a few controls, you can make the calls in-process.

An automation client generally follows a standard set of steps when operating on an automation tree. These include the following:

▶ Determine criteria for locating an element. This can be specified with a `PropertyCondition` or a complex combination of `AndCondition`, `OrCondition`, or `NotCondition`.

▶ Locate element in the automation tree using the `FindFirst` or `FindAll` methods of the `AutomationElement`.

▶ Check whether the control implements the required control patterns.

▶ Look up values of specific properties and/or set up listeners for events fired on the automation element.

▶ Take any desired action on the automation element. For example, if the located element implements the `InvokePattern` (via the `IInvokeProvider` interface), you could call `Invoke()` on the automation element:

▶ Navigate to parent/child/sibling from the current position.

Let's see how we can perform the preceding operations using the client-side automation APIs.

Locating Elements in the Automation Tree

Locating elements in the automation tree is equivalent to doing a search on the `AutomationTree` with some conditions. The following snippet shows several ways in which you can retrieve `AutomationElements`:

```
// Locate the application from the window handle
_handle = new WindowInteropHelper(Application.Current.MainWindow).Handle;
var windowElt = AutomationElement.FromHandle(_handle);

// Locate the UserControl with AutomationId
var ucElt = windowElt.FindFirst(TreeScope.Descendants,
        new PropertyCondition(AutomationElement.AutomationIdProperty,
"ID_AutomationClient"));

// Find all its children who are Buttons
var childElts = ucElt.FindAll(TreeScope.Descendants,
        new PropertyCondition(AutomationElement.ClassNameProperty, "Button"));
```

Note that we should perform these operations on a separate thread so as to not block the UI thread. This can be done by wrapping the calls into a delegate that can be called on a thread-pool thread, like so:

```
WaitCallback callback = delegate(object state)
                    {
// Automation calls
                    };

ThreadPool.QueueUserWorkItem(callback);
```

If you refer to the sample code (AutomationClientAPIExample.xaml.cs), you see the preceding snippet being used for all the examples.

Checking for Control Patterns

In the following snippet, we loop through all of the child controls and print out those that implement the ScrollPattern:

```
PropertyCondition c = new PropertyCondition(AutomationElement.IsControlElementProp-
➥erty,
true);
AutomationElementCollection elements = ucElt.FindAll(TreeScope.Descendants, c);

StringBuilder sb = new StringBuilder();
sb.Append("—-=== Checking for Control Patterns ===—-\n");
sb.Append("Controls supporting the ScrollPattern:\n");
foreach (AutomationElement elt in elements)
{
        var patterns = from pattern in elt.GetSupportedPatterns()
                    where pattern.Id == ScrollPattern.Pattern.Id
                    select pattern.ProgrammaticName;
        if (patterns.Count() > 0)
        {
                sb.Append(elt.Current.ClassName);
                sb.Append(Environment.NewLine);
        }
}
```

In the preceding code, we are firing a LINQ query that goes through all of the supported patterns (retrieved via GetSupportedPatterns) on the automation element and specifically picking ScrollPattern. Note how we check for the pattern using ScrollPattern.Pattern.Id. Internally WPF stores all of the patterns with pattern identifiers for easy lookup. We could have also checked for this pattern using GetCurrentPattern, as shown here:

```
object objPattern = elt.GetCurrentPattern(ScrollPattern.Pattern);
if (objPattern != null)
{
        ScrollPattern pattern = objPattern as ScrollPattern;
        // Further operations
}
```

Looking Up Property Values

Reading property values is similar to the API for reading control patterns. The following snippet shows you how you can get all the supported properties on an AutomationElement and read their values:

```
StringBuilder sb = new StringBuilder();
AutomationProperty[] properties = ucElt.GetSupportedProperties();
foreach (AutomationProperty property in properties)
{
        sb.Append("\t" + property.ProgrammaticName + ": " +
ucElt.GetCurrentPropertyValue(property));
        sb.Append("\n");
}
```

GetSupportedProperties gives you all the supported automation properties, whereas a single property can be queried using GetCurrentProperty. If you want to know the values of the automation properties set on different controls, you can use a tool called UISpy that ships with the Windows SDK. The tool also allows you to navigate the automation tree starting at the root element (desktop) and shows more in-depth information about the automation element. For more information about UISpy, see this MSDN article: http:/ /msdn.microsoft.com/en-us/library/ms727247.aspx.

Listening to Events

You can subscribe to automation events using the public static Add*EventHandler methods on the Automation class. These include AddAutomationEventHandler, AddAutomationFocusChangedEventHandler, AddStructureChangedEventHandler, and AddAutomationPropertyChangedEventHandler. There are similarly named Remove*EventHandler methods as well. Additionally, you also have the option of removing all event handlers registered on any automation element with the RemoveAllEventHandlers method.

The following snippet shows event registration of a custom control. Here we subscribe to property changes on the ValuePattern.ValueProperty. By limiting to TreeScope.Element, we make sure that we get notified only for property changes happening on the element directly.

```
Automation.AddAutomationPropertyChangedEventHandler(rangeSelectorElt,
TreeScope.Element,
```

18

```
        TakeActionForEvent,
        new[] { ValuePattern.ValueProperty });

private void TakeActionForEvent(object sender, AutomationPropertyChangedEventArgs
args)
{
        // Some action
}
```

RemoveAutomationPropertyChangedEventHandler is the symmetrical method for removing
the event handler.

```
Automation.RemoveAutomationPropertyChangedEventHandler(rangeSelectorElt,
TakeActionForEvent);
```

Navigating to the Parent, Child, or Sibling

Navigation on the automation tree can be performed by calling methods on the
TreeWalker class, such as GetFirstChild, GetLastChild, GetPreviousSibling,
GetNextSibling, and GetParent. The following snippet shows how you can walk up the
tree until you hit the RootElement, the desktop:

```
AutomationElement parent = rangeSelectorElt;
StringBuilder sb = new StringBuilder();
while (parent != null)
{
        string className = parent == AutomationElement.RootElement ? "RootElement
(Desktop)" : parent.Current.ClassName;
        sb.Append("\t" + className + "\n");
        parent = TreeWalker.RawViewWalker.GetParent(parent);
}
```

Performing Operations on Automation Elements

Performing operations on an automation element is equivalent to calling methods on the
element's supported control patterns. For example, in the following code, we are making
sure the element implements the WindowPattern and calling the pattern's
SetWindowVisualState method:

```
AutomationElement windowElt = AutomationElement.FromHandle(_handle);

WindowPattern pattern = windowElt.GetCurrentPattern(WindowPattern.Pattern) as
WindowPattern;
if (pattern != null) // Button implements the IInvokeProvider interface
{
        pattern.SetWindowVisualState(WindowVisualState.Normal);
}
```

Automation of a Custom Control

Now that you have seen how you can use the client-side APIs, let's go to the other side of the automation story, the provider. As mentioned in an earlier section, a control supports UI automation if it overrides the protected method OnCreateAutomationPeer and returns an instance of an AutomationPeer. This method is actually defined on the UIElement, which by default returns null.

By subclassing the AutomationPeer, you can expose capabilities of the control that can be programmatically used by automation clients. Typically, you would not subclass AutomationPeer directly but instead use one of its derived classes available in the framework. WPF provides automation peers for all its standard controls, and they are all part of the System.Windows.Automation.Peers namespace in PresentationCore.dll and PresentationFramework.dll.

You should pick a peer class that closely represents the functionality of your control. For example, if your control behaves like a Button, you should pick ButtonBaseAutomationPeer. Similarly if you have a custom NumericTextBox control that only accepts numeric strings, you should subclass TextBoxAutomationPeer. As a final example, ItemsControlAutomationPeer is a good choice for a custom ItemsControl derived control.

To help steer our discussion on automation peers, let's consider a custom control called RangeSelector for which we build the automation peer. As the name suggests, RangeSelector allows you

FIGURE 18.5   Range selector.

to select a range within a minimum and a maximum value. The default template for this control looks similar to a slider, but instead of a single thumb two thumbs allow you to set the start and end of a range. This can be seen in Figure 18.5.

We don't cover this control in any more detail to keep our focus on the automation side of the control. This control has some interesting aspects, especially the property coercion that you will find useful. Make sure you peruse the RangeSelector.cs file provided in the sample code with this book.

Picking a Base Peer Class

RangeSelector contains four dependency properties that define the range and the minimum, maximum values. These are appropriately named RangeStart, RangeEnd, Minimum, and Maximum, each of type double. To implement the automation peer for RangeSelector, we need to pick a base class from one of the many classes from the System.Windows.Automation.Peers namespace. Our first reaction might be to pick the SliderAutomationPeer or its base class RangeBaseAutomationPeer. However, this wouldn't be an ideal choice since both of these classes are useful if you are picking a single value between a minimum and maximum. RangeBaseAutomationPeer implements the IRangeValueProvider pattern interface, which gives us properties like Minimum, Maximum, Value, LargeChange, and SmallChange. Although RangeBaseAutomationPeer comes pretty close to what we need, it doesn't fit well with our control. We need a more generic class than `RangeBaseAutomationPeer` that does not already implement a pattern interface, giving us the option to pick our own control patterns.

The class `FrameworkElementAutomationPeer` fits this description perfectly. It is a fairly generic class and does not implement any pattern interfaces. Thus, the automation peer for our custom control can subclass `FrameworkElementAutomationPeer` and add a suitable pattern interface. It is a common practice to name the automation peer by suffixing the control name with `AutomationPeer`, such as `RangeSelectorAutomationPeer` for our `RangeSelector` control.

Picking Pattern Interfaces, aka the Control Patterns

The next step after picking the base peer class is to determine which pattern interfaces to implement. We already ruled out `IRangeValueProvider` because it does not adequately represent the "range" in our `RangeSelector` control. However, we could have been a little creative and still gone ahead with this interface. But is that the right way to go? Since this interface comes pretty close to what we need, we could have still used it by repurposing its properties. In other words, we could have creatively mapped the interface-supported properties to the properties defined on the `RangeSelector` control. This, however, is not considered a good practice mostly because the ultimate goal of UI automation is to provide information to assistive technologies and also aid in UI testing. Misrepresenting the control with a pattern interface that doesn't quite fit the bill is going to convey wrong information and also break the assumptions made by automation clients. Remember, when you choose a particular control pattern, you are telling the outside world that your control behaves like what the pattern says and supports the pattern's functionality. It is always better not to violate the assumptions made by the clients, and that is exactly the reason why we are not choosing this pattern interface.

But that still leaves our question unanswered: "Which pattern interface do we choose?" It is common for a custom control like ours to not fit nicely with any of the control patterns. In fact, you might be hard-pressed to find a control pattern that fits well for a highly specialized control that has nonconventional interaction behavior. This only means we do a careful study of the available pattern interfaces for our `RangeSelector` control.

After a simple elimination process, we decided to go with the `IValueProvider` interface or the `ValuePattern` that supports a singular string-based value. The following snippet shows this interface in its entirety:

```
public interface IValueProvider
{
        void SetValue(string value);
        string Value { get; }
        bool IsReadOnly { get; }
}
```

Why did we pick this out of all others? (Note: You may want to refer to Figure 18.3 as you read further.) Most of the other interfaces were too specialized and did not fit our needs. Either they contained irrelevant properties and methods (such as `IDockProvider`, `IWindowProvider`, `ITransformProvider`, and so on) or had some properties that matched but also had some extra ones (such as `IRangeValueProvider`).

There is no one-to-one correspondence between a control type and a control pattern. A control may implement many control patterns, and a control pattern may be implemented by many controls.

Even though `IValueProvider` is a simplistic interface with a single string-based `Value` property, we can use it satisfactorily by representing our range as a comma-separated string value: `"<RangeStart>, <RangeEnd>"`, for example, "25,75". The output of our control is really a range, with its components being the `RangeStart` and `RangeEnd`. By representing the range as a string, we are at least conveying the right information to screen readers and also giving room for automation test clients to parse our string for component values.

With the `FrameworkElementAutomationPeer` as our base peer class and `IValueProvider` as the pattern interface, we are all set to implement the `RangeSelectorAutomationPeer`.

Building RangeSelectorAutomationPeer

Here is the code for the peer with some overridden methods:

```
        public class RangeSelectorAutomationPeer : FrameworkElementAutomationPeer,
➡IValueProvider
        {
                private string _currentValue;

                public RangeSelectorAutomationPeer(RangeSelector owner)
                        : base(owner)
                {
                }

                protected override AutomationControlType GetAutomationControlType
➡Core()
                {
                        return AutomationControlType.Custom;
                }

                protected override string GetClassNameCore()
                {
                        return OwningRangeSelector.GetType().Name;
                }

                public override object GetPattern(PatternInterface patternInter
➡face)
```

18

```
        {
                switch (patternInterface)
        {
                        case PatternInterface.Value:
                                return this;
                }

                return base.GetPattern(patternInterface);
        }

        public void SetValue(string value)
        {
                string[] range = value.Split(new[] { ',' });
                if (range.Length == 2)
                {
                        double start, end;

                        // Set the range only if both values parse correctly
                        if (double.TryParse(range[0], out start) &&
                                double.TryParse(range[1], out end))
                        {
                                OwningRangeSelector.RangeStart = start;
                                OwningRangeSelector.RangeEnd = end;
                        }
                }
        }

        public string Value
        {
                get
                {
                        return FormatValue(OwningRangeSelector.RangeStart,
OwningRangeSelector.RangeEnd);
                }
        }

        private static string FormatValue(double start, double end)
        {
                return string.Format("{0:F2},{1:F2}", start, end);
        }

        public bool IsReadOnly
        {
                get { return false; }
        }
```

```
private RangeSelector OwningRangeSelector
{
        get { return (RangeSelector)Owner; }
}

public void RaiseRangeChangedEvent(double start, double end)
{
        string newValue = FormatValue(start, end);
```

```
RaisePropertyChangedEvent(ValuePatternIdentifiers.ValueProperty,
_currentValue, newValue);
```

```
        _currentValue = newValue;
}
```

Note that several other protected methods can be overridden. In the preceding code, we are passing back the control type as `AutomationControlType.Custom` since our control doesn't behave like one of the standard controls. We do this in the `GetAutomationControlTypeCore` override. `AutomationControlType` is an enumeration of the following values:

```
public enum AutomationControlType
{
        Button, Calendar, CheckBox, ComboBox, Edit, Hyperlink,
        Image, ListItem, List,Menu, MenuBar, MenuItem,
        ProgressBar, RadioButton, ScrollBar, Slider,
        Spinner, StatusBar, Tab, TabItem, Text, ToolBar,
        ToolTip, Tree, TreeItem, Custom, Group, Thumb, DataGrid,
        DataItem, Document, SplitButton, Window, Pane, Header,
        HeaderItem, Table, TitleBar, Separator
}
```

Let's look at some of the other overrides. The `GetClassNameCore` override returns the control name, and the `GetPattern` override returns the instance of the peer if the requested pattern interface is `PatternInterface.Value`, since we are specifically implementing this pattern. `PatternInterface` is an enumeration for the different interfaces described earlier. It is possible for a control to respond to different patterns dynamically depending on its runtime configuration. For example, a multiline `TextBox` will respond for `PatternInterface.Text` by default, but it can also respond to `PatternInterface.Scroll` if the scroll viewer is visible.

The `Value` property and the `SetValue` method are implementations of the `IValueProvider` interface. The `RangeSelectorAutomationPeer` allows the read/write access of the range value as a string.

`RaiseRangeChangedEvent` is a custom method called by `RangeSelector` to raise an automation event whenever the range changes. When the `RangeStart` or `RangeEnd` dependency properties change, the control calls its private `RaiseRangeChangedEvent`, which internally calls the same-named method on the `RangeSelectorAutomationPeer`. The following snippet shows how the automation event is raised (in `RangeSelector.cs`):

```
private void RaiseRangeChangedEvent(double start, double end)
{
        if (AutomationPeer.ListenerExists(AutomationEvents.PropertyChanged))
        {
                RangeSelectorAutomationPeer peer = (RangeSelectorAutomationPeer)
UIElementAutomationPeer.FromElement(this);
                if (peer != null)
                {
                        peer.RaiseRangeChangedEvent(start, end);
                }
        }

        var args = new RangeChangedEventArgs(start, end);
        args.Source = this;

        RaiseEvent(args);
}
```

And in `RangeSelectorAutomationPeer.cs`:

```
public void RaiseRangeChangedEvent(double start, double end)
{
        string newValue = FormatValue(start, end);
        RaisePropertyChangedEvent(ValuePatternIdentifiers.ValueProperty, _current-
Value,
newValue);

        _currentValue = newValue;
}
```

RangeSelector forwards the call to the peer only if there is an automation client listening to `AutomationEvents.PropertyChanged` event. `AutomationEvents` is an enumeration consisting of the following different event values:

```
        public enum AutomationEvents
        {
                ToolTipOpened,
                ToolTipClosed,
                MenuOpened,
                MenuClosed,
                AutomationFocusChanged,
                InvokePatternOnInvoked,
                SelectionItemPatternOnElementAddedToSelection,
```

```
            SelectionItemPatternOnElementRemovedFromSelection,
            SelectionItemPatternOnElementSelected,
            SelectionPatternOnInvalidated,
            TextPatternOnTextSelectionChanged,
            TextPatternOnTextChanged,
            AsyncContentLoaded,
            PropertyChanged,
            StructureChanged
    }
```

Finally, to make the automation peer available to clients, the RangeSelector overrides the OnCreateAutomationPeer and serves an instance of the RangeSelectorAutomationPeer, as shown here:

```
            protected override AutomationPeer OnCreateAutomationPeer()
            {
                    return new RangeSelectorAutomationPeer(this);
            }
```

We pass in the instance of the RangeSelector to the peer, which is used internally to query the properties on the control. The peer can also use this to check for runtime changes on the control and respond differently in the GetPattern override.

Additional Resources

If your primary motivation for using UI automation is UI testing, then in addition to the techniques in this chapter, you can check out a library available on CodePlex called TestAPI. This library provides a broader set of APIs for testing various aspects of the UI. Test API is made available through Microsoft's WPF Test Team (http://www.codeplex.com/testapi).

The WPF Application Quality guide is also a good addendum to UI automation, especially in the context of UI testing (http://windowsclient.net/wpf/white-papers/wpf-app-quality-guide.aspx).

18

Summary

This chapter provided a walk-through of the UI automation capabilities of WPF. These capabilities can be harnessed for automated or semi-automated UI testing. In addition, you can use the control discovery, navigation, and interrogation capabilities of the UI automation framework for accessibility-related tools such as screen readers.

Numbers

A

ink-based functionality, attached properties, encapsulating as, 146
InkCanvas class, 28-29, 143-146
INotifyPropertyChanged, 282
input devices, evolution of, 7
Input priority level (Dispatcher), 286
InputBinding class, 266
interactive search bars, 22
interactivity, 2D-on-3D surfaces, 200-201
interfaces, 2
  GUI development
    design patterns, 301-304
    pixel shaders, effect mapping, 235-239
  UIs (user interfaces), 2-3
    commands, 255-266
    deferring operations, Dispatcher, 287
    routed events, 243-255
    visual tree, 332
internal resource dictionaries, 295-296
internal state management, scoped dependency properties, 296
interpolation, 216
  Bézier interpolation, 214
  linear interpolation, 214, 218
intrinsic functions, HLSL (High Level Shading Language), 227
Invalid priority level (Dispatcher), 286
Inversion of Control (IoC) containers, 298
IoC (Inversion of Control) containers, 298
IScrollInfo, 115-116, 123-124, 127, 322-323
  bounds, controlling, 116
  custom scrolling functionality, adding, 119-122
  Thumb
    location management, 116
    logical scrolling, 117
  user-requested scrolling, responding to, 116
IsValidDataObject method, 110
ItemContainerGenerator, UI virtualization, 132-135
ItemContainerStyle, customizing, 74-77
ItemContainerStyle property (ItemsControl class), 21
ItemsControl class, 21-22, 29
  customizing, 72-74
  ItemContainerStyle, 21
  ItemsPanel, 21
  ItemTemplate, 21
  RelativeSource.PreviousData property, 284
  Template, 21
  UI virtualization, 131-133
ItemsControl control, 70
ItemsPanel property (ItemsControl class), 21, 131-133

ItemsPanelTemplate class, 27-29, 77-78
ItemsPresenter class, 29
ItemTemplate, customizing, 77-78
ItemTemplate property (ItemsControl class), 21
IWeakEventListener, weak events, delivering, 254-255

J–K

JetBrains DotTrace, 329

Kaxaml tool, 313-314
keyboard focus, 266
  events, 267-270
  properties, 267-270
keyboard navigation (focus), 271-273
Keyboard.Focus() method, 266
keyframe animations, 207-209
keywords, HLSL (High Level Shading Language), 226
Kutruff, Andrew, 292

L

Language Integrated Query (LINQ), 291
lasso selection tools, creating, 143-146
layered structures, custom controls, 39
layout, 5, 49-52
  3D layout, 200
  absolute layout, 85
  circular layouts, 63
  conversations, 51-52
  events, 66, 68
  layout logic, custom scrolling, 117-119
  layout space, 51
  transformations, 63-68
  UIElement class, 5, 50
layout animations, attached properties, 102
layout logic, custom scrolling, creating, 117-119
layout patterns, 23
layout space, 51
LayoutTransforms, 66-67
light
  3D worlds, 186-187
  refraction, 187
light sources, 3D scenes, 186
line charts, RelativeSource.PreviousData property, 283
linear interpolation, 214, 218
LinearGradientBrush class, 25-26
LINQ (Language Integrated Query), 291
list data, 2
list-based controls, 34

How can we make this index more useful? Email us at indexes@sampublishing.com

Q-R

automation tree, navigating, 336-338
AutomationElement class, 333-335
AutomationPeer class, 333-335
control patterns, 333-335
    checking for, 340
custom controls, 343-349
events, listening to, 341-342
namespaces, 333
object model, 332-338
properties, 335-336
property values, reading, 341
resources, 349
**UI controls, helper objects, attached
properties, 103**
UI virtualization, 130-131
3D virtualization, 140-142
classes, 131-132
component interaction, 132-133
containers, 130-131
    recycling, 140
deferred scrolling, 139-140
ItemContainerGenerator, 133-135
viewports, 130-131
virtualized controls, creating, 135-139
UIElement class, 5, 15-16, 50
UIs (user interfaces), 2-3
commands, 255-258
    components, 257
    ICommandSource interface, 262-266
    request requery, 261-262
    routed commands, 259
deferring operations, Dispatcher, 287
routed events, 243-245
    attached events, 246-248
    class handlers, 249-250
    event triggers, 245-246
    property mirrors, 246
    weak events, 250-255
visual tree, 332
UISpy, 341
UndockFrontChild() method, 150, 152
undocking controls, 149-154
UniformGrid panel
layout, 50
properties, 71
unit testing, 111
UpdateScrollInfo method, 121
UseHover attached property, building, 95-100
user experience, accounting for, 8-9
user input, 6, 8
user-requested scrolling, responding to, 116
UserControl class, 22-23, 29
UX guidelines, visual design, 308

V

value converters, data transformations, 32-33
VanishingPointPanel, 56-58
vector graphics, designing, Adobe Illustrator, 309
vertex shaders, pixel shaders, compared, 223
vertical ScrollBars, 79
**vertical scrolling, user-requested scrolling,
responding to, 116**
vertices, mesh surfaces, 219
Video Memory Usage category (Perforator), 329
view refactoring, 23
Viewport3D class, 27-29
Viewport3D element, 186-192
viewports, UI virtualization, 130-131
views, transitions
applying, 159-161
creating, 154-161
handling, 157-159
Virtual Earth, 130
virtualization, 129-130, 142. *See also*
UI virtualization
performance, 322-323
Virtual Earth, 130
Visual class, 13-16, 29
visual classes, 11
Adorner, 29
Adorner class, 24
Brush, 29
Brush-related classes, 25-27
ContentControl, 29
ContentControl class, 20
ContentPresenter, 29
ContentPresenter class, 20-21
Control, 29
Control class, 19-20
ControlTemplate class, 27
DataTemplate, 29
DataTemplate class, 27
Decorator, 29
Decorator class, 24
DependencyObject, 29
DependencyObject class, 12, 16
DispatcherObject, 29
DispatcherObject class, 12, 16
DrawingVisual, 29
DrawingVisual class, 13-15
FlowDocument, 18-19, 29
FrameworkElement, 29
FrameworkElement class, 15-16
GlyphRuns, 18-19, 29
hierarchy, 11-12
Image, 29
Image class, 25